INTERPRETATION
WORKING WITH SCRIPTS

with love,
David

INTERPRETATION

WORKING WITH SCRIPTS

Charles J. Lundy
Faculty of Education
University of Toronto

David W. Booth
Faculty of Education
University of Toronto

55 Barber Greene Road, Don Mills, Ontario M3C 2A1

Canadian Cataloguing in Publication Data

Lundy, Charles J., 1939-
Interpretation

ISBN 0-7747-1210-4

1. Drama—Explication. I. Booth, David W. (David Wallace), 1938- II. Title.

PN1707.L86 808.2 C83-098138-1

ISBN 0-7747-1210-4

89 88 87 86 85 84 83 1 2 3 4 5 6 7

Editor: Sharon Jennings
Editorial Consultant: David Perlman
Photographer: Arn Jacenty
Make-up Artist: Jack Medhurst
Composition: CompuScreen Typesetting Ltd.

Printed and Bound in Canada

For Kathleen Gould Lundy
and Howard Reynolds

We extend our warmest thanks to the following people who helped in the development of this book:

The drama teachers who studied and taught with us in courses at the Faculty of Education over the past decade;

Marguerite McNeil for all her work on the manuscript;

Jack Medhurst for the excellent makeup;

Theodore Dragonieri, Mike Kilpatrick, Carol Ricker Wilson, Susan Wilson and the class of '82;

Linda Genesi-Williams, who was involved from the beginning.

Contents

Prologue

This book is about interpreting scripts, about bringing life to words written by a playwright, perhaps a year ago, perhaps two thousand years ago. Interpretation is a learning process which starts when you begin to explore a script for meaning. The process continues as you discover how a playwright builds and develops a script, as you examine the artistic concepts and history of theatre, and as you learn about the technical preparation that is needed in order to share a script with an audience. At the same time you will learn something about yourself and about working with other people, and, in turn, this knowledge will add further insight to your own understanding of the script. Eventually, you may want to share your understanding with an audience in a dramatization of the script. Finally, after having gone through this entire learning and creative process, you will understand more fully how the different roles in theatre—playwright, performer, director, and audience—overlap, and how each contributes to the process of interpretation.

Throughout this book you will have several opportunities to take on the roles of playwright, performer, director, and audience. The book, which is divided into three sections, introduces you to a number of contemporary scripts as well as to scripts from the classical repertoire. Section A, *Theatre Scripts*, calls on you to be the playwright's voice. Strategies are presented that will assist you in examining a variety of scripts, in analysing scripts, in interpreting character, and in rehearsing and sharing your interpretation.

Section B, *Alternative Scripts*, encourages you to be not only performer, but also playwright and director. You will explore various dramatic techniques for creating scripts from such unconventional material as poems, articles, and cartoons. Your theatrical understanding will grow as you learn from your creations.

Section C, *The Cycle of Theatre*, encourages you to explore scripts from the past, present, and future. As you work with the cycle of theatre, with the universal truths that have been explored for centuries through the art of theatre, you will have opportunities to compare styles and attitudes, concepts and techniques, and to understand the social exchange that theatre generates: the effect of actor upon audience and audience upon actor.

Each section, which begins with an explanatory "Introduction," is divided into chapters, and each chapter has its own introduction, called "The Program." For every script selection there is a further explanatory note, called "Playbill," and a set of "Activities." At the end of most chapters is a "Workshop" that provides you with activities related to the overall theme of the chapter. Since the scripts in this book are connected through the themes of theatre, the sections can be explored in any order, and the chapters completed in any sequence. At times the suggestion is made in the Playbill or Activities that you read a chapter or a selection further along in the book. Read ahead only if you wish; the instruction is not there to complicate matters, but to indicate how closely the scripts in this book are related, no matter what chapter they are found in. Finally, to further assist you, there is a Glossary at the end of this book.

In every section of this book, you will use improvisation (your own words) to bring meaning to script (the words of others). You will learn and grow each time you attempt to probe the experiences that lie beneath the words of the script. With every script the learning begins afresh.

In everyday life, 'if' is a fiction, in the theatre 'if' is an experiment.

In everyday life, 'if' is an evasion, in the theatre 'if' is the truth.

When we are persuaded to believe in this truth, then the theatre and life are one.

This is a high aim. It sounds like hard work.

To play needs much work. But when we experience the work as play, then it is not work any more.

A play is play.

Peter Brook,
The Empty Space

SECTION A: Theatre Scripts

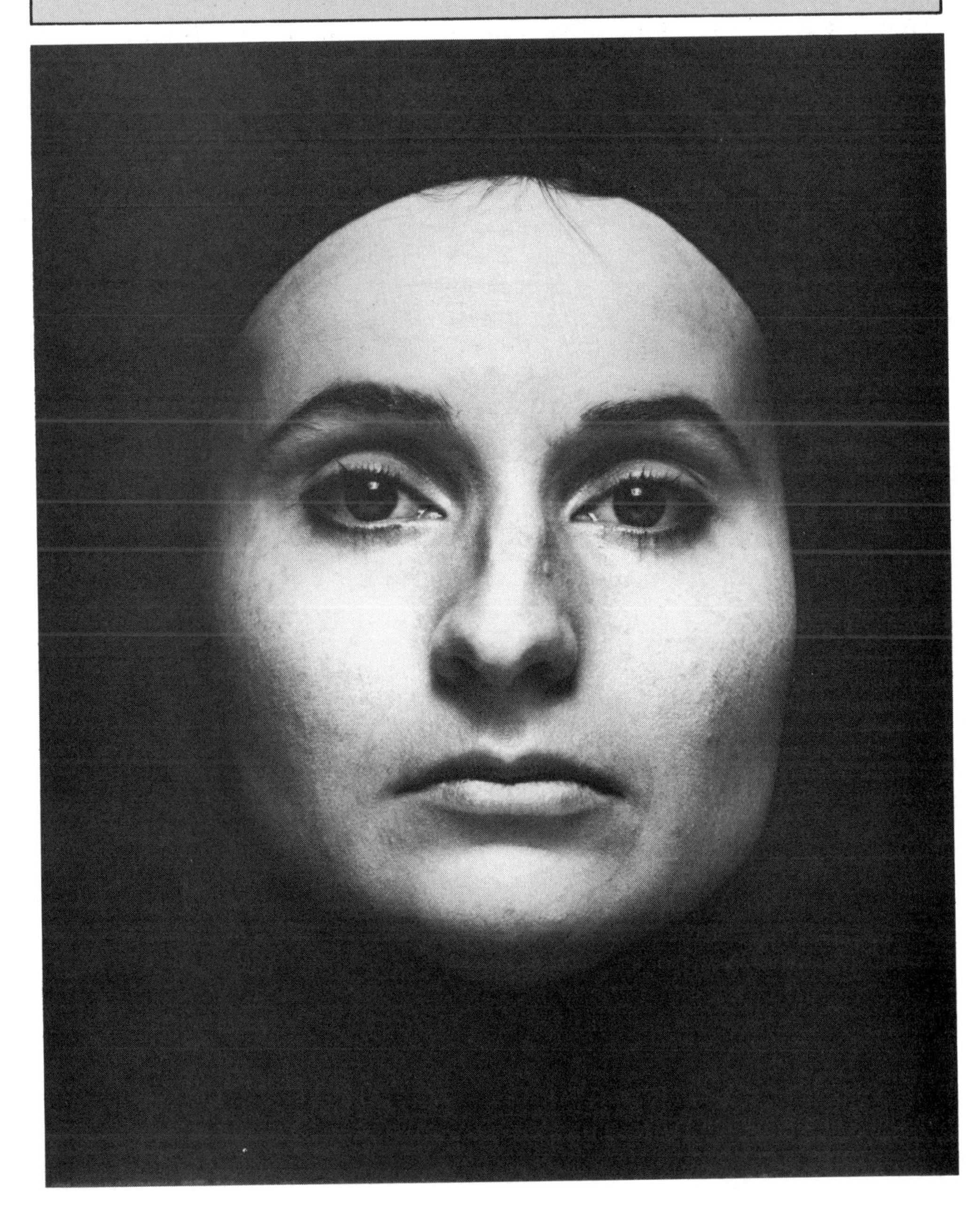

Introduction

This section, entitled *Theatre Scripts*, does two things: it introduces you to various types of scripts, and it examines the many different ways in which you can explore a script for deeper understanding. Eventually, when you are ready to share this understanding, the work you have done will allow you to communicate your interpretation clearly.

Script is literature that speaks. It speaks to us and about us, and it speaks with the voices of flesh and blood human beings—the voices of those who translate the playwright's words into speech and action. However, drama is not merely a matter of reciting lines and performing actions. An actor must search for meaning in a script and attempt to communicate that meaning to others. By working with the scripts in this book, you will develop powers of analysis and imagination—powers that will help you to find and to share meaning. Through the roles you explore, you will enter into the thoughts and feelings of many kinds of characters living many kinds of lives. In so doing, you will not only learn more about these characters created through the art form of script writing, but you will also deepen your understanding of yourself. As well, since working with scripts is a co-operative endeavor, you will improve your ability to work and communicate with other people.

Working in drama is an intensive form of problem solving. As you work through what a script means to you, you must also consider what your interpretation will mean to others, and how you can best make your interpretation clear to them. You will find that your analytical and creative abilities are often taxed to the limit, since this is demanding and engrossing work, requiring a deep consideration of human behavior. A script is only the skeleton of a situation. It is your interpretation which must provide the flesh and breath to make the script come alive.

In the best cases, the creativity needed to interpret the play equals the original creative act of writing the play. The words and lines of the play must be examined closely, analysed thoroughly, and translated from print into real speech by real people playing the parts of the characters in the play. This is the task that the selections in this section of the book have set for you.

There is a scene in Shakespeare's *Hamlet* in which Hamlet instructs a group of travelling players to:

> . . . Suit the action to the word, the word to the action, with this special observance; that you o'erstep not the modesty of nature; for the purpose of playing is to hold, as 'twere, the mirror up to nature. . . .

This is as good a description as any of the method and purpose of drama. It remains as true today as it was when it was written, over four hundred years ago.

1: What is a script?

THE PROGRAM

Script is the branch of literature which is the easiest to identify, since it has a shape and form which make it distinct. The characteristics which make a script recognizable are: identification of speakers by their names or other designations; stage directions, which are usually written in italics and give some indication of the actions and thoughts of the characters; and division of the dialogue into acts and scenes in longer plays.

On the surface, scripts appear to be simple in structure, but beneath that simplicity lies an incredibly complex web of meanings. While a script can be examined and appreciated as literature, it usually only has life when it is performed for spectators. To find the life of a script requires intense work and a deep examination into the meaning of the words.

The author of a script, the playwright, begins the process by devising the plot and writing the words that the character or characters say. These characters are placed in a particular setting, at a particular time, and say their given lines to accomplish a dramatic purpose within the play. The playwright may also have in mind another purpose: to communicate to the audience a view of the world and the people in it, to show how people interact, and to show the consequences of this interaction.

Unlike other writers, playwrights usually do not communicate directly with their audience. Rather, the play or script must be turned over to a group who will interpret it and then communicate the meanings that they have found to the audience. Simply put, the playwright writes, the actors interpret through rehearsal, and then the play is presented to an audience. Sometimes the playwright does work with the actors, but usually actors must work only with the words on paper.

Before you can attempt to communicate to an audience, you must have practice at finding meaning in a script and at translating that meaning into speech and physical action. You will have to practise working with others and listening to their concepts and ideas about the script. Above all, you will have to experiment with each role you undertake to find ways of bringing it to life, so that your character moves and speaks in a way which is not artificial.

The selections in this chapter provide you with the opportunity to explore various types of script. *Juve* is a script written by a group of young people about themselves and their world. Originally, the script was created by the group by improvising situations in their lives and setting the words down after the dramatic form had been found. *Juve* is an example of a situation in which the performing group is also the playwright.

The Elephant Man is a more traditional script than *Juve* and follows the pattern outlined at the beginning of this chapter. It is a serious drama based on a historical incident. *Come and Go* is a complete play although it is very short. It will tax your interpretive powers because the meaning—rich in possibilities—is hidden beneath a deceptively simple surface.

What Glorious Times They Had introduces the concept of "a play within a play." The actors must adopt a role within the role they are already playing, and, therefore, they must examine the meaning of the script on two levels. Other examples of this concept will be found throughout this book.

The last selection, from *Barefoot in the Park*, is from the theatrical form known as the "Broadway comedy." As you work with this scene, you will find that the lines have been cleverly structured in order to draw laughs. You will have to develop a pattern of pacing and timing the lines so that these laughs are not lost. Working with comedy is as demanding as working with serious material.

As you work with the selections in this chapter, be aware of the similarities of the scripts as well as their differences. Each script will present a new set of problems to solve and a new group of characters and situations to explore.

FROM

JUVE

by Campbell Smith

CHARACTERS

Alan
Chris
Michael
Frank
Joan
Diana
Terry

(The stage is empty and all members of the cast are scattered through the audience. The Band begins to play and the cast sings out from the audience. When the Band breaks into Juve *the cast runs onstage, playing tag, skateboarding, playing basketball and football.)*

Juve (Theme Song)

E
Here I am

D
Here we are

A
We're new

B
We're blue

E
What to do

D
What to try

A
Where to go

D A
We're the new stars on the horizon

D F
Shootin' fast before we fall

E
On our marks

D
Here we go

A
On this marathon

E
Headin' up

D
Headin' down

A
Headin' round

D A
At a breakneck speed tryin' for the lead

D F
With both feet off the ground

C#min
Playin' hard

Playin' fast

Amaj7
Playin' tough

B♭ Amaj7 C#min
Want to try our own identities

Amaj7
Don't want to goose step into history

Amaj7
And join the big parade

D A
Let us do it our own way

D F
Hallelujah I'm a bum

G
I'm someone.

PLAYBILL

As was pointed out in The Program to this chapter, *Juve* does not have a single playwright or author. Rather, the play is a collective creation in which Campbell Smith, after interviewing hundreds of West Coast teenagers, used a cast drawn from Vancouver-area high schools to develop improvisations based on his interviews. The dialogue was written down after the improvisations were fully developed, and then music and songs were added.

As you read this selection, begin thinking of how you can say the dialogue to make it sound natural and unforced. Also note the use of chants and song and the use of choral speaking (all characters speaking in unison). All of these are very old theatrical techniques.

All: Are we in
Well I guess
High School, High School
Yes, yes, yes.
Ye-e-e-a-a-a-h . . .
HIGH SCHOOL!!

Girls and boys come out to play
The moon doth shine as bright as day
Come with a whoop or come with a call
But come with a good will or not at all.

Terry: Ready or not
You must be caught
First one caught's it
Hiding around the goal post's it!

Michael: Homefree!

Joan & Diana: Blue bells, cockle shells
Evey, ivy over
I love coffee
I love tea
I love the boys
And the boys love me.

Frank: Strike three! You're out!

Alan: What do you mean, "out"?

Chris: Kill the ump!

All: *(Voices adding one by one)* One potato, two potato, three potato, four. Five potato, six potato, seven potato more.

Joan & Diana: Bumped his head on the edge of the bed

All: And couldn't get up in the morning.

(School bell rings.)

All: Lesson two!

Alan: I like hockey because it's an exciting game. Some people think the game is too violent, but it's just part of the game. It makes me feel good when the other team hits one of the guys on the team I like. Then the good team piles on that guy and then the other team piles up on the good team. After the referee pulls all the guys off, the guy on the bottom is so squashed he can't play hockey anymore. That's what I like about hockey.

Chris: Pushups!

*(*ALL *do pushups.)*

Chris: On the second day of my summer vacation I got up, got dressed, ate breakfast and went downtown to look for a job. Then I hung out in front of the drugstore.

(School bell rings.)

Michael: My dad came home on September 22, 1978. It was a Wednesday. I found him in the phone book. I was just looking through it one day and I found his name. So I phoned. And this guy answered.

Frank: *(as Michael's father)* Hello.

Michael: Hello. Are you my father?

Frank: No. Who are you?

Michael: Mike Fera.

Frank: Oh.

(They hang up.)

Michael: A few days later there was this phone call at my house. Hello?

Frank: Hi turkey. You don't know who this is, do you?

Michael: No.

Frank: Your dad.

Michael: It was my dad! A few days later he came by and we talked. He wasn't anything like the pictures. But he's a real nice guy. I'm going to like him a lot. But right now he's in jail for armed robbery. But I get to see him every Sunday.

Diana: Guess who I was talking to this morning.

Chris: The guy who talks to trees?

Diana: No.

Chris: The human fly?

Diana: No.

Chris: Who?

Diana: Denos Konakis.

Chris: Macho Man. What'd he say?

Diana: The usual.

Diana & Chris: Football! YOU BET!

Michael: Hi.

Terry: *(as Michael's father)* Hi. How're you doing?

Michael: Good.

Terry: How's school?

Michael: Great. I passed with a C+ average.

Terry: Great.

Michael: If I keep up that average that means I go to Royal Military College in four years.

Terry: Good.

(Silence.)

Michael: Thank you for the plane. It's great. It's got a blue propellor. And everything. Terry and I built it together.

Terry: Who's Terry?

Michael: A friend of mine at school. He's great. We do a lot of stuff together. He's blind, right? But that doesn't matter. Next week we're going to see the car show. There'll be cars and everything.

(Silence.)

Terry: How's your mother?

Michael: Good. She says hi. Hi.

(Silence.)

Michael: So do they feed you good in here?

Terry: Sure. Last night we had fish and chips for supper.

Michael: That's good.

Terry: Fried in three year old motor oil.

Michael: Really?

Terry: No.

(A bell rings.)

Michael: Does that mean I have to go?

Terry: Ya.

*(*MICHAEL *moves to go.)*

Terry: Hey listen. How'd you like to go to Calgary next summer?

Michael: Calgary? I've never been to Calgary.

Terry: So would you like to go?

Michael: Just you and me?

Terry: Just you and me.

Michael: Oh wow! Ya.

Terry: Okay. Next summer then for sure. We'll go see the Stampede.

Michael: Wait until I tell Terry. Maybe I'll bring him with me next week so you can meet him.

Terry: Sure.

(Silence.)

Michael: I guess I'd better be going. See you next week.

Terry: I'll be here.

Frank: My brothers and their friends are real geniuses in engines. Right now they're driving stunt in the derbies, rollin' and stuff like that. So I think I might do that. Like everybody drives kind of nuts when they get their first car. You don't have to wreck your car, but if it's a real crummy car, you can just moff it right out.

Alan: We did that up at Alice Lake, his brothers took us. We came along in a GT Ford and we just slid, put the whole axle out of place. That was excellent!

Frank: Like there's this one road, I can't tell you where. It's secret, right? Where everybody goes to drag.

Alan: It's a great place, just excellent.

Frank: Like it seems kinda weird, it seems like the 50's, but it still happens. Archie gets into his car, this 396, man. Revs it up and goes.

Alan: One time they had a drag with this guy with a 400 Turbo, 4 speed, that was a great race. It hit 145 miles an hour.

Frank: Like we've seen accidents, roll overs, and stuff like that, but nobody's ever been killed.

Alan: Like that just happens when somebody gups out and hits the brakes, right?

Frank: Sometimes we have drags where you come flying at each other. This one guy came in and just went flying over the other car.

Both: What a mess!

ACTIVITIES

1. One of the challenges of this script is to create effective transitions between scenes. First determine where you feel changes in scenes occur, and then experiment with various techniques that will make the action flow from one scene to another. Some suggestions are: an action (or series of actions) which is repeated between scenes; a series of tableaux at each scene change; a sound effect or musical bridge which signals the transition. Be prepared to experiment with many techniques until the whole group is satisfied.

2. In the Playbill, we mentioned the term choral speaking. This type of dramatization is examined in Chapter 7, and you may want to read The Program for Chapter 7 now. Choral speaking involves many voices speaking in unison, and this kind of dramatization has great importance in the ritual beginnings of theatre. In *Juve*, you have a chance to use choral speech when delivering the nursery rhymes, chants, and song, all of which are forms of ritual. Experiment with a variety of ways of combining your voices. Vary your loudness, pitch, tone, etc.

3. In this selection from *Juve*, the teenage boys talk about hockey, planes, cars, and engines. The teenage girls chant rhymes like, "I love the boys and the boys love me." Do you find this portrayal of young men and women convincing, or is it a stereotype? What changes would you make to the script in order to better represent your own lifestyle?

4. You can recreate the process by which *Juve* was evolved. In groups choose an incident which one person has experienced and retells to you now. Develop an improvisation based on this story, and work until the improvisation is satisfactory. Then have someone write down the dialogue as it is spoken. You may have to edit and revise the dialogue until you are sure that it conveys the story accurately and effectively.

5. After developing a script in Activity 4, give the script to another group to dramatize. After they have rehearsed your script, have them present it to you; then explore what changes their interpretation has made to your script. Be particularly aware of how the group has created full or "real" characters rather than stereotypes or one-dimensional characters.

FROM

THE ELEPHANT MAN

by Bernard Pomerance

PLAYBILL

Unlike *Juve*, this selection is a conventional play written by a single playwright. It is based on the life of John Merrick, a horribly deformed man who lived in London, England, in the latter part of the nineteenth century. Frederick Treves, a doctor, rescued Merrick from a life as a freak in side-shows and contributed to Merrick's intellectual development. Merrick was an intelligent, perceptive person who became a celebrity in London society through his cleverness and gentle kindness.

When you read the scenes, be aware of how Merrick's inner depth of character overrides the image of his external appearance as described in Treves' opening speech.

CHARACTERS

Frederick Treves, a doctor
John Merrick, the elephant man
Voice at the lecture
Carr Gomm, administrator of the London Hospital
Porter, a hospital orderly
Snork, a hospital orderly

SCENE III

WHO HAS SEEN THE LIKE OF THIS?

*(*TREVES *lectures.* MERRICK *contorts himself to approximate projected slides of the real Merrick.*[1]*)*

Treves: The most striking feature about him was his enormous head. Its circumference was about that of a man's waist. From the brow there projected a huge bony mass like a loaf, while from the back of his head hung a bag of spongy fungous-looking skin, the surface of which was comparable to brown cauliflower. On the top of the skull were a few long lank hairs. The osseous growth on the forehead, at this stage about the size of a tangerine, almost occluded one eye. From the upper jaw there projected another mass of bone. It protruded from the mouth like a pink stump, turning the upper lip inside out, and making the mouth a wide slobbering aperture. The nose was merely a lump of flesh, only recognizable as a nose from its position. The deformities rendered the face utterly incapable of the expression of any emotion whatsoever. The back was horrible because from it hung, as far down as the middle of the thigh, huge sack-like masses of flesh covered by the same loathsome cauliflower stain. The right arm was of enormous size and shapeless. It suggested but was not elephantiasis, and was overgrown also with pendant masses of the same cauliflower-like skin. The right hand was large and clumsy—a fin or paddle rather than a hand. No distinction existed between the palm and back, the thumb was like a radish, the fingers like thick tuberous roots. As a limb it was useless. The other arm was remarkable by contrast. It was not only normal, but was moreover a delicately shaped limb covered with a fine skin and provided with a beautiful hand which any woman might have envied. From the chest hung a bag of the same repulsive flesh. It was like a dewlap suspended from the neck of a lizard. The lower limbs had the characters of the deformed arm. They were unwieldy, dropsical-looking, and grossly misshapen. There arose from the fungous skin growths a very sickening stench which was hard to tolerate. To add a further burden to his trouble, the wretched man when a boy developed hip disease which left him permanently lame, so that he could only walk with a stick. *(To* MERRICK*)* Please. (MERRICK *walks.)* He was thus denied all means of escape from his tormentors.

Voice: Mr. Treves, you have shown a profound and unknown disorder to us. You have said when he leaves here it is for his exhibition again. I do not think it ought to be permitted. It is a disgrace. It is a pity and a disgrace. It is an indecency in fact. It may be a danger in ways we do not know. Something ought to be done about it.

Treves: I am a doctor. What would you have me do?

Voice: Well. I know what to do. *I* know.

(Silence as lights fade out.)

SCENE VIII

MERCY AND JUSTICE ELUDE OUR MINDS AND ACTIONS

(MERRICK *in bath.* TREVES, GOMM.*)*

Merrick: How long is as long as I like?

Treves: You may stay for life. The funds exist.

Merrick: Been reading this. About homes for the blind. Wouldn't mind going to one when I have to move.

Treves: But you do not have to move; and you're not blind.

Merrick: I would prefer it where no one stared at me.

Gomm: No one will bother you here.

Treves: Certainly not. I've given instructions.

(PORTER *and* SNORK *peek in.)*

Porter: What'd I tell you?

Snork: Gawd almighty. Oh. Mr. Treves. Mr. Gomm.

Treves: You were told not to do this. I don't understand. You must not lurk about. Surely you have work.

Porter: Yes, sir.

Treves: Well, it is infuriating. When you are told a thing, you must listen. I won't have you gaping in on my patients. Kindly remember that.

Porter: Isn't a patient, sir, is he?

Treves: Do not let me find you here again.

Porter: Didn't know you were here, sir. We'll be off now.

[1]Anyone playing the part of Merrick is cautioned to be very careful of back strain and not to maintain the contorted posture for too long.

Gomm: No, no, Will. Mr. Treves was precisely saying no one would intrude when you intruded.

Treves: He is warned now. Merrick does not like it.

Gomm: He was warned before. On what penalty, Will?

Porter: That you'd sack me, sir.

Gomm: You are sacked, Will. You, his friend, you work here?

Snork: Just started last week, sir.

Gomm: Well, I hope the point is taken now.

Porter: Mr. Gomm—I ain't truly sacked, am I?

Gomm: Will, yes. Truly sacked. You will never be more truly sacked.

Porter: It's not me. My wife ain't well. My sister has got to take care of our kids, and of her. Well.

Gomm: Think of them first next time.

Porter: It ain't as if I interfered with his medicine.

Gomm: That is exactly what it is. You may go.

Porter: Just keeping him to look at in private. That's all. Isn't it?

(SNORK *and* PORTER *exit.)*

Gomm: There are priorities, Frederick. The first is discipline. Smooth is the passage to the tight ship's master. Merrick, you are safe from prying now.

Treves: Have we nothing to say, John?

Merrick: If all that'd stared at me'd been sacked—there'd be whole towns out of work.

Treves: I meant, "Thank you, sir."

Merrick: "Thank you sir."

Treves: We always do say please and thank you, don't we?

Merrick: Yes, sir. Thank you.

Treves: If we want to properly be like others.

Merrick: Yes, sir, I want to.

Treves: Then it is for our own good, is it not?

Merrick: Yes, sir. Thank you, Mr. Gomm.

Gomm: Sir, you are welcome. (*Exits.*)

Treves: You are happy here, are you not, John?

Merrick: Yes.

Treves: The baths have rid you of the odor, have they not?

Merrick: First chance I had to bathe regular. Ly.

Treves: And three meals a day delivered to your room?

Merrick: Yes, sir.

Treves: This is your Promised Land, is it not? A roof. Food. Protection. Care. Is it not?

Merrick: Right, Mr. Treves.

Treves: I will bet you don't know what to call this.

Merrick: No, sir, I don't know.

Treves: You call it, Home.

Merrick: Never had a home before.

Treves: You have one now. Say it, John: Home.

Merrick: Home.

Treves: No, no, really say it. I have a home. This is my. Go on.

Merrick: I have a home. This is my home. This is my home. I have a home. As long as I like?

Treves: That is what home is.

Merrick: That is what is home.

Treves: If I abide by the rules, I will be happy.

Merrick: Yes, sir.

Treves: Don't be shy.

Merrick: If I abide by the rules I will be happy.

Treves: Very good. Why?

Merrick: Why what?

Treves: Will you be happy?

Merrick: Because it is my home.

Treves: No, no. Why do rules make you happy?

Merrick: I don't know.

Treves: Of course you do.

Merrick: No, I really don't.

Treves: Why does anything make you happy?

Merrick: Like what? Like what?

Treves: Don't be upset. Rules make us happy because they are for our own good.

Merrick: Okay.

Treves: Don't be shy, John. You can say it.

Merrick: This is my home?

Treves: No. About rules making us happy.

Merrick: They make us happy because they are for our own good.

Treves: Excellent. Now: I am submitting a follow-up paper on you to the London Pathological Society. It would help if you told me what you recall about your first years, John. To fill in gaps.

Merrick: To fill in gaps. The workhouse where they put me. They beat you there like a drum. Boom boom: scrape the floor white. Shine the pan, boom boom. It never ends. The floor is always dirty. The pan is always tarnished. There is nothing you can do about it. You are always attacked anyway. Boom boom. Boom boom. Boom boom. Will the children go to the workhouse?

Treves: What children?

Merrick: The children. The man he sacked.

Treves: Of necessity Will will find other employment. You don't want crowds staring at you, do you?

Merrick: No.

Treves: In your own home you do not have to have crowds staring at you. Or anyone. Do you? In your home?

Merrick: No.

Treves: Then Mr. Gomm was merciful. You yourself are proof. Is it not so? (*Pause.*) Well? Is it not so?

Merrick: If your mercy is so cruel, what do you have for justice?

Treves: I am sorry. It is just the way things are.

Merrick: Boom boom. Boom boom. Boom boom.

(Fadeout.)

ACTIVITIES

1. This script requires that the physical features of the Elephant Man be conveyed by suggestion rather than by extensive makeup and costume. Experiment with one person forming the shape of Merrick while another reads Treves' speech in Scene III. Determine which physical shapes and movements convey the features Treves describes.

2. Examine the speeches of Merrick in Scene VIII to determine all you can about his inner life. Experiment with ways of playing the role so that his qualities are clearly expressed despite his external features.

3. Analyse the relationship between Treves and Merrick as expressed through their dialogue in Scene VIII. Play the scene in a variety of ways: between a parent and child, a doctor and patient, and as two children. How does the scene change?

4. When Will, the hospital porter, is "sacked," each of the characters involved had thoughts and feelings about the action. Each person who has a role in this scene can improvise a monologue in which those thoughts and feelings are said aloud. This technique is used later in *Countdown* (Section A, Chapter 3).

5. This play presents a theme which examines the contrast between a person's inner reality and the way others perceive that person. This theme will reappear in other selections, which you may want to read now: *The Farm Show* (Section A, Chapter 3), and *The Good Person of Szechwan* (Section C, Chapter 20). With other members of a group, develop an improvisation which expresses this theme in a contemporary setting.

COME AND GO

by Samuel Beckett

PLAYBILL

This is the text of a complete play. Initially it may appear to be very simple, but when you examine it more closely, you will find that it has a number of possible meanings. Before working on the play, read Beckett's Notes on this page. In them he gives some advice on positions, lighting, costumes, props, exits, voices, and sounds. Then, during your first read-through of the play, pay particular attention to the stage directions and the actions they indicate. Attempt to duplicate these actions, and determine how they enhance or change your interpretation of the script.

CHARACTERS

Flo
Vi } Age undeterminable
Ru

(Sitting centre side by side stage right to left FLO, VI, *and* RU. *Very erect, facing front, hands clasped in laps. Silence.)*

Vi: Ru.

Ru: Yes.

Vi: Flo.

Flo: Yes.

Vi: When did we three last meet?

Ru: Let us not speak.

(Silence. Exit VI *right. Silence.)*

Flo: Ru.

Ru: Yes.

Flo: What do you think of Vi?

Ru: I see little change. (FLO *moves to centre seat, whispers in* RU*'s ear. Appalled.*) Oh! (*They look at each other.* FLO *puts her finger to her lips.*) Does she not realize?

Flo: God grant not.

(Enter VI. FLO *and* RU *turn back front, resume pose.* VI *sits right. Silence.)*

Flo: Just sit together as we used to, in the playground at Miss Wade's.

Ru: On the log.

(Silence. Exit FLO *left. Silence.)*

Ru: Vi.

Vi: Yes.

Ru: How do you find Flo?

Vi: She seems much the same. (RU *moves to centre seat, whispers in* VI*'s ear. Appalled.*) Oh! (*They look at each other.* RU *puts her finger to her lips.*) Has she not been told?

Ru: God forbid.

(Enter FLO. RU *and* VI *turn back front, resume pose.* FLO *sits left. Silence.)*

Ru: Holding hands . . . that way.

Flo: Dreaming of . . . love.

(Silence. Exit RU *right. Silence.)*

Vi: Flo.

Flo: Yes.

Vi: How do you think Ru is looking?

Flo: One sees little in this light. (VI *moves to centre seat, whispers in* FLO*'s ear. Appalled.*) Oh! (*They look at each other.* VI *puts her finger to her lips.*) Does she not know?

Vi: Please God not.

(Enter RU. VI *and* FLO *turn back front, resume pose.* RU sits right. Silence.)

Vi: May we not speak of the old days? (*Silence.*) Of what came after? (*Silence.*) Shall we hold hands in the old way?

(After a moment they join hands as follows: VI*'s right hand with* RU*'s right hand,* VI*'s left hand with* FLO*'s left hand,* FLO*'s right hand with* RU*'s left hand,* VI*'s arms being above* RU*'s left arm and* FLO*'s right arm. The three pairs of clasped hands rest on the three laps. Silence.)*

Flo: I can feel the rings.

(Silence.)

NOTES

Successive positions

1	Flo	Vi	Ru
2	Flo		Ru
		Flo	Ru
3	Vi	Flo	Ru
4	Vi		Ru
	Vi	Ru	
5	Vi	Ru	Flo
6	Vi		Flo
		Vi	Flo
7	Ru	Vi	Flo

Hands

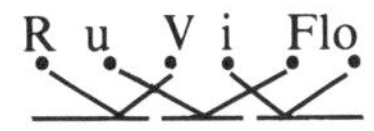

Lighting
Soft, from above only and concentrated on playing area. Rest of stage as dark as possible.

Costume
*Full-length coats, buttoned high, dull violet (*RU*), dull red (*VI*), dull yellow (*FLO*). Drab nondescript hats with enough brim to shade faces. Apart from color differentiation three figures as alike as possible. Light shoes with rubber soles. Hands made up to be as visible as possible. No rings apparent.*

Seat
Narrow benchlike seat, without back, just long enough to accommodate three figures almost touching. As little visible as possible. It should not be clear what they are sitting on.

Exits
The figures are not seen to go off-stage.

They should disappear a few steps from lit area. If dark not sufficient to allow this, recourse should be had to screens or drapes as little visible as possible. Exits and entrances slow, without sound of feet.

Ohs
Three very different sounds.

Voices
As low as compatible with audibility. Colorless except for three "ohs" and two lines following.

ACTIVITIES

1. Read through the script several times aloud exactly as it is written, following as closely as possible all the stage directions and notes. Afterwards discuss with your group what the script means to each of you. If there is agreement, continue to elaborate and extend that meaning. If there is a different perception of the meaning, do the script according to each of the different interpretations and discuss how it changes each time.

2. Determine what each character says in the whispered conversation. How does the play change when what is whispered is trivial instead of very serious?

3. Change the style of the script in a radical way. Do it in the style of *Juve*, using chanting and choral speaking when delivering the lines. What effect does this style-change have on the meaning of the script?

4. This script is an example of "theatre of the absurd." Similar scripts, such as *The Bald Soprano* (Section C, Chapter 20) and *The Real Inspector Hound* (Section A, Chapter 2), are found in other sections of this book. You may want to read these scripts now, or, when working on them later, refer back to your work on *Come and Go.*

FROM

WHAT GLORIOUS TIMES THEY HAD

by Diane Grant and Company

PLAYBILL

This play is based on actual events which occurred in Manitoba just before the First World War. Nellie McClung and a dedicated group of suffragists were determined to change society so that women would be allowed to vote. The scenes presented here also demonstrate the theatrical convention of "a play-within-a-play," other examples of which can be found elsewhere in this book. When you read this play, be aware of the need for some characters to play two different roles: one in the play and another in the play-within-a-play.

CHARACTERS

Sir Rodmond Roblin, the Premier of Manitoba
P.T. Fletcher, the parliamentary secretary to Sir Rodmond Roblin
Nellie McClung, a social reformer, novelist and suffragist
Frances Beynon, a journalist and suffragist
Lillian Beynon Thomas, a journalist and suffragist, Frances' sister
E. Cora Hind, an agriculture expert and journalist
Delegate, male member of Franchise for Fellows Society
Various members of the Legislative Assembly, male cast members
Various members of the Mock Parliament, female cast members

(CORA *enters from upstage left with "Vote With Women" banners which she distributes. The women put them on and stand in front of stage right chairs,* NELLIE *in front of upstage chairs, next* CORA, LILLIAN *and* FRANCES, *respectively.* ROBLIN, *carrying Union Jack, enters from downstage left, followed by* FLETCHER *carrying balloons. The men cross upstage centre, then left.* FLETCHER *stands behind the small desk, still carrying balloons.* ROBLIN *crosses to large desk and sits.* FLETCHER *and the women sit.)*

Roblin: (*sotto voce*) Are the boys all here, Fletcher?

Fletcher: Yes, Mr. Premier.

Roblin: (*stands*) Members of the Committee. We are pleased to have with us today the charming members of the Political Equality League, who are here to petition for suffrage. The first spokesman—uh—spokeswoman will be Mrs. Nellie McClung. Mrs. McClung.

Fletcher: Here, here.

Nellie: (*stands*) I want to thank you for your gracious reception of our delegation. (*Applause from the women.* ROBLIN *nods graciously.*) We are not here to ask for mercy but for justice. Do we not have brains to think, hands to work, hearts to feel and lives to live? Do we not bear our part in citizenship? Do we not help to build the empire? We want the women's point of view represented in our legislation. How would you, Sir Rodmond, like to be governed by a parliament of women?

Roblin: I have a good wife. She governs me well enough.

(FLETCHER *laughs.)*

Nellie: The Premier has a good wife. He, at least, is not afraid to trust the women with the franchise. (*The women laugh.*) However, there are some who say that the government is afraid to give us the vote.

Women: Here, here. True, true. Go on.

Roblin: Some people will say anything.

Nellie: Indeed, they will. Some even say that politics is too corrupt for women. But why should politics be corrupt? There is nothing inherently vicious about politics, and the politician who says it is corrupt is admitting one of two things—either that he is a party to that corruption, or that he is unable to prevent it.

(The women applaud.)

Women: Here, here. True, true. Go on.

Nellie: In either case, he is sounding the alarm and we are willing, even anxious to come to the rescue.

(The women laugh and applaud. ROBLIN *rises in anger and interjects.)*

Roblin: *(shouting)* When you say things are corrupt, it is only the imaginings of a vile and wicked mind.

*(*FLETCHER *pounds his desk.)*

Women: No, no. Shame, shame. Go on, Nellie, go on.

Roblin: I did not dispute you when you were speaking. You will be good enough to listen to my reply. (NELLIE *sits down.* ROBLIN *regains composure.*) Now. The question raised today is not a new one, and it is not confined to Manitoba, for the claim of women for equal suffrage is being made in a great many civilized countries, mostly English-speaking ones.

Fletcher: Here, here.

Roblin: As you know, we draw our inspiration in legislation, theology, art and science from the motherland. Now, that being a fact that none will deny, can you, can anyone, say with confidence that what we have today will be preserved and not destroyed? So surely as the sun arose today in the east and will set in the west, so surely, if you are right, the franchise will come. But, consider the example of England. There, when Mrs. Pankhurst and her militant supporters were briefly disappointed in their cause, they became hysterical, endangered life, and destroyed millions of dollars worth of property. As I have listened, I have thought how delighted Lloyd George, Asquith, and other British statesmen would have been if they had been approached in the same ladylike manner as I have been today. A mother has a hundredfold more influence in shaping public opinion around her dinner table than she would have in the market place, hurling her eloquent phrases to the multitude. I believe that woman suffrage would break up the home. It would throw the children into the arms of the servant girls! *(The women stand, applauding vigorously.* FLETCHER *applauds and then, hearing the applause, stops, perplexedly.* ROBLIN *turns and stares at the women. He turns to* FLETCHER.) Come on, boys.

(Music: "The Maple Leaf Forever." Lights slowly fade. ROBLIN *and* FLETCHER, *with balloons, exit downstage right, followed by* NELLIE, CORA, LILLIAN *and* FRANCES *respectively.* NELLIE *carries with her the Union Jack. Lights come up slowly.)*

SCENE 2
THE WALKER THEATRE

Nellie: *(entering from upstage right, carrying bunting)* I've got the bunting.

*(*NELLIE *crosses to large desk.* FRANCES *enters from downstage right, carrying newspaper. She crosses and gives newspaper to* NELLIE. NELLIE *and* FRANCES *move large desk upstage centre.* LILLIAN *enters from downstage right.)*

Lillian: I want to talk to Mr. Walker.[1] Won't be a moment.

*(*LILLIAN *crosses to small desk, wheels it out upstage left.* NELLIE *puts newspaper on chair upstage right, and drapes bunting on large desk.* FRANCES, *facing front, talks out.)*

Frances: Frank?[2] May I please see the spotlight for the last speech?

(Blackout. Spot up, which wavers about. CORA *enters from upstage right and is hit by the spot. She is carrying the balloons.)*

Cora: What is going on? I can't see a blasted thing. And where is Lillian?

(The spot continues to wander about the stage. LILLIAN *enters from upstage left with mace.* CORA *places balloons on stage right chairs, except for first chair, downstage right.)*

Lillian: I can't find Mr. Walker. We've only got five minutes.

(She crosses upstage centre and places mace on large desk. LILLIAN *exits downstage right.)*

Frances: Oh, Frank. That will never do.

(Blackout.)

Lillian: *(offstage right)* Frances, your hat is here. Come and put it on.

Frances: Coming, Lillian. For heaven's sake, Frank. Turn something on.

*(*FRANCES *exits downstage left. All lights come up.* LILLIAN *enters from downstage right, carrying hat.)*

Lillian: Where's Frances?

Nellie: Trying on her hat.

[1]the theatre owner
[2]the stage manager

*(*LILLIAN *puts the hat on the large desk.* FRANCES *enters from downstage left.)*

Frances: Wonderful news. We're all sold out.

All: *(simultaneously)* Marvellous. Isn't that splendid! Hurray!

(Blackout. NELLIE *moves downstage centre.* CORA *stands in front of chair, downstage right.* LILLIAN *stands in front of chair, downstage left.* FRANCES *crosses upstage centre, puts on hat and picks up mace.)*

Cora: *(whispers)* Good luck, everybody.

(Spot up on NELLIE. *All lights come up slowly.)*

Nellie: Ladies and gentlemen, may I remind you that for the next short while, positions in society will be reversed. The women will have the vote and the men will have to beg for it.

(Spot out. All lights are up. NELLIE *crosses to upstage left chair and stands in front of it.)*

Frances: *(Speaker of the House)* No idiot, lunatic, criminal or man shall vote. *(Raps mace three times.)* I hereby declare this parliament in session.

(All converge centre stage and talk at once, as follows.)

Nellie: I just adore that mace. It's the prettiest thing.

Frances: Thank you. I love your hat.

Nellie: This old thing?

Lillian: Did you hear that Mrs. Armstrong had a boy?

Frances: Order, order, ladies.

Cora: A boy? She must be so disappointed.

Nellie: That makes five boys. Tsk, tsk.

Frances: Order, order, ladies.

Lillian: Five!

Cora: Have you seen that new Sears catalogue?

Nellie: Aren't the short skirts ghastly?

Frances: *(raising her voice)* Order! *(Silence.* NELLIE, CORA *and* LILLIAN *sit down.* FRANCES, *sweetly—)* Shall we begin, ladies? *(Pause)* The first item on the agenda is the question of the franchise for men.

Lillian: *(as Government, stands)* Madame Speaker. It's a well-known fact, and I speak as a mother, that the male child is more difficult to toilet train than the female child, and the same would undoubtedly hold true when training men in parliamentary procedures. (*Sits.*)

Cora: (*as Opposition, stands*) Red herring. Red herring.

Frances: (*Speaker*) Order. Order. I recognize the Honorable Leader of the Opposition.

Cora: (*Opposition*) Speaking as one who is rather keen on men, I submit that it is poppycock to shut out half of the world's population simply because of a minor biological difference. (*Sits.*)

Lillian: (*as Government, stands*) Madame Speaker, may I retort?

Cora: (*as Opposition, stands*) That's a nickel word.

Frances: (*Speaker*) Order. Order. Perhaps the Honorable member of the Opposition will allow the Honorable member from Brandon-Souris to reply.

Cora: (*Opposition*) Don't you mean retort?

Frances: (*Speaker*) Order!

(CORA—*the Opposition—sits.)*

Lillian: (*Government*) This difference. A minor one, you say? Let me appeal to your finer sensibilities, woman to woman. Would you want this room, this very room, filled with the reek of cigar smoke? Would you want to hear the clink of brandy glasses in caucus? Would you want the halls festooned wth spitoons, echoing with ribald laughter? Think. Can you, in all honesty, still say a minor difference?

Cora: (*Opposition*) Balderdash. Poppycock. Emotional hogwash.

Frances: (*Speaker*) Order. Order. Time has expired. Chair recognizes the. . . .

Lillian: (*Government*) And have you considered the suggestive nature of male attire—the colored waist-coats, the embroidered suspenders, the bay rum behind the ears, the waxed ends of moustaches and the tight trousers? (*Sits.*)

Cora: (*Opposition*) Yes, yes, yes.

Frances: (*Speaker, rapping mace*) May I have order! We have reached the end of the question period.

Cora: (*as Opposition, stands*) I would like to address. . . .

Frances: (*Speaker*) I gather that the Honorable Leader of the Opposition has a supplementary question.

Cora: (*Opposition*) I address my question to the Honorable member from Brandon-Souris. I speak on behalf of the fathers of Manitoba. Should they not have legal guardianship rights over their children? They plant the seed, should they not have a share in the harvest? (*Sits.*)

Lillian: (*as Government, stands*) Who brings the child forth in pain and travail? The mother. Who nurtures it at her breast? The mother. Who teaches it to walk, talk and sing?

All: (*sing together*) Put them all together, they spell "Mother."

*(*CORA*—the Opposition, and* LILLIAN*—the Government, speak together, neither listening to the other. They are face to face.)*

Cora: (*Opposition*) Furthermore, I find it disgusting that you should use this important question as an opportunity for oratory.

Lillian: (*Government*) My husband doesn't want the vote. He's the power behind the throne. That's good enough for him.

(As they argue, DELEGATE *enters from upstage left. He is wearing a banner which says "Votes For Men." He crosses downstage right and attempts to get past* LILLIAN *and* CORA. *They pay no attention to him. The Speaker attempts to restore order as* DELEGATE *pushes through the two women and stands downstage right. He, the delegate, is a timid soul but he knows that right is on his side.)*

Frances: (*Speaker*) Order! (*Silence.* CORA *and* LILLIAN *sit.* FRANCES, *sweetly—*) The chair recognizes the delegate from the Franchise for Fellows Society.

Delegate: Ladies and . . . ladies. I am here on behalf of the Franchise for Fellows Society to ask, nay to beg for the vote.

We have been shut out too long and we're knocking at the door.
We bring home the bacon, may we not cook it?
We lie in the beds, may we not make them?
We have one less rib, why not one more privilege?
We have the brains, why not the vote?

(Pause. All look at NELLIE *who is hidden behind the newspaper. She slowly lowers newspaper, looks around and gets to her feet.)*

Nellie: (*The Premier*) We wish to compliment the delegation on its splendid gentlemanly appearance. (*All whistle a wolf whistle.*) If, without exercising the vote, such splendid specimens of manhood can exist, such a system of affairs should not be interfered with. If the leader of the delegation is as intelligent as he is attractive, we should have no problem. As I have listened, I have thought how delighted Lady Lloyd George, Queen Mary, and other British stateswomen would have been if they had been approached in as gentlemanly a manner as I have been today. As to the work of woman, woman has toiled early and woman has toiled late so that the idol of her heart might have the culture and accomplishment that we see here in this man today. So surely as the sun arose today in the east and will set in the west, so surely, if we extend the vote to men, they will take a backward step—and fall off their pedestals. Why upset yourselves? Politics is an unsettling business, and unsettled men mean unsettled bills, broken furniture, broken vows and divorce! (*The women and the delegate gasp in horror.*) Come on, girls.

*(*NELLIE *exits downstage left, followed by* LILLIAN, FRANCES, *and* CORA, *who picks up balloons and carries them out.)*

ACTIVITIES

1. As you work with this script, examine the opportunities and problems that exist in doing a play within a play. Be aware of the intent of the second play and determine if it is intended to parody an existing situation. You will have to decide on whether to present the scene in a comic or serious manner. Experiment with both modes and decide which is more effective.

2. These scenes present examples of stereotypical thinking—that is, seeing certain people as a group rather than as unique individuals. The stereotype presented here might be summed up as "all women should remain at home, raise children and look after their husbands." This play examines stereotypes by reversing the situation: women form the government and men are seeking the vote. In a group, examine aspects of contemporary life in which stereotyping takes place. Using a technique similar to this play, create an improvisation where the roles are reversed between those regarded as stereotypes and those who do the stereotyping.

3. Other chapters in this book look at the conventions you are working with in this script. The dramatic convention of a play within a play is encountered again in *The Real Inspector Hound* (Section A, Chapter 2), *Jitters* (Section A, Chapter 2), *A Midsummer Night's Dream* (Section A, Chapter 4), *Rosencrantz and Guildenstern are Dead* (Section C, Chapter 18), and *Six Characters in Search of an Author* (Section C, Chapter 20). The dramatization of historical material is dealt with in Section B, Chapter 10 "Scripting" and Chapter 12 "Docudrama."

FROM

BAREFOOT IN THE PARK

by Neil Simon

PLAYBILL

Paul and Corie Bratter are newly married and have moved to an apartment on the sixth floor of a building with no elevator. Paul is just beginning practice as a lawyer, and Corie, full of life and adventure, wants to prevent him from becoming "stuffy." In her efforts to do so, she often sounds and acts like a stereotypical "wife." For you to understand this role more fully, you should read *Love and Marriage Lazzi Style* in Chapter 17 at some point during your work with this scene.

When this scene from *Barefoot in the Park* begins, the furniture has arrived and Corie is busy setting up the apartment. Mr. Velasco lives in a loft above their apartment and uses their roof and window ledge to get to his home. As you read this script be aware of the comic structure of the dialogue. Be particularly aware of how timing increases the effectiveness of line delivery. Experiment with pauses, slow line delivery and rapid line delivery to find the best comic effect. Remember that comedy is never funny to the actors, only to those who watch. Consequently, the characters must treat the situation seriously.

CHARACTERS

Corie Bratter
Paul Bratter
Corie's mother

(There is no one on-stage. The apartment is dark except for a crack of light under the bedroom door, and faint moonlight from the skylight. Suddenly the front door opens and CORIE *rushes in, carrying a pastry box and a bag containing two bottles. After switching on the lights at the door, she puts her packages on the coffee table, and hangs her coat in the closet.* CORIE *wears a cocktail dress for the festivities planned for tonight, and she sings as she hurries to get everything ready. She is breathing heavily but she is getting accustomed to the stairs. As she takes a bottle of vermouth and a bottle of gin out of the bag, the doorbell buzzes. She buzzes back, opens the door, and yells down the stairs.)*

Corie: (*Yells*) Paul? (*We hear some strange, incoherent sound from below*) Hi, love . . . (*She crosses back to the coffee table, and dumps hors d'oeuvres from the pastry box onto a tray*) Hey, they sent the wrong lamps . . . but they go with the room so I'm keeping them. (*She crosses to the bar, gets a martini pitcher and brings it back to the coffee table*) . . . Oh, do you have an Aunt Fern? . . . Because she sent us a cheque . . . Anyway, you have a cheap Aunt Fern . . . How you doing? (*We hear a mumble from below.* CORIE *opens both bottles and pours them simultaneously into the shaker so that she has martinis made with equal parts of gin and vermouth*) . . . Oh, and your mother called from Philly . . . She and Dad will be up a week from Sunday . . . And your sister has a new boy friend. From Rutgers . . . He's got acne and they all hate him . . . including your sister. (*She takes the shaker and while mixing the cocktails she crosses to the door*) . . . Hey, lover, start puckering your lips 'cause you're gonna get kissed for five solid minutes and then . . . (*She stops*) Oh, hello, Mr. Munshin. I thought it was my husband. Sorry. (*A door slams. She shrugs sheepishly and walks back into the room, closing the door behind her. As she goes into the kitchen, the door opens and* PAUL *enters, gasping. He drops his attaché case at the railing, and collapses on the couch.* CORIE *comes out of the kitchen with the shaker and ice bucket*) It *was* you. I thought I heard your voice. *(She puts the ice bucket on the bookcase and the shaker on the end table)*

Paul: (*Gasp, gasp*) Mr. Munshin and I came in together. (CORIE *jumps on him and flings her arms around his neck; he winces in pain*) Do you have to carry on—a whole personal conversation with me—on the stairs?

Corie: Well, there's so much I wanted to tell you . . . and I haven't seen you all day . . . and it takes you so long to get up.

Paul: Everyone knows the intimate details of our life . . . I ring the bell and suddenly we're on the air.

Corie: Tomorrow I'll yell, "Come on up, Harry, my husband isn't home." (*She takes the empty box and bag, and throws them in the garbage pail in the kitchen*) Hey, wouldn't that be a gas if everyone in the building thought I was having an affair with someone?

Paul: Mr. Munshin thinks it's *him* right now.

Corie: (*Crossing back to the couch*) Well?

Paul: Well what?

Corie: What happened in court today? Gump or Birnbaum?

Paul: Birnbaum!

Corie: (*Jumps on his lap again. He winces again*) Oh, Paul, you won.

You won, darling. Oh, sweetheart, I'm so proud of you. (*She stops and looks at him*) Well, aren't you happy?

Paul: (*Glumly*) Birnbaum won the protection of his good name but no damages. We were awarded six cents.

Corie: Six cents?

Paul: That's the law. You have to be awarded something, so the court made it six cents.

Corie: How much of that do you get?

Paul: Nothing. Birnbaum gets the whole six cents . . . And I get a going-over in the office. From now on I get all the cases that come in for a dime or under.

Corie: (*Opening his collar and rubbing his neck*) Oh, darling, you won. That's all that counts. You're a good lawyer.

Paul: Some lawyer . . . So tomorrow I go back to sharpening pencils.

Corie: And tonight you're here with me. (*She kisses his neck*) Did you miss me today?

Paul: No.

Corie: (*Gets off his lap and sits on the couch*) Why not?

Paul: Because you called me eight times . . . I don't speak to you that much when I'm home.

Corie: (*Rearranging the canapés*) Oh, you're grouchy. I want a divorce.

Paul: I'm not grouchy . . . I'm tired . . . I had a rotten day today . . . I'm a little irritable . . . and cold . . . and grouchy.

Corie: Okay, grouch. I'll fix you a drink. (*She crosses to the bar and brings back three glasses*)

Paul: (*Crosses to the closet, takes off his overcoat and jacket, and hangs them up*) I just couldn't think today. Couldn't think . . . Moving furniture until three o'clock in the morning.

Corie: Mr. Velasco moved. You complained.

(She pours a drink)

Paul: Mr. Velasco *pointed*! *I* moved! . . . He came in here, drank my liquor, made three telephone calls, and ordered me around like I was one of the Santini Brothers.

(He takes the drink from CORIE*, and crosses to the dictionary on the table under the radiator. He takes a gulp of his drink and reacts with horror. He looks at* CORIE*, who shrugs in reply)*

Corie: Temper, temper. We're supposed to be charming tonight.

Paul: (*Taking off his tie*) Yeah, well, I've got news for you. This thing tonight has "fiasco" written all over it.

Corie: (*Moves to the mirror on the washstand on the bedroom landing*) Why should it be a fiasco? It's just conceivable they may have something in common.

Paul: (*Folding his tie*) Your mother? That quiet, dainty little woman . . . and the Count of Monte Cristo? You must be kidding.

(He puts the tie between the pages of the dictionary, and slams it shut)

Corie: Why?

(She puts on a necklace and earrings)

Paul: (*Crosses to the closet and gets another tie*) You saw his apartment. He wears Japanese kimonos and sleeps on rugs. Your mother wears a hairnet and sleeps on a board.

Corie: What's that got to do with it?

Paul: (*Crossing back to the mirror under the radiator and fixing his tie*) Everything. He skis, climbs mountains, and the only way into his apartment is up a ladder or across a ledge. I don't really think he's looking for a good cook with a bad back.

Corie: The possibility of anything permanent never even occurred to me.

Paul: Permanent? We're lucky if we get past seven o'clock . . .

(The doorbell buzzes and PAUL *crosses to the door)*

Corie: That's her. Now you've got me worried . . . Paul, did I do something horrible?

Paul: (*Buzzing downstairs*) Probably.

Corie: Well, do something. Don't answer the door. Maybe she'll go home.

Paul: Too late. I buzzed. I could put a few Nembutals in his drink. It won't stop him but it could slow him down. (*He opens the door and yells downstairs*) Mom?

Mother's voice: (*From far below*) Yes, dear . . .

Paul: (*Yelling through his hands*) Take your time. (*He turns back into the room*) She's at Camp Three. She'll try the final assault in a few minutes.

Corie: Paul, maybe we could help her.

Paul: (*Getting his blazer out of the closet*) What do you mean?

Corie: (*Behind the couch*) A woman puts on rouge and powder to make her face more attractive. Maybe we can put some make-up on her personality.

Paul: (*Puts his attaché case on the bookcase*) I don't think I want to hear the rest of this.

Corie: All I'm saying is, we don't have to come right out and introduce her as "my dull fifty-year-old housewife mother."

Paul: (*Crosses to the bar and pours a drink of Scotch*) Well, that wasn't the wording I had planned. What did you have in mind?

Corie: (*Moves around the couch and sits on the right side of the couch*) Something a little more glamorous . . . A former actress.

Paul: Corie—

Corie: Well, she *was* in *The Man Who Came to Dinner*.

Paul: Your mother? In *The Man Who Came to Dinner*? . . . Where, in the West Orange P.T.A. show? (*He moves to the couch*)

Corie: No! . . . On Broadway . . . And she was in the original company of *Strange Interlude* and she had a small singing part in *Knickerbocker Holiday*.

Paul: Are you serious?

Corie: Honestly. Cross my heart.

Paul: Your mother? An actress?

(He sits next to CORIE*)*

Corie: Yes.

Paul: Why didn't you ever tell me?

Corie: I didn't think you'd be interested.

Paul: That's fascinating. I can't get over it.

Corie: You see. *Now* you're interested in her.

Paul: It's a lie?

Corie: The whole thing.

Paul: I'm going to control myself.

(He gets up and crosses back of the couch)

Corie: (*Gets up and crosses to him at right of the couch*) What do you say? Is she an actress?

Paul: No.

(He moves toward the door)

Corie: A fashion designer. The brains behind Ann Fogarty.

Paul: (*Points to the door*) She's on her way up.

Corie: A mystery writer . . . under an assumed name.

Paul: Let's lend her my trench coat and say she's a private eye.

Corie: You're no help.

Paul: I didn't book this act.

Corie: (*Moves to* PAUL) Paul, who is she going to be?

Paul: She's going to be your mother . . . and the evening will eventually pass . . . It just means . . . that the Birdman of Forty-eighth Street is not going to be your father. (*He opens the door*) Hello, Mom.

(MOTHER *collapses in, and* PAUL *and* CORIE *rush to support her. They quickly lead her to the armchair at right of the couch)*

Corie: Hello, sweetheart, how are you? (*She kisses* MOTHER, *who gasps for air*) Are you all right? (MOTHER *nods*) You want some water?

(MOTHER *shakes her head "No" as* PAUL *and* CORIE *lower her into the chair. She drops her pocketbook on the floor)*

Mother: Paul . . . in my pocketbook . . . are some pink pills.

Paul: (*Picks up her bag, closes the door, and begins to look for the pills*) Pink pills . . .

(CORIE *helps* MOTHER *take off her coat)*

Mother: I'll be all right . . . Just a little out of breath . . . (CORIE *crosses to the coffee table and pours a drink*) I had to park the car six blocks away . . . then it started to rain so I ran the last two blocks . . . then my heel got caught in the subway grating . . . so I pulled my foot out and stepped in a puddle . . . then a cab went by and splashed my stockings . . . if the hardware store downstairs was open . . . I was going to buy a knife and kill myself.

(PAUL *gives her a pill, and* CORIE *gives her a drink)*

Corie: Here, Mom. Drink this down.

Paul: Here's the pill . . .

(MOTHER *takes the pill, drinks, and coughs)*

Mother: A martini? To wash down a pill?

Corie: It'll make you feel better.

Mother: I *had* a martini at home. It made me sick . . . That's why I'm taking the pill . . .

(CORIE *puts the drink down on the table)*

Paul: (*Sitting on the end table*) You must be exhausted.

Mother: I'd just like to crawl into bed and cry myself to sleep.

Corie: (*Offering her the tray of hors d'oeuvres*) Here, Mom, have an hors d'oeuvre.

Mother: No, thank you, dear.

Corie: It's just blue cheese and sour cream.

Mother: (*Holds her stomach*) I wish you hadn't said that.

Paul: She doesn't feel like it, Corie . . . (CORIE *puts the tray down and sits on the couch.* PAUL *turns to* MOTHER) Maybe you'd like to lie down?

Corie: (*Panicky*) Now? She can't lie down now.

Mother: Corie's right. I can't lie down without my board . . . (*She puts her gloves into a pocket of her coat*) Right now all I want to do is see the apartment.

Paul: (*Sitting on the couch*) That's right. You haven't seen it with its clothes on, have you?

Mother: (*Rises and moves to the left*) Oh, Corie . . . Corie . . .

Corie: She doesn't like it.

Mother: (*Exhausted, she sinks into the armchair at left of the couch*) Like it? It's magnificent . . . and in less than a week. My goodness, how did you manage? Where did you get your ideas from?

Paul: We have a decorator who comes in through the window once a week.

Corie: (*Crossing to the bedroom*) Come take a look at the bedroom.

Mother: (*Crossing to the bedroom*) Yes, that's what I want to do . . . look at the bedroom. Were you able to get the bed in? (*She looks into the room*) Oh, it just fits, doesn't it?

Paul: Just. We have to turn in unison.

Mother: It looks very snug . . . and did you find a way to get to the closet?

Corie: Oh, we decided not to use the closet for a while.

Mother: Really? Don't you need the space?

Paul: Not as much as we need the clothes. It flooded.

Mother: The closet flooded?

Corie: It was an accident. Mr. Velasco left his bathtub running.

Mother: Mr. Velasco . . . Oh, the man upstairs . . .

Paul: (*Taking her arm*) Oh, then you know about Mr. Velasco?

Mother: Oh, yes. Corie had me on the phone for two hours.

Paul: Did you know he's been married three times?

Mother: Yes . . . (*She turns back to* CORIE) If I were you, dear, I'd sleep with a gun. (*She sits in the bentwood armchair*)

Paul: Well, there's just one thing I want to say about this evening . . .

Corie: (*Quickly, as she crosses to the coffee table*) Er . . . not before you have a drink. (*She hands* MOTHER *the martini*) Come on, Mother. To toast our new home.

Mother: (*Holding the glass*) Well, I can't refuse that.

Corie: (*Making a toast*) To the wonderful new life that's ahead of us all.

Paul: (*Holds up his glass*) And to the best sport I've ever seen. Your mother.

Mother: (*Making a toast*) And to two very charming people . . . that I'm so glad to be seeing again tonight . . . your mother and father.

(CORIE *sinks down on the sofa)*

Paul: (*About to drink, stops*) My what?

Mother: Your mother and father.

Paul: What about my mother and father?

Mother: Well, we're having dinner with them tonight, aren't we? . . . (*To* CORIE) Corie, isn't that what you said?

Paul: (*Sits next to* CORIE *on the sofa*) Is that right, Corie? Is that what you said?

Corie: (*Looks helpless, then plunges in*) Well, if I told you it was a blind date with Mr. Velasco upstairs, I couldn't have blasted you out of the house.

Mother: A blind date . . . (*She doesn't quite get it yet*) With Mr. Velasco . . . (*Then the dawn*) The one that . . .? (*She points up, then panics*) Good God! (*She takes a big gulp of her martini*)

Paul: (*To* CORIE) You didn't even tell your mother?

Corie: I was going to tell her the truth.

Paul: (*Looks at his watch*) It's one minute to seven. That's cutting it pretty thin, isn't it?

Mother: Corie, how could you do this to me? Of all the people in the world . . .

Corie: (*Gets up and moves to* MOTHER) I don't see what you're making such a fuss about. He's just a man.

Mother: My *accountant's* just a man. You make him sound like Douglas Fairbanks, Junior.

Corie: He looks *nothing* like Douglas Fairbanks, Junior, . . . does he, Paul?

Paul: No . . . He just jumps like him.

Mother: I'm not even dressed.

Corie: (*Brushing her* MOTHER*'s clothes*) You look fine, Mother.

Mother: For Paul's parents I just wanted to look clean . . . *He'll* think I'm a nurse.

Corie: Look, Mother, I promise you you'll have a good time tonight. He's a sweet, charming, and intelligent man. If you'll just relax I *know* you'll have a perfectly nice evening. (*There is a knock on the door*) Besides, it's too late. He's here.

Mother: Oh, no . . .

Corie: All right, now don't get excited.

Mother: (*Gets up and puts her drink on the coffee table*) You could say I'm the cleaning woman . . . I'll dust the table. Give me five dollars and I'll leave.

Corie: (*Stops* MOTHER) You just stay here . . .

Paul: (*Going to* MOTHER) It's going to be fine, Mom.

(*He crosses to the door)*

Corie: (*Leads* MOTHER *back to the sofa*) And smile. You're irresistible when you do. And finish your martini.

(*She takes it from the table and hands it to* MOTHER*)*

Mother: Do you have a lot of these?

Corie: As many as you need.

Mother: I'm going to need a lot of these.

(*She downs a good belt)*

Paul: Can I open the door?

Corie: Paul, wait a minute . . . Mother . . . your hair . . . in the back . . .

Mother: (*Stricken, she begins to fuss with her hair*) What? What's the matter with my hair?

Corie: (*Fixing* MOTHER'S *hair*) It's all right now. I fixed it.

Mother: (*Moves toward* PAUL) Is something wrong with my hair?

Paul: (*Impatient*) There's a man standing out there.

Corie: Wait a minute, Paul . . . (PAUL *moves back into the room and leans against the back of the armchair.* CORIE *turns* MOTHER *to her*) Now, Mother . . . The only thing I'd like to suggest is . . . well . . . just try and go along with everything.

Mother: What do you mean? Where are we going?

Corie: I don't know. But wherever it is . . . just relax . . . and be one of the fellows.

Mother: One of what fellows?

Corie: I mean, don't worry about your stomach.

(*There is another knock on the door)*

Mother: Oh, my stomach.

(*She sinks down on the couch)*

Paul: Can I open the door now? . . .

Corie: (*Moving to the right of the couch*) Okay, okay . . . open the door.

ACTIVITIES

1. In addition to the need to concentrate on line delivery in comedy, you must also be aware of comic action. Examine the stage directions for indications of what you must do in the scene. Include those actions which are useful to your interpretation and be ready to invent actions which will enhance the overall comic effect of the script. Be sure that your actions are appropriate because, as you will see in other chapters, there are many different types of comedy. See *The Real Inspector Hound* (Section A, Chapter 2), *Count Dracula* (Section A, Chapter 4) *The Birds* (Section C, Chapter 15), and "Commedia dell'Arte" (Section C, Chapter 17).

2. Continue the scene by improvising what happens when the door is opened. Examine the script to determine what sort of person Mr. Velasco is. What happens to the improvisation if Mr. Velasco is different than the stereotype we expect to see? Experiment with the changes in the improvisation as a result of Mr. Velasco being a shy, timid person, a loud-mouthed, overbearing person, a very sophisticated and snobbish person.

3. Experiment with the scene by using the technique discussed in *What Glorious Times They Had*, Activity 2. That is, reverse the roles of Corie and Paul. Examine the changes which occur in the scene if Corie is the lawyer and Paul is arranging the furniture and worrying about his mother.

WORKSHOP

1. Compare and contrast the five scripts you have encountered in this chapter. Examine their similarities, and pick out their differences. Discuss which role was your favorite and which role you liked least. Give reasons for your preference. Which role gave you the greatest problems in terms of understanding the character, situation, and action? Which script was the easiest to understand? List the features which distinguish these scripts from other forms of writing.

2. With your group, choose an event reported in a newspaper (any political, human interest, bizarre or comic event). Interpret it as it would be told by a town crier, a modern day newscaster, a playwright, and as it might be depicted by a movie. Pay particular attention to how the "script" form changes from one interpretation to the other. Could your event be mimed or danced? If so, examine how this method would change the "script" form.

3. Take one simple line from any of the plays in this chapter—a line that is important in showing action, emotion, or a climax of a scene. Repeat the line many times with many different inflections. Say it using different levels of intensity; then repeat it going up and down the scale. By stretching the vocal qualities, you may well bring more color and tone to the line, adding to its meaning and clarity.

4. Take a story about the life of a real person from history. Improvise what might have been his/her relationship with a close friend, a family member, an enemy, etc. Try to visualize how this person would talk and react in a given situation; for example, Napoleon talking to an aide the night before the Battle of Waterloo; Cleopatra preparing to commit suicide and talking to her maid; the leader of a country getting dressed before giving an inaugural address or after some great emergency; a movie star who is on his/her way to an Academy Award ceremony, hoping he/she might win the award.

5. Describe a simple situation in life which you have observed. In your description establish such specifics as setting, character, action, mood, the objectives of the characters, motivating forces, the effect of the elements on those involved in this incident. Try to discover the emotional reactions of those involved. Improvise a scene bringing this incident to life.

6. To discover how scripts can be modified, expanded, or even changed, find a piece of music which expresses the "mood" of a situation similar to that in one of the scripts. Stage this scene to the music. How does this different art form change the substance or expression of the script?

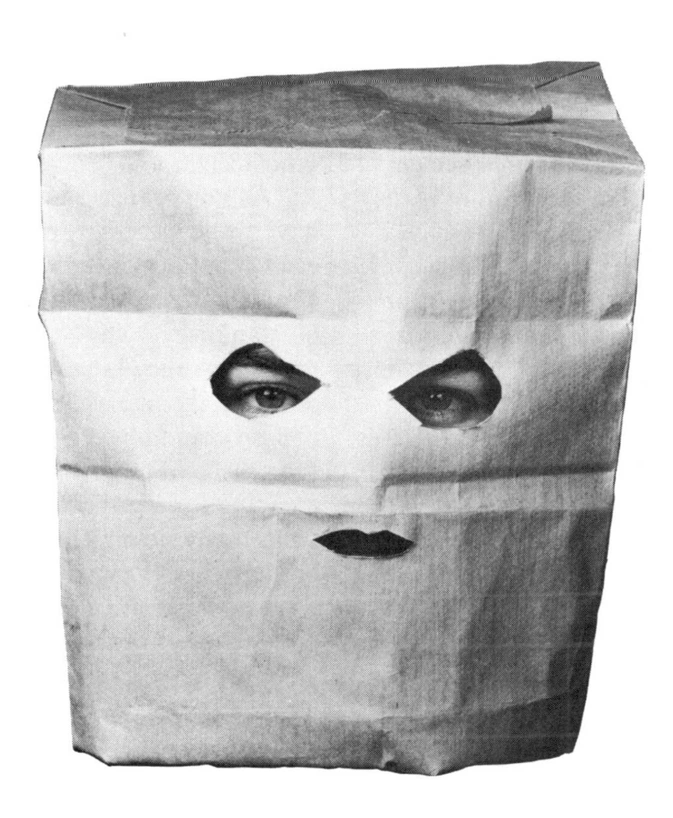

2: Analysing the script

THE PROGRAM

Since script is dialogue written down, it is logical that the first step in script analysis is to read the play aloud with your group. Many of the problems you encounter in saying a speech are not evident in silent reading. It is usually best to read the scene aloud several times before you begin an in-depth analysis so that you become familiar with the characters and the situation.

A scene, like a complete play, can be analysed on the basis of its structure. One aspect of structure is the expository material at the beginning of a play which gives us information on *where* the scene takes place, *when* the scene is placed in time—the past, present or future—*who* the people in the scene are, and *what* is going on among them. Determining where, when, who, and what helps you analyse another aspect of structure—conflict. Every scene is based on conflict, and it is important that you be able to define this conflict. The rising action of the scene results from the attempts of the characters to resolve the conflict. Often this resolution is complicated because of obstacles placed in the characters' way. Each play has a climax at which point the conflict is resolved, however, and many scenes have a minor climax. (Since a scene from a play is only part of a larger whole, there may not be a climax in every selection in this book.) After the resolution of the conflict, the scene may have a denouement in which the loose ends of the plot are tidied up. In most scenes climax, resolution, and denouement can be established fairly quickly. Once they have been established you can discuss and decide with your group what the overall meaning of the scene is. Perhaps you can agree on a simple statement of what you think the scene is about, such as: "this scene is about two people who cannot get along but cannot bear to be apart." This statement will be useful in your more detailed analysis, but you should be willing to alter it as you find out more about the scene.

The next step is to engage in a very close reading of the lines, paying attention to all the details and noting any inconsistencies or puzzling things you find. You will begin to discover that what appears to be superficially very simple is actually very complex. This stage is called sub-textual analysis. You will discover that what the line of dialogue means to the person who is speaking is frequently not what the line means on the surface. A script can be compared to an iceberg; that part which is above the water line is the text (the words on paper), and the two thirds below water is the sub-text (the many possible meanings which exist in those words). As you develop your understanding of the sub-text, you increase your insight and sensitivity regarding the script.

As you search for meaning, you will find that you have to be aware of what is happening every moment to each character in the scene. This awareness comes from close examination of the characters and from your understanding of why they are doing and saying the things they do as they interact with the other characters. Until you find the internal action of the script, you will not be able to communicate the meaning of the script to others. Do not be in too much of a rush to settle on a single meaning for the script. Rather, be open to exploring a great many possible meanings. With your partner or group, work through the script in a variety of different ways, and discard only those approaches which do not develop any further insight.

Once you have defined precisely what the scene or play means to you and your partner or group, you can begin to examine what you want the scene to say to others.

The scenes in this chapter will provide numerous opportunities for you to find the internal action of a script. *After Liverpool* is a series of short scenes concerned with human relationships. The appearance of simplicity should not deceive you; these scenes require a great deal of sub-textual analysis before their complex web of meanings becomes clear. *The Real Inspector Hound* is an example of a complicated plot structure. You will have to analyse this script closely to determine what is going on and how the characters relate to each other. *Jitters*, like *The Real Inspector Hound*, is an example of a play within a play. In *Jitters* you will have to investigate the plot structure on two different levels, and develop the skill of playing two characters in the same scene.

FROM

AFTER LIVERPOOL

by James Saunders

PLAYBILL

Like *Juve*, which was the first selection in Chapter 1, *After Liverpool* is not conventional in form. It consists of short scenes without definite characters or stage directions. To find meaning, you are required to examine and analyse the dialogue very closely. Here is how the author described the play:

> *After Liverpool* is not a play but a suite of pieces, to be performed by one or more actors and one or more actresses. The order in which the pieces are played is not specified. Using a musical analogy, the script gives some themes, within and between which any number of variations are possible.

When you begin work with this selection, stick to the order of scenes as they appear. See if you can determine what it is that could hold the scenes together if played in this particular order. Later, you can pull the scenes together in other combinations.

1

M: How do you do?

W: How do you do?

M: We haven't met. My name is.

W: How do you do?

M: How do you do? I'm a friend of.

W: My name is.

M: How do you do? I come from. I live with.

W: I was born in.

M: How interesting.

W: Not really.

M: I work at. I go to. I drive past. I walk up.

W: That must be a bore.

M: Not really. I get up. I run over. I fly past. I come across. I knock back. All grist to the mill.

W: I put over. I take from. I take out, I take out, I take out.

M: Tiresome.

W: Not really.

M: I put on. I put off, I hang up, I run down, I take, from, I. I saw you across the room. I wanted to meet you.

W: Well, here we are.

M: And now we know each other.

W: Not really.

M: Not really.

2

W: Do you want an apple?

M: Yes, please.

W: Here you are.

M: Is that the only one?

W: Yes. Go on, have it.

M: No no. I wouldn't dream of it.

W: Go on.

M: What about you?

W: Don't worry about me.

M: Don't you want one?

W: Look, I'm offering it to you, aren't I?

M: I don't want it if you want it.

W: I thought you said you did want it.

M: Not if you want it. Not the last one.

W: The last one tastes the same as all the others. Whether I want it or not.

M: Of course it doesn't. Look, do you really expect me to sit here eating the last apple knowing you might like it yourself? Do you? Honestly, you have such a low opinion of me.

3

W: Do you want an apple?

M: Are you having one?

W: Do you want an apple?

M: I'll have one if you do.

W: Why if I do? Do you want one or not?

M: All right, let's both have an apple.

W: There's only one apple.

M: Only one? You have it.

W: But I don't want it.

M: I wish you wouldn't bother me with your problems.

4

M: Are there any apples?

W: Yes, there's one left.

M: Only one?

W: Yes.

M: I'll leave it then.

W: Have it.

M: No, I won't take the last one.

W: Why not?

M: Someone might want it.

W: But you want it.

M: Not really.

5

W: There's one apple left.

M: Oh?

W: You'd better have it.

M: Why me?

W: I don't want you feeling aggrieved because I've taken the last apple.

M: Don't be ridiculous. If you want it, have it. If you don't, leave it where it is.

W: All right.

M: You're really going to eat it are you? The last bloody apple.

6

W: I'd love an apple, wouldn't you?

M: Mm.

W: Oh, there's only one left.

M: You have it, darling.

W: No, you have it, darling.

M: No you have it darling.

W: No you have it darling.

M: No you have it darling.

W: No you have it. Darling.

7

W: Here is an apple. See the apple. I want the apple. Do you want the apple?

M: I want the apple. I also want you to have the apple.

W: I also want you to have the apple. Shall we split the apple?

M: But if we split the apple, we shall have nothing to argue about.

8

W: Hey.

M: Hm?

W: Catch.

M: Thanks.

W: Eat.

M: Catch.

W: Thanks.

M: Eat.

W: Catch . . .

9

W: So you're going at last.

M: Seems like it.

W: Is that yes or no?

M: Unless you've got some other idea.

W: I've run out of ideas. Why, do you have any other ideas?

M: If I had I suppose I wouldn't be going, would I?

W: I suppose not. Anyway, I've tried everything.

M: *You've* tried everything?

W: We've both tried everything, I suppose. I suppose there's no point in hanging on. No point in trying again. No point in going over the same old ground again and again and again. Best to give up, I suppose. Cut one's losses. Go, go. Try with somebody else.

M: There's nobody else.

W: You'll find somebody else.

M: So will you.

W: I daresay. Not to worry about me.

M: We did agree it would be best.

W: I know we agreed. I'm saying, go, go. Only.

M: Only what?

W: It's your decision.

M: My decision!

W: Just so long as you realize. It's your decision.

M: We both agreed. . . .

W: We both agreed but it's your decision, it's still your decision. You're the one who's going.

M: One of us has to go.

W: And you're the one. You've made the decision to go. I haven't. I can't make decisions for you. Just so long as you realize.

M: Do you want me to go?

W: I want you to make your own decision and do your own thing. I'm not going to hold you back. If you want to go. I also don't want to be—held responsible—if you do.

M: Do you want me to go?

W: I want you to do as you think fit!

M: Do you want me to go!
Do you want me to go!!

W: No.
Do you want to go?

M: No.
Oh, what else is there to say?

W: We'll find something.

10

(*The* MAN is talking)

W: Just a minute, can you stop?

M: What's the matter?

W: I'm bored with this conversation.

M: You're what?

W: The conversation doesn't interest me.

M: Oh?

W: Can you talk about something else?

M: Certainly, if you want me to. I do apologize for boring you.

W: Not you, your conversation. You weren't to know, I was trying to look interested. My fault.

M: You mean you should have looked bored?

W: No, I should have told you straight away I wasn't interested.

M: Hm. Does this often happen?

W: What?

M: Finding yourself saddled with a crashing bore?

W: You are not a crashing bore.

M: Just an ordinary bore.

W: I've offended you.

M: Me? Why should I be offended. You're the one who should be offended, having to put up with a crashing bore.

W: You are not. . . .

M: After all, if one's a crashing bore it's best that one's told. Thank you. For telling me. That I'm a. . . .

W: Stop it.

M: Am I boring you again?

W: Listen. Stop it and listen, be quiet and shut up and listen. It's quite simple. You were talking about something which didn't interest me. I should have let you know at once. Instead I pretended to be interested. It was my mistake. I apologize.

M: Oh, don't apologize, I should apologize, I'm the bore.

W: You're not *listening*. . . .

M: And now I have news for you. May I tell it, at the risk of boring you?

W: Go on.

M: This conversation is boring *me*. So shall we change the subject? Or better still, since we both find each other such crashing bores, perhaps I'll put the television on.

W: I don't want television, I want to talk to you.

M: In spite of the fact that I'm. . . .

W: Please. Stop it, please, please.

M: The sad thing is, I was only telling you that story because I thought you might be interested. It was of no interest to me.

11

M: How would you like to go to the cinema tonight?

W: Tonight?

M: If you're not doing anything else.

W: No, I'm not doing anything else.

M: How about it then?

W: Erm. Yes, all right. If you like.

M: Not if I like. If you like. Do you want to go?

W: You want to go, don't you?

M: If you do.

W: Mm. All right, then.

M: You don't sound terribly enthusiastic. Is there anything else you want to do?

W: No no.

M: Or we could stay in. We don't have to go out.

W: We may as well. No reason why not.

M: The reason why not would be if you didn't want to go.

W: I've told you, I'll come if you're going.

M: I don't want to drag you out just because you think I want to go.

W: Don't you want to go then?

M: I want to go if you want to go. Do you want to go to the cinema or not?

W: Yes. Erm. Yes, yes.

M: You're sure?

W: I'm sure, yes.

M: You don't sound very sure.

W: I'm easy. If you're going I'll come with you.

M: Just because I'm going?

W: I don't care either way, honestly. I'll

stay in or I'll go out. I honestly don't give a damn either way.

M: Oh, well, let's stay in, for God's sake.

W: Why?

M: There's no point going if you don't want to go.

W: There is a point. *You* want to go.

M: I don't want to go to the bloody cinema. I just thought you might like to go to the cinema. I do wish you'd say what you want now and then.

W: So. We're in for another jolly evening at home, are we?

12

M: What's wrong?

W: Hm?

M: What's the matter?

W: With what?

M: With you.

W: Nothing as far as I know. Why?

M: Something obviously is.

W: Why, what have I said?

M: You haven't said anything.

W: Well then.

M: You still manage to make it pretty obvious you're upset about something.

W: I don't know what gives you that idea. You're probably feeling a bit morose, so you imagine I'm upset.

M: I'm not morose.

W: No? You're not exactly cheerful, are you?

M: Do you expect me to be cheerful when you're like this?

W: Like what?

M: You know very well.

W: Are you blaming me for it?

M: For what?

W: For your moroseness.

M: I'm not morose and I'm not blaming you for anything.

W: Oh do leave me alone.
I don't know why it is you take everything so personally.

M: What are you talking about?

W: The minute I'm a little under the weather you go around as if it's the end of the world. You make me feel so guilty.

M: If you'd just tell me what I've done wrong.

W: Why shouldn't I feel a bit low now and then? You're depressed often enough. I don't automatically assume it's something I've done.

M: I know you don't.

W: You mean it usually is something I've done.
Oh do leave me alone.
If I'm such a depressing influence why don't you go out?

M: I don't want to go out and leave you like this.

W: You're not doing much good staying in, are you? Face as long as a fiddle.
You're only making me feel guilty.

M: Look, I can't help it if I'm affected by your moods.

W: Moods. Is that what you think they are?

M: I can't be happy if you're upset. I'm sorry. . . .

W: Well I'm very sorry but there's nothing I can do about it.

M: I'm not saying there is.

W: Well then. Go out, leave me alone. Go out and have a drink or something. I'll be all right. No point in both of us being miserable.

M: Oh God. . . .
I'm no help, am I?

W: Obviously not.

M: Well am I? Is there anything I can do?

W: No. I said no.

M: I'm going out then.

W: Where to?

M: I don't know. For a walk.
All right?

W: Wait.

M: What?

W: Don't leave me.

13

W: Well
Goodbye

M: Oh
You're going

W: Yes
It's been

M: Yes

W: Well

M: It's been

W: Erm
Thank you for

M: Yes
Thank you
Look, I don't

W: No
It's all right
No need to

M: Well anyway
Thank you anyway and

W: Yes

(Silence)

M: You have an eyelash on your cheek.

W: Have I?

M: Just there.

W: Here?

M: There.

W: Is it gone?

M: No.
There. It's gone.
So.

W: I hope you don't

M: No
It's been
We've

W: It's

M: I

W: I

M: I

(She cries)

W: I

M: I

W: I

M: I

14

(Looking at each other, smiling)

M: Hallo.

W: We met. Remember?

M: So we did. Yesterday, wasn't it?

W: What a good memory you have.

M: And the day before?

W: So we did. The day before as well.

M: And the day before that?

W: And the day before that and the day before that and the day before that.
How are you today?

M: I'm very well. How are you?

W: All the better for meeting you.

M: What are you laughing at?

W: You.

M: Me?

W: I'm laughing at meeting you again. It is very funny. Every morning I wake up and there's this familiar stranger waiting for me to meet him again.

M: How do you do?

W: How do you do?
What on earth are we laughing at?

M: Goodbye. It's been pleasant meeting you.

W: Goodbye. Won't it be.

(Exit)

ACTIVITIES

1. One way to help you define your understanding of the "sub-text" of a character's lines is to say aloud or write out the thoughts of the character as he or she says each line. Choose one short scene and experiment with this technique.

2. Each of the scenes is a complete unit. That is, each can exist on its own without reference to another scene. However, the power of the material comes from the way each scene varies the theme. With others in the class, experiment with a different scene order. Try leaving some scenes out and reorganizing others. This technique of deciding on the most effective dramatic order of material will be encountered again in "Anthology" (Section B, Chapter 11).

3. Pay particular attention to the last line in each scene. Be careful not to "throw away" this line since it clarifies and comments on all the action which preceded it. Experiment with various ways of saying these lines.

4. Scenes 1 and 14 appear to make little sense. In this way they are similar to *Come and Go* in Chapter 1. You may have to use some of the techniques suggested for *Come and Go* to find meaning in these scenes. What happens if you put more than two people in these or other scenes?

5. Sometimes radical experiments enhance the meaning of scenes. Do these scenes in unusual circumstances such as: *Where*—on a desert island, in a crowded subway. . . . *Who*—knights of the Round Table, Adam and Eve.

FROM

THE REAL INSPECTOR HOUND

by Tom Stoppard

PLAYBILL

Moon and Birdboot, two drama critics, are in a theatre reviewing a play. In between scenes, each is preoccupied with his own thoughts. Moon's ambition is to become the senior critic on his paper, and he has considered murdering his superior. (A junior critic on Moon's paper, Puckeridge, is mentioned in this extract but does not appear in it.) Birdboot has been thinking about an actress with whom he wishes to start an affair.

The first act of the play that Moon and Birdboot are reviewing has concluded. In this first act it was revealed that a madman had escaped in the vicinity of Muldoon Manor and is being pursued by Inspector Hound. It was also revealed that there is a romantic triangle between the characters Simon, Felicity, and Lady Cynthia Muldoon. The scene you watch takes place in the drawing-room of Muldoon Manor, and the characters are listening to a police bulletin on the radio. A dead body, which

CHARACTERS

Moon, a newspaper drama critic
Birdboot, a newspaper drama critic
Mrs. Drudge, the maid
Cynthia, married to Lord Albert Muldoon who has disappeared in Canada
Felicity, a house guest and friend of Cynthia
Magnus, Cynthia's half-brother
Simon, a stranger and a cad
Inspector Hound
Voice on Radio
Body on stage

(Between MOON *and* BIRDBOOT *and the auditorium is an acting area which represents, in as realistic an idiom as possible, the drawing-room of Muldoon Manor. French windows at one side. A telephone fairly well upstage (i.e. towards* MOON*). The* BODY *of a man lies sprawled face down on the floor in front of a large settee. This settee must be of a size and design to allow it to be wheeled over the body, hiding it completely. Silence.)*

Birdboot: Well now—shaping up quite nicely, wouldn't you say?

Moon: Oh yes, yes. A nice trichotomy of forces. One must reserve judgement of course, until the confrontation, but I think it's pretty clear where we're heading.

Birdboot: I agree. It's Magnus a mile off.

(Small pause.)

Moon: What's Magnus a mile off?

Birdboot: If we knew that we wouldn't be here.

Moon: *(clears throat)* Let me at once say that it has *élan* while at the same time avoiding *éclat*. Having said that, and I think it must be said, I am bound to ask—does this play know where it is going?

Birdboot: Well, it seems open and shut to me, Moon—Magnus is not what he pretends to be and he's got his next victim marked down—

Moon: Does it, I repeat, declare its affiliations? There are moments, and I would not begrudge it this, when the play, if we can call it that, and I think on balance we can, aligns itself uncompromisingly on the side of life. *Je suis*, it seems to be saying, *ergo sum*.[1] But is that enough? I think we are entitled to ask. For what in fact is this play concerned with? It is my belief that here we are concerned with what I have referred to elsewhere as the nature of identity. I think we are entitled to ask—and here one is irresistibly reminded of Voltaire's cry, "*Voila!*"—I think we are entitled to ask—*Where is God?*

Birdboot: *(stunned)* Who?

Moon: Go-od.

Birdboot: *(peeping furtively into his program)* God?

Moon: I think we are entitled to ask.

(The phone rings. The set re-illumines to reveal CYNTHIA, FELICITY

[1]The reference is to Descartes's famous saying, "*Cogito, ergo sum*"—I think, therefore I am.

and MAGNUS *about to take coffee, which is being taken round by* MRS. DRUDGE. SIMON *is missing. The* BODY *lies in position.)*

Mrs. Drudge: (*into phone*) The same, half an hour later? . . . No, I'm sorry—there's no one of that name here. (*She replaces phone and goes round with coffee. To* CYNTHIA) Black or white, my lady?

Cynthia: White please.

(MRS. DRUDGE *pours.)*

Mrs. Drudge: (*to* FELICITY) Black or white, miss?

Felicity: White please.

(MRS. DRUDGE *pours.)*

Mrs. Drudge: (*to* MAGNUS) Black or white, Major?

Magnus: White please.

(Ditto.)

Mrs. Drudge: (*to* CYNTHIA) Sugar, my lady?

Cynthia: Yes please.

(Puts sugar in.)

Mrs. Drudge: (*to* FELICITY) Sugar, miss?

Felicity: Yes please.

(Ditto.)

Mrs. Drudge: (*to* MAGNUS) Sugar, Major?

Magnus: Yes please.

(Ditto.)

Mrs. Drudge: (*to* CYNTHIA) Biscuit, my lady?

Cynthia: No thank you.

Birdboot: (*writing elaborately in his notebook*) The second act, however, fails to fulfil the promise. . . .

Felicity: If you ask me, there's something funny going on.

(MRS. DRUDGE'*s approach to* FELICITY *makes* FELICITY *jump to her feet in impatience. She goes to the radio while* MAGNUS *declines his biscuit, and* MRS. DRUDGE *leaves.)*

Radio: We interrupt our program for a special police message. The search for the dangerous madman who is on the loose in Essex has now narrowed to the immediate vicinity of Muldoon Manor. Police are hampered by the deadly swamps and the fog, but believe that the madman spent last night in a deserted cottage on the cliffs. The public is advised to stick together and make sure none of their number is missing. That is the end of the police message.

lay undetected on-stage through the first act, is still in place.

Like *What Glorious Times They Had*, this is a play within a play. Initially, you may be confused by events, but close attention to the action should reveal what is going on. Unlike *After Liverpool*, this play relies heavily on plot—the step-by-step ordering of events. Note that the play being reviewed is a parody of a standard British murder mystery. When you play any of the "actors" in this play, remember to do so with absolute seriousness.

(FELICITY *turns off the radio nervously. Pause.)*

Cynthia: Where's Simon?

Felicity: Who?

Cynthia: Simon. Have you seen him?

Felicity: No.

Cynthia: Have you, Magnus?

Magnus: No.

Cynthia: Oh.

Felicity: Yes, there's something foreboding in the air, it is as if one of *us*—

Cynthia: Oh, Felicity, the house is locked up tight—no one can get in—and the police are practically on the doorstep.

Felicity: I don't know—it's just a feeling.

Cynthia: It's only the fog.

Magnus: Hound will never get through on a day like this.

Cynthia: (*shouting at him*) *Fog!*

Felicity: He means the Inspector.

Cynthia: Is he bringing a dog?

Felicity: Not that I know of.

Magnus:—never get through the swamps. Yes, I'm afraid the madman can show his hand in safety now.

(A mournful baying hooting is heard in the distance, scary.)

Cynthia: What's that?!

Felicity: (*tensely*) It sounded like the cry of a gigantic hound!

Magnus: Poor devil!

Cynthia: Ssssh!

(They listen. The sound is repeated, nearer.)

Felicity: There it is again!

Cynthia: It's coming this way—it's right outside the house!

(MRS. DRUDGE *enters.)*

Mrs. Drudge: Inspector Hound!

Cynthia: A *police* dog?

(Enter INSPECTOR HOUND. *On his feet are his swamp boots. These are two inflatable—and inflated—pontoons with flat bottoms about two feet across. He carries a foghorn.)*

Hound: Lady Muldoon?

Cynthia: Yes.

Hound: I came as soon as I could. Where shall I put my foghorn and my swamp boots?

Cynthia: Mrs. Drudge will take them out. Be prepared, as the Force's motto has it, eh, Inspector? How very resourceful!

Hound: (*divesting himself of boots and foghorn*) It takes more than a bit of weather to keep a policeman from his duty.

(MRS. DRUDGE *leaves with chattels. A pause.)*

Cynthia: Oh—er, Inspector Hound—Felicity Cunningham, Major Magnus Muldoon.

Hound: Good evening.

(He and CYNTHIA *continue to look expectantly at each other.)*

Cynthia and Hound: (*together*) Well?—Sorry——

Cynthia: No, do go on.

Hound: Thank you. Well, tell me about it in your own words—take your time, begin at the beginning and don't leave anything out.

Cynthia: I beg your pardon?

Hound: Fear nothing. You are in safe hands now. I hope you haven't touched anything.

Cynthia: I'm afraid I don't understand.

Hound: I'm Inspector Hound.

Cynthia: Yes.

Hound: Well, what's it all about?

Cynthia: I really have no idea.

Hound: How did it begin?

Cynthia: What?

Hound: The . . . thing.

Cynthia: What thing?

Hound: (*rapidly losing confidence but exasperated*) The trouble!

Cynthia: There hasn't *been* any trouble!

Hound: Didn't you phone the police?

Cynthia: No.

Felicity: I didn't.

Magnus: What for?

Hound: I see. (*Pause.*) This puts me in a very difficult position. (*A steady pause.*) Well, I'll be getting along, then. (*He moves towards the door.*)

Cynthia: I'm terribly sorry.

Hound: (*stiffly*) That's perfectly all right.

Cynthia: Thank you so much for coming.

Hound: Not at all. You never know, there might have been a serious matter.

Cynthia: Drink?

Hound: More serious than that, even.

Cynthia: (*correcting*) Drink before you go?

Hound: No thank you. (*Leaves.*)

Cynthia: (*through the door*) I do hope you find him.

Hound: (*reappearing at once*) Find who, Madam?—out with it!

Cynthia: I thought you were looking for the lunatic.

Hound: And what do you know about that?

Cynthia: It was on the radio.

Hound: Was it, indeed? Well, that's what I'm here about, really. I didn't want to mention it because I didn't know how much you knew. No point in causing unnecessary panic, even with a murderer in our midst.

Felicity: Murderer, did you say?

Hound: Ah—so that was not on the radio?

Cynthia: Whom has he murdered, Inspector?

Hound: Perhaps no one—yet. Let us hope we are in time.

Magnus: You believe he is in our midst, Inspector?

Hound: I do. If anyone of you have recently encountered a youngish good-looking fellow in a smart suit, white shirt, hatless, well-spoken—someone possibly claiming to have just moved into the neighborhood, someone who on the surface seems as sane as you or I, then now is the time to speak![1]

Felicity: I——

Hound: Don't interrupt!

Felicity: Inspector——

Hound: Very well.

[1]Inspector Hound is describing the character Simon Gascoyne.

Cynthia: No. Felicity!

Hound: Please, Lady Cynthia, we are all in this together. I must ask you to put yourself completely in my hands.

Cynthia: Don't, Inspector. I love Albert.

Hound: I don't think you quite grasp my meaning.

Magnus: Is one of us in danger, Inspector?

Hound: Didn't it strike you as odd that on his escape the madman made a beeline for Muldoon Manor? It is my guess that he bears a deep-seated grudge against someone in this very house! Lady Muldoon—where is your husband?

Cynthia: My husband?—you don't mean——?

Hound: I don't know—but I have a reason to believe that one of you is the real McCoy!

Felicity: The real what?

Hound: William Herbert McCoy who as a young man, meeting the madman in the street and being solicited for sixpence for a cup of tea, replied, "Why don't you do a decent day's work, you shifty old bag of horse manure," in Canada all those many years ago and went on to make his fortune. (*He starts to pace intensely.*) The madman was a mere boy at the time but he never forgot that moment, and thenceforth carried in his heart the promise of revenge! (*At which point he finds himself standing on top of the corpse. He looks down carefully.*)

Hound: Is there anything you have forgotten to tell me?

(*They all see the corpse for the first time.*)

Felicity: So the madman has struck!

Cynthia: Oh—it's horrible—horrible—

Hound: Yes, just as I feared. Now you see the sort of man you are protecting.

Cynthia: I can't believe it!

Felicity: I'll have to tell him, Cynthia—Inspector, a stranger of that description has indeed appeared in our midst—Simon Gascoyne. Oh, he had charm, I'll give you that, and he took me in completely. I'm afraid I made a fool of myself over him, and so did Cynthia.

Hound: Where is he now?

Magnus: He must be around the house—he couldn't get away in these conditions.

Hound: You're right. Fear naught, Lady Muldoon—I shall apprehend the man who killed your husband.

Cynthia: My husband? I don't understand.

Hound: Everything points to Gascoyne.

Cynthia: But who's that? (*Points to the corpse.*)

Hound: Your husband.

Cynthia: No, it's not.

Hound: Yes, it is.

Cynthia: I tell you it's not.

Hound: *I'm* in charge of this case!

Cynthia: But that's not my husband.

Hound: Are you sure?

Cynthia: For goodness sake!

Hound: Then who is it!

Cynthia: I don't know.

Hound: Anybody?

Felicity: I've never seen him before.

Magnus: Quite unlike anybody I've ever met.

Hound: This case is becoming an utter shambles.

Cynthia: But what are we going to do?

Hound: (*snatching the phone*) I'll phone the police!

Cynthia: But you are the police!

Hound: Thank God I'm here—the lines have been cut!

Cynthia: You mean——?

Hound: Yes!—we're on our own, cut off from the world and in grave danger!

Felicity: You mean——?

Hound: Yes!—I think the killer will strike again!

Magnus: You mean——?

Hound: Yes! One of us ordinary mortals thrown together by fate and cut off by the elements, is the murderer! He must be found—search the house!

(*All depart speedily in different directions leaving a momentarily empty stage.* SIMON *strolls on.*)

Simon: (*entering, calling*) Anyone about?—funny. . . .

(*He notices the corpse and is surprised. He approaches it and turns it over. He stands up and looks about in alarm.*)

Birdboot: This is where Simon gets the chop.

(*There is a shot.* SIMON *falls dead.* INSPECTOR HOUND *runs on and crouches down by* SIMON*'s body.*

CYNTHIA *appears at the french windows. She stops there and stares.)*

Cynthia: What happened, Inspector?!

*(*HOUND *turns to face her.)*

Hound: He's dead. . . . Simon Gascoyne, I presume. Rough justice even for a killer—unless—unless—We assumed that the body could not have been lying there before Simon Gascoyne entered the house . . . but . . . (*he slides the sofa over the body*) there's your answer. And now—who killed Simon Gascoyne? And why?

("Curtain," freeze, applause, exeunt.)

Moon: Why not?

Birdboot: Exactly. Good riddance.

Moon: Yes, getting away with murder must be quite easy provided that one's motive is sufficiently inscrutable.

Birdboot: Fickle young pup! He was deceiving her right, left and centre.

Moon: (*thoughtfully*) Of course. I'd still have Puckeridge behind *me*——

Birdboot: She needs someone steadier, more mature——

Moon:—And if I could, so could he——

Birdboot: Yes, I know of this rather nice hotel, very discreet, run by a man of the world——

Moon: Uneasy lies the head that wears the crown.

Birdboot: Breakfast served in one's room and no questions asked.

Moon: Does Puckeridge dream of me?

Birdboot: (*pause*) Hello—what's happened?

Moon: What? Oh yes—what do you make of it, so far?

Birdboot: (*clears throat*) It is at this point that the play for me comes alive. The groundwork has been well and truly laid, and the author has taken the trouble to learn from the masters of the genre. He has created a real situation, and few will doubt his ability to resolve it with a startling denouement. Certainly that is what it so far lacks, but it has a beginning, a middle and I have no doubt it will prove to have an end. For this let us give thanks, and double thanks for a good clean show without a trace of smut. But perhaps even all this would be for nothing were it not for a performance which I consider to be one of the summits in the range of contemporary theatre. In what is possibly the finest Cynthia since the war——

Moon: If we examine this more closely, and I think close examination is the least tribute that this play deserves, I think we will find that within the austere framework of what is seen to be on one level a country-house week-end, and what a useful symbol that is, the author has given us—yes, I will go so far—he has given us the human condition——

Birdboot: More talent in her little finger——

Moon: An uncanny ear that might have belonged to a Van Gogh——

Birdboot:—a public scandal that the Birthday Honors[1] to date have neglected——

Moon: Faced as we are with such ubiquitous obliquity, it is hard, it is hard indeed, and therefore I will not attempt, to refrain from invoking the names of Kafka, Sartre, Shakespeare, St. Paul, Beckett, Birkett, Pinero, Pirandello, Dante and Dorothy L. Sayers.

Birdboot: A rattling good evening out. I was held.

(The phone starts to ring on the empty stage. MOON *tries to ignore it.)*

Moon: Harder still——Harder still if possible——Harder still if it is possible to be——Neither do I find it easy——Dante and Dorothy L. Sayers. Harder still——

Birdboot: Others taking part included—*Moon*!

(For MOON *has lost patience and is bearing down on the ringing phone. He is frankly irritated.)*

Moon: (*picking up phone, barks*) Hello! (*Pause, turns to* BIRDBOOT*, quietly.*) It's for you. (*Pause.*)

*(*BIRDBOOT *gets up. He approaches cautiously.* MOON *gives him the phone and moves back to his seat.* BIRDBOOT *watches him go. He looks round and smiles weakly, expiating himself.)*

Birdboot: (*into phone*) Hello. . . . (*Explosion.*) Oh, for God's sake, Myrtle!—I've told you never to phone me at work! (*He is naturally embarrassed, looking about with surreptitious fury.*) What? Last night? Good God, woman, this is hardly the time to—I assure you, Myrtle, there is absolutely nothing going on between me and—I took her to dinner simply by way of keeping *au fait* with the world of the paint and the motley——Yes, I promise——Yes, I do——Yes, I *said* yes—I *do*—and you are mine too, Myrtle—darling—I can't—(*whispers*) *I'm not alone*—(*up*). No, she's not!—(*He looks around furtively, licks his lips and mumbles.)* All *right*! I love your little pink ears and you are my own fluffy bunny-boo——Now for God's sake——Good-bye, Myrtle—(*puts down phone*).

[1]The Birthday Honors List is published on the reigning monarch of England's birthday. It names those people who are to be given titles.

ACTIVITIES

1. The plot of the play being performed in this script is very complex. Most murder mystery melodramas are. To clarify the action of this play within a play, rehearse only the melodrama itself, without any reference to Moon and Birdboot. Rehearse the Moon and Birdboot parts separately. Examine the changes that occur when Moon and Birdboot are watching and when they are not.

2. Examine the ending of this excerpt. Notice how "reality" in the form of the drama critics has been drawn into the "illusion" of the play by the telephone call. What other examples in the script can you find of "absurdity"—those things for which there is no rational explanation. Invent a continuation of this scene by having Act 3 of the murder mystery commence while Birdboot is still onstage.

3. Note how all the characters in the melodrama are stereotypes. Can you do the scene by making these characters "real" people in the manner of *After Liverpool*? How does the murder mystery change?

FROM

JITTERS

by David French

CHARACTERS

Patrick Flanagan, plays the part of Frank
Jessica Logan, plays the part of Lizzie
Phil Mastorakis, plays the part of Eric
George Ellsworth, the director
Robert Ross, the playwright
Nick, the stage manager (optional)
Susi, the prompter (non-speaking role, optional)

PLAYBILL

The actors in this play within a play are rehearsing *The Care and Treatment of Roses*, a new play which will open for previews in the evening. The cast, all Canadian actors, is especially nervous because it is expecting a New York critic to be in the audience. (An interesting comparison you might think about is your own nervousness as an actor and the fragile egos and tenseness displayed by the actors here.) As you read through this scene, be aware of the fact that one of the roles you play is not *your* role, but your *character's* role. When you fully understand your character, he/she will become a certain kind of actor in *The Care and Treatment of Roses.*

Patrick: (*an Italian accent*) Why'd you get so upset for, Lizzie? All I asked is how long is he going to stay.

Jessica: (*watering plants*) He's home for the holidays. That's all I know. What do you want me to do, tell him to go to a hotel? He's my son.

Patrick: I don't like the way he looks at me. Like I'm not good enough to sit on the furniture. He'd better not start that today, because if he does, he'll wish like hell he didn't.

Jessica: I don't want trouble, Frank.

Patrick: (*sits at the table*) Then put his nose back in joint or I'll do it for him.

(The doorbell rings.)

Jessica: That's Eric, now. (*She sets down the watering-can and switches off the hi-fi.*)

Patrick: Where the hell are my shoes?

Jessica: Honestly, you're worse than Jimmy. (*She stands behind his chair and strokes his chest.*) Your shoes are upstairs. And would you please put on a shirt?

Patrick: Lizzie, I'll give the kid two weeks. Either he's gone or I go. Make up your mind. (*He rises.*)

Jessica: Don't threaten me.

Patrick: Two weeks, baby. (*He exits upstairs.*)

(The doorbell rings again. JESSICA *crosses into the hallway out of sight. We hear the door open and close.)*

Phil: (*off*) Hello, Elizabeth.

Jessica: (*off*) Hi, Eric. Come in. You look half-frozen.

*(*PHIL *and* JESSICA *enter,* PHIL *taking off his overcoat. He glances into the living-room. He seems quite relieved to find it empty.)*

Jessica: Here. Let me take your coat. (*She hangs his hat, coat, and scarf on the hatrack.*) I appreciate this, Eric. I wouldn't have called if it wasn't important.

Phil: I know that. That's why I'm here. (*He crosses near the sofa.*) What is it? Frank?

Jessica: No, it's Jimmy.

Phil: Oh?

Jessica: Sit down. I just made a fresh pot of coffee. Have you eaten?

Phil: Nothing for me, I had breakfast at the rectory . . . What's happened, Sis?

Jessica: He's quit school.

Phil: Jimmy quit school? (*He sits on the sofa, near the arm.*)

Jessica: He says he's had all he can take of university and wants to stay here until he figures out what he wants to do. (*She sits on the arm of the sofa.*) I don't want him to make a mistake, Eric. I don't want him to do something he'll regret later on.

Phil: Well, maybe university isn't what he needs right now.

Jessica: (*puts her hand on his*) Please, I want you to talk to him. You're the only one who can. He won't listen to me.

Phil: And how's Frank feel about all this?

Jessica: He doesn't know yet. All he knows is Jimmy's home for the winter break.

*(*PHIL *nods. And nods. Clears his throat.)*

George: Patrick, that was your cue.

Patrick: (*off*) I beg to differ. My cue is Phil's line, "I see." I didn't hear it.

Phil: I didn't say it.

George: Did you forget?

Phil: No, I thought I'd try not saying it. Don't you feel the silence is more telling?

Patrick: (*off*) The only actor I know who likes to cut his lines.

Phil: That's because I can *act* them.

Patrick: (*off*) Act all you want, mate, only don't act my cues. I'll be up here all night.

George: (*to* ROBERT) What do you think?

Robert: Cut the line. He doesn't need it.

George: Okay, Patrick, take your cue from Jessica's, "Jimmy's home for the winter break." Jess, take it back to, "Let me take your coat."

Phil: George, can I look away when she starts that stuff about Jimmy. I did this time. It felt better.

George: (*angrily*) Look we can't have these interruptions! We have a preview tonight! Let's just get on with it! When you're ready, Jess. Thank you.

*(*PHIL *gives* GEORGE *a look. Then he and* JESSICA *get into position. He takes his overcoat off the hatrack and glances again up at* GEORGE.*)*

Jessica: Here. Let me take your coat. (PHIL *thrusts it at her.*) I appreciate this, Eric. I wouldn't have called if it wasn't important.

Phil: (*irritably*) I know that. That's why I'm here. (*He crosses near the sofa.*) What is it? Frank?

Jessica: No, it's Jimmy.

Phil: Oh?

Jessica: Sit down. I just made a fresh pot of coffee. Have you eaten?

Phil: Nothing for me. I had brunch at the rectory . . . What's happened, Sis?

Jessica: He's quit school.

Phil: Jimmy quit school? (*He sits on the sofa, near the arm.*)

Jessica: He says he's had all he can take of university and wants to stay here until he figures out what he wants to do. (*She sits on the arm of the sofa.*) I don't want him to make a mistake, Eric. I don't want him to do something he'll regret later on.

Phil: Well, maybe university isn't what he needs right now. (*He sneers up at* GEORGE.)

Jessica: (*puts her hand on his*) Please, I want you to talk to him. You're the only one who can. He won't listen to me.

Phil: And how's Frank feel about all this?

Jessica: He doesn't know yet. All he knows is Jimmy's home for the winter break.

(PATRICK *comes down the stairs, laughing.*)

Phil: (*rises*) Hello, Frank.

Patrick: (*to* JESSICA) You ought to see that kid of yours. He can't even get his socks on. What, they don't teach him to drink in college? (*To* PHIL) So how's it going, Father? You still dipping into the poorbox?

Jessica: Frank, you're awful. (*To* PHIL) He's just pulling your leg.

Phil: Is he?

Patrick: Did she tell you? The kid took a swing at me last night.

Phil: (*puts a cigarette in his mouth*) No, Elizabeth never mentioned it . . . (*He fishes in his pockets for matches.*)

Patrick: He thought he could drink me under the table. (*He brings out his lighter and lights* PHIL*'s cigarette.*)

Phil: Thanks . . . He's going through a very difficult period, Jimmy.

Patrick: Well, he better get over it fast or he'll get his ass kicked.

Jessica: Frank, please.

Patrick: I mean it, Lizzie.

Phil: He needs understanding right now, not brute force.

Patrick: Is that so? (*He sits on the sofa and stares at* PHIL.)

Jessica: (*moves behind* PATRICK) Honey, let Eric handle it. He knows how to talk to Jimmy. Okay? (*She leans over to kiss the top of* PATRICK's head but as she does so, PATRICK *ducks and leaps to his feet. He stares at* GEORGE, *grimacing.*)

George: (*moves to the stage*) What's wrong?

Patrick: I don't like that kiss. I've never liked it. I can't do it.

George: Patrick, we can't keep starting and stopping like this. We'll never get through the play.

Phil: How come he doesn't get hell? I notice you don't say he's interrupting. With him it's starting and stopping.

George: (*to* PATRICK) What's wrong with the kiss?

Patrick: I don't believe her.

Jessica: (*angrily*) Listen, you. I was doing leading ladies when you were failing to get through adolescence. So don't tell me how to act.

Patrick: I forgot: she's worked with Mike Nichols. Let's all curtsy.

Jessica: At least I've got the guts to work outside this country.

Patrick: Then what the hell are you doing back here? And don't hand me that crap about your kids needing a mother. I don't buy it. The truth is your last two Broadway plays died in the first week. You haven't acted in theatre for two years. You're living in the past, lady.

George: Okay, take it easy. Let's just solve the problem and get back to work. We're running behind. (*To* PATRICK) What is it about the kiss you don't believe?

Patrick: First of all, the priest hates my guts. He resents the fact we're living together, and here she is kissing me after I've just insulted him. Not only is it unbelievable, it's maudlin.

Jessica: It's not maudlin, it's tender. And perfectly in character.

Patrick: Well, it's not in character for me to let you. At that moment Frank doesn't want to be touched. It makes his skin crawl.

Jessica: Well, if you think I personally enjoy it, you're greatly mistaken. But we do make sacrifices, don't we? Now let's get on with it.

George: Yes, we're wasting time. Maybe there's another way to make the same point. (*He looks out at* ROBERT.) What do you think, Robert?

Robert: I don't see the problem. I think it works.

Patrick: How predictable.

Robert: It's worked all along, hasn't it? Why does it suddenly not work?

Patrick: Why? Because I've never questioned it before. I've always done it because those were the stage directions. *Your* stage directions.

Robert: I see.

Patrick: That's Phil's line. It's been cut.

Robert: Why're you so hostile? What did I do? (*He starts down the aisle.*)

Patrick: I criticize his masterpiece, and suddenly I'm hostile.

Robert: That's not what I meant, and you know it. If you've got a beef, tell me.

George: (*to* ROBERT) Okay, don't get hot under the collar. (*To* PATRICK) Let's just cut the kiss and get on with it. (*To* JESSICA) Put your hand on his shoulder. That'll make the same point.

* * *

(GEORGE *steps off the stage and takes his seat on the aisle. The theatre is now in blackness.*)

George: Stay on book, Susi, but forget what I said before. At this stage of the game, harping on lines would only demoralize them more.

(*Lights up on stage.* JESSICA *is alone on stage, watering the hanging plants. After a moment,* PATRICK *comes down the stairs. He is shirtless, and is doing up his belt. He glances at* JESSICA, *who ignores him. He crosses to the table and pours himself a cup of coffee.*)

Patrick: (*an Italian accent*) Why'd you get so upset for, Lizzie? All I asked is how long is he going to stay.

Jessica: He's home for the holidays. That's all I know. What do you want me to do, tell him to go to a hotel? He's my son.

Patrick: I don't like the way he looks at me. Like I'm not good enough to sit on the furniture. He'd better not start that today, because if he does, he'll wish like hell he didn't.

Jessica: I don't want trouble, Frank.

Patrick: (*sits at the table*) Then put his nose back in joint or I'll do it for him.

(*Slight pause*)

Jessica: Did you hear the doorbell?

(GEORGE *leaps to his feet and glares at the control booth, jabbing his finger in the direction of the front door. Suddenly there is a knocking on the door.* GEORGE *sits and shakes his head.)*

Jessica: That's Eric, now. (*She sets down the watering-can and switches off the hi-fi.*)

Patrick: Where the hell are my shoes?

Jessica: Honestly, you're worse than Jimmy. (*She stands behind his chair and strokes his chest.*) Your shoes are upstairs. And would you please put on a shirt?

Patrick: Lizzie, I'll give the kid two weeks. Either he's gone or I go. Make up your mind. (*He rises.*)

Jessica: Don't threaten me.

Patrick: Two weeks, baby. (*He exits upstairs.*)

(A second knock on the door. JESSICA *crosses into the hallway out of sight. We hear the door open and close.)*

Phil: (*off*) Hello, Elizabeth.

Jessica: (*off*) Hi, Eric. Come in. You look half-frozen.

Phil: (*as he enters*) Not half as frozen as that doorbell.

Nick: (*over the PA*) Sorry.

Jessica: Here. Let me take your coat. (*She hangs his hat, coat, and scarf on the hatrack.*) I appreciate this, Eric. I wouldn't have called if it wasn't important.

Phil: I know that. That's why I'm here. (*He crosses near the sofa.*) What is it? Jimmy?

Jessica: No, it's—Yes, it is Jimmy, as a matter of fact.

Phil: Oh?

Jessica: Sit down. I just made a fresh pot of coffee. Have you eaten?

Phil: Nothing for me. I just had a snack at the rectory . . . What's happened, Sis?

Jessica: He's quit school.

Phil: Jimmy quit school? (*He sits on the sofa, far from the arm.*)

Jessica: He says he's had all he can take of university and wants to stay here until he figures out what he wants to do. (*She sits on the arm of the sofa.*) I don't want him to make a mistake, Eric. I don't want him to do something he'll regret later on.

Phil: Well, maybe university isn't what he needs right now.

Jessica: (*In order to put her hand on his, she has to lean and stretch.*) Please, I want you to talk to him. You're the only one who can. He won't listen to me.

Phil: And how's Frank feel about all this?

Jessica: He doesn't know yet. All he knows is Jimmy's home for the winter break.

*(*PATRICK *comes down the stairs, laughing.)*

Phil: I see.

*(*PATRICK*'s laughter stops, then starts again.)*

Phil: (*rises*) Hello, Frank.

Patrick: I see. I see, I see, I see . . . (*To* JESSICA) Well, you ought to see that kid of yours. He can't even get his socks on. What, they don't teach him to drink in college? (*To* PHIL) So, Father, I see you, I see you. How's it going? You still dipping into the poorbox?

Jessica: Frank, you're awful. (*To* PHIL) He's just pulling your leg.

Phil: I see.

Patrick: Did she tell you? The kid took a swing at me last night.

Phil: (*puts a cigarette in his mouth*) No, Elizabeth never mentioned it . . . (*He fishes in his pockets for matches.*)

Patrick: He thought he could drink me under the table. (*He brings out his lighter to light* PHIL*'s cigarette.* PHIL *bends to accept the light, and as he does so, a tall flame shoots up like a blowtorch from the adjustable lighter.* PHIL *recoils instinctively. He reaches for the vase of red roses on the coffee table and hurls the roses and water into* PATRICK*'s face.* PHIL *dashes around the table, and with a wild look of outrage* PATRICK *starts after him.)*

*(*GEORGE *rushes down the aisle to the stage.)*

George: Cut! Cut! Cut!

(Blackout.)

ACTIVITIES

1. If you play two roles in this script you must remember that the second role is a character played by the first role—an actor. Analyse both roles carefully, and decide how your voice, movements, and actions can make it very clear that the actor and the actor-as-character are the same person.

2. From the evidence you have in this excerpt, describe the type of play you think *The Care and Treatment of Roses* is. It may be helpful to do just this part of the script without the interruptions. Continue the plot of *The Care and Treatment of Roses* by improvising what happens next. Can you find another script in this text which is similar in style?

3. As you have already seen, there are other scripts in this book which involve actors rehearsing a play during a play. Discuss why dramatists would be attracted to this theme.

4. Examine the character of each "actor" in this script. Improvise scenes where the actors continue their interaction; for example, at lunch or after rehearsals.

WORKSHOP

1. For any scene in this chapter, find the moment(s) of "discovery." Such a moment may be an intellectual discovery of any character in the play regarding him/herself or any other character. It may be a discovery about an event, about the world, about humanity, or philosophy. A moment of discovery could be a physical act directed at or involving any character in the play. When you have found a moment of discovery, run through the scene and concentrate on working towards this moment. This technique can be applied to any script in this book.

2. Improvise scenes based on what happens before any of the scenes in this chapter begin, such as scenes where the characters are first introduced. Then, improvise what happens after the end of the scene to show what develops as a result of the actions and emotions of the scene.

3. To develop your understanding of a script, have your group read the text, in role, aloud. Put the script aside and tell the story of the scene sequentially in an informal mode, each of the group members telling part of the scene. Discuss the characters, interpretation, and problems in the play. Reread the text. Put the script aside and improvise the scene again.

4. To help you understand the actions of characters in a script, it is helpful to describe aloud in the third person all the actions a character does, such as: "He/she goes onto the stage to answer the phone, not sure of why he/she is going." For any of the roles you play describe your actions in this way and then say your dialogue. Be sure to include a description of how your character is feeling about the action.

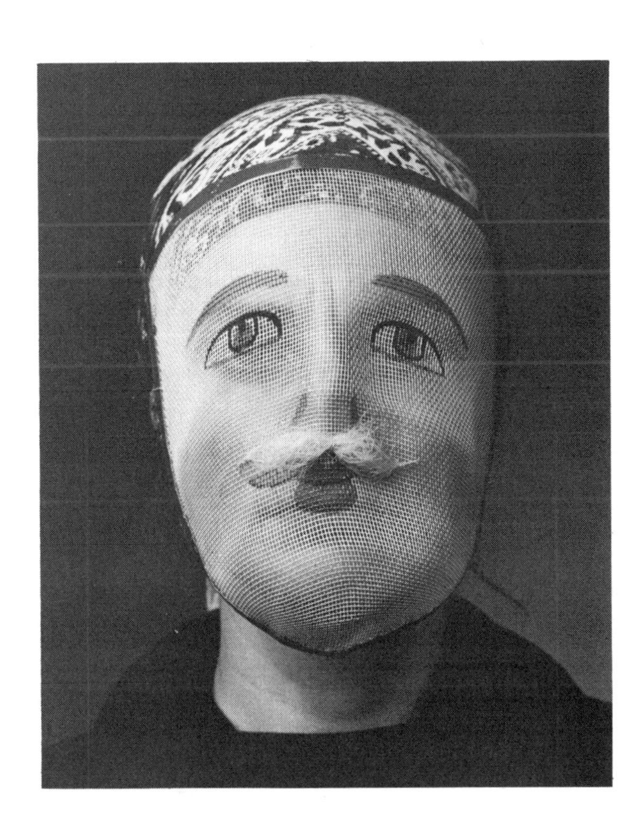

3: Developing a character

THE PROGRAM

Plays are about people, even if these people are presented in the guise of animals or inanimate objects. Plays examine the nature of the human condition by exploring relationships among people and the relationship of people to the world. If you are to work with scripts, one thing needing intense concentration is the task of adopting the role of another person in circumstances which are different from your own. To do this, you have to find out all you can about that other person and his or her internal life, and then develop techniques which will communicate to others the qualities of the character you are playing.

The first step is to examine the script for all the details you can find about your character. Look at what your character says about himself or herself and to whom your character says it. Examine what your character says about other people (what we say about others is often an indication of how we feel about ourselves). Examine how your character responds, in speech and in actions, to situations in the play and to other characters. Are your character's actions consistent with what your character says? What do other characters say about you, and how do they treat you? Once you have examined and analysed all this information, write a short biography about your character, *as* the character; for example, "My name is ________ and I live at ________." This is called backgrounding the character and requires that you invent information which is logically consistent with the information you have gathered from the text. You should be able to provide all the information necessary to give your character an inner life.

One of the most difficult problems you will encounter is that of finding physical actions for your role. An important way of finding these actions is the use of the following question from the acting method of Constantin Stanislavski:

"What would I do if I were this character in these circumstances?" By providing answers to this question, you gain insight into the character you are playing. But be sure you understand the question! "What would *I* do. . . ." By stressing the "I" you recognize that although you can never "be" another person, you can bring all your own resources and understanding to the interpretation of the character.

"Do" is the operative word in the sentence. It is not "feel" or "think" but "do," which means creating physical action. If you concentrate on the physical action of a character, feelings in the role will arise naturally rather than be imposed artificially on the character. As you determine what your character does (stand, sit, walk, run, gesture, etc.), you will be defining who your character is.

Every person has motivations, known or unknown, for every action he or she does, and it is important that you define your character's motivations. You can discover your character's motivation by defining the intentions the character has. An intention is a determination to do or accomplish certain things or to behave in a certain way. Your character may have few or many intentions in the course of a scene, and it is important that you be able to define them by stating them in sentences. When you write down an intention, be sure to structure the sentence so that it expresses a state of "doing" not a state of "being" (sad, happy, etc.). A statement of intention should be in the form of "I want to get revenge for . . .", or "I am going to acquire all the money I can."

In a dramatic structure or a script, a character's intentions are usually only accomplished by overcoming obstacles. These obstacles can be physical or psychological. It is important that you define the obstacles your character is working against, and that you be aware of the strategies the character undertakes to overcome them.

Above all, you must develop belief in the character you play. The actions you develop must be true to the character. They must feel right to you, and they must enhance the interpretation of the character and the scene.

The scenes that follow will provide a variety of roles for you to explore using the techniques outlined here. *Whose Life Is It, Anyway?* is a serious drama about a character in an extreme situation. Anyone playing the major role will discover the importance of physical action in life since the possibility of physical action has been removed from the role. *Countdown* gives opportunities for participants to directly experience the inner thoughts of characters. The two scenes from *The Farm Show* present marked contrasts in style, tempo, and content, and show how varied the presentation of characters can be. The lead character of *The Tragedy of Dr. Faustus* is surrounded by characters which will test your ingenuity and inventiveness since you have to create devils, angels, and other fantastic characters. Finally, *Antigone* demands that you investigate deeply the motivating forces of two strong people bent on achieving conflicting goals.

As you undertake these challenges, keep in mind that your primary task is to develop your belief in the character and the situation. No one will ever believe a character you do not believe yourself.

FROM

WHOSE LIFE IS IT ANYWAY?

by Brian Clark

PLAYBILL

Ken Harrison, a talented sculptor, has suffered a serious spinal injury in a car accident which has left him paralysed from the neck down. The play is concerned with Ken's struggle to decide whether to live or die. As you read this play, be aware of the inner thoughts of the characters and how these thoughts might conflict with the dialogue actually spoken.

CHARACTERS

Ken Harrison, the patient
Sister Anderson, the ward supervisor
Nurse Kay Sadler, a nurse in training
Dr. Clare Scott, a young doctor
Dr. Michael Emerson, a medical specialist

Dr. Scott: You're bright and chirpy this morning.

Ken: (*Ironically*) It's marvelous, you know. The courage of the human spirit.

Dr. Scott: (*Dryly*) Nice to hear the human spirit's OK. How's the lungs? (*She takes her stethoscope from her pocket. She puts the stethoscope to* KEN*'s chest*)

Ken: (*sings*) Boom boom.

Dr. Scott: Be quiet. You'll deafen me.

Ken: Sorry. (*She continues to listen.*) And what does it say?

Dr. Scott: (*Gives up*) What does what say?

Ken: My heart, of course. What secrets does it tell?

Dr. Scott: It was just telling me that it's better off than it was six months ago.

Ken: It's a brave heart. It keeps its secrets.

Dr. Scott: And what are they?

Ken: Did you hear it going boom boom, like that? Two beats.

Dr. Scott: Of course.

Ken: Well, I'll tell you. That's because it's broken, broken in two. But each part carries on bravely, yearning for a woman in a white coat.

Dr. Scott: And I thought it was the first and second heart sounds.

Ken: Ah! Is there a consultant's round this morning?

Dr. Scott: That's right.

Ken: I suppose he will sweep in here like Zeus from Olympus, with his attendant nymphs and swains.

Dr. Scott: I don't think that's fair.

Ken: Why not?

Dr. Scott: He cares; he cares a lot.

Ken: But what about?

Dr. Scott: His patients.

Ken: I suppose so.

Dr. Scott: He does. When you first came in he worked his guts out to keep you going; he cares.

Ken: I was a bit flip, wasn't I . . .

Dr. Scott: It's understandable.

Ken: But soon we shall have to ask the question why.

Dr. Scott: Why?

Ken: Why bother. You remember the mountain labored and brought forth not a man but a mouse. It was a big joke. On the mouse. If you're as insignificant as that, who needs a mountain for a mummy?

Dr. Scott: I'll see you later . . . with Dr. Emerson.

Ken: And Cupbearers Limited.

Dr. Scott: Oh no . . . I assure you . . . We're not at all limited. (*She goes out. She opens the door of* SISTER*'s room. The* SISTER *is writing at the desk.*) Sister. It's Mr. Harrison. He seems a little agitated this morning.

Sister: Yes, he's beginning to realize what he's up against.

Dr. Scott: I'm changing the prescription and putting him on a small dose of Valium. I'll have a word with Dr. Emerson. Thank you, Sister. (*She closes the door and looks up the corridor toward* KEN*'s room.* NURSE SADLER *is just going in with a feeding cup.*)

Ken: An acolyte, bearing a cup.

Nurse: I beg your pardon?

Ken: Nothing. I was joking. It's nothing.

Nurse: It's coffee.

Ken: You're joking now.

Nurse: I'm not.

Ken: What you have there is a coffee-flavored milk drink.

Nurse: Don't you like it?

Ken: It's all right, but I would like some real coffee, hot and black and bitter so that I could chew it.

Nurse: I'll ask the Sister.

Ken: I shouldn't.

Nurse: Why not?

Ken: Because in an hour's time, you'll be bringing round a little white pill that is designed to insert rose-colored filters behind my eyes. It will calm me and soothe me and make me forget for a while that you have a lovely body.

Nurse: Mr. Harrison . . . I'm . . .

Ken: (*genuinely concerned*) I'm sorry. Really, I *am* sorry. I don't want to take it out on you—it's not your fault. You're only the vestal virgin . . . Sorry I said virgin.

Nurse: You'd better drink your coffee before it gets cold. (*She feeds him a little, sip by sip.*)

Ken: I was right; it's milky . . . What made you become a nurse?

Nurse: I'm not a nurse yet.

Ken: Oh yes you are. (NURSE SADLER *smiles.*) *Nurse* Sadler.

Nurse: You must have thought me a real twit.[1]

Ken: Of course not!

Nurse: The Sister-Tutor told us we would say it.

Ken: Well then . . .

Nurse: But I was so sure I wouldn't.

Ken: You haven't told me what made you become a nurse.

Nurse: I've always wanted to. What made you become a sculptor?

Ken: Hey there! You're learning too fast!

Nurse: What do you mean?

[1]This is a reference to an earlier scene in which the nurse introduced herself as Kay Sadler instead of Nurse Sadler as hospital rules require.

Ken: When you get a personal question, just ignore it—change the subject, or better still, ask another question back. (NURSE SADLER *smiles.*) Did Sister-Tutor tell you that too?

Nurse: Something like it.

Ken: It's called being professional, isn't it?

Nurse: I suppose so.

Ken: I don't want any more of that, it's horrid. Patients are requested not to ask for credit for their intelligence, as refusal often offends.

Nurse: You sound angry. I hope I . . .

Ken: Not with you, Kay. Not at all. With myself I expect. Don't say it. That's futile isn't it?

Nurse: Yes. (SISTER *opens the door.*)

Sister: Have you finished, Nurse? Dr. Emerson is here.

Nurse: Yes, Sister. I'm just coming.

Sister: Straighten that sheet. (*She goes, leaving the door open.*)

Ken: Hospitals are weird places. Broken necks are acceptable, but a wrinkled sheet! . . . (NURSE SADLER *smooths the bed. She goes out as* DR. EMERSON *comes in with* SISTER *and* DR. SCOTT.)

Dr. Emerson: Morning.

Ken: Good morning.

Dr. Emerson: How are you this morning?

Ken: As you see, racing around all over the place. (DR. EMERSON *picks up the chart and notes from the bottom of the bed.*)

Dr. Emerson: (*to* DR. SCOTT) You've prescribed Valium, I see.

Dr. Scott: Yes.

Dr. Emerson: His renal function looks much improved.

Dr. Scott: Yes, the blood urea is back to normal and the cultures are sterile.

Dr. Emerson: Good . . . Good. Well, we had better go on keeping an eye on it, just in case.

Dr. Scott: Yes, of course, sir.

Dr. Emerson: Good . . . Well, Mr. Harrison, we seem to be out of the woods now . . .

Ken: So when are you going to discharge me?

Dr. Emerson: Difficult to say.

Ken: Really? Are you ever going to discharge me?

Dr. Emerson: Well, you'll certainly be leaving *us* soon, I should think.

Ken: Discharged or transferred?

Dr. Emerson: This unit is for critical patients; when we have reached a position of stability, then you can be looked after in a much more comfortable, quiet hospital.

Ken: You mean you only grow the vegetables here—the vegetable store is somewhere else.

Dr. Emerson: I don't think I understand you.

Ken: I think you do. Spell it out for me, please. What chance have I of only being partly dependent on nursing?

Dr. Emerson: It's impossible to say with certainty what the prognosis of any case is.

Ken: I'm not asking for a guarantee on oath. I am simply asking for your professional opinion. Do you believe I will ever walk again?

Dr. Emerson: No.

Ken: Or recover the use of my arms?

Dr. Emerson: No.

Ken: Thank you.

Dr. Emerson: What for?

Ken: Your honesty.

Dr. Emerson: Yes, well . . . I should try not to brood on it if I were you. It's surprising how we can come to accept things. Dr. Scott has prescribed something which will help. (*To* DR. SCOTT) You might also get Mrs. Boyle along . . .

Dr. Scott: Yes, of course.

Dr. Emerson: You'll be surprised how many things you will be able to do. Good morning. (*They go into the corridor area.*)

Dr. Emerson: What dose was it you prescribed?

Dr. Scott: Two milligrams T.I.D.

Dr. Emerson: That's very small. You might have to increase it to five milligrams.

Dr. Scott: Yes, sir.

Dr. Emerson: We ought to aim to get him moved in a month at most. These beds are very precious.

Dr. Scott: Yes.

Dr. Emerson: Well, thank you, Doctor. I must rush off. Damned committee meeting.

Dr. Scott: I thought you hated those.

Dr. Emerson: I do, but there's a new heart monitoring unit I want . . . very much indeed.

Dr. Scott: Good luck, then.

Dr. Emerson: Thank you, Clare. (*He goes.* DR. SCOTT *looks in at* SISTER*'s office.*)

Dr. Scott: Did you get that Valium for Mr. Harrison, Sister?

Sister: Yes, Doctor. I was going to give him the first at twelve o'clock.

Dr. Scott: Give him one now, will you?

Sister: Right.

Dr. Scott: Thank you. (*She begins to walk away, then turns.*) On second thoughts . . . give it to me. I'll take it. I want to talk with him.

Sister: Here it is. (*She hands a small tray with a tablet and a feeding cup of water.*)

Dr. Scott: Thank you. (*She walks to* KEN*'s room and goes in.*) I've brought something to help you.

Ken: My God, they've got some highly qualified nurses here.

Dr. Scott: Only the best in this hospital.

Ken: You're spoiling me you know, Doctor. If this goes on I shall demand that my next enema is performed by no one less than the Matron.

Dr. Scott: Well, it wouldn't be the first she'd done, or the thousandth either.

Ken: She worked up through the ranks, did she?

Dr. Scott: They all do.

Ken: Yes, in training school they probably learn that at the bottom of every bed pan lies a potential Matron. Just now, for one or two glorious minutes, I felt like a human being again.

Dr. Scott: Good.

Ken: And now you're going to spoil it.

Dr. Scott: How?

Ken: By tranquilizing yourself.

Dr. Scott: Me?

Ken: Oh, I shall get the tablet, but it's you that needs the tranquilizing; I don't.

Dr. Scott: Dr. Emerson and I thought . . .

Ken: You both watched me disturbed, worried even perhaps, and you can't do anything for me—nothing that really matters. I'm paralysed and you're impotent. This disturbs you because you're a sympathetic person and as someone dedicated to an active sympathy doing something—anything even—you find it hard to accept you're impotent. The only thing you can do is to stop me thinking about it—that is—stop me disturbing you. So I get the tablet and you get the tranquility.

Dr. Scott: That's a tough diagnosis.

Ken: Is it so far from the truth?

Dr. Scott: There may be an element of truth in it, but it's not the whole story.

Ken: I don't suppose it is.

Dr. Scott: After all, there is no point in worrying unduly—you know the facts. It's no use banging your head against a wall.

Ken: If the only feeling I have is in my head, and I want to feel, I might choose to bang it against a wall.

Dr. Scott: And if you damage your head?

Ken: You mean go bonkers?

Dr. Scott: Yes.

Ken: Then that would be the final catastrophe, but I'm not bonkers—yet. My consciousness is the only thing I have and I must claim the right to use it and, as far as possible, act on conclusions I may come to.

Dr. Scott: Of course.

Ken: Good. Then you eat that tablet if you want tranquility, because I'm not going to.

Dr. Scott: It is prescribed.

Ken: Oh come off it, Doctor. I know everyone around here acts as though those little bits of paper have just been handed down from Sinai. But the writing on those tablets isn't in Hebrew . . .

Dr. Scott: . . . Well, you aren't due for it till twelve o'clock. We'll see . . .

Ken: That's what I always say. If you don't know whether to take a tranquilizer or not—sleep on it. When you tell Dr. Emerson, impress on him I don't need it . . . (DR. SCOTT *smiles. She leaves and goes to the* SISTER*'s room.*)

Dr. Scott: Sister, I haven't given it to him . . . Leave it for a while.

Sister: Did you alter the notes?

Dr. Scott: No . . . Not yet. (*She picks up a pile of notes and begins writing.*)

ACTIVITIES

1. For the person playing the role of Ken, this scene provides an opportunity to examine fully the internal life of the character. When you practise the scene, try to immobilize your body except for the head and neck. How expressive can you be using only these parts? Since you cannot move or use gestures, your facial expressions and vocal inflections will have to convey Ken's feelings. Experiment with a variety of expressions until members of your group indicate that you are conveying the feelings of the character.

2. The roles of Dr. Scott and Dr. Emerson require clear statements of each person's intentions in this scene. As suggested in The Program, be sure to formulate your statements in terms of actions. For each doctor can you determine what obstacle he or she will encounter in achieving his or her intentions? It would be useful to determine those things the doctors do *not* say in order to understand what they *do* say.

3. Examine the dialogue on pages 31-32 between Ken and Nurse Sadler. Notice the contrast between the nurse and the doctors in terms of "professionalism." Nurse Sadler's emotions are much more evident, and Ken interacts with her differently than with the others. (Nurse Sadler is embarrassed that she has revealed her first name, something a professional nurse is never to do.) Decide on what physical actions would be appropriate for Nurse Sadler in this scene.

4. Themes of medicine and hospitals have long been popular in drama. From this script, can you determine the basis for that popularity? In this book you will find other scripts on the same theme. In Section C, Chapter 17, the theme is treated in a comic manner in four different scripts. *The Elephant Man* (Section A, Chapter 1) and *An Enemy of the People* (Section C, Chapter 20) treat the matter seriously.

FROM

COUNTDOWN

by Alan Ayckbourn

PLAYBILL

This play is about the relationship of a husband and wife who have been married for many years. In the scene presented here, which takes place after supper, the couple is going through the ordinary action of having a cup of tea. What is unusual about the script is that in addition to the lines of dialogue, the playwright has given the inner thoughts of the characters, and these thoughts must be spoken aloud. This gives you the opportunity to explore

CHARACTERS

Wife

Husband

(*Pause. The* WIFE *enters carrying the tray.*)

Wife: What's happened to him this evening? Must be a world crisis if he's actually forgotten to come padding out to carry this tray. Perhaps he's finally given it up. Thank heavens for that. Forever running in and out with this tray. Why doesn't he behave like a man? I'd like to know what he's done with the whistle off that kettle. Where is he then? (*She begins pouring the tea.*)

(*He enters.*)

Husband: Oh there she is. (*Loudly.*) *Oh there you are, dear.*

Wife: What does one say to that? (*Loudly.*) *Here I am.*

Husband: *Good.* That's a nasty piece of sarcasm if ever I heard one.

Wife: *Tea.*

Husband: *Oh, tea! That's nice.* (*He takes cup from her.*)

Wife: Surprise, surprise . . .

Husband: The way she hands me that tea, you'd think it was a cheque for a hundred pounds. I bet she hid that whistle on purpose. So I wouldn't hear her come out, so she can accuse me of inconsideration . . . I'm tired. I'm really tired. If she wasn't here . . . I'd a good mind to . . . I'm so tired. Dog tired. Flaked out. If she wasn't here . . . I'd be tempted to yawn. But since she is here . . . Can't have her see me yawning. I'll have to swallow the thing and risk giving myself wind.

Wife: His eyes are watering. It's that small print. I knew he needed glasses. If he wasn't so vain.

(He starts to stir his tea.)

Go on, go on stir away. I've had three cups by the time he's finished stirring his first. I wouldn't mind if he'd remembered to put sugar in it. And if he expects me to sugar it for him, just so he can complain it's too sweet . . . I'm so tired . . .

Husband: Had an extraordinary dream the other night about a motor mower. Whatever made me? We don't even own a motor mower. No grass. Except for that bit at the side. I suppose that counts as grass. What there is of it. You could cut that with the nail scissors, there's so little of it. Except that I don't think we've got any nail scissors either. I couldn't find them last night for my toe nails. They were catching in the sheet. Serve her right if I'd torn it. She should put things back . . . bathroom cabinet, second shelf. I put the screw eye in there especially. Then she goes and hangs her sponge bag on it instead, so that the door won't shut, so the mirror's at the wrong angle, so I have to shave with one foot in the bath . . . I bet she hasn't put any sugar in this. . .

Wife: *It's not sugared.*

Husband: *Oh no?* Thank you very much. Calmly watches me spraining my wrist stirring the thing . . .

Wife: That'll teach him . . . but maybe I should have told him sooner, now I've got to sit through a second performance.

Husband: (*laughing loudly*) *Hey! Do you know what's in the sugar basin . . . the whistle, the whistle off the kettle!*

Wife: (*laughing*) *Oh really? Fancy. How silly of me.*

Husband: *Silly you!* (*They both laugh gaily at some length.*) *Oh dear.*

Wife: *Oh dear.*

Husband: How stupid can you get?

Wife: That's made his evening. Well, as long as he doesn't start reading his paper to me. (*The* HUSBAND *laughs at something he's reading.*) Ah, we've got to the cartoons already. That laugh's for my benefit. I'm supposed to ask him what it's about; well I'm not going to . . .

Husband: This laugh'll keep her in suspense. She's dying to know what it is. Well let her wait . . . (*He laughs again.*)

Wife: I know. (*She laughs suddenly.*)

Husband: What's she laughing at? She's waiting for me to ask, isn't she? Well I'm not going to.

Wife: I must try and keep my eyes open.

Husband: Man here pushed his wife under a bus. I'll make sure she reads that.

Wife: Why's my husband such an old man? He's always been old. When he was young he was old. (*The* HUSBAND *folds his newspaper.*) Oh no . . . I know what that means . . .

Husband: Oh well, here we go . . . conversation time.

> the intentions behind the characters' lines. (Note that the lines of dialogue are printed in italics.) As you read the play, experiment with ways of saying the internal thoughts of the characters in such a way that they are clearly distinguishable from the dialogue.

ACTIVITIES

1. This scene demonstrates a very valuable rehearsal technique: one where the characters say their inner thoughts aloud. You can use this technique when you rehearse any scene by speaking the thoughts you think are in your character's mind. Improvise the continuation of this scene from *Countdown* using this technique.

2. Examine other scripts you have worked with in this book and determine which characterizations could be strengthened by using this technique. For example, use it for the characters in *Whose Life Is It Anyway?* and *After Liverpool.*

3. Try this scene wearing neutral masks which show no emotions. Examine how the masks affect the action of the scene. As a further activity, you might tape the internal monologues of the characters and have the tape played while doing the scene with the masks. (Note: simple masks can be made using paper bags, paper plates, or cardboard.)

4. Invent other scenes in which this internal/external technique can be used. You can improvise very ordinary scenes in which the internal monologues reveal unusual levels of feeling and tension.

FROM

THE FARM SHOW

by Theatre Passe Muraille and Paul Thompson

PLAYBILL

Like *Juve* in Chapter 1, this play is a collective creation. Using the theme of rural life, it was developed by the actors in a theatre group. The actors lived in a farming community for a summer and dramatized the stories and characters they encountered. The scenes were developed by improvisations, and the written form of the script evolved from these improvisations. While the two scenes presented here do not appear to be related, the characters live in the same community, and in some of your activities you may want to shift characters from one scene to the other.

Act I, Scene VIII.

CHARLIE WILSON.

CHARACTERS

Janet
Charlie Wilson, an eccentric
Men and women in the community (up to 17)

(One actor plays Charlie Wilson consistently. Other members of the cast are visible, but this scene is largely a voice portrait drawn from the memories of people who knew him.)

Janet: Last summer we asked one of the farmers if he knew anyone in the area who was considered eccentric. Someone who was a bit strange and outside of the community. He said the only man he could think of was a man named Charlie Wilson.

Man: Well, I can tell you one thing about Charlie Wilson—he's dead.

Janet: Well, we went around and asked people what they remembered about Charlie.

Woman: Charlie had two shacks that he lived in, one for the summer and one for the winter. His winter shack would be, oh, about this (*paces it off*) long and about that wide. He had a bed, a wood stove, and a table. He didn't have a chair, he would pull the table up to the bed and he had some boxes for his books and his groceries.

Charlie: (*reading from letter*) "Mr J.E. Little, South Street, Goderich. Hello, Ern. I received the parcel you sent me last Christmas."

Woman: He had what, I guess you'd call a tic, on the side of his face, and he'd work it and rub it and his tongue would roll out the side of his mouth, so it was very difficult to understand what he was saying. Oh, I didn't know him very well. Alma used to . . .

Man: You could always tell one of Charlie's tools. He would go out and find a discarded head of a shovel, or an adze, and if he couldn't find a handle, he would go out in the brush and cut a limb, and then just carve it down till it fit. Then he would go out and find all kinds of nuts and bolts and wire things and then put them together. Well, it looked funny, but it worked.

Man: He was a lonely man. He spent a lot of time just by himself. But he used to come over to our house every Thursday night exactly at 6:00 for supper and then he'd watch *Bonanza.* I was one of the few people who ever saw the inside of his shack.

Charlie: "The severity of my tic prevented me acknowledging receipt before this. Dante's *Divine Comedy* contains some interesting historical notes, such as that purgatory was introduced to the Papal form of Christianity in the 6th Century by Pope Gregory."

Woman: I can tell you exactly what Charlie looked like. He had a long lean face that looked like it was hewn out of white elm. He was very pale and he had a square jaw and his chin stuck out just a little. He was always clean-shaven, but occasionally you could see his beard, and it would be white.

Man: Charlie? Oh, Charlie was a corker, he'd get off some good ones—I remember once he started in . . .

Woman: He was one of the best educated men I knew—and he was self-educated. He used to come over to play cards with Fred. He wouldn't stay for dinner because he was ashamed of his tic. I knew him for fifty-three years.

Charlie: (*moves to different spot on-stage*) Now, that's Brassica Oleracia. *You'd* call it wild cabbage. You can tell by the waxy texture of the leaves. Now, that's a young plant. Some of them grow one—two feet high. The waxy texture of the leaves protects them from freezing in a temperate climate.

Woman: He would always wear a clean, blue shirt, and when you passed by his two shacks, you would see hanging out on the line, between them, a pair of blue striped overalls and a blue shirt. Now in summer he wore a rail-roader's hat, and in winter he had sort of a fur cap. (CHARLIE *moves back into "shack".*)

Man: Work? Oh yeah, Charlie worked, and he had a pension and a bit of land. But most of the time he did odd jobs. Now if you hired Charlie for an odd job, he'd be by at nine in the morning, wanting to know what's to be done and he'd start in doing it. Then at twelve noon, he'd quit and be gone till one. Then he'd be back and he'd work until five o'clock or until the job was done. But I tell you, don't get Charlie talking, 'cause if you get him talking you wouldn't get a thing done. Now I remember once he was talking to me . . .

Woman: Women and the Bible! Charlie didn't have any use for either of them. The things he used to say would curl your hair.

Man: In the middle of winter he used to walk the mile or so to our place and when he'd get inside, he'd sit almost as if he was in a trance for half an hour, and then he'd rub his cheek. The kids were kind of repulsed by that.

Charlie: My tic, my tic *dally roo,* bothers me so much sometimes that

I can't get to sleep. I often think I would like to go down to the Maitland and chop a hole in the ice and jump in. But with my luck (*laughing tone*) the axe handle would probably break.

Woman: Well, he chewed tobacco and he took snuff and the smell of his pipe was enough to knock an elephant over.

Man: Oh, you could argue with Charlie, but he didn't have any sense of . . . ah . . . humor!

Woman: Charlie Wilson had a wonderful wit! Now that Les Jervis, well everyone knows he's full of it.

Man: I remember when old Bert Lobb went to visit him in the hospital, Charlie had cancer and he showed Bert his open sore. Well, Bert was so mad at those doctors for keeping him alive and in pain he nearly took the roof off that hospital.

Man: He was odd and kept apart, but he's in heaven!

Charlie: "Wishing you the compliments of the season and again thanking you for your kindness, I remain, your friend, Charlie Wilson . . . Address, J. Chas. Wilson, RR 2, Clinton Ontario." (*exit*)

Act I, Scene X.

WASHING WOMAN.

Marion, the washing woman
Jim, her husband
Boy, their son
Jane, their daughter
Mary, another daughter
Feed man
Woman buying eggs

(Woman appears pushing washing machine to centre stage, or, if no wheels, she gets her husband to help.)

Marion: You know, if you'd get that thing fixed, we wouldn't have to carry it out here every time. (*to audience*) I was *so* busy yesterday, I had so much to do that when I woke up this morning I had a headache and I had to take an aspirin. Well, I feel better now, but I've decided to take it easy today. I'm going to stay right here in this house (*climbs into washing machine and squats down*) and maybe do a little housework.

If there's one thing you've got to have on a farm, it's your *health.* If you're not healthy, you're no good to anyone. (*begins dusting machine*) Oh, just look at that.

I'll just give you an idea of what I did yesterday. I started out at five thirty and collected my eggs. Well I do that every morning. You see, I have five hundred new pullets, year-old chickens, and I'm the only one who can collect the eggs because they get very excited . . . (JIM*'s speech below overlaps last sentence.*)

Jim: Marion! Marion, I have to go to the dealers. I'll be back about one-thirty . . .

Marion: What? What did you say, dear?

Jim: I said I have to go down to the dealers for shear-pins. I'll be back about one or one-thirty. So if we could have dinner . . .

Marion: But I took you in yesterday!

Jim: I know. But they shear off in tough hay. We'll need you out on the tractor about three. So, if you could . . .

Marion: No! I'm not going out of this house today. I need a rest.

Jim: Well, you're the only one left, so I'll see you on the tractor at three . . . (*exit*)

Marion: Well, maybe Jane could help you! That girl never does a thing around here ! Maybe she could . . . Oh well, I must remember to speak to Jane. Then I made breakfast as usual but I didn't have a chance to do the dishes because I had to take the boys to their hockey practice. They have hockey practice on Tuesdays and Saturdays and baseball practice on, uh, let me see, Thursdays, yes, but Elizabeth takes them on Thursdays, so that's all right. Then I decided to do my grocery shopping at the same time and kill two birds with one stone after I dropped Jim off at the implement dealers, but I forgot my list. Wouldn't you know! And I forgot the cheese. Well, I was . . .

Boy: (*enters with old cap advertising Funk's corn*) Mom . . .? Mom . . .? Mom? (*finally gets her attention*)

Marion: What is it dear? (*to audience*) Excuse me.

Boy: Mom, would you wash my Funk's hat please? Thank you.

Marion: Just a *minute*! You come here! Now I've told you *three* times to get rid of this filthy old thing. If I see it again, I'll *burn* it!

Boy: (*whining*) Aw, come on, Mom. It's my lucky Funk's hat. I gotta have it. If I don't have it, we'll lose the game!

Marion: I'm not washing it. No son of mine is going to be seen wearing a hat like that!

Boy: Pleeeeeeeease?

Marion: (*sighs*) Oh, all right. But this is the *last time*!

Boy: Thanks Mom. I knew it. (*Kisses her*) I love you! (*exit*)

Marion: Excuse me, I'll just start the washing. Oh, yes. Well, I was having some ladies in and wouldn't you know it the one thing that Mrs. Hislop loves is cheese?

Jane: (*enters carrying laundry*) Would you wash this please? I'm going to the dance tonight. Thank-you. (*exit*)

Marion: Jane? Jane! Your father wants you on the tractor at three o'clock. (*overlays Jane's speech above*) And don't you talk to me like that young lady or you'll get no . . . (*sigh*) Excuse me while I get this laundry in. (*starts to gyrate*) Well, I had to go back and get some cheese and by the time I go back at eleven thirty the eggs were all over the place.

Mary: (*enters carrying bag*) Mom this isn't garbage!

(Knock on door off-stage)

Marion: I've put it out three times. Could you answer the door please? I thought that you . . . The pullets you see, don't know how to lay in the nests yet. And then I had to get the boys . . . (*phone rings*) Hello? Oh, hello Elizabeth. No, I thought you were . . .

Man: (*enters with* MARY) Feed man! Could you sign here ma'am.

Mary: You're new around here, aren't you?

(Knock on door off-stage)

Marion: Do you have a pencil? My husband is out in the barn. (*to* ELIZABETH *on the phone*) I can't pick up the boys. I have to take it easy today.

Woman: (*enters with basket*) I've come for my eggs! I ordered three dozen this morning.

Marion: Mary, try and find a pencil. (*to audience*) Then the card party arrived and I hadn't time to do the dishes all day. (*to* EGG WOMAN) Well, I'm sorry, the bakery has bought all the eggs.

Man: (*to* MARY) No, I don't have a pencil. (*to* MARION) Your husband isn't out in the barn. I've gone out there for the last . . .

*(*BOY *enters holding a hurt thumb, gets into an argument with his sister and chases her around washer,* WOMAN *and* FEED MAN *wait impatiently,* MARION*'s speech has been gradually speeding up until now, gyrating furiously, she is incomprehensible. With a loud squawk and flap,* MARION *turns into a chicken.)*

Jim: (*pause*) What's for dinner!

ACTIVITIES

"Charlie Wilson"

1. In this scene most of the information about the character of Charlie Wilson comes from what people say about him. To develop your understanding of Charlie, improvise scenes which are referred to in the text; for example, Charlie doing an "odd job" for a farmer.

2. Finding physical actions for all the people in this scene can prove difficult. Try doing the scene with all the speakers in tableau, perhaps unfreezing only when they speak. Can you find significant actions for Charlie when others are speaking about him? Find appropriate music to play in the background during the scene.

3. Do the scene as a television documentary. How does this change the scene? How can you present the parts where Charlie—a dead man—speaks?

ACTIVITIES

"Washing Woman"

1. As you develop this scene, attempt to "speed up" the lines and the action each time so that the person playing Marion begins to feel the hectic pace of the character's life.

2. Examine these two significant actions in the scene and attempt to determine why they occur: Marion getting into the washing machine (a wringer-washer); Marion turning into a chicken. Can you replace these actions with other significant ones?

3. Improvise a scene in which Marion tells her best friend about her life, her family, and her work. If you are playing the friend, try to convince Marion that her life on the farm must be wonderful compared to your hectic life in the city.

4. Develop an improvisation in which Marion hires Charlie Wilson to do odd jobs around the farm. How is your understanding of both characters enhanced?

5. The techniques of dramatizing real people and events presented in this script will be encountered in other sections of this book: "Docudrama" (Section B, Chapter 12) and "Scripting" (Section B, Chapter 10) explore the techniques, and *Juve* (Section A, Chapter 1) and *1837: The Farmer's Revolt* (Section A, Chapter 4) are examples of other scripts using similar techniques.

FROM

THE TRAGEDY OF DR. FAUSTUS

by Christopher Marlowe

PLAYBILL

Written in 1588, this play tells the story of Dr. Faustus, a scholar who made a bargain with the devil. In return for surrendering his soul, Faustus would gain twenty-four years of earthly power and access to all knowledge. In the scene preceding this one, Faustus has just signed the pact in blood despite the pleas of the Good Angel. To most Elizabethans the devil was very real, and the audience would have found such a scene especially horrifying. As you read the following scene, you may find the language difficult and often obscure. It will

CHARACTERS

Faust
Mephistophilis
Good Angel
Evil Angel
Lucifer
Belzebub
Pride
Covetousness
Wrath
Envy
Gluttony
Sloth
Lechery
(Pride through Lechery: the **Seven Deadly Sins**)

SCENE VI

(Enter FAUST *in his Study, and* MEPHISTOPHILIS.*)*

Faust: When I behold the heavens, then I repent
And curse thee, wicked Mephistophilis,
Because thou hast deprived me of those joys.

Meph: Why, Faustus,
Thinkst thou heaven is such a glorious thing?
I tell thee, 'tis not half so fair as thou,
Or any man that breathes on earth.

Faust: How provest thou that?

Meph: It was made for man; therefore is man more excellent.

Faust: If it were made for man 'twas made for me.
I will renounce this magic and repent.

(Enter GOOD ANGEL *and* EVIL ANGEL.*)*

G. Ang: Faustus, repent; yet God will pity thee.

E. Ang: Thou art a spirit; God cannot pity thee.

Meph: As are the elements, such are the spheres,
Mutually folded in each other's orb;
And jointly move upon one axletree
Whose terminine is termed the world's wide pole;
Nor are the names of Saturn, Mars, or Jupiter
Feigned, but are erring stars.

Faust: But tell me, have they all one motion, both *situ et tempore*?[1]

Meph: All jointly move from East to West in twenty-four hours upon the poles of the world, but differ in their motion upon the poles of the zodiac.

Faust: Tush, these slender trifles Wagner can decide.
Hath Mephistophilis no greater skill?
Who knows not the double motion of the planets?
The first is finished in a natural day;
The second thus, as Saturn in thirty years, Jupiter in twelve, Mars in four, the Sun, Venus, and Mercury in a year, the Moon in Twenty-eight days. Tush, these are freshmen's suppositions. But tell me, hath every sphere a dominion or *Intelligentia*?[2]

Meph: Ay.

Faust: How many heavens or spheres are there?

Meph: Nine: the seven planets, the firmament, and the empyreal heaven.

Faust: But is there not *coelum igneum, et crystallinum*?[3]

Meph: No, Faustus, they be but fables.

Faust: Well, resolve me in this question: why have we not conjunctions, oppositions, aspects, eclipses, all at one time, but in some years we have more, in some less?

Meph: *Per inequalem motum respectu totius.*[4]

Faust: Well, I am answered. Tell me, who made the world?

Meph: I will not.

Faust: Sweet Mephistophilis, tell me.

Meph: Move me not, for I will not tell thee.

Faust: Villain, have I not bound thee to tell me anything?

Meph: Ay, that is not against our Kingdom; but this is.
Think thou on hell, Faustus, for thou art damned.

Faust: Think, Faustus, upon God that made the world!

Meph: Remember this!

(Exit.)

[1]*situ et tempore*: in time and place

[2]*Intelligentia*: a ruling spirit

[3]*coelum igneum, et crystallinum*: a burning heaven and a crystalline heaven. In the Ptolemaic system, the belief which prevailed when this play was written, the universe consisted of nine concentric spheres with the earth at the centre.

[4]*Per inequalem motum respectu totius*: because of the unequal motion in relation to the whole

help if you focus on the intentions of each of the characters and the means they use to achieve their goals. You may wish to look back at the techniques you used to handle rhyme and chant in *Juve*.

Faust: Ay, go, accursed spirit, to ugly hell;
'Tis thou has damned distressed Faustus' soul. Is't not too late?

(Enter GOOD ANGEL *and* EVIL ANGEL.*)*

E. Ang: Too late.

G. Ang: Never too late, if Faustus can repent.

E. Ang: If thou repent, devils shall tear thee in pieces.

G. Ang: Repent, and they shall never raze thy skin.

(Exeunt ANGELS.*)*

Faust: Ah Christ, my Savior!
Seek to save distressed Faustus' soul.

(Enter LUCIFER, BELZEBUB, *and* MEPHISTOPHILIS.*)*

Luc: Christ cannot save thy soul, for he is just; There's none but I have interest in the same.

Faust: O who art thou that lookst so terrible?

Luc: I am Lucifer,
And this is my companion prince in hell.

Faust: O Faustus, they are come to fetch away thy soul!

Luc: We come to tell thee thou dost injure us:
Thou callst on Christ, contrary to thy promise.
Thou shouldst not think of God; think of the Devil,—
And of his dam too.

Faust: Nor will I henceforth. Pardon me in this,
And Faustus vows never to look to heaven,
Never to name God or to pray to him,
To burn his Scriptures, slay his ministers,
And make my spirits pull his churches down.

Luc: Do so, and we will highly gratify thee. Faustus, we are come from hell to show thee some pastime: sit down, and thou shalt see all the Seven Deadly Sins appear in their proper shapes.

Faust: That sight will be as pleasing unto me as paradise was to Adam, the first day of his creation.

Luc: Talk not of paradise nor creation, but mark this show; talk of the Devil and nothing else. Come, away!

(Enter the SEVEN DEADLY SINS*)*

Now, Faustus, examine them of their several names and dispositions.

Faust: What are thou, the first?

Pride: I am Pride. I disdain to have any parents. I am like to Ovid's flea: I can creep into every corner of a wench; sometimes like a periwig I sit upon her brow; next like a necklace I hang about her neck, or like a fan of feathers I kiss her lips; and then turning myself to a wrought smock do what I list. But fie, what a scent is here! I'll not speak another word except the ground were perfumed and covered with cloth of arras.

Faust: Thou art a proud knave indeed. What art thou, the second?

Covet: I am Covetousness, begotten of an old churl in an old leathern bag; and, might I have my wish, I would desire that this house and all the people in it were turned to gold, that I might lock you up in my chest. O my sweet gold!

Faust: What art thou, the third?

Wrath: I am Wrath. I had neither father nor mother; I leaped out of a lion's mouth when I was scarce half an hour old, and ever since I have run up and down the world with this case of rapiers, wounding myself when I had nobody to fight withal. I was born in hell; and look to it, for some of you shall be my father.

Faust: What art thou, the fourth?

Envy: I am Envy, begotten of a chimney-sweeper and an oyster-wife. I cannot read, and therefore wish all books were burned. I am lean with seeing others eat. O that there would come a famine through all the world, that all might die, and I live alone; then thou shouldst see how fat I would be! But must thou sit and I stand? Come down, with a vengeance!

Faust: Away, envious rascal! What art thou, the fifth?

Glut: Who, I, sir? I am Gluttony. My parents are all dead, and the devil a penny they have left me but a bare pension, and that is thirty meals a day and ten bevers—a small trifle to suffice nature. O I come of a royal parentage: my grandfather was a gammon of bacon, my grandmother a hogshead of claret wine. My godfathers were these: Peter Pickle-herring and Martin Martlemas-beef. O but my godmother—she was a jolly gentlewoman, and well beloved in every good town and city: her name was mistress Margery March-beer. Now, Faustus, thou hast heard all my progeny; wilt thou bid me to supper?

Faust: No, I'll see thee hanged! Thou wilt eat up all my victuals.

Glut: Then the Devil choke thee.

Faust: Choke thyself, glutton. What art thou, the sixth?

Sloth: I am Sloth. I was begotten on a sunny bank, where I have lain ever since, and you have done me great injury to bring me from thence; let me be carried thither again by Gluttony and Lechery. I'll not speak another word for a king's ransom.

Faust: What are you, mistress minx, the seventh and last?

Lech: Who, I, sir? I am one that loves an inch of raw mutton better than an ell of fried stockfish, and the first letter of my name begins with L—echery.

Luc: Away, to hell, to hell! (*Exeunt the* SINS.) Now, Faustus, how dost thou like this?

Faust: O this feeds my soul!

Luc: Tut, Faustus, in hell is all manner of delight.

Faust: O that I might see hell and return again, how happy were I then!

Luc: Thou shalt. I will send for thee at midnight. In mean time take this book, peruse it thoroughly, and thou shalt turn thyself into what shape thou wilt.

Faust: Great thanks, mighty Lucifer; This will I keep as chary as my life.

Luc: Farewell, Faustus, and think on the Devil.

Faust: Farewell, great Lucifer. Come, Mephistophilis.

(Exeunt omnes.)

ACTIVITIES

1. To understand more fully how Faustus is feeling about his pact with the devil, improvise a scene between the Good Angel and Evil Angel in which each makes further arguments for Faustus repenting or continuing his pact. Make the arguments as convincing as you can. At the conclusion Faustus can express which argument he finds more convincing.

2. Examine the speeches of the Seven Deadly Sins. They are written in the common speech of Marlowe's time and are difficult to understand today. See if you can get the sense of what they say. With your group create contemporary equivalents of the Seven Deadly Sins, and, using today's language, improvise a scene in which they appear to Faustus. Use makeup and costume, if possible, to enhance your characterizations.

3. When you create contemporary equivalents for the Seven Deadly Sins, investigate creating characters who are the opposite of the stereotypes suggested by the sins. That is, instead of playing Pride as a self-centred person concerned about appearance, find other ways that a person can be excessively proud. In a similar manner, what if Gluttony were a very thin person who ate very little? Attempt to create characters who express their "sin" in very subtle ways. Employ the technique, presented in *Countdown*, of saying the internal thoughts and feelings of the characters aloud.

4. Investigate techniques which would enhance the characterizations in this scene. Use masks, costumes, make-up, and props to elaborate character, and, if possible, develop lighting, sound effects, and music to build atmosphere. Attempt to recreate the horror that the original Elizabethan audience felt while watching this scene.

5. Other examples of Elizabethan theatre will be found in the selection *A Midsummer Night's Dream* (Section A, Chapter 4) and in the chapter "Shakespeare's People" (Section C, Chapter 18). You may want to read ahead in order to develop a better understanding of Elizabethan drama.

FROM

ANTIGONE

by Jean Anouilh

PLAYBILL

Oedipus's two sons, Eteocles and Polynices, were to rule Thebes in alternate years after Oedipus's death. A civil war broke out when Eteocles refused to step down after his first year, and the two brothers killed each other in single combat. Creon, Oedipus's brother-in-law, ascended the throne and buried Eteocles, with whom he had sided, with full

CHARACTERS

Chorus (can be one or several people)
First Guard
Second Guard
Third Guard
Antigone
Creon
Page (non-speaking)

Chorus: The spring is wound up tight. It will uncoil of itself. That is what is so convenient in tragedy. The least little turn of the wrist will do the job. Anything will set it going: a glance at a girl who happens to be lifting her arms to her hair as you go by; a feeling when you wake up on a fine morning that you'd like a little respect paid to you today, as if it were as easy to order as a second cup of coffee; one question too many, idly thrown out over a friendly drink—and the tragedy is on.

The rest is automatic. You don't need to lift a finger. The machine is in perfect order; it has been oiled ever since time began, and it runs without friction. Death, treason and sorrow are on the march; and they move in the wake of storm, of tears, of stillness. Every kind of stillness. The hush when the executioner's axe goes up at the end of the last act. The silence inside you when the roaring crowd acclaims the winner—so that you think of a film without a sound-track, mouths agape and no sound coming out of them, a clamor that is no more than a picture; and you, the victor, already vanquished, alone in the desert of your silence. That is tragedy.

Tragedy is clean, it is restful, it is flawless. It has nothing to do with melodrama—with wicked villains, persecuted maidens, avengers, sudden revelations and eleventh-hour repentances. Death, in a melodrama, is really horrible because it is never inevitable. The dear old father might so easily have been saved; the honest young man might so easily have brought in the police five minutes earlier.

In a tragedy, nothing is in doubt and everyone's destiny is known. That makes for tranquillity. There is a sort of fellow-feeling among characters in a tragedy: he who kills is as innocent as he who gets killed: it's all a matter of what part you are playing. Tragedy is restful; and the reason is that hope, that foul, deceitful thing, has no part in it. There isn't any hope. You're trapped. The whole sky has fallen on you, and all you can do about it is to shout.

Don't mistake me: I said "shout": I did not say groan, whimper, complain. That, you cannot do. But you can shout aloud; you can get all those things said that you never thought you'd be able to say—or never even knew you had it in you to say. And you don't say these things because it will do any good to say them: you know better than that. You say them for their own sake; you say them because you learn a lot from them.

In melodrama, you argue and struggle in the hope of escape. That is vulgar; it's practical. But in tragedy, where there is no temptation to try to escape, argument is gratuitous: it's kingly.

(Voices of the GUARDS *and scuffling sounds heard through the archway.* CHORUS *looks in that direction, then, in a changed tone)*

The play is on. Antigone has been caught. For the first time in her life, little Antigone is going to be able to be herself.

*(*CHORUS *exits through arch. A pause, while the off-stage voices rise in volume, then the* FIRST GUARD *enters, followed by* SECOND *and* THIRD GUARDS, *holding the arms of* ANTIGONE *and dragging her along. The* FIRST GUARD, *speaking as he enters,*

honors. Creon decreed that Polynices's body was to be left in the open to rot and that anyone who attempted to bury Polynices would be put to death. In the following scenes, Antigone, the daughter of Oedipus, tries to bury her brother and is caught.

The playwright has based this play on the original Greek tragedy written by Sophocles around 441 B.C., but Anouilh has made the language and the characters contemporary. One example of change is the number of people in the chorus. In the original play the chorus was a group of speakers; in this play the chorus can be a single speaker. It is important to note that this play was written and presented in Paris in 1942 during the German occupation. Thus, the characters and the plot had a wider meaning for the audience, and the conflict was one which they readily understood.

crosses swiftly to end of the table. The TWO GUARDS *and* ANTIGONE *stop downstage.)*

First Guard: (*recovered from his fright*) Come on, now, Miss, give it a rest. The chief will be here in a minute and you can tell him about it. All I know is my orders. I don't want to know what you were doing there. People always have excuses; but I can't afford to listen to them, see. Why, if we had to listen to all the people who want to tell us what's the matter with this country, we'd never get our work done. (*To the* GUARDS.) You keep hold of her and I'll see that she keeps her face shut.

Antigone: They are hurting me. Tell them to take their dirty hands off me.

First Guard: Dirty hands, eh? The least you can do is try to be polite, Miss. Look at me: I'm polite.

Antigone: Tell them to let me go. I shan't run away. My father was King Oedipus. I am Antigone.

First Guard: King Oedipus' little girl! Well, well, well!

• • •

Antigone: I should like to sit down, if you please.

(A pause, as the FIRST GUARD *thinks it over.)*

First Guard: Let her sit down. But keep hold of her. (*The two* GUARDS *start to lead her towards the chair at the end of table. The curtain upstage opens, and* CREON *enters, followed by his* PAGE. FIRST GUARD *turns and moves upstage a few steps, sees* CREON.) 'Tenshun! (*The three* GUARDS *salute.* CREON, *seeing* ANTIGONE *handcuffed to* THIRD GUARD, *stops on the top step, astonished.*)

Creon: Antigone! (*To the* FIRST GUARD.) Take off those handcuffs! (FIRST GUARD *crosses above table to left of* ANTIGONE.) What is this? (CREON *and his* PAGE *come down off the steps.*)

(FIRST GUARD *takes key from his pocket and unlocks the cuff on* ANTIGONE'*s hand.* ANTIGONE *rubs her wrist as she crosses below table towards chair at end of table.* SECOND *and* THIRD GUARDS *step back to front of arch.* FIRST GUARD *turns upstage towards* CREON.)

First Guard: The watch, sir. We all came this time.

Creon: Who is guarding the body?

First Guard: We sent for the relief.

(CREON *comes down.)*

Creon: But I gave orders that the relief was to go back to barracks and stay there! (ANTIGONE *sits on chair at left of table.*) I told you not to open your mouth about this!

First Guard: Nobody's said anything, sir. We made this arrest, and brought the party in, the way you said we should.

Creon: (*to* ANTIGONE) Where did these men find you?

First Guard: Right by the body.

Creon: What were you doing near your brother's body? You knew what my orders were.

First Guard: What was she doing? Sir, that's why we brought her in. She was digging up the dirt with her nails. She was trying to cover up the body all over again.

Creon: Do you realize what you are saying?

First Guard: Sir, ask these men here. After I reported to you, I went back, and first thing we did, we uncovered the body. The sun was coming up and it was beginning to smell, so we moved it up on a little rise to get him in the wind. Of course, you wouldn't expect any trouble in broad daylight. But just the same, we decided one of us had better keep his eye peeled all the time. About noon, what with the sun and the smell, and as the wind dropped and I wasn't feeling none too good, I went over to my pal to get a chew. I just had time to say "thanks" and stick it in my mouth, when I turned round and there she was, clawing away at the dirt with both hands. Right out in broad daylight! Wouldn't you think when she saw me come running she'd stop and leg it out of there? Not her! She went right on digging as fast as she could, as if I wasn't there at all. And when I grabbed her, she scratched and bit and yelled to leave her alone, she hadn't finished yet, the body wasn't all covered yet, and the like of that.

Creon: (*to* ANTIGONE) Is this true?

Antigone: Yes, it is true.

First Guard: We scraped the dirt off as fast as we could, then we sent for the relief and we posted them. But we didn't tell them a thing, sir. And we brought in the party so's you could see her. And that's the truth, so help me God.

Creon: (*to* ANTIGONE) And was it you who covered the body the first time? In the night?

Antigone: Yes, it was. With a toy shovel we used to take to the seashore when we were children. It was Polynices' own shovel; he had cut his name in the handle. That was why I left it with him. But these men took it away; so the next time, I had to do it with my hands.

First Guard: Sir, she was clawing away like a wild animal. Matter of fact, first minute we saw her, what with the heat haze and everything, my pal says, "That must be a dog," he says. "Dog!" I says, "That's a girl, that is!" And it was.

Creon: Very well (*Turns to the* PAGE) Show these men to the ante-room. (*The* PAGE *crosses to the arch, stands there, waiting.* CREON *moves behind the table. To the* FIRST GUARD.) You three men will wait outside. I may want a report from you later.

First Guard: Do I put the cuffs back on her, sir?

Creon: No. (*The three* GUARDS *salute, do an about-turn and exit through arch, right.* PAGE *follows them out. A pause.*) Had you told anybody what you meant to do?

Antigone: No.

Creon: Did you meet anyone on your way—coming or going?

Antigone: No, nobody.

Creon: Sure of that, are you?

Antigone: Perfectly sure.

Creon: Very well. Now listen to me. You will go straight to your room. When you get there, you will go to bed. You will say that you are not well and that you have not been out since yesterday. Your nurse will tell the same story. (*He looks towards arch, through which the* GUARDS *have exited.*) And I'll get rid of those three men.

Antigone: Uncle Creon, you are going to a lot of trouble for no good reason. You must know that I'll do it all over again tonight.

(*A pause. They look one another in the eye.*)

Creon: Why did you try to bury your brother?

Antigone: I owed it to him.

Creon: I had forbidden it.

Antigone: I owed it to him. Those who are not buried wander eternally and find no rest. If my brother were alive, and he came home weary after a long day's hunting, I should kneel down and unlace his boots, I should fetch him food and drink, I should see that his bed was ready for him. Polynices is home from the hunt. I owe it to him to unlock the house of the dead in which my father and my mother are waiting to welcome him. Polynices has earned his rest.

Creon: Polynices was a rebel and a traitor, and you know it.

Antigone: He was my brother.

Creon: You heard my edict. It was proclaimed throughout Thebes. You read my edict. It was posted up on the city walls.

Antigone: Of course I did.

Creon: You knew the punishment I decreed for any person who attempted to give him burial.

Antigone: Yes, I knew the punishment.

Creon: Did you by any chance act on the assumption that a daughter of Oedipus, a daughter of Oedipus' stubborn pride, was above the law?

Antigone: No, I did not act on that assumption.

Creon: Because if you had acted on that assumption, Antigone, you would have been deeply wrong. Nobody has a more sacred obligation to obey the law than those who make the law. You are a daughter of lawmakers, a daughter of kings, Antigone. You must observe the law.

Antigone: Had I been a scullery maid washing my dishes when that law was read aloud to me, I should have scrubbed the greasy water from my arms and gone out in my apron to bury my brother.

Creon: What nonsense! If you had been a scullery maid, there would have been no doubt in your mind about the seriousness of that edict. You would have known that it meant death; and you would have been satisfied to weep for your brother in your kitchen. But you! You thought that because you come of the royal line, because you were my niece and were going to marry my son, I shouldn't dare have you killed.

Antigone: You are mistaken. Quite the contrary. I never doubted for an instant that you would have me put to death.

(*A pause, as* CREON *stares fixedly at her.*)

Creon: The pride of Oedipus! Oedipus and his head-strong pride all over again. I can see your father in you—and I believe you. Of course you thought that I should have you killed! Proud as you are, it seemed to you a natural climax in your existence. Your father was like that. For him as for you human happiness was meaningless; and mere human misery was not enough to satisfy his passion for torment. (*He sits on stool behind the table.*) You come of people for whom the human vestment is a kind of straitjacket: it cracks at the seams. You spend your lives wriggling to get out of it. Nothing less than a cosy tea party with death and destiny will quench your thirst. The happiest hour of your father's life came when he listened greedily to the story of how, unknown to himself, he had killed his own father and dishonored the bed of his own mother. Drop by drop, word by word, he drank in the dark story that the gods had destined him, first to live and then to hear. How avidly men and women drink the brew of such a tale when their names are Oedipus—and Antigone! And it is so simple, afterwards, to do what your father did, to put out one's eyes and take one's daughter begging on the highways.

Let me tell you, Antigone: those days are over for Thebes. Thebes has a right to a king without a past. My name, thank God, is only Creon. I stand here with both feet firm on the ground; with both hands in my pockets; and I have decided that so long as I am king—being less ambitious than your father was—I shall merely devote myself to introducing a little order into this absurd kingdom; if that is possible.

Don't think that being a king seems to me romantic. It is my trade; a trade a man has to work at every day; and like every other trade, it isn't all beer and skittles. But since it is my trade, I take it seriously. And if, tomorrow, some wild and bearded messenger walks in from some wild and distant valley—which is what happened to your dad—and tells me that he's not quite sure who my parents were, but thinks that my wife Eurydice is actually my mother, I shall ask him to do me the kindness to go back where he came from; and I shan't let a little matter like that persuade me to order my wife to take a blood test and the police to let me know whether or not my birth certificate was forged. Kings, my girl, have other things to do than to surrender themselves to their private feelings. (*He looks at her and smiles.*) Hand *you* over to to killed! (*He rises, moves to end of table and sits on the top of table.*) I have other plans for you. You're going to marry Haemon; and I want you to fatten up a bit so that you can give him a sturdy boy. Let me assure you that Thebes needs that boy a good deal more than it needs your death. You will go to your room, now, and do as you have been told; and you won't say a word about this to anybody. Don't fret about the guards: I'll see that their mouths are shut. And don't annihilate me with those eyes. I know that you think I am a brute, and I'm sure you must consider me very prosaic. But the fact is, I have always been fond of you, stubborn though you always were. Don't forget that the first doll you ever had came from me. (*A pause.* ANTIGONE *says nothing, rises and crosses slowly below the table towards the arch.* CREON *turns and watches her; then*) Where are you going?

Antigone: (*stops downstage. Without any show of rebellion*) You know very well where I am going.

Creon: (*after a pause*) What sort of game are you playing?

Antigone: I am not playing games.

Creon: Antigone, do you realize that if, apart from those three guards, a single soul finds out what you have tried to do, it will be impossible for me to avoid putting you to death? There is still a chance that I can save you; but only if you keep this to yourself and give up your crazy purpose. Five minutes more, and it will be too late. You understand that?

Antigone: I must go and bury my brother. Those men uncovered him.

Creon: What good will it do? You know that there are other men standing guard over Polynices. And even if you did cover him over with earth again, the earth would again be removed.

Antigone: I know all that. I know it. But that much, at least, I can do. And what a person can do, a person ought to do.

(Pause.)

Creon: Tell me, Antigone, do you believe all that flummery about religious burial? Do you really believe that a so-called shade of your brother is condemned to wander for ever homeless if a little earth is not flung on his corpse to the accompaniment of some priestly abracadabra? Have you ever listened to the priests of Thebes when they were mumbling their formula? Have you ever watched those dreary bureaucrats while they were preparing the dead for burial—skipping half the gestures required by the ritual, swallowing half their words, hustling the dead into their graves out of fear that they might be late for lunch?

Antigone: Yes, I have seen all that.

Creon: And did you never say to yourself as you watched them, that if someone you really loved lay dead under the shuffling, mumbling ministrations of the priests, you would scream aloud and beg the priests to leave the dead in peace?

Antigone: Yes, I've thought all that.

Creon: And you still insist upon being put to death—merely because I refuse to let your brother go out with that grotesque passport; because I refuse his body the wretched consolation of that mass-production jibber-jabber, which you would have been the first to be embarrassed by if I had allowed it. The whole thing is absurd!

Antigone: Yes, it's absurd.

Creon: Then why, Antigone, why? For whose sake? For the sake of them that believe in it? To raise them against me?

Antigone: No.

Creon: For whom then if not for them and not for Polynices either?

Antigone: For nobody. For myself.

(A pause as they stand looking at one another.)

Creon: You must want very much to die. You look like a trapped animal.

Antigone: Stop feeling sorry for me. Do as I do. Do your job. But if you are a human being, do it quickly. That is all I ask of you. I'm not going to be able to hold out for ever.

Creon: (*takes a step towards her*) I want to save you, Antigone.

Antigone: You are the king, and you are all-powerful. But that you cannot do.

Creon: You think not?

Antigone: Neither save me nor stop me.

Creon: Prideful Antigone! Little Oedipus!

Antigone: Only this can you do: have me put to death.

ACTIVITIES

1. In this scene there are two very strong characters, each of whom believes he/she is "right" and has very clear objectives. Examine all the evidence you have in the script about each person, and draw up lists of the positive and negative qualities each possesses. Also pick out the merits of each person's arguments. To be sure you see both sides, play each role when going through the script. When you have understood all aspects of each side, have other members of your group create a jury that will hear the arguments of Antigone and Creon. When all arguments have been made, the jury will decide how the conflict is to be resolved.

2. Examine the role of the chorus in this play. In the original Greek tragedy, the chorus was a group of people who spoke together. An example of this type of chorus can be seen in *Oedipus The*

King (Section C, Chapter 15). But in *Antigone* the chorus is presented as a character, and anyone playing this role must determine what sort of person this is by examining the dialogue. Experiment with many different ways of saying this speech. Have several people say this speech chorally and compare the effect with that of a single person's delivery.

3. Imagine you are members of the original French audience which saw this play in 1942. Have a discussion about this scene with other audience members in the lobby at intermission. Be aware that there would be German army officers in the lobby also.

4. Examine the speech by Antigone on page 41 beginning "I owed it to him." That speech may appear offensive since it seems to cast a woman in a subservient role. However, the meaning changes if it is treated metaphorically, that is, "the hunt" refers to French resistance activities against the German occupation in World War II, and Antigone is expressing the French population's support of the resistance. Find other examples of lines which could have a second meaning.

WORKSHOP

1. Two people (A and B) are chosen from a group. B goes out of earshot. A then announces to the group "I want B to tell me he is sorry" (or hop on one foot, or touch the floor). A then goes out of earshot and B announces to the group "I want A to sing a song" (or any other objective).

Once the participants have announced their objectives, the other members of the group, who will be the audience, give A and B roles and a situation which could be drawn from a script in this book. "You are a husband and wife going to have tea after supper." A and B now play their scene each trying to make the other fulfill the stated objective. The game ends when one of the pair succeeds in getting the other to do what he/she wants. There should be a time limit set, so that the scene does not ramble on or disintegrate into a pushing match, and if there is no winner, it is all right. The point of stating and working toward an objective has been made.

2. Choose a character from one of the plays studied so far, and prepare a mask which depicts the most outstanding characteristic or quality of this character, be it physical, emotional, or a depiction of the "inner" character. Choice of color, expression, type of mask, type of material, can all be important elements in creating the whole character with one mask.

3. Have a press conference where the person being interviewed is a character from one of the plays. The others are reporters who ask very specific questions about the character's life, problems, feelings, etc. At the end of the press conference the reporters can decide if the character is really the person presented or an imposter. Reasons for either judgment should be given.

4. As you did with the characterizations of the Seven Deadly Sins in *Dr. Faustus*, use the opposite way of interpreting a character in any of the other plays to see how the interpretation changes. Some examples are:
—Ken in *Whose Life Is It Anyway?* is complaining and feeling sorry for himself;
—the couple in *Countdown* are loving and tender with each other;
—Creon doesn't care what happens to Antigone.

5. Experiment with putting one or two characters from one play into another play to comment on the action as it unfolds. What happens if they get involved in the action of the play? For example, what would happen if Corie, from *Barefoot in the Park*, were to become a part of *Countdown*?

6. Do a scene as if all the characters were animals. Choose an animal which might be reflective of the character you are playing, and go through the scene saying the dialogue and doing the actions, but play the character throughout as if it were this animal. Does the animal movement help delineate your character? Does the animal characteristic truly reflect the role you are playing, or change your own attitude about the role? Does the animal movement free the body and give you new insights into the character? Observe the others, and allow yourself to react to the other animal characters in the play. If one is an ape, do you feel more threatened by the movements than before? Choose the animals carefully, and do the scene several times as different animals. This technique is very valuable for any script in this book.

4: Rehearsing the Script

THE PROGRAM

You probably have discovered by now that working with scripts is a difficult but rewarding process. Every script presents new problems to be solved and demands creative thought and action from you.

Polishing a script through rehearsals is a continuation of the work you have begun, and it will make even greater demands upon you. One of the greatest pitfalls in rehearsing a scene or play is allowing yourself and the group to get stale. To avoid this, each rehearsal must provide something new for the interpretation of the script and the characters. Continually re-doing the scene without freshness does not benefit anyone.

Another problem you may encounter is the difficulty of working in a group for a sustained period. It is essential that everyone be committed to the work and that everyone express their commitment by being at rehearsals on time and by doing what was promised to be done. It is also vital that communication skills be practised by listening to each other's ideas and encouraging all group members to express their thoughts and feelings. Drama is a co-operative art and demands that all group members contribute to the success of their work.

Memorization of lines is always difficult and most performers experience problems. You should not attempt to memorize too soon. Rather, give yourself plenty of time and practice at saying the lines aloud so that they become a part of the expression of the character you are playing. As your understanding of your role grows the lines will become more easily assimilated.

Rehearsal should be a time of exploration and experimentation. Avoid being too rigid in matters of physical action (blocking) and line delivery (diction, articulation, and projection). Instead, use the time to find different and varied means of expression. The following suggestions are designed to help you look at the script in different ways. After you have tried a technique with your group, analyse what was achieved and what could be retained for the final interpretation.

REHEARSAL TECHNIQUES

1. At any time during rehearsal, before memorization, put the scripts aside and improvise the scene. Examine what was left out of the improvisation; this material has probably not been fully understood or internalized.

2. To develop concentration on the physical actions in the scene, do the scene without any dialogue or speech.

3. Beginnings and endings of scenes are very important. A scene can start with physical action before the first line is spoken and can often continue after the last line has been said. Investigate the possibilities of extending your scene at the beginning and at the end with significant physical actions.

4. Decide on a significant property (cane, glass, pen, book, etc.) or costume piece (hat, scarf, cloak) for your character, and, during rehearsal, use the prop or costume piece to enhance your characterization. You will likely over-use it initially, but you may find some significant actions which are useful.

5. To gain fresh insight into the script, rehearse the scene in the following ways:
   a) run through the script saying aloud only the stage directions which apply to your character. Can you find new actions?
   b) Choose one significant word from each speech your character says. (Not each line but each *speech*, which is the lines of dialogue that occur after your character is designated to speak.) After each group member has done the same for his or her character, run through the scene saying only that one word for each speech. Can you retain the quality and feeling of the scene? Note what changes have occurred.

6. Can you put an additional non-speaking person into your scene in a significant way?

7. Every play has events which happen "outside" of the play and have importance for the characters. To understand what happened in these "unwritten scenes" improvise them with other members of your group.

8. Every play and scene has a certain style in which it is usually played. Often fresh insights can be gained by radically altering that style. Here are some suggestions for new styles in which to rehearse the scene. (Try a number of styles and use anything in speech or movement which enhances your interpretation of your character and the scene.) Rehearse the scene as if it were: a western movie; a television soap opera; a ballet; a grand opera; a detective or spy story; a story with small children playing all the parts.

9. The following techniques are designed to enable you and your group to concentrate on a specific task as you rehearse. Often, new speech patterns and physi-

cal movements, which can be incorporated into the final interpretation, will result. These techniques will also enliven a stale rehearsal. After each rehearsal discuss what can be retained from the unusual way in which you have done the scene.

a) You must touch each character to whom you speak. You cannot break this contact until you speak to another person.
b) Run through the scene at triple speed doing all the actions and saying all the lines.
c) Do the scene in "slow motion," saying all speeches at slow speed.
d) If there is an argument or heated discussion between characters in a scene, do the scene saying the lines while having a mock arm-wrestling contest. Examine the push and pull of the power struggle.
e) Have some characters laugh after every speech they say, while others cry after each speech.
f) Do the scene as robots or animals.
g) Have your character say his/her inner thoughts aloud before or after every speech.
h) Change your character to a person who is totally illogical and irrational in movements so that the physical actions you do have no relation to what you say.

10. Find appropriate music which can be played during your rehearsal so that the mood and feeling of the scene is enhanced.

The above techniques are designed to help you and your group investigate, experiment, and find fresh life in the scene you are working on. They will help you accomplish the difficult task of finding your interpretation of the scene.

The scripts in this chapter give you ample opportunity to utilize the rehearsal suggestions given above. *1837: The Farmer's Revolt* is full of physical action and requires creative inventiveness in order to develop an interpretation. *A Midsummer Night's Dream* provides a model of a rehearsal script in order for you to see how other theatre groups work. *The Shadow Box* requires concentration on creating mood through line delivery and tempo. The final selection, *Count Dracula*, demands investigation into special effects, props, and costumes which can enhance the interpretation of a scene.

FROM

1837: THE FARMER'S REVOLT

THE CANADIAN FARMER'S TRAVELS IN THE U.S.A.

by Rick Salutin

PLAYBILL

This dramatization of the events surrounding the Upper Canada Rebellion of 1837 is based on historical fact. The scene presented here revolves around the disparity in outlook between Americans and Canadians at that time. It also shows how Canadians saw themselves and others. As you read through the scene be aware of the opportunities for inventing physical action to enhance the ideas presented. Also take into account the number of roles that are available, and consider how you will rehearse the scene with fewer people than there are roles.

CHARACTERS
Robert Davis
Parts for up to 20 actors

*(*ROBERT DAVIS, *Upper Canada farmer, drags himself out from the bottom of the brawl during the election of 1836.)*

Davis: Would you believe that was an election? I would! Lost two teeth in it—and that proves it's an election around here. My name's Robert Davis. I have a small town here in Nissouri Township. Lived here all my life. Got two fine kids. Taught myself to read and write. But this election was just about the end for me. Why we've been working for reform for fifteen years—and now things in Upper Canada are worse than ever. I'd about lost hope. And I needed to get my hope back somehow. So I decided I'd take a trip to the United States. I'd heard things were different down there, and I thought—if I can see that someone else has succeeded, maybe I can keep on trying myself. So I started out. (*Walks.*) Now the first place I came to on my way to the border was the little town of Chatham. Beautiful little place for a town, but very sleepy . . .

(The TOWN COUNCIL *of Chatham comes to order.)*

Mayor: My friends, as members of the Town Council of Chatham I think we should establish what is going to be happening here for the next twenty years.

Davis: Good. I'd like to see that. What have you got in mind?

(The members of the COUNCIL *yawn, fall flat on their backs, and snore.)*

Davis: See that! That's despair—I'm not going to stay around here. (*Walks.*) So I kept on, till I came to the town of Sandwich, that's right across the river from Detroit. Look around. There's nothing happening here.

Boatman: All aboard for Detroit.

Davis: Can you take me to Detroit?

Boatman: Yup. Get aboard fast. Miss this boat and there isn't another one for a week.

Davis: That's ridiculous—one boat a week!

(They start across the river.)

Davis: And as we left Sandwich snoozing in the sunshine, I could see a kind of stir on the other side of the river. And sounds—sounds like I'd never heard before—

(The bustling sounds of Detroit begin to come up.)

Davis: And suddenly we were surrounded by boats, big and little, carrying grain, and goods, and *people*—

Boatman: (*Yelling*) Detroit! Gateway to the American Dream—

(The sounds of industry and trade explode around poor DAVIS. *People rush back and forth past him, happy, productive—)*

American: Howdy stranger. I'd like to stay and shoot the breeze, but I'm too busy getting rich.

Davis: Look at all these people—and this *industry*, and—and—two thousand immigrants a day—most of them from Upper Canada!

Immigrant: (*Kissing the ground*) America! America!

Runaway Slave: (*To* DAVIS) Excuse me sir, I'm a runaway slave. Which way is Canada?

Davis: No, no. Don't go there. It's terrible. Stay here, I'm sure things will get better for you. (*Turning.*) Oh—look. A four-storey brick building! (*Someone plays it.*) Isn't it wonderful?

Wrecker: 'Scuse me fella. Gotta tear down this four-storey building.

Davis: (*Horrified*) Why?

Wrecker: (*Knocking it down*) 'Cause we're gonna put up a *six*-storey one in its place! There—*Whoosht—up it goes.*

Davis: Oh—and look at what it says on it—Museum!

Museum: Sure. Come on in—

*(*DAVIS *enters, sees statues of American heroes—"We got more than we know what to do with"—Whistler's Mother, or some such nonsense. By the way, this scene has never been "set."* DAVIS *has seen different things nearly every time he has taken his trip.)*

Davis: This is all fine, but you know I'm a farmer, and I'll really know what to make of your country when I see what's happening outside the cities. So can you tell me how I get to the country?

American: Sure. How'd you like to go?

Davis: How? I thought I'd walk—

American: Pshaw—nobody walks down here. Now you can go by coach, or canal—

Davis: Don't talk to me about canals! Did you ever hear of the Welland Canal? They've been building it for twelve years. It's only twelve miles long. It's cost us millions of dollars and you *still* have to dig your way through!

American: No kidding. Well we've got the Erie Canal. Five hundred miles and clear straight through—

Davis: (*Stunned*) Five hundred miles . . .

American: But if you don't like that, you can always take the train.

Davis: Train? What was that word you just said?

(Zip. He is suddenly in the country.)

Davis: So I went to the country. Acre after acre of cleared, fertile land—

Farmer: Excuse me friend, would you mind moving your foot?

Davis: My foot? Why?

Farmer: Well, do you feel something moving under it?

Davis: Moving? Why yes—I do!

Farmer: Just move it aside—there.

(They both watch as a crop of wheat grows from the floor to the ceiling.)

Farmer: Crop of wheat I planted this morning. A little small this year. Well, watch yourself while I harvest it. (*With his axe.*) Timber!

Davis: Wheat—and apple orchards—and thousands of head of cattle—and sixty pound cheeses!

(These appear—or fail to do so—at the whim of the other actors onstage. The most fun occurs when someone introduces into the scene something DAVIS *and the others have not expected.)*

Davis: And then I went to one of the hundreds of thriving country towns—

Schoolhouse: Bong! Bong! Come on kiddies—everybody into school for your free universal education.

Davis: Free? Universal? You mean your schools aren't just for your aristocracy?

Schoolhouse: You watch your language down here. We don't use words like that!

Davis: Everyone can go to school? Does it work?

Schoolhouse: Hah! Where's that dumb kid. C'mere kid, get inside.

(The DUMB KID *walks through one door of the* SCHOOLHOUSE *and emerges from the other.)*

Formerly Dumb Kid: $E=MC^2$.

Church: Ding Dong—Methodist.

Another: Ding Dong—Lutheran.

Another: Ding Dong—Quaker.

(Somebody has not declared himself.)

Davis: What are you?

Townsman: I'm an atheist.

Davis: You allow atheists down here too?

Church: We don't like them but we allow them.

Davis: But which one is your established church, you know, the official church?

(They all laugh.)

Townsman: Say—you must be a Canadian.

Davis: (*Delighted*) I am. How'd you know?

Townsman: Say house.

Davis: House.

Townsman: Say about.

Davis: About.

Townsman: I knew it. Now excuse us, we're going to have an election.

Davis: (*Panicking*) An election? Let me out of here—I'm going to hide—I've lost enough teeth.

(He watches from a distance.)

First Voter: Having searched my conscience, I have decided to cast my vote as a Democrat.

(The next VOTER *steps up.* DAVIS *winces in expectation of the clash.)*

Second Voter: Well, in that case, I'm going to vote Republican.

Third Voter: Then I vote Democrat.

Fourth Voter: Let's see—the Republicans won last time, so I'll vote Democrat too.

All: Hurray!

(They all commiserate with the lone REPUBLICAN.)

Davis: Hey—wait a minute. When does the fight start?

Voter: Fight? What do you mean? This is an election. Now come here, uh, what's your name?

Davis: Davis.

Voter: No, I mean your first name. We all use first names here.

Davis: Bob.

Voter: Well, Bob, I'd like you to meet the new governor of our state. This is Ole. Ole, this is Bob, from Canada—

Ole: (*A very slow-speaking farmer*) Well, how do you do. You wouldn't like to buy a pig would you?

Davis: Pig? You mean you're the governor of this state and you still work as a farmer.

Ole: Well, gotta make some money somehow—

Davis: You know, you've all given me new hope. You've proven to me it can be done. This is what we've been working for years, and I can go home now and—

Voter: Home? Wait a minute Bob. Why don't you stay right here with us and make this your new home?

Davis: Here? But why should I?

Another Voter: Because it's the best darned country in the world. That's why.

Davis: But—but I've got my family back there.

Another: Bring 'em down here. Bring your whole country.

Davis: But—but there's my farm.

Another: Tell you what we'll do Bob. We'll give you a four hundred acre cleared farm right here. Just for you.

Davis: (*Getting excited*) Cleared? (*Suspicious.*) How much?

Another: Nothing. Just take good care of it.

Davis: I can have that farm?

Another: Sure. We'll just sweep those Indians off of it and—

Davis: Why that's wonderful! You're all so generous! This must be the finest—

Another: See. He's starting to act like an American already. Being happy and talking loud—

Davis: No. No, I can't do it.

Another: Those words don't exist in America.

Davis: I can't stay. You see—it's not my home. I can't just leave Canada. It's up to us to do there what you've done here. But you've given me hope. Now I know it can be done—(*He is leaving.*) So I went home.

(Lethargic, snoring, apathetic CANADIANS *surround him.)*

Davis: And I said—Don't lie around. Get up. Help each other. You can do it. (*He drags them to their feet. They are rubbery-legged. They cling to each other and anything they can find.*) I've seen it now. I know it can be done. We can do it too, if we stay together. Now is not the time for Reformers to fawn and crouch. Now is the time to unite and fight!

ACTIVITIES

1. The scenes provide many opportunities for the actors to be inventive. Using movement and tableau, how can your group create many of the actions and things which are suggested? Try working on the following: the town council of Chatham, the boat across the river to Detroit, the qualities and people of Detroit, a four storey building being torn down, American heroes in a museum, a train trip to the country, a crop of wheat growing, the school, the churches.

2. Some rehearsal techniques mentioned in The Program which might be applied profitably in rehearsing this scene are: #1—improvising the scene; #2—concentrating on physical action; #4—using props and costume pieces; and #10—finding appropriate music.

3. While there is only one main character in this script, there are many small parts which should be divided among the group. Everyone in the group should be involved in significant ways throughout the scenes. Try rehearsing the scenes so that no one exits or enters, and everyone is in a role, or changing to another role, at all times in the scene. That is, no one should be seen to "drop" their role; when you stop being one person or thing, you become another person or thing immediately.

4. The rehearsal techniques developed here are of great value for some of the scripts you have already worked on. For example, *Juve* and *The Farm Show*, like *1837*, were both based on real people and events. *The Elephant Man* and *Antigone* both used the technique of direct address to the audience. If you do further work on these scripts, you may want to use some of the methods explored in this chapter.

FROM

A MIDSUMMER NIGHT'S DREAM

by William Shakespeare

PLAYBILL

Theseus, Duke of Athens, is about to marry Hippolyta and has commanded that celebrations be arranged. In this scene, Bottom the weaver and his friends meet to prepare a play which will be performed after the wedding. They are tradesmen, not professional actors, and have little theatrical background. The script that you use in this book contains the notations for physical action (called "blocking") which were developed in rehearsals by the Royal Shakespeare Company. As you read the script be aware of what actions were done by the actors in this production to convey their interpretation of the play. However, it is not intended that you slavishly follow what others have done, but rather that you use the material as a basis for your own interpretation. As Peter Brook, the director of this production, said in his book *The Empty Space*,

> A word does not start as a word—it is an end product which begins as an impulse,

CHARACTERS
Quince, the carpenter
Snug, the joiner
Bottom, the weaver
Flute, the bellows maker
Snout, the tinker
Starveling, the tailor

[1] SNUG *enters carrying block (a wooden cube 40 cm by 40 cm by 40 cm) and places it DSC.* QUI *lifts finger for silence.*
[2] *Answering noises from* SNO *(SL side of orchestra),* FLU *(rear of orchestra),* STA *(SR side of orchestra).* BOT *climbs on stage SL, crosses to* QUI
[3] BOT *turns to audience.*
[4] STA + FLU *to SR side of orchestra;* SNO *to SL side of orchestra;* BOT *making for DSL.*
[5] BOT *crosses back to* QUI.

[1] *Enter* QUINCE *the carpenter, and* SNUG *the joiner, and* BOTTOM *the weaver, and* FLUTE *the bellows-mender, and* SNOUT *the tinker, and* STARVELING *the tailor*

Quince: Is all our company here? [2]
Bottom: You were best to call them generally, man by man, according to the scrip.
Quince: Here is the scroll of every man's name which is thought fit through all Athens to play in our interlude before the Duke and the Duchess on his wedding day at night.
Bottom: First, good Peter Quince, say what the play treats on; then read the names of the actors; and so grow to a point.
Quince: Marry, our play is *The most lamentable comedy and most cruel death of Pyramus and Thisbe.*
Bottom: [3] A very good piece of work, I assure you, and a merry. Now, good Peter Quince, call forth your actors by the scroll. Masters, spread yourselves. [4]
Quince: Answer as I call you. Nick Bottom, the weaver. [5]
Bottom: Ready!—Name what part I am for, and proceed.
Quince: You, Nick Bottom, are set down for Pyramus.
Bottom: What is Pyramus?—a lover or a tyrant?
Quince: A lover that kills himself, most gallant, for love.

[1] BOT *picks up block,* QUI *having removed book.*
[2] *Block down.*
[3] *Imitation of Samson, pushes block over.*
[4] QUI *sits on block.*
[5] BOT *picks up block;* QUI *puts book back on it.*
[6] BOT *clears SL.*
[7] FLU *on to stage from SR, crosses to* QUI; QUI *eases to* BOT.
[8] QUI *crosses to* FLU.
[9] BOT *eases SC, pulls vest over face.*
[10] BOT *backs SL.*

[11] BOT *vest off face.*

[12] STA *on stage from SR, crosses to* QUI.

Bottom: That will ask some tears in the true performing of it. If I do it, let the audience look to their eyes! I will move storms. I will condole, in some measure. To the rest.—Yet my chief humor is for a tyrant. I could play Ercles rarely, [1] or a part to tear a cat in, [2] to make all split: [3]

The raging rocks
And shivering shocks
Shall break the locks
Of prison gates,
And Phibbus' car
Shall shine from far [4]
And make and mar
The foolish Fates.

This was lofty! [5] Now name the rest of the players.—This is Ercles' vein, a tyrant's vein. A lover is more condoling. [6]

Quince: Francis Flute, the bellows-mender? [7]

Flute: Here, Peter Quince.

Quince: Flute, you must take Thisbe on you.

Flute: What is Thisbe?—a wandering knight? [8]

Quince: It is the lady that Pyramus must love.

Flute: Nay, faith, let not me play a woman—I have a beard coming.

Quince: That's all one: you shall play it in a mask, and you may speak as small as you will.

Bottom: [9] An I may hide my face, let me play Thisbe, too. I'll speak in a monstrous little voice: "Thisne, Thisne!" [10] "Ah, Pyramus, my lover dear; thy Thisbe dear, and lady dear."

Quince: No, no; you must play Pyramus; and Flute, you Thisbe.

Bottom: Well, proceed. [11]

Quince: Robin Starveling, the tailor? [12]

Starveling: Here, Peter Quince.

[1] STA *delighted.*

[2] SNO *on stage from SL, shakes hands with* BOT.

[3] *All call for* SNUG, *towards auditorium.* SNUG *eventually puts head around SL door and coughs.* QUI *crosses to him, shakes hands, pulls him DS.*

[4] QUI *turns back DS.*

[5] QUI *crosses back to* SNUG.

[6] SNUG *roars.*

stimulated by attitude and behavior, which dictates the need for expression. This process occurs inside the dramatist; it is repeated inside the actor.

[7] BOT *crosses to* QUI.

[8] SNUG *hurls mallet at US wall, crosses down to* BOT *(SC), roars.* BOT *shakes head, puts hat on block, roars,* FLU *claps, silenced by* QUI. SNUG *roars, crashes against DSL wall.* QUI *crosses to him as he stops.*

[9] QUI *crosses back to block.*

[10] BOT *off stage SL, into orchestra and up to back of auditorium.* QUI *and others rush to front of stage and follow his progress.*

[11] BOT *coming back.*

Quince: Robin Starveling, you must play Thisbe's mother. [1] Tom Snout, the tinker? [2]

Snout: Here, Peter Quince.

Quince: You, Pyramus' father; myself, Thisbe's father; Snug, the joiner, [3] you the lion's part; and I hope here is a play fitted.

Snug: Have you [4] the lion's part written? Pray you, if it be, give it me; for I am slow of study.

Quince: You may do it extempore; [5] for it is nothing but roaring. [6]

Bottom: Let me play the lion too. [7] I will roar that I will do any man's heart good to hear me. I will roar that I will make the Duke say "Let him roar again; let him roar again!" [8]

Quince: An you should do it too terribly you would fright the Duchess and the ladies that they would shriek; and that were enough to hang us all.

Flute: That would hang us.

Starveling: Every mother's son. [9]

Bottom: I grant you, friends, if you should fright the ladies out of their wits they would have no more discretion but to hang us. But I will aggravate my voice so that I will roar you as gently as any sucking dove. I will roar you an 'twere any nightingale.

Quince: You can play no part but Pyramus; [10] for Pyramus is a sweet-faced man; a proper man as one shall see in a summer's day; a most lovely, gentlemanlike man. Therefore you must needs play Pyramus.

Bottom: Well, I will undertake it. [11] What beard were I best to play it in?

Quince: Why, what you will.

Bottom: I will discharge it in either your straw-color beard, your orange-tawny beard, your purple-in-grain beard, or your French-crown-color beard, your perfect yellow.

[1] *All line up:* BOT *first,* SNUG *last. All collect parts and cross around to SR. (*BOT, FLU, STA, SNO, SNUG*)*

[2] *All hands piled on block.* SNUG *lifts mallet. All wince.*

[3] *Hands away. All exit,* SNO *striking block out SL door.*

Quince: Some of your French crowns have no hair at all; and then you will play bare-faced! But, masters, here are your parts, [1] and I am to entreat you, request you, and desire you to con them by tomorrow night, and meet me in the palace wood a mile without the town by moonlight. There will we rehearse; for if we meet in the city we shall be dogged with company, and our devices known. In the meantime I will draw a bill of properties such as our play wants. I pray you, fail me not.

Bottom: We will meet [2] and there we may rehearse most obscenely and courageously. Take pains, be perfect. Adieu!

Quince: At the Duke's oak we meet.

Bottom: Enough; hold, [3] or cut bowstrings.

(Exeunt BOTTOM *and his fellows)*

ACTIVITIES

1. This example of a rehearsal script is presented to demonstrate the careful and meticulous planning which goes into any stage presentation.

It is important to know that the "blocking" of this play did not occur before rehearsal but rather in a notation of what actions and interpretations the actors and director arrived at during countless hours of experimentation, trials, and failures during rehearsals. When you rehearse the scene, attempt to follow every stage direction. You will begin to see that this blocking was created as the result of a particular interpretation of the play.

2. After you investigate the existing blocking for this scene, can you find a new series of physical actions based on your understanding and interpretation of the characters and the scene? Develop your interpretation by ignoring the indicated actions and working only with the lines of dialogue. As you develop your interpretation, note it down in blocking diagrams.

3. Some useful rehearsal techniques mentioned in The Program which could be applied to this scene are: #1—improvising the scene; #5b—choosing one significant word; #8—finding a new style; #9f—doing the scene as animals; and #9g—saying inner thoughts aloud.

4. This script is another "play within a play" and is similar to other scripts in this book such as *The Real Inspector Hound* (Section A, Chapter 2), *Jitters* (Section A, Chapter 2), *What Glorious Times They Had* (Section A, Chapter 1), *Rosencrantz and Guildenstern are Dead* (Section C, Chapter 18) and *Six Characters in Search of an Author* (Section C, Chapter 20). You may want to return to the earlier scripts in this book and use the blocking technique explored here. You should also keep blocking in mind when you reach the two other scripts mentioned.

5. If you wish to see how the performance of Bottom's and his friends' play was received, you can examine Act V, Scene 1 of Shakespeare's *A Midsummer Night's Dream.*

FROM

THE SHADOW BOX

by Michael Cristofer

PLAYBILL

This play is set on the grounds of a hospital for the terminally ill. It concerns the interactions of family and friends with a dying person and that person's coming to grips with the one inescapable fact of life. This is the last scene in the play. Compare this scene to preceding ones in this book in terms of physical action. When reading through this script, it is important to be aware that stillness and pauses in dialogue are significant dramatic techniques.

CHARACTERS

Joe, a patient
Steve, his young son
Maggie, his wife
Brian, a patient
Beverly, his ex-wife
Mark, a friend
Felicity, an elderly woman
Agnes, her daughter

Brian: People don't want to let go. Do they. They think it's a mistake. They think it's supposed to last forever . . .

Joe: There's a few things—I could talk to you about them . . .

Brian: I suppose it's because . . .

Joe: . . . you don't expect it to happen.

Brian: You don't expect it to happen to you.

Joe: But it happens anyway, doesn't it? It doesn't matter what you do, you can't stop it.

Brian: You try.

Mark: (*In the living room*) You keep thinking, there's got to be some way out of this.

Brian: You want to strike a bargain . . . make a deal.

Mark: You don't want to give in.

Joe: You want to say no.

Maggie: . . . no . . .

Mark: . . . no . . .

Brian: Your whole life goes by—it feels like it was only a minute.

Beverly: You try to remember what it was you believed in.

Mark: What was so important?

Maggie: What was it?

Beverly: You want it to make a difference.

Maggie: You want to blame somebody.

Brian: You want to be angry.

Joe: You want to shout, "Not me!"

Brian: Not me!

Maggie: Not me!

Felicity: What time is it, Agnes?

Agnes: I don't know, Mama.

Brian: And then you think, someone should have said it sooner.

Mark: Someone should have said it a long time ago.

Beverly: When you were young.

Brian: Someone should have said, this living . . .

Mark: . . . this life . . .

Beverly: . . . this lifetime . . .

Brian: It doesn't last forever.

Maggie: A few days, a few minutes . . . that's all.

Brian: It has an end.

Joe: Yes.

Mark: This face.

Beverly: These hands.

Mark: This word.

Joe: It doesn't last forever.

Brian: This air.

Mark: This light.

Brian: This earth.

Beverly: These things you love.

Maggie: These children.

Beverly: This smile.

Maggie: This pain.

Brian: It doesn't last forever.

Joe: It was never supposed to last forever.

Mark: This day.

Maggie: This morning.

Beverly: This afternoon.

Mark: This evening.

Felicity: What time is it, Agnes?

Agnes: I don't know, Mama. It's time to stop. Please, Mama. It's time to stop.

Brian: These eyes . . .

Mark: These things you see.

Maggie: It's pretty.

Joe: Yes.

Mark: Yes.

Brian: These things you hear.

Mark: This noise.

Beverly: This music.

Steve: I can play for you now. It's not good, but it's not bad either.

Maggie: Yes.

Beverly: Yes.

Brian: They tell you you're dying, and you say all right. But if I *am* dying . . . I must still be alive.

Felicity: What time is it?

Mark: These things you have.

Maggie: Yes.

Joe: This smell, this touch.

Mark: Yes.

Beverly: This taste.

Brian: Yes.

Maggie: This breath.

Steve: Yes.

Mark: Yes.

Brian: Yes.

Maggie: Yes.

Beverly: Yes.

Joe: Yes.

Brian: This moment.

(Long pause. Lights fade.)

ACTIVITIES

1. This scene provides opportunities to concentrate on rehearsing very quiet, contemplative material. You will have to stress the speeches of the characters and the timing, pacing, and inflection of the lines. Since there is very little action indicated you will also have to decide on an effective grouping of the characters. Perhaps you might find opportunities to insert very significant movements which will enhance the mood of the scene. This is the final scene of the play so your staging and delivery should be rehearsed to give the scene a strong emotional impact.

2. Some useful rehearsal techniques for this scene as outlined in The Program are: #5b—choosing one significant word; #6—adding non-speaking characters; #9g—saying inner thoughts aloud; and #10—adding appropriate music.

3. This scene is similar in style to the "Charlie Wilson" scene in *The Farm Show* (Section A, Chapter 4), because they both use the techniques of Readers Theatre. Readers Theatre is explored in Section B, Chapter 8, and when you reach that chapter, you can use *The Farm Show* and *The Shadow Box* as extra material for the Activities.

FROM

COUNT DRACULA

by Ted Tiller

PLAYBILL

Mina Murray has been visiting her friend Sybil Seward at Sybil's father's asylum for the insane. Mina has become ill recently, and no apparent cause can be found. Jonathan, her fiance, has arrived greatly concerned, and Dr. Seward has sent for Henrich van Helsing, a noted authority on vampires and mysterious illnesses. The only clue to Mina's illness is that it occurred just after a dinner at which Count Dracula was a guest. This version of Bram Stoker's famous story is set in England, just north of London, in the early years of the present century. The style of this play is "melodrama," a genre that the chorus in *Antigone* (Chapter 3) discussed. It is essential that you avoid trying to make this play comic. Instead, you should play it very seriously to allow the melodramatic qualities to emerge.

CHARACTERS

Sybil Seward
Dr. Arthur Seward, brother of Sybil
Jonathan Harker
Mina Murray
Count Dracula
Hennessey, butler

Sybil: (*Off Right upstairs*) Careful, dear. You haven't been downstairs in three days. Slowly now, Mina. Slowly! (JONATHAN *rises, goes to staircase.* MINA *appears descending the Right stairs, her progress hindered by* SYBIL*'s death grip. Despite illness and pallor,* MINA MURRAY *is a most attractive young woman. At her neck she wears an old fashioned cameo on a wide velvet "choker" which conceals the lower part of her throat.)*

Mina: Jonathan, dear!

Jonathan: Mina! You look beautiful, darling! Not sick at all.

Mina: I feel fine. Just a little weak.

Jonathan: (*Takes her arm*) Here, let me help you.

Mina: No, truly, I don't need help.

Sybil: Yes, she does. If I let go, she'd slump right to the floor!

Jonathan: I have her, Miss Seward. Sit here, darling. (*He guides* MINA *into Right corner of the sofa. As he goes above sofa to come around and sit by her,* SYBIL *crosses below sofa, plops herself down at* MINA*'s Left side, leaving* JONATHAN *neatly thwarted.*)

Seward: (*Tries to catch* SYBIL*'s eye*) Oh, Sybil?

Sybil: (*Spreading her gown, taking up more room*) Yes, Brother?

Seward: Nothing. (JONATHAN *gets tuffet from downstage Left, carries it to Right of sofa, sits on it near* MINA. SYBIL *watches affably, unaware that she is a cul-de-sac for Cupid.*)

Sybil: Now, everybody comfy? . . . You're right, Mr. Harker. She does look well. (*Puts on her bifocals and studies* MINA.) Oh, I see. It's make-up.

Seward: Sybil, *come have a sherry!*

Sybil: (*Instantly on her feet*) Oh, jolly! I was just beginning to flag a bit. (*She goes to bar where* SEWARD *gives her a sherry and a glare.* JONATHAN *moves over, sits by* MINA, *patting her hand affectionately.* SYBIL *starts back toward sofa but is detoured by* SEWARD *into the swivel chair.*)

Jonathan: I've been terribly worried about you.

Mina: No need, darling. Now that you're here, just watch me astound the medical profession. It will be known as The Mina Murray Cure, or Instant Recovery.

Jonathan: (*Laughing, embraces her*) Oh, dearest, dearest Mina!

Sybil: (*Squinting at wristwatch*) I

wonder if Count Dracula has stepped into a quagmire?

Seward: Why on earth would he?

Sybil: Well, he *could*, you know, if he walked through the woods. He's late.

Mina: (*Gets out of* JONATHAN*'s embrace, sits forward, spine erect, staring oddly*) But he *is* coming?

Jonathan: Mina, what is it? You like this man?

Mina: (*A moment*) No. He fascinates me, but I don't like him.

Jonathan: (*After a puzzled glance at* SEWARD) Oh, I almost forgot. I brought you a present. (*Goes to briefcase, takes out oblong plush jewellery box.*)

Sybil: Oh, how nice! (*Under her breath to* SEWARD) Is today Mina's birthday?

Seward: (*Patting her shoulder*) No, dear.

Jonathan: Here, darling.

Mina: A jewel case! Oh, Jonathan, you've done something you shouldn't.

Jonathan: I don't know why not. It's just another way to say I love you. Go on, open it.

Mina: (*Lifts out a triple strand of pearls*) Jonathan! They're *exquisite!* (*Murmurs of approval from* SYBIL *and* SEWARD. JONATHAN *steps behind sofa, reaches for clasp of* MINA*'s velvet choker.*)

Jonathan: Dear, let me take this off. Let's see how they look on you.

(Sound: Fade in Dogs howling in distance.)

Mina: (*Covering throat with both hands*) No! *Don't!*

Jonathan: But, darling, why not?

Mina: I mean not now. Not—not in this dress. Pearls don't really go well with—*Tomorrow!* Tomorrow I'll—I'll wear a different gown for dinner and they'll—They're lovely, Jonathan, and I thank you—but don't ask me to put them on. Not yet. When I'm really well, I'll—(*She begins to cry.*)

(Sound: Dogs howling grows louder. SEWARD *and* SYBIL *glance toward window but do not move.)*

Jonathan: (*Sitting quickly, cradles her*) Of course, Mina. Of course you don't have to wear them now. Here, darling. (*Gives her his breast pocket handkerchief.*)

Mina: I'm shivering. Hold me close, Jonathan. There's a cold wind blowing round me.

Sybil: (*Rises, starts Left*) Perhaps the hall window is open.

Seward: It isn't. Please get her a shawl, Sybil.

(SYBIL *turns, starts toward Right stairs. All lights flicker off and on rapidly, then on again. Involuntarily everyone looks up at chandelier.)*

(Sound: Howling increases and seems nearer, a great melancholy chorus, deep throated, sustained and terrifying.)

Mina: Listen!

Sybil: (*Stopped on first step*) It's as though every dog for miles around is—is trying to warn us. Arthur, you remember mother's superstition about dogs howling in the night? She said it meant someone nearby—would die before morning.

Mina: (*Pushing free of* JONATHAN, *leans forward, staring again*) No, they're wolves. They sound like wolves! (MINA *rises as though mesmerized, moves slowly to the windows and stands motionless, looking out.*)

Jonathan: (*Following her*) There are no wolves here, Mina darling.

Mina: How still it is down there. Not a leaf stirring. Sybil is right. It's like death.

(Sound: The howling begins to fade away, overlapped and replaced by eerie music of The Dracula Leitmotif. All lights flicker again and go out, leaving only the glow from the fireplace and a dim light from Left hallway, spilling down the stairs.)

Sybil: (*Frightened, goes to* SEWARD) Arthur! What is it?

Seward: (*Crossing below her to Right*) The electric power. Don't be alarmed. I'll try the switch. (*He flicks wall switch by Right bookcase several times.*) Nothing. It must be the main fuse.

(Music swells as COUNT DRACULA *enters at top of Left stairway, his shadow rippling down the steps. His countenance is arresting, lupine, cruel and coldly handsome. He is immaculately attired in white tie and tails. Over his shoulders is an evening cape of costly black satin lined with vibrant red silk and with a stiff, high standing collar which frames his head.* DRACULA *holds his silk opera hat inverted in one hand and drops his white kid gloves into it with a gesture that is the quintessence of arrogance. When he speaks his accent is slightly Continental and his voice not only insinuates but threatens.)*

Dracula: (*A mocking bow*) Good evening. (*Music dies out. They all turn to him in surprise and* MINA *comes away from the windows, looking at him fixedly.*)

Seward: (*Holds near Right bookcase*) Good evening. (*As* DRACULA *comes down the steps,* SYBIL *crosses to him.*)

Sybil: Count Dracula, how good of you to come. We're sorry about the lights.

Dracula: The lights?

Sybil: They seem to have quite gone out. Quite.

Dracula: (*Kissing her hand*) What matter? You illuminate the room. (*He looks at the chandelier, makes the most casual of gestures toward it and instantly all stage lights come up full.*)

Sybil: Oh, good! *There* they are. Now why do you suppose they went off?

Dracula: (*Shrugs*) Perhaps a case of temporary electrical indisposition. (*Puts silk hat with gloves on desk, crosses to* MINA, *bends over her hand and kisses it.*) My dear Miss Murray, how beautiful you are tonight. You are a feast—for the eyes.

Mina: We—we are honored to have you with us.

Dracula: It is I who am honored, to be your guest and that of the eminent Doctor and his interesting sister. And this gentleman—?

Mina: Is my fiance. Count Dracula, may I present Mr. Jonathan Harker?

Jonathan: (*Holds out his hand*) How do you do?

Dracula: (*Ignores the proffered hand*) Ah, yes. The young architect.

Jonathan: (*Mild surprise*) How did you know? Did Mina—?

Mina: No. I never mentioned it. (*All four look at him curiously.*)

Dracula: I surmised. You look like an architect, Mr. Harker. You yourself are so symmetrically built.

Seward: Sybil, take Count Dracula's cape and hat, please. Hang them in the hall while I fix him a drink. (SYBIL *starts immediately for* DRACULA, *arms raised to remove his cape.*)

Dracula: If you will permit me, Doctor—(*Gracefully steps aside, dodging the oncoming* SYBIL.) and Miss Seward, I'll retain the cape. There's a chill in the autumn air. As for the libation, thank you, no. I never drink—socially. (SYBIL *gets his hat and gloves from the desk.* DRACULA *gives her a lordly wave of dismissal. She all but curtseys, floats up the Left stairs, hat clutched to her bosom, and exits.* DRACULA *moves to French windows, stands in profile looking out.* JONATHAN *goes to* MINA, *reaching for her hand but she draws away.*)

Mina: Don't Jonathan. Now now. (*She crosses to fireplace, watching* DRACULA, *leaving* JONATHAN *puzzled and hurt.*)

Dracula: What an interesting vista. From here my castle looks like a huge, crumbling tombstone.

Sybil: (*Enters Left stairs, descends breathlessly*) Arthur, there's a car coming up the drive. I spotted it through the hall window.

Seward: (*Starts for French windows*) Good. It's bound to be my old friend from Holland.

Sybil: Professor—

Sybil and Dracula: (*Together*) Heinrich Van Helsing. (*Though they started in spoken duet,* DRACULA *finishes the name alone,* SYBIL'*s voice having faded away in her astonishment.*)

Seward: Why—yes.

Dracula: (*As though searching memory*) In a rather ancient motorcar which he keeps in London—for his frequent trips from Amsterdam—to confer with your English specialists.

Seward: Why, how—Are you clairvoyant? (DRACULA *smiles, shakes his head.*) How do you know these things?

Dracula: Merely a hobby. I collect facts, trivial or momentous, and store them away for future use.

Seward: I see. Excuse me. I'll go let him in. (SEWARD *crosses to Left stairs, stops part way up for another look at his baffling guest, then exits above.* DRACULA *steps out onto balcony, holding out the edges of his cape at the railing, making him resemble a great black bat blotting out the sky. Trance-like,* MINA *moves closer to the windows watching him.*)

Sybil: Mr. Harker, I'll ring for an attendant to take your luggage upstairs. (*She starts toward bell cord.*) You must want to change for dinner.

Jonathan: (*Half hears, studying* MINA) To change?—Oh, yes, of course. Don't bother to ring, Miss Seward. (*Getting his luggage.*) I'll take my things up myself. Which room is it?

Sybil: It's at the end of the passage. It—I'd better show you. You might get it mixed up with the linen closet. (*She notices jewellery case and pearls on sofa, scoops them up.*) You may as well take these along. I don't believe Mina likes your gift. Pity. (*She sails ahead of him, starts up Right stairway.*)

Jonathan: (*Another glance at* MINA *whose back is to him*) Perhaps not. She's behaving very strangely.

Sybil: Oh, this is one of her *good* days. Come along, Mr. Harker. (SYBIL *beckons with the jewel case, exits above and* JONATHAN *follows her with luggage. Instantly* DRACULA *whirls and faces* MINA. *His movement is so sudden she draws back with a gasp.*)

Dracula: Ah, Miss Murray, we are alone. How opportune. (*Takes her hand, leads her toward sofa.*) You seem perturbed, my dear. I want you to sit down, empty your mind of all trepidation.

Mina: (*Slowly pulls her hand free, starts toward desk chair*) I'll—I'll sit here, Count Dracula.

Dracula: (*Takes her by both hands, gently but inexorably leads her to sofa, seats her*) Please. I know what is best for a lovely convalescent. T-r-u-s-t me, my dear. Relax. Lean back and close your eyes. (*His voice, his hypnotic eyes have a mesmeric effect on* MINA. *She does exactly as told.* DRACULA *gives the chandelier a glance and a casual gesture and all lights go out except fire glow, faint off-stage hall lights and the feeble light of distant stars. Ominous music begins softly. He looks down triumphantly upon the unseeing* MINA, *glides to above sofa and stands directly behind her.*) There, that's better, isn't it? The gloom is soothing to your beautiful, tired eyes. (*Adjusts her head, unfastens her neck band and cameo.*) Let me remove this velvet choker. It is constrictive and conceals your lovely throat.

Mina: (*Weakly, her protesting hands go to her throat*) No, no—

Dracula: Sh-hh! You must be absolutely still. You must rest. R-e-l-a-x. (*He drops choker on floor behind sofa, murmuring hypnotically:*) You are going to sleep—to sleep—a quiet, dreamless sleep. You are floating, drifting through space—now you are falling, slowly, slowly—falling into oblivion! (MINA *gives a little sigh and her head rolls to one side. She is asleep. Music surges slightly and* DRACULA *begins to laugh. Then he bares his teeth in a hideous grin, slowly lowers his head toward* MINA'*s throat, his jaws working like an animal salivating over raw meat. Just as he is above her throat,* HENNESSEY *enters Left stairs with a small refreshment tray, snaps on wall switch by Left bookcase on his way down steps. Stage lights up full. Music Out. With a snarl of fury,* DRACULA *leaps back.*)

Hennessey: (*Offering tray*) Canapes, sir?

ACTIVITIES

1. Much of the action of this play is concerned with special effects, costumes, and properties. In a classroom setting, a lot of the special equipment necessary may not be available to you. However, it is surprising how effective ingenious substitution can be. You can adapt or revise many of the special effects needed and still interpret this script effectively. Decide on those things you have to adapt, and rehearse the play incorporating the changes.

2. Read the stage directions given in this particular script. Remember that they indicate what was done in one production of the play, and do not have to be slavishly followed. Are there stage directions which you wish to change or eliminate? As you rehearse the scene, be prepared to find your own actions so that you find your own interpretation.

3. Useful rehearsal techniques for this script as outlined in The Program might be: #2—doing only physical action; #5a—saying aloud only stage directions in character; #9a—touching character to whom you speak; #9b—delivering lines at triple speed; #9e—laughing/crying after each line; #9h—finding irrational actions; and #10—finding appropriate music.

4. Improvise the scene in which Count Dracula came to dinner for the first time. Retain the style and mood of the play and retain the characterizations. Focus on the need of Count Dracula to get Mina alone.

5. Other scripts in the text which are in the style of melodrama are *Black Ey'd Susan* (Section C, Chapter 19) and the play within the play in *The Real Inspector Hound* (Section A, Chapter 2). Compare *Count Dracula* to *The Real Inspector Hound*, and, if you wish to read ahead, look at *Black Ey'd Susan*.

WORKSHOP

1. Any scene in a script can be sub-divided into smaller scenes or "beats." These beats change when there is a significant change in action, direction, emotion, or mood. They can also change when one character achieves an objective and new intentions are formed. Choose any play and practise sub-dividing it into beats. Rehearse each beat thoroughly before moving on to the next.

2. After reading a script, try to discover if the author has verbalized the conflict of the play, or if he/she has hidden it and it has to be dug out of the words and actions. Is the hidden meaning revealed in subtle or perhaps absurd ways, as in *Come and Go*? Does the author verbalize the conflict, or does he/she show the real human conflict through action and emotions? Improvise any scenes which you feel the author has "left out."

3. Create prompt cards which give specific directions to those who are rehearsing a scene. On the cards you can write such directions as "happy," "sad," "silly," "tragic," "mime," "very fast," "very slow," and so on. While a group is rehearsing, one person selects and holds up a card. The group immediately adjusts to the direction and continues the rehearsal. The prompt card can be changed several times. At the end of the rehearsal the group will discuss the changes that occurred and which changes they can use in their interpretation.

4. Before a rehearsal, everyone is informed that one of the actors will steal an important prop during the rehearsal. All the actors must prevent this from happening. The rehearsal begins after one actor has been secretly informed that he or she is the thief. At the end of the rehearsal, everyone is asked to identify the thief and the property which was stolen. The purpose of this activity is to increase observation of other actors in the scene and to add a super-objective for all actors.

5. Instead of speaking the lines, dance or mime the scene being rehearsed, using music carefully selected to reflect the mood of the script. Dance the scene as if it were a ballet or modern jazz dance, and try to communicate through movement the emotions, climaxes, objectives, problems, or mood changes. While moving, try to find physical actions which reflect the character you will play and use props which will be utilized in the play. Afterwards, decide which new physical actions you can incorporate in your interpretation.

6. Divide the class into two groups. Each group reads the text in role, aloud, then puts the book aside, and tells the story of the scene sequentially in an informal mode, with each of the students telling part of the scene. Discuss the characters, interpretation, and problems in the play. Re-read the text. Put the book aside and improvise the text seated in a circle. Now combine the two groups. Group 1 sits in a circle and reads the text in-role. It is the "outside," that is, the literal, objective text. Group 2 sits in a circle within circle 1, each student facing the character whose role he or she will take. This group is the "inside," that is, the subjective, the subtext—the thinking and feeling part of the role.

The actors "outside" begin to read the scene. At the end of each line take a silent count of 3 before the next actor picks up the next line. During the silent count, any one of the "inside" characters may pick up the line and express a reaction usually left unspoken. This may result in a series of comments and reactions from the other "inside" characters. When these comments stop, the next "outside" character takes the next line, pauses for silent count of three, and, if there is no reaction from "inside" characters, the next line is read. Continue until the scene is concluded. The "inside" characters need not comment on every line, but should be given opportunities to speak the relevant unspoken reactions of characters they represent. When the scene is completed, reverse the "inside" and "outside" groups. This technique should produce a marked deepening of interpretation of role, character, and scene.

5: Sharing the script

THE PROGRAM

Working with scripts involves communication on all levels. It is natural that you will want to communicate to others the interpretation your group has worked out for the script you are doing. This can be an exciting and rewarding activity. Your presentation to an audience can be one of many different types, from informal sharing in the classroom to a complete theatrical event given on-stage. Be sure that the time available to you is adequate for the type of presentation you choose to do.

Before your group can communicate to an audience, there must be a consensus within the group about *what* is to be communicated and *how* it is to be communicated. Decisions will have to be made about the style of the scene or play, and about how to get the audience's attention focussed on the important events in the material.

Most important of all is for your group to present the material in such a way that it will appear to the audience to be happening for the first time, regardless of the number of hours you have rehearsed. Freshness, vitality, belief, and commitment are qualities which will involve the audience in your presentation. These qualities cannot be feigned; they must come from the depth of involvement of each member of the presenting group.

Technical effects such as lighting, costumes, sound effects, and makeup can greatly enhance your presentation, but they are not essential. Nor can these effects disguise a presentation which has not been fully rehearsed or does not have the complete involvement of all the cast members. Remember, if you are using technical effects, be sure to incorporate them into the rehearsals early enough for all cast members to be comfortable using them.

The composition and the design of your presentation must be considered in terms of how to communicate clearly with the audience. Simply stated, in the rehearsal stage your presentation should be looked at in terms of how to direct your audience's attention towards those things which are important for it to see. Perhaps the teacher or other class members can help your group evaluate this. No matter how clever the action may be, you must eliminate anything which will draw the audience's attention away from the important focus.

Another aspect which must be attended to is how well the audience can hear the lines. Projection of the voice must be such that the dialogue can be heard without the voices sounding strained. Diction—the articulation and pronunciation of words, phrases, and sentences—will have to be worked on so that what is being said is clear.

It is important that you get feed-back from your audience. This can often be done informally and will provide you with invaluable reactions to the effectiveness of your group's communication. It is very hard to hear criticism without becoming defensive, but valid comments, genuinely intended to help, should be considered as valuable aids to your learning.

Up to this point in the book you have studied many aspects of working with a script. In Chapter 1 you realized that a deep examination of the structure of a play is necessary to bring the play to life. In Chapter 2 you sought ways of finding the internal action or subtext of a script. Chapter 3 was about developing belief in a character's internal life, and Chapter 4 helped you keep your work fresh and alive as you prepared for performance. Now it is time to bring together all that you have learned. The play *Us and Them* presents you with many problems to be solved and tests your skills and creativity. As you will see from the Playbill and from your first reading of the play, your examination and exploration of structure, character, words, and actions will call for a great deal of creative interpretation from you.

Finally, a note of caution. All plays are protected by copyright and should not be performed for any audience until permission to do so has been obtained from the author, publisher, or agent controlling the rights. The acknowledgement section of this book will indicate the party to contact.

FROM

US AND THEM

by David Campton

PLAYBILL

"This play was written to be performed by a company of almost any size, of any age, and of either sex. The number against a character (A1, B2) is intended to indicate who makes a statement, asks a question, replies, or interjects, but the dialogue should be shared among the whole company. That is to say, although an A1 character should not speak B2 lines, there can be any number of A1 characters.

However, because the lines have been shorn of characterizing devices, the characters should not be treated as featureless machines. They are people. Character should be projected on to the lines (which is a reversal of the usual process).

The effect to aim at is of one conversation, emphasizing the fact that there is no difference between the people on either side of the wall. They are really part of one group."

David Campton

(A bare stage. The RECORDER *enters with a large book and pen. He looks around.)*

Recorder: How odd. I felt sure there was someone here. Just a minute ago. There's still the trace of an echo. I could have been mistaken, though. They come and go.... Well, it's my job to wait and see. (*He makes himself comfortable*) I may have to wait some time.... But there's nothing I can do about that. Time passes. (*Pause*) Listen. Footsteps coming from this direction. And more footsteps coming from that direction. Something is about to happen. I must make a note.

(Parties A *and* B *enter from opposite sides. They pause wearily.)*

"Party A from the East. Party B from the West. Worn out with travelling they come to rest." (*He ponders over the last note*) Verse in an official record? (*He crosses out the last words*) "At first they are too exhausted for words." ... That's better. "Gradually they look around them, at first critically, then with growing admiration and delight. But too taken with their own concerns to notice the other group."

A1: Here?

B1: Here.

A1: It's a good place.

B1: Yes, it's a good place.

A2: Better than any other place we've seen.

B2: It's a good place all right.

A1: To pause at.

B1: To stay at.

A2: To make our own.

B2: For ever and ever.

A1: This is our place.

B1: Ours.

A2: Ours.

B2: We took long enough to find it.

A3: It was a long journey.

B3: But it was worth every day we searched.

A1: It was worth every mile we tramped.

B1: Look at it.

A2: Just look.

B2: Look here.

A3: Look there.

B3: Look.

A1: Look.

(They point out things that please them.)

Recorder: Of course, they could have commented on the natural advantages of the place—such as the average hours of sunshine, the mean rainfall, the geological structure, the chemistry of the topsoil, and the lush pasturage. They'll find the words in time. But next they notice each other.

(From pointing out the delights of the place, the parties point to each other.)

A1: Look.

B1: Look.

A2: Look!

B2: Look!!

(The groups chatter excitedly among themselves.)

Recorder: Party A goes into a huddle, looking warily at Party B. Party B goes into a huddle, looking warily at Party A. Nothing to comment on there. It's the usual pattern. Any minute now the Spokesmen will face up to each other.

(A SPOKESMAN *from Party* B *steps forward.)*

Spokesman B: Who are you?

(A SPOKESMAN *from Party* A *steps forward.)*

Spokesman A: Who are *you*?

Spokesman B: We've come a long way.

Spokesman A: *We've* come a long way.

(The SPOKESMEN *return to their groups for quick conferences. After a few seconds they face each other again.)*

Spokesman A: We want to live here.

Spokesman B: *We* want to live here.

(The SPOKESMEN *return to their groups for quick conferences. After a few seconds they face each other again.)*

Spokesman B: We won't let you drive us away.

Spokesman A: We don't want to drive you away.

(The SPOKESMEN *return to their groups for conferences.)*

Recorder: One man, one vote. It takes time, but that's Democracy. There's no guarantee that they'll come to the right decision in the end, but that's Democracy, too. Not that I'm complaining about Democracy. It encourages a sense of responsibility. In theory, anyway.

(The SPOKESMEN *turn and face each other.)*

Spokesman A: Isn't there enough room for all of us?

Spokesman B: There's enough room for everybody.

Spokesman A: You could have all you see from there to here.

Spokesman B: You could have all you see from here to there.

Spokesman A: Agreed?

Spokesman B: Agreed.

(The As *and* Bs *shout "Agreed." The* SPOKESMEN *shake hands.)*

Spokesman A: Do you mind if we pause in negotiations?

Spokesman B: For a conference?

Spokesman A: Agreed.

(They go into conference again.)

Recorder: Proposals, counter-proposals, resolutions, amendments, points of order, appeals to the chair, motions, votes, polls, divisions, objections, and recounts. Everybody has a say. It can become tedious, but it has one advantage—if anything goes wrong, everyone is to blame.

Spokesman A: We have come to a conclusion.

Spokesman B: A conclusion is a good thing to come to. We have reached an agreement.

Spokesman A: It's always as well to reach an agreement.

Spokesman B: That you take that stretch of country with all its natural amenities, grazing rights, water rights, hunting rights, fishing rights, arable land, and mineral deposits.

Spokesman A: And that you take that stretch of land with all its natural amenities, etcetera, etcetera, etcetera.

Spokesman B: Furthermore . . .

Spokesman A: Furthermore?

Spokesman B: Yes, furthermore. For the benefit of all concerned . . .

Spokesman A: Does that include us?

Spokesman B: It includes everybody. That a line be drawn.

Recorder: (*musing aloud*) A line?

Spokesman B: A line. That a line be drawn to mark the place where your land ends and ours begins.

Spokesman A: Ah, yes. I was just about to add that a line be drawn to mark the place where our land ends and yours begins.

Spokesman B: Good fences make good neighbors.

Spokesman A: Good neighbors make good fences.

Spokesman B: Shall we mark it now?

Spokesman A: Why not?

Spokesman B: Chalk?

Spokesman A: String.

*(*SPOKESMAN A *produces a length of string and the two groups join forces in surveying the ground, and pegging out the string in a straight line. Everyone has his own idea how the job should be done, but eventually it is finished.)*

Recorder: I don't know who gave me this job. I seem to have been doing it as long as I can remember. Not that I'm complaining—someone has to do it. The record has to be kept. Who knows—one day someone may learn from it.

(The groups stand back and admire their handiwork.)

Spokesman A: It's a good line.

Spokesman B: Though I say it myself.

A1: I don't know.

Spokesman A: Are you criticizing this line?

Spokesman B: Perhaps you could make a better line.

Spokesman A: We're all listening. What have you got against this line?

A1: Chickens.

As and Bs: Chickens? What have chickens got to do with it? Take no notice. Got chickens on the brain.

A1: I know something about chickens, I do. There's not much you can tell me about chickens. I was brought up with chickens. And I'll tell you this: chickens can't read.

Spokesman B: Chickens can't read?

Spokesman A: What difference does that make to this line?

A1: None at all to your line.

Spokesman B: Or to your chickens for that matter.

A1: No use putting up your "Beware of the Bull" signs. No use sticking up your "Trespassers will be Prosecuted" notices. And you might as well forget your "One-Way Streets," your "Diversions," and your "Roads Closed." The chickens go where they want to go. No use drawing a line, and expecting the chickens to stay on this side of it. Or on that side of it for that matter.

As and Bs: True. That's a point. I never saw a chicken reading. Or taking any notice of a line.

Spokesman B: But what does it matter where the chickens go?

A1: Oh, if it doesn't matter there's no more to be said.

Spokesman A: Good. Now we can get on with . . .

A2: But suppose it should be sheep.

B1: Sheep?

A2: Sheep can't read either. At least I never saw a sheep reading. Ignorant animals really.

B1: A line won't keep a sheep from straying.

B2: Especially if they can't read.

A3: Or cows from wandering.

B3: Or horses from getting lost.

A2: And as for rabbits . . .

Spokesman B: All right. What do you want?

Spokesman A: Schools for animals?

A1: What we need are fences.

B1: Walls.

A2: Thick enough to stop cows from breaking through.

B2: High enough to stop chickens from flying over.

A3: Good walls make good neighbors.

B3: Good neighbors make good walls.

Spokesman A: You want walls?

Spokesman B: Shall we build walls?

A1: Before we do anything else.

*(*SPOKESMAN A *and* SPOKESMAN B *take opposite ends of the piece of string, and raise it about six inches off the ground.)*

Spokesman A: This high?

B1: Higher. Think of the cows.

(The string is raised waist high.)

Spokesman B: This high?

A2: Higher. Think of the horses.

(The string is raised shoulder high.)

Spokesman A: This high?

B2: Higher. Think of the chickens.

(The string is held as high as the SPOKESMEN *can reach, standing on tiptoe.)*

Spokesman B: I think that should do.

B1: Yes, that should do.

Spokesman A: It had better do. Now make it fast.

(The ends of the string are tied to posts.)

Spokesman B: And build the wall.

(The wall is built. This can be done in a number of ways. Blocks could be built up to the height of the string, or more string could be tied between the posts, or material could be draped over the string. At all events it is achieved after a great deal of activity. Meanwhile, the RECORDER *looks on, and takes notes.)*

Recorder: I won't say they're right. I won't say they're wrong. It's my job merely to record events. Events speak for themselves. They wanted a wall: they've got a wall. Neither side can see over, or through, or round. That's a wall.

(Now all the As *are on one side of the wall, and all the* Bs *are on the other side.)*

Spokesman A: That's a wall. That ought to last.

Spokesman B: Nothing we need to learn about making a wall.

Recorder: Except how to make a way over, or through, or round.

Spokesman A: Are you there?

Spokesman B: We're here. Are you all satisfied?

Spokesman A: Everything went according to plan. What now?

Spokesman B: We settle down. And you?

Spokesman A: We settle down, too. It's good land.

Spokesman B: It's very good land. We're lucky. We've got good neighbors.

Spokesman A: We've got good neighbors, too. It's a good wall.

Spokesman B: Good walls make good neighbors.

Spokesman A: Good neighbors make good walls.

Spokesman B: Good-bye, then. There's work to be done.

Spokesman A: Good-bye. Must get down to work.

(Shouting "Good-bye" the two groups pick up their belongings, and move away. The "Good-byes" die away in the distance.)

Recorder: Nothing left but the wall. And the chickens on each side of the wall. And the sheep on each side of the wall. And the cows on each side of the wall. And the horses on each side of the wall. And the people on each side of the wall . . .

(The groups re-appear on each side of the wall. They are all working.)

It's a busy life—and the great advantage with being busy is that it occupies the mind. Working keeps thoughts under control. Thoughts are more apt to run wild than any sheep. Thoughts can fly higher than any chickens. In fact walls make thoughts fly even higher. But as long as thoughts are kept under control there's no harm done. Except that there comes a time when all the chickens have been fed; all the cows have been milked; all the sheep have been rounded up in the fold—and thoughts are free to stray.

(Gradually the groups give up work, and make themselves comfortable.)

A1: I wonder what they're doing over there.

A2: Over there?

B1: Over there. What do you think they're doing?

A2: Why?

A1: Why not?

A2: Why do you wonder what they're doing over there?

B1: We can't see them, can we?

B2: They can't see us.

A1: I just wondered.

B1: Anybody can wonder.

A1: Just a thought—like do spring and summer come before autumn and winter, or do autumn and winter come first?

B1: Like—can a worm think?

A1: Like—what are they doing over there?

A2: The usual things, I suppose.

B2: They'll be doing the usual things.

A1: What do you mean—the usual things?

A2: Things that you usually do.

B2: Things that we usually do.

B1: Not the things that *they* usually do?

A2: The things that they usually do.

B1: You said the things that *we* usually do.

A2: They're the same things.

B1: Are they the same?

A2: Why shouldn't they be the same?

B2: Why should they be the same?

A1: They're not like us.

A2: Aren't they?

B1: It stands to reason.

A1: Work it out for yourself.

B1: Just work it out.

A1: For instance—you're not like me, are you?

A2: Not much.

B1: You're not a bit like me.

A2: So they're not like us.

B2: So they're not a bit like us.

A2: We're on this side of the wall.

B2: They're on the other side of the wall.

A1: Fancy living on the other side of the wall.

B1: Fancy wanting to live on the other side of the wall.

A2: When you could be living here.

B2: Fancy not wanting to live here.

A1: Funny.

B1: They've got some funny ways.

A1: Yes, they've got some funny ways.

B2: Have they?

A2: Of course. You've got some funny ways, too.

B1: They look funny to me all right.

A2: We've all got funny ways.

B2: But their ways are funnier. Over there.

B1: We don't even know what ways they've got.

A2: If they've got ways we don't know about, they must be funny ways.

A1: Still, as long as they're on the other side of the wall, it doesn't matter.

B1: It doesn't matter as long as they're on that side, and we're on this.

A2: I'm not so sure.

A1: What do you mean?

B1: I've been thinking. They're very quiet.

B2: We're quiet.

B1: We've got nothing to make a noise about.

A2: What about them, eh?

A1: What about them?

A2: What have they got to be so quiet about?

B1: It's unnatural.

A1: It's unusual.

B2: It's disturbing.

A2: It's disquieting.

B1: It's abnormal.

A1: It's uncomfortable.

B2: It's sinister.

A2: It's not as it should be.

B1: It's enough to send cold shivers down your back.

A1: It's enough to make your hair stand on end.

B2: Just thinking about it.

A2: Just wondering.

B1: What are they up to?

A2: What are they doing behind that wall?

B2: They could be doing anything behind that wall.

B1: Like what?

A2: Just think.

B1: Ah!

B2: Oh!

A1: They wouldn't.

B2: Not that!

A2: I wouldn't put it past 'em.

B2: Not them!

A1: Not that!

A2: Not what?

A1: Not what you're thinking.

B2: Oh, would they really?

B1: They're not to be relied on.

A1: You're exaggerating.

A2: Exaggerating?

A1: You wouldn't expect anybody to do that.

B2: We wouldn't do it.

B1: We're not like them.

A2: They're not like us.

B2: But they wouldn't. Not . . .

B1: Like . . .

A2: For instance . . .

B1: Or even . . .

A1: Not to mention . . .

A2: Just you wait.

A1: Wait for what?

B1: You'll see. You'll believe me then.

A2: Just you wait till you see it happening.

B2: I don't believe it.

A1: Oh!

A2: You will.

B1: If you ask me, they're wicked.

B2: Stands to reason. They're a wicked lot.

A1: They wouldn't get up to that sort of thing if they weren't wicked.

A2: Well, as long as they're wicked on their side of the wall . . .

A1: Wickedness spreads.

B1: Wickedness creeps.

A2: How long will they go on being wicked on their side of the wall?

B2: It's a high wall.

A1: It's a thick wall.

B3: Let them do what they like on their side of the wall.

A3: They can't interfere with us.

A1: Can't they?

B1: What can they do to us?

A2: They could be making plans now.

B2: Think. Just think.

A1: They could be spying on us now.

B3: Don't be silly.

A3: That's absurd.

A1: Is it?

B1: Perhaps we ought to check.

A2: It wouldn't do any harm to look.

A3: You can look if you like.

B3: I'm not making a fool of myself.

A3: I'll tell you what they're doing on the other side.

A2: What?

B3: I know what they're doing.

B2: Tell us.

A3: They're lying down in the sun like sensible people, maybe chewing long bits of grass.

B3: They're looking up at the sky, and working out tomorrow's weather.

A3: Or they're counting chickens.

B3: Or counting sheep.

A3: They're doing what we're doing.

B3: They're doing exactly what we're doing.

A1: I knew they weren't to be trusted.

B1: Have a look quickly.

A2: Look at them.

B2: Look.

A1: Look.

B1: How?

A2: Climb up.

B2: Look over the top.

(They prepare to climb the wall with whatever means are at hand—blocks, furniture, or each other.)

Recorder: At this point there is always the temptation to shout "stop." But a Recorder mustn't. It's a Recorder's job to record: no more, no less. And, my goodness the fuss that's made about handwriting and spelling! As if spelling mattered after . . . they've taken the first steps, you see. And after the first steps the others follow naturally. All a Recorder can do is to record. They climb to the top of the wall, and . . .

(The A's who have now reached the top of the wall, come face to face with the B's. They all shriek, and clamber down again.)

A1: It's all true.

B1: They were.

A1: Looking over.

B1: Spying.

A1: On us.

B1: On us.

A1: It's a good job we looked.

B1: We caught them at it.

A1: And were they surprised!

B1: They never expected that.

A1: They were fairly caught.

B1: Caught in the Act.

A2: But why were they doing it?

B2: Why would they want to do it?

A2: Why?

B2: Why?

A1: Ah-ha.

B1: We can guess.

A1: That's only half the story.

B1: That's only the tip of the iceberg.

A1: They're up to no good.

B1: They're ready for something.

A1: We must be ready for them.

B2: Ready for what?

A1: Ready for anything.

B1: Anything might happen.

A1: They're not like us.

B1: They're a bad lot.

A1: They're cruel.

B1: They're ruthless.

A1: Devilish.

B1: Fiendish.

A1: Wild.

B1: Savages.

A1: Peeping Toms.

B1: Sneaks.

A3: But let's consider.

B3: Let's think carefully.

A3: We looked over the wall, too.

B3: We'd never have seen them if we hadn't peeped.

A1: It's as well that we did.

B1: Where should we be now if we hadn't?

A3: Wait, though. Couldn't we forget that it happened?

B3: Couldn't we make allowances?

A1: Oh, yes, indeed.

B1: Why not, indeed?

A1: If we *want* to be made into mince.

B1: If we want to wake up with our throats cut.

A2: But what can we do?

B2: What's to be done?

A1: One thing's certain.

B1: There's no doubt at all.

A1: We can't live here any longer with them just there.

B1: We'll either have to fight or move on.

A1: Either they go, or we'll have to go.

B1: It's them or us.

As and Bs: Them.

A3: But we've got the wall.

B3: There's always the wall.

As and Bs: Pull it down. Pull it down.

(Both sides attack the wall.)

Recorder: It's odd: even sensible actions that would never be taken in the cause of peace are taken in the name of war. Like all pulling together.

Like breaking down walls. But the result isn't the same. As for instance . .

(The wall falls. For a second the two sides stare at each other. Then, with a cry, they rush at each other. They fight. Some are forced off-stage. Some run off-stage and are pursued. Some fall and are dragged away by friends.)

They fight. No, I'm not recording all the details. Any battle is just like any other battle. There are some acts of chivalry, some deeds of treachery, a hint of courage, a touch of cowardice. But the heroes, and the cowards, and the patriots, and the traitors have one thing in common: they all end up as dead as each other. This is nothing. I've seen battles that make this look like a squabble between sticklebacks. Not that I'm offering any prizes for the best battle. Every battle ends in the same way. One side thinks it has won; the other side thinks it ought to have won. Someone cleans up the mess, and the ground is left clean and tidy—ready for someone else to fight over another time. I could moralize. I could draw conclusions. But the conclusion is so obvious. The facts speak for themselves. They fight until . . . Oh, is it over already?

(The stage is clear.)

Now, is there anything to add before I draw the line? No? I had a feeling that there might be. Like the last spark in a dying fire. Like the last syllable of a fading echo. Ah, I thought as much.

(An A *and a* B *limp on to the stage from opposite sides. They come face to face where the wall once stood.)*

A: Going?

B: Going.

A: You could stay—now.

B: No, we can't stay—now.

A: It's good land.

B: It was good land.

A: We—we didn't want to—to . . .

B: If only we hadn't . . .

A: But you . . .

B: We?

A: We, too.

B: It was the wall, you know.

A: The wall was to blame.

B: The wall.

A: The wall.

B: We should have made it stronger.

A: Thicker.

B: Higher.

A: Longer.

B: It was the wall.

(They go out on opposite sides. The RECORDER *slams the book shut, and jumps up angrily.)*

Recorder: I don't want to know any more. It's all down here. Over and over again. History. The record is kept because someday someone may learn from it. Now I'm required elsewhere. Oh, this all becomes so monotonous. (*He starts to walk away, but pauses*) Someday. Somewhere. Someone. Is it possible? Hah!

(He goes. Black-out.)

ACTIVITIES

1. Re-read the playwright's note about this play. As he states, "character should be projected on to the lines . . ." and, therefore, when you are assigned a role that is only a letter and a number (A1, B2, etc.) you must decide many things. Read your lines and decide the following about your character: sex? age? occupation? temperament? physical attributes? marital status? relationship with the other characters? Create a complete personality for your character before rehearsals begin. During rehearsals, note how your character changes when you begin interacting with the other actors' characters.

2. Everyone in the group should offer suggestions about the character of the Recorder. Is the Recorder very serious and concerned, or can the lines be delivered lightly, mocking the foibles of the human race? How will the character of the Recorder change your interpretation of the play? Compare the role of the Recorder to roles in "Charlie Wilson" from *The Farm Show* (Section A, Chapter 3). What techniques are used there that might be of help now?

3. As your group works with this script, a number of the rehearsal techniques outlined in The Program to Chapter 4 can be used to help you find your interpretation of this play. When you experiment with these techniques, keep in mind that you are "trying things out" to see how they affect your understanding of the play. You are not bound to use all or any of them in your final presentation. You can use these techniques for the whole play or for segments of it. Here is a suggested sequence of rehearsal techniques you may use in preparing *Us and Them.*

a) Read the play through several times after allocating roles. Discuss and analyse the play thoroughly.
b) Subdivide the play into scenes which can be rehearsed separately.
c) Begin to rehearse each scene by adding actions. Use the rehearsal techniques outlined in Chapter 4 and other suggestions in previous chapters.
d) Begin to incorporate significant props and/or costume pieces.
e) Begin to set the scripts aside and rehearse with lines memorized.
f) Start to establish your interpretation by running through the play as a whole without interruptions.
g) Add any technical effects you are going to use and incorporate them into rehearsals.
h) Have several final run-throughs until you are satisfied that the performance is polished and everything happens "on cue."

WORKSHOP

1. With your group, visit a rehearsal in progress at a school, in a community group, in a local college group, or in a professional theatre group. Observe the work of the director and actors. Arrange an in-depth discussion with the director and other production people and ask questions about what you have observed and about the roles of the various people involved in the planning of a production.

2. Divide your group into committees, each with the job of researching one area of play production; for example, stage managing, costuming, lighting, prop acquisition, stage design, directing, box office duties, publicity, etc. Set a time for each committee to make a full report on their findings. Encourage the development of a library of resource materials and of a list of people in each area.

3. In a brain-storming session after these reports, prepare a chart which shows how a production staff is organized and the delegation of authority. Indicate the scheduling necessary to meet production deadlines and requirements.

4. As a group, discuss a rehearsal schedule for a play which you could produce in your class or school.

5. As a group, visit a school auditorium or stage area and find the following: a) the proscenium; b) size and depth of the floor of the stage; c) any exits which can be utilized; d) the size of the acting area; e) the light and control board; f) where scenery can be stored for easy moving and disposal; g) the lights and light bars; h) the curtains and audience sight lines. Locate areas where scenery and costumes could be built or stored. Become familiar with all the hardware and equipment available and determine how much is needed for your specific play.

6. Arrange workshops, films, slide-shows, or lectures by known experts in the fields of make-up, costuming, directing, and play production for the class. Allow for a question and answer period where you will get in-depth information.

SECTION B: Alternative Scripts

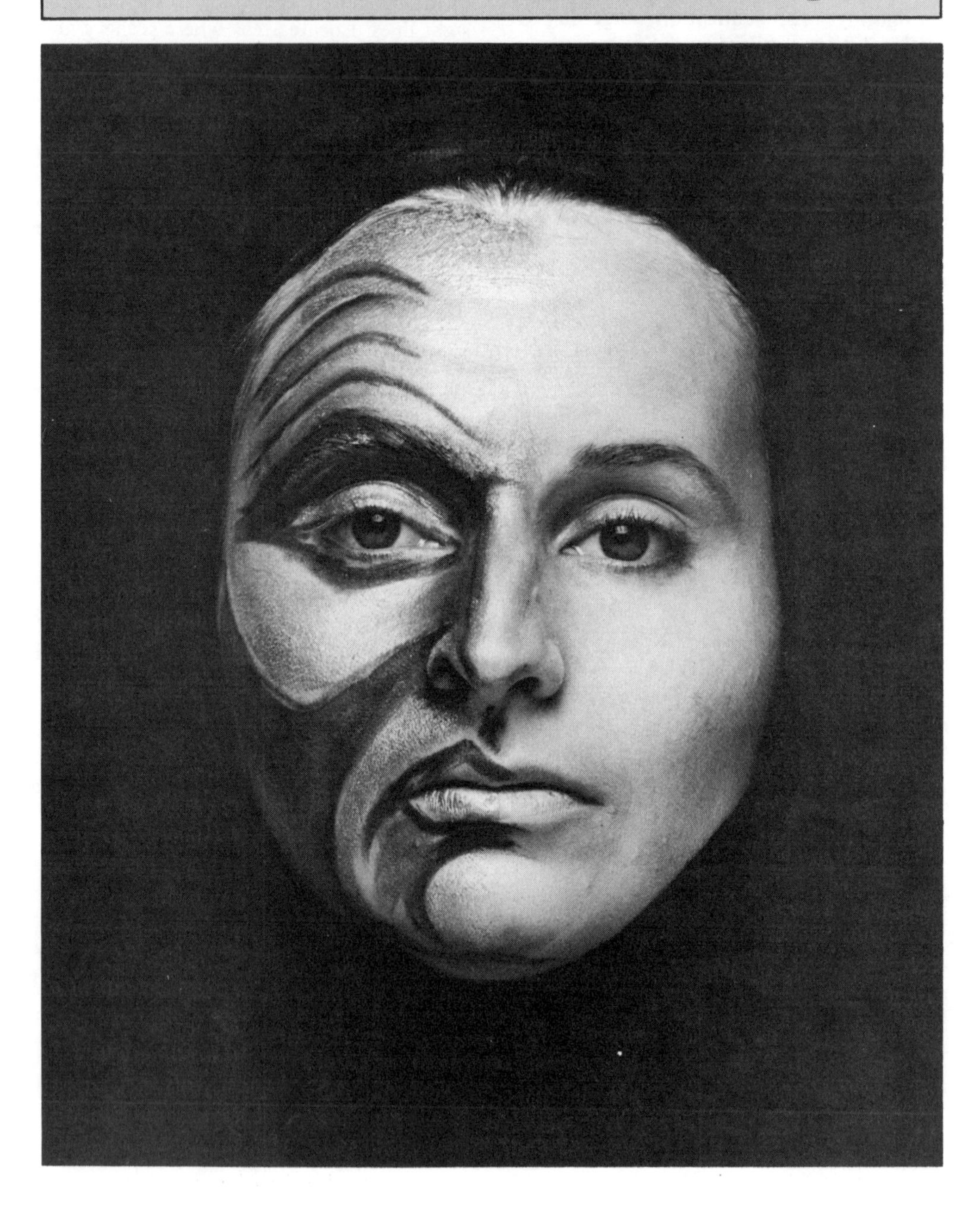

Introduction

Section A of this book examines and works with a wide variety of scripted material actually presented in theatres. Generally, the scripts in Section A use common elements: the speaker is indicated, the dialogue is written down, and stage directions are usually given to indicate something of the characters' actions, thoughts, and feelings. Many of these common elements are also found in the plays of Section C. Section C offers a look at scripts used throughout recorded history, including many contemporary scripts. There are thousands of such scripts available for you to examine, explore, and share.

This section, Alternative Scripts, contains many forms of literature that are not often thought of as script. In it you will explore how poems, novels, short stories, historical texts, children's stories, folk tales, biographies, diaries, and newspaper articles can be used as script. You will learn techniques for transposing various types of writing into dramatic form. You will discover how to locate dialogue in poems, novels, and other writings; how to dramatize narration; and how to write a script from first person accounts of events. In addition, you will develop alternative dramatic forms for the presentation of non-scripted writing such as Readers Theatre, Story Theatre, and Children's Theatre, and you will learn how to put together a dramatic anthology, and a presentation based on documents.

The techniques you learn in this section will be very valuable for you. For example, if a conventional script does not satisfy the needs of your group, or if your group wishes to dramatize a piece of writing that cannot be enacted in conventional ways in its present form, you can turn to other forms of writing, or transpose non-dramatic literature into dramatic form. These techniques will also help you solve some of the problems that frequently trouble theatre groups: too few roles for females or males; too few or too many parts for the members of the group; or plays with one major and several minor roles.

As you work with the material in this section of the book and become comfortable with the innovations involved, you will find that you are undertaking the role of playwright. In other words, you will not just be exploring and interpreting someone else's script; you will be the creator, or the source, of your own script. You will work with the *process* of drama as well as the end *product*. Your search for meaning in a script and your efforts to make a script come alive will, in this section, be from a perspective different than your work in Sections A and C. However, the work you do here will help you bring new and creative interpretive skills to the traditional script forms found elsewhere in this book.

6: Scripts from other sources

THE PROGRAM

Unlike the materials in Sections A and C of this book, the selections in this chapter are not written in traditional script form. For example, you will find here poems, parts of a novel, an advertisement, and a cartoon. Each piece of writing does contain dialogue, however, and that dialogue can be explored using standard drama techniques, many of which are explored and explained in Section A. As you work with the selections in this chapter you will become aware of the possibilities that exist, in most types of writing, for defining roles, speaking words aloud, and finding appropriate movement. This understanding of the dramatic potential in writing will enable you to develop the alternative forms of script explored in subsequent chapters in this section.

Before you dramatize any of these selections you will have to make the following decisions:

WHO is speaking? How many parts are there? From what each character says, what can you determine about that character?

WHERE is the scene taking place? How does the scene change when you vary the setting?

WHAT is happening in terms of physical action? Are the characters seated very quietly or is there a lot of movement?

WHEN is this scene taking place? Does the scene change if you put it in the past? the present? the future?

WHY are these characters saying these lines? (This is the same as determining the *sub-text* as discussed in Chapter 2.) Some of the material in this chapter is written in a very concise way, and you will have to experiment with a variety of possible reasons for saying the lines before you find a meaningful sub-text.

As you proceed through this chapter you will note that some of the selections are grouped together. This is because the selections in each group explore a common theme. You will have to make decisions about a) what the theme is, and b) how to organize the selections to best convey that theme.

Be aware that because of the nature of the material in this chapter, you will be able to vary the decisions you make. These variations can result in quite different interpretations.

PLAYBILL

In these selections, dialogue is presented in three very different formats. "What is he?" is a poem; "How One Simple Phone Call . . ." is an advertisement, and "Boy, Girl, Boy, Girl" is a cartoon. However, because of the dialogue, each can be regarded as a script. As you read each selection, pay attention to the male and female roles. Are the roles stereotypes, or does the writing work against stereotypical thinking?

What Is He?

What is he?
—A man, of course.
Yes, but what does he do?
—He lives and is a man.
Oh quite! but he must work. He must have a job of some sort.
—Why?
Because obviously he's not one of the leisured classes.
—I don't know. He has lots of leisure. And he makes quite
beautiful chairs.—
There you are then! He's a cabinet maker.
—No no!
Anyhow a carpenter and joiner.
—Not at all.
But you said so.
—What did I say?
That he made chairs, and was a joiner and carpenter.
—I said he made chairs, but I did not say he was a carpenter.
All right then, he's just an amateur.
—Perhaps! Would you say a thrush was a professional flautist,
or just an amateur?—
I'd say it was just a bird.
—And I say he is just a man.
All right! You always did quibble.

D.H. LAWRENCE

ACTIVITIES

1. In working with this poem you must make decisions about who, where, what, when, and why as outlined in The Program, page 64. Experiment with many variables. For example, "where" could be the entrance to heaven; "why" could be determining if the person should be allowed to join an exclusive club; "who" could be changed to a doctor. With each change, vary the dialogue accordingly. What happens to the dramatization of the poem when the first two lines are altered to read:

"What is she?
—A woman, of course.";

or:

"What are they?
—People, of course."

2. As you explore the dramatic possibilities of this poem, be sure to investigate possible roles for the two people speaking. How do the lines change if the people are a lawyer and a witness, a husband and a wife, or two friends? When you decide who the speakers are, you will also need to make a decision about where the scene takes place.

ACTIVITIES

1. This dialogue is slightly "idealized" in that both parties are courteous and considerate. Read the script aloud several times until you feel you understand the people. Then change the script by varying the circumstances slightly. For example, what if the consultant has just been fired for being rude to callers, and this is the last telephone call he/she will take?

2. As you did with "What is he?", the roles in this script can be altered. Does your interpretation change if the caller is a man and the consultant is a woman?

3. Use this example as a model for creating your own scripted dialogue of telephone conversations. For example: you call to complain about a product you just bought, and the person who sold it to you does not want to exchange or repair the product. After running through your improvisation a few times, write down the dialogue in script form.

Boy, Girl, Boy, Girl

JULES FEIFFER

ACTIVITIES

1. Cartoons are excellent sources of script material. Not only do they provide you with dialogue, but they also provide you, through the drawings, with information about roles and physical actions. Enact the script in this cartoon several times with a partner until you have fully explored the roles, dialogue, and action.

2. Explore the situation presented in this cartoon a little further by improvising what happened before this scene occurred. Continue this scene beyond the last panel to discover what happens next.

The Three Selections

1. You have probably already noted how the first two selections present a stereotypical view of females and males, and how the last gives a reverse view of this stereotype. This last selection uses role reversal to look at a typical situation from an opposite viewpoint. Find other examples of advertising, cartoons, and poetry which seem to present stereotypes, and explore them dramatically using role reversal.

2. Because of common themes, these three selections can form one dramatic unit. Perform the three selections in the order they are given, then change this order around. You will have to decide what order is the most effective, and what means you can use (such as setting, extra lines of dialogue) to unite the selections. What statement is your dramatization making?

PLAYBILL

Through the use of dialogue, these three poems explore human relationships. In order to set up the context for the dialogue and the roles of the speakers, you will have to use the techniques suggested in The Program. As you read the poems, attempt to determine the theme which unites them.

Two Friends

I have something to tell you.
I'm listening.
I'm dying.
I'm sorry to hear.
I'm growing old.
It's terrible.
It is, I thought you should know.
Of course and I'm sorry. Keep in touch.
I will and you too.
And let me know what's new.
Certainly, though it can't be much.
And stay well.
And you too.
And go slow.
And you too.

DAVID IGNATOW

ACTIVITIES

1. You probably realized that the surface simplicity of the dialogue is deceiving. In order to find meaning in this script, you will have to explore the "sub-text" of the dialogue. (Many of the techniques for doing this are given in Section A—Chapter 2.) Experiment with a number of different interpretations of this poem before making a final decision. If other groups are also doing this poem compare your interpretation with theirs.

Get off this estate

'Get off this estate.'
'What for?'
'Because it's mine.'
'Where did you get it?'
'From my father.'
'Where did he get it?'
'From his father.'
'And where did he get it?'
'He fought for it.'
'Well, I'll fight you for it.'

CARL SANDBURG

ACTIVITIES

1. After dramatizing this poem, try doing it entirely in mime. Can you still convey the meaning of the poem? Continue the scene by improvising the dialogue that occurs following the last line. How does the scene develop when one speaker refuses to fight?

Battle Won Is Lost

They said, "You are no longer a lad."
I nodded.
They said, "Enter the council lodge."
I sat.
They said, "Our lands are at stake."
I scowled.
They said, "We are at war."
I hated.
They said, "Prepare red war symbols."
I painted.
They said, "Count coups."
I scalped.
They said, "You'll see friends die."
I cringed.
They said, "Desperate warriors fight best."
I charged.
They said, "Some will be wounded."
I bled.
They said, "To die is glorious."
They lied.

PHIL GEORGE

ACTIVITIES

1. This poem presents an opportunity to work in groups larger than pairs, and to interpret narrative material and dialogue. Decide how you will deal with the "they said" lines and the short statement lines of the speaker. Can you use movements to elaborate what is suggested in the poem?

The Three Selections

1. After discussing the common themes of these three poems, decide on an order of presentation and on techniques of unifying them into a single dramatic statement. You may find that simple masks (made out of paper bags) will be useful in your interpretation.

PLAYBILL

Here are three poems which create a definite atmosphere or mood although they consist only of dialogue. Examine the subtext of each line of dialogue, and then determine the underlying meaning of each poem. As you read, pay attention to the roles in all three poems. How are they similar, and how do they differ?

Wait Till Then

"A dull day."
"And yet it is a day."
"What else? What could it be?"
"Why, nothing."
"Oh."
"You still don't understand, my child.
A dark day is so much more than no day—
Some day, none—"
"I see."
"But you don't see. With eyes as warm as yours,
As moist, as large—"
"And so I should see everything."
"Except nothing. Wait till then."
"When?"
"Forget, forget it. I must hold my tongue."
"No, tell me."
"Will not, cannot. Wait, I say,
Till any light at all is so much more
Than no light—oh, it blinds me, thinking of it,
As this day does, compared. I thank this day
For being. That's enough, that's fire and flame,
That's rockets bursting, that's one great
White ball of brightness breaking, that's
Lightning in the night—it shows the shapes
Of dear things still there—still there—"
"I see them."
"Not as I do, not as I do. Wait."
"Till when?"

MARK VAN DOREN

ACTIVITIES

1. In order to interpret this poem dramatically, you will have to answer the who, where, what, when, and why questions referred to in The Program. You should experiment with a variety of roles for the second speaker. Some possibilities are a parent, a teacher, or an older person. What if the speaker was a person such as Merlin, or Joan of Arc's mother or father? Would the interpretation of the poem change?

A Frosty Night

"Alice, dear, what ails you,
Dazed and lost and shaken?
Has the chill night numbed you?
Is it fright you have taken?"

"Mother, I am very well,
I was never better.
Mother, do not hold me so,
Let me write my letter."

"Sweet, my dear, what ails you?"
"No, but I am well.
The night was cold and frosty—
There's no more to tell."

"Ay, the night was frosty,
Coldly gaped the moon,
Yet the birds seemed twittering
Through green boughs of June.

"Soft and thick the snow lay,
Stars danced in the sky—
Not all the lambs of May-day
Skip so bold and high.

"Your feet were dancing, Alice,
Seemed to dance on air,
You looked a ghost or angel
In the star-light there.

"Your eyes were frosted star-light;
Your heart, fire and snow.
Who was it said, 'I love you'?"
"Mother, let me go!"

ROBERT GRAVES

ACTIVITIES

1. This poem raises many questions which you will have to answer. Some of these questions are: why is the daughter "shaken"? to whom is she writing? what is in the letter? To develop answers, improvise what happened before the poem began, and what will occur afterwards. Although you may not choose to continue the poetic form of the dialogue, you should attempt to keep the spirit and tone of the writing.

ACTIVITIES

1. As in "A Frosty Night," you will have to explore the many questions this poem raises. When you read the poem aloud, discuss and make decisions about the areas of ambiguity.

The Horn

"Oh, hear you a horn, mother, behind the hill?
My body's blood runs bitter and chill.
The seven long years have passed, mother, passed,
And here comes my rider at last, at last.
I hear his horse now, and soon I must go.
How dark is the night, mother, cold the winds blow.
How fierce the hurricane over the deep sea!
For a seven years' promise he comes to take me."

"Stay at home, daughter, stay here and hide.
I will say you have gone, I will tell him you died.
I am lonely without you, your father is old;
Warm is our hearth, daughter, but the world is cold."

"Oh mother, Oh mother, you must not talk so.
In faith I promised, and for faith I must go,
For if that old promise I should not keep,
For seven long years, mother, I would not sleep.
Seven years my blood would run bitter and chill
To hear that sad horn, mother, behind the hill.
My body once frozen by such a shame
Would never be warmed, mother, at your hearth's flame.
But round my true heart shall the arms of the storm
For ever be folded, protecting and warm."

JAMES REEVES

The Three Selections

1. Create a context in which all three selections can be dramatized. Decide on an order for the poems, and, in your work, stress the settings and the roles of each.

FROM

I'VE GOT VIKTOR SCHALKENBURG

PLAYBILL

This selection presents an entirely different source of dialogue for dramatization. The material is from a novel, and it has striking similarities to the conventional script forms found in Sections A and C. However, as you read, you will find that you have to examine the dialogue closely to determine who the speakers are, what the actions are, and what the setting is.

TAPE NUMBER 1

O.K., we're in business.

A tape recorder?

Don't be worried. I'm sorry about all this, the gun and all. And what I've done to keep you here. It was the only way.

Who the hell are you?

I'm nobody to fear.

I suggest that you let me go. Free me before the authorities find out about this. Kidnapping is a crime here.

This isn't kidnapping, Viktor.

My name isn't Viktor. You have my wallet.

You're Viktor Schalkenburg.

I'm Johann Valken.

Naturally, I don't expect you to admit it immediately.

Is this your home?

You know very well it isn't.

I didn't think it was, you're right.

Why not?

You're from America. A tourist.

Why do you say that?

Your clothes, your sunburn.

I'm a teacher. A college professor. My name is Vail.

I think you had better let me go, Professor Vail.

I will, in a few days.

Let me go now and we'll both forget it.

No chance for that. I want to talk to you.

You have a bad cold.

Yes, I came down here to rest and relax and get rid of my cold and now I've got Viktor Schalkenburg.

What is it with this name? Who is this Viktor person?

Very convincing. Look, all I want to do is to talk to you, that's all. I'm no policeman. I'm a history professor.

What do you want?

I want to talk to you.

Listen to me. My name is Johann Valken. There's a hundred ways you can check my credentials. My passport. I am well known here. You think I'm this. . . . Good God. Listen, will you make one telephone call?

What would it prove?

That I'm not this person you think I am.

Who'd be able to prove that?

My doctor.

No. No calls. Do you want a beer?

A beer?

We'll be here for a time so we might as well relax and get comfortable. Again you have nothing to fear. I'm not a policeman of any sort. I will not turn you over to your enemies. This is no Eichmann thing. So have a beer and do not be afraid of me. I'm. . . .

You're crazy, that's what you are, my American friend. I think you better go back to the Aruba Hilton or wherever you came from.

I want to talk to you. That's all I want. You were with the Einsatzgruppen in the Crimea.

You're absolutely mad. Is that what you think I am? Some sort of Nazi? A war criminal? My God. . . .

I recognized you. Then I went to some trouble to prove I was right. This is no ruse, no trick. I have a strong interest in the Third Reich. You are, to me, invaluable. A fantastic find.

You're serious, aren't you?

Yes, I'm serious. You're one of the few links with many important things . . . you were in the Fuehrerbunker, Viktor.

I'm *not* this person.

I don't expect you to admit it, of course; that would surprise me.

Will you please let me go before it's too late.

What's that mean? Too late.

This is a very serious crime.

Yes, I gave it a great deal of thought, believe me.

You bring me here by force, with a pistol, and then chain me. I do not know the details of the law here but one can imagine that what you have done . . . my God. It might be a capital crime.

I guess I better forget the whole thing then and tip off the police that you're here—that Viktor Schalkenburg is here.

Do that. Phone them now.

You're good, Viktor. I admire you. If I picked up that phone you'd start screaming.

Call them!

Beautiful. You're beautiful.

Why don't you call them?

The phone isn't connected, Viktor. I was only kidding anyway. Now listen. There is no need to get excited. I'm not going to turn you over to your enemies. Have a beer and don't worry. We'll just talk, you and I, talk about the old days. O.K.?

But there is only one problem. I'm not this Viktor Schalkenburg.

Nice. Very nice. Wait until I show you the proof. When you've seen my proof and still insist that you're not Schalkenburg then my plan fails, naturally. Then I'll have to give my proof to the police here and let them decide, let you work it out with them.

Proof? What proof?

Photographs. Slides. Thirty-five millimetre slides.

Dear God. . . .

This, Viktor, will save us a lot of time. Would you like a Heineken?

Bring me one. Anything to humor you.

TAPE NUMBER 2

There. That's better. It wasn't quite in focus.

Is that fellow supposed to be me?

Yes, the sergeant behind the officer in the long coat.

Where is this?

The Crimea. Nineteen forty-one.

You must be crazy to do a thing like this. Absolutely crazy.

Here's a better shot of you. From the SS files at Bad Tölz.

Where did you get these pictures?

The Waffen SS archives in the Pentagon. We've got tons of material there. Most of it has never been touched. Your stuff had been culled out by some of the Nuremberg people. It was easy for me to get this stuff and have it photographed. I have a friend who's very big there.

If I were this man, why would I talk to you?

To save yourself.

How?

You talk and I'll promise to wait two years before I release anything. I want to do a book on you. If you refuse to talk I'll turn you over to the people who are hunting you. The Russians. The Jews.

Two years?

That's time enough to get away from here, cover your tracks and assume a new identity.

This Schalkenburg, he might solve the problem by killing you.

No.

Why not?

It would destroy him. If something happens to me—well, certain people, very efficient people with world-wide connections—they'd have you in a net within a few days. There would be no time to get away. No time to hide.

But you take this risk?

Yes—but there is really no risk as you see. You admit now that you're Schalkenburg?

Of course not—but that one does resemble me, doesn't he? I can see why you got excited. . . . What assurances would this man have that he wouldn't be handed over to his enemies once you have gotten whatever it is that you want?

None. None except my word.

You are an FBI man and all this is a pose to throw the man off guard. Too bad it's the wrong man.

You leave me no alternative, Viktor.

How many days is this supposed to take?

A few days. Three, four. Then I'll leave Aruba.

To return to New England. I say that from your accent.

That's true.

You sound a bit like John F. Kennedy.

Are you Schalkenburg?

Yes, I'm Viktor Schalkenburg.

ACTIVITIES

1. Because the dialogue presented here does not contain any of the material a conventional script might have, such as stage directions and speaker identification, you will have to examine the dialogue closely to develop your interpretation. In groups, create a "background" for the dialogue. Decide on the following: stage directions, setting, the character of each speaker, actions, and use of props. When you have completed your background, write this new information into the existing script. Each group can act out its interpretation for the other groups.

2. In groups, develop an improvisation to continue the scene. Make sure this improvised material is consistent with the background you developed in the previous activity.

WORKSHOP

1. Examine other written material for its dramatic potential. For example, look through an anthology of poetry for poems which contain dialogue; choose cartoons and comic strips which have dramatic content; search through novels for passages of dialogue.

2. Investigate newspapers for the "scripts" that occur within them. Often you will find reports which contain direct quotations of dialogue. Assemble these scripts and work on dramatizing them.

3. Create your own scripts by cutting out words, phrases, and sentences from magazines and newspapers. Put these lines of dialogue in some sort of order and glue them to a page. Dramatize the script you have created.

4. Using the techniques of *Viktor Schalkenburg*, tape record conversations (with the participants' permission!), and transcribe parts of this dialogue into writing. Can you create a dramatic interpretation of the dialogue?

5. Using a tape recorder again, interview a person who has interesting stories to tell about your neighborhood or community. Find ways of transforming these stories into dramatic form.

7: Choral dramatization

THE PROGRAM

In the early days of humanity, tribal chants and rituals had a magical and mystical quality. The power and effect of a group of people chanting together was recognized by the first playwrights. The use of a "chorus"—a group of performers that speaks lines in unison and moves in a co-ordinated manner—became one of the earliest dramatic techniques. The chorus was a part of Greek theatre, and its use is recorded in plays written over 2000 years ago. The chorus commented on the action on-stage and related to the audience events which had occurred off-stage. In order to enhance their work, playwrights since the time of ancient Greece have often used a chorus. As you work with choral dramatization, you also will discover this centuries-old theatrical convention.

Choral dramatization begins with choral speech, of which there are many kinds. In unison choral speech, the entire chorus speaks as a unit. Articulation must be carefully executed, and everyone must begin and finish each phrase with precision. No single voice should dominate the group. In two-part choral speaking, selections may be divided into "dark" and "light" tones. Dark tones are lines that are most effectively delivered by low-pitched and loud voices. Light tones are lines that are most effectively delivered by higher-pitched and soft voices. In multi-part choral speaking a piece may be divided into parts for solo speakers and parts for small groups. The groups and soloists must pick up their cues so that the selection sounds as if it were spoken by one person. A selection may reach a climax and the number of voices increase, perhaps ending in unison. A conductor who is not part of the group may be used to unify the interpretation and to make final decisions about mood, theme, and pace, or a leader who is an actual member of the group may be positioned so that the others can see him or her begin the action.

Once the group has become familiar with the words of the text, physical action can be added to dramatize the selection. This can be done in a number of ways; part of the group can do the actions while another part chorally speaks the lines; the whole group can do both the speech and the movement; or various small groups can alternate movement and speech. Whichever way is chosen, be sure that the flow of the language, the rhythm, and the cadence of the speech is enhanced by movements which deepen the meaning of the writing. (If you want to free your hands, write the script on a blackboard or use an overhead projector.) If you wish, you can use costumes and masks, and add music and sound effects to your choral dramatizations.

For the purpose of this chapter, choral dramatization is regarded as a *mode* of dramatic interpretation. However, keep in mind that choral work is also a *technique* which can be used in the dramatization of a wide variety of material such as scripts, poems, and stories. Opportunities for the use of choral work as a technique will occur in subsequent chapters in this section and in other sections of this book. (Section A of this book contains examples of the use of a chorus and choral dramatization such as the choral speaking of nursery rhymes in *Juve*, the single character acting as the chorus in *Antigone*, and the opportunities for choral speaking in *Us and Them*. Section C provides examples of the dramatic function of a chorus in such plays as *Oedipus the King*, *The Birds*, and *Murder in the Cathedral*.)

The selections that follow allow you to experiment with the techniques of choral dramatization and to build skills that you can utilize in interpreting other dramatic material.

PLAYBILL

A litany is defined as "a prayer consisting of a series of invocations and supplications by the leader with alternate response by the congregation" (Webster's *New Collegiate Dictionary*). "A Litany for Rain" could be the prayer of a primitive tribe which needed rain for the success of its food crops. As you read this material aloud, experiment with ways of delivering the lines. For example, increase the number of speakers giving the recitative lines, beginning with one speaker and adding more voices as the selection develops.

A Litany for Rain

RECITATIVE:	RESPONSE:
We overcome this wind.	We overcome.
We desire the rain to fall, that it be poured in showers quickly.	Be poured.
Ah, you rain, I ask you to fall. If you fall, it is well.	It is well.
A drizzling confusion.	Confusion.
If it rains and our food ripens, it is well.	It is well.
If the young men sing, it is well.	It is well.
A drizzling confusion.	Confusion.
If our grain ripens, it is well.	It is well.
If our women rejoice,	It is well.
If the children rejoice,	It is well.
If the young men sing,	It is well.
If the aged rejoice,	It is well.
An overflowing in the granary,	Overflowing.
A torrent in flow,	A torrent.
If the wind veers to the south, it is well.	It is well.
If the rain veers to the south, it is well.	It is well.

ACTIVITIES

1. Divide into four groups, and assign each group four lines from the recitative column and four lines from the response column. For example, group one could take recitative lines 1, 5, 9, 13 and response lines 2, 6, 10, 14. The other three groups can divide the rest of the lines in a similar style. Practise multi-part choral speaking for small groups as outlined in The Program to this chapter.

2. Imagine that this litany is a ritual of a tribe that lived long ago. Develop actions and vocal expressions which will give the piece dignity and formality. Keep in mind how important rain would have been to primitive people.

PLAYBILL

The origins of this material from Innuit life are apparent. The song-poem clearly portrays what is important to sustain life in the Innuit's harsh environment, and shows how human relationships are shaped by the Innuit's need of the hunter and food-gatherer. Although there is only one speaker, find opportunities for adding voices to the choral speaking of this passage. Try to maintain a song-like rhythm in your delivery.

Orpingalik's Song: My Breath

(This is what I call this song, for it is just as necessary to me to sing it as it is to breathe.)

I will sing a song.
A song that is strong.
  Unaya-unaya.

Sick I have lain since autumn,
Helpless I lay, as were I
My own child.

Sad, I would that my woman
Were away to another house
To a husband
Who can be her refuge,
Safe and secure as winter ice.
  Unaya-unaya.

Dost thou know thyself?
So little thou knowest of thyself.
Feeble I lie here on my bench
And only my memories are strong!
  Unaya-unaya.

Beasts of the hunt! Big game!
Often the fleeting quarry I chased!
Let me live it again and remember,
Forgetting my weakness.
  Unaya-unaya.

Let me recall the great white
Polar bear,
High up its back body,
Snout in the snow, it came!
He really believed
He alone was a male
And ran towards me.
  Unaya-unaya.

It threw me down
Again and again,
Then breathless departed
And lay down to rest,
Hid by a mound on a floe.
Heedless it was, and unknowing
That I was to be its fate.
Deluding itself
That he alone was a male.
And unthinking
That I too was a man!
  Unaya-unaya.
I shall ne'er forget that great
  blubber-beast,
A fjord seal,
I killed from the sea ice
Early, long before dawn,
While my companions at home
Still lay like the dead,
Faint from failure and hunger,
Sleeping.
With meat and with swelling blubber
I returned so quickly
As if merely running over ice
To view a breathing hole there.

And yet it was
An old and cunning male seal.
But before he had even breathed
My harpoon head was fast
Mortally deep in his neck.

That was the manner of me then.
Now I lie feeble on my bench
Unable even a little blubber to get
For my wife's stone lamp.

The time, the time will not pass,
While dawn gives place to dawn
And spring is upon the village.
  Unaya-unaya.

But how long shall I lie here?
How long?
And how long must she go a-begging
For fat for her lamp,
For skins for clothing
And meat for a meal?
A helpless thing—a defenceless woman.
  Unaya-unaya.

Knowest thou thyself?
So little thou knowest of thyself!
While dawn gives place to dawn,
And spring is upon the village.
  Unaya-unaya.

ORPINGALIK

Translated from an Eskimo dialect by W.E. Calvert

ACTIVITIES

1. Find lines in this song-poem that are effective if spoken by "dark" or "light" voices only. Choose a partner with a voice quality different to your own, and decide which lines are dark and which ones are light.

2. After practising the song-poem with a partner, form a larger group and keep working with the dark-light interpretation.

3. The stories in "Orpingalik's Song" give you an opportunity for dramatization. You can act out the stories as you speak the lines, or one group can mime the actions while the lines are being spoken by another group.

FROM
RUNAWAYS
by Elizabeth Swados

PLAYBILL

This excerpt from a modern play shows how choral speaking is used in a contemporary litany. Compare this piece with "A Litany for Rain" and note any similarities. As you read this selection, be aware of the opportunities it provides for physical action.

FIND ME A HERO

Company: Find me a hero.
Make the old fairytales come true.
Put him on a horsey.
Give him a shield and a crown.
Find me a hero.

Solo: Don't mean no sandwich
So many different variations of unhappy endings are coming my way,
I think I've got me a Lancelot and then I clap my hands and he's gone away.

Company: Find me a hero.
Make the old fairytales come true.
Put him on a skateboard.
Give him a shield and a crown.
Find me a hero.

Solo: Don't mean no Blimpie.
I want him to be President, yes.
I want him to be a winner.
Walking with a marching band,
And I won't accept a sinner.

Company: Find me a hero.
Make the old fairytales come true.
Put him on a moped.
Give him some gloves and a helmet.
Find me a hero.

Solo: Don't mean no meatloaf.

Company: Hero, hero, I want a hero.
Make me a hero, don't let me down.
Find me a reason. Give me a leader.
Give me confidence.
Don't let me down.
Hero, hero, I want a hero. Make me a hero, don't let me down.
Find me a reason. Give me a leader.
Give me confidence.
Don't let me down.

Solo: Don't want him sad. Don't want confusion.

Company: Don't want that boring preaching, or false conclusions.

Solo: Don't want no bitterness or violent action.

Company: No easy answers. No quick reactions.
Find me a hero.
Make the old fairytales come true.
Put him on a horsey.
Give him a shield and a crown.
Find me a hero.
Find me a hero.
Find me a hero.
YEE HAH!

ACTIVITIES

1. Work through this selection as it is presented—one person as the solo part and the rest of the class as the company. Then divide into two groups to recite the lines. Finally, ignore the given division of lines, and divide the lines up in whatever way you feel is effective, perhaps again using dark and light voices. Invent physical actions to enhance your choral work.

2. Using the ideas above, experiment acting out the selection in different roles. Some suggestions are: corporate executives at a board meeting, people at a political rally, young children singing a nursery rhyme.

3. Have the hero appear at the end of the selection. This hero need not fit the stereotype suggested in the selection—male, young, brave, a "winner." Experiment with a number of alternative heroes.

4. Material of a similar nature can be found in *Juve*, Section A, Chapter 1. Examine that script and compare it with this selection.

PLAYBILL

Here is a choral passage which closely resembles "A Litany for Rain." However, you will note that the response is written in a language you have never seen or heard. This "made-up" language will give you an opportunity to decide on the meaning these new words will have. You will have to convey your meaning through the way in which you say the words and through the physical actions you invent to accompany the choral speaking. Indeed, you could make this a ritual performed by some unheard-of tribe from the past (or future).

Canedolia: an off-concrete scotch fantasia

oa! hoy! awe! ba! mey!

who saw?

rhu saw rum. garve saw smoo. nigg saw tain. lairg saw
lagg. rigg saw eigg. largs saw haggs. tongue saw luss. mull
saw yell. stoer saw strone. drem saw muck. gask saw noss.
unst saw cults.
echt saw banff. weem saw wick. trool saw tatt.

how far?

from largo to lunga from joppa to skibo from ratho to
shona from ulva to minto from tinto to tolsta from soutra
to marsco from braco to barra from alva to stobo from
fogo to fada from gigha to gogo from kelso to stroma
from hirta to spango.

what is it like there?

och it's freuchie, it's faifley, it's wamphray, it's frandy, it's
sliddery.

what do you do?

we foindle and fungle, we bonkle and meigle and
maxpoffle. we scotstarvit, armit, wormit, and even whifflet.
we play at cross-stobs, leuchars, gorbals, and finfan. we
scavaig, and there's aye a bit of tilquhilly. if it's wet,
treshnish and mishnish.

what is the best of the country?

blinkbonny! airgold! thundergay!

and the worst?

scrishven, shiskine, scrabster, and snizort.

listen! what's that?

catacol and wauchope, never heed them

tell us about last night

well, we had a wee ferintosh and we lay on the quiraing. it
was pure strontian!

but who was there?

petermoidart and craigenkenneth and cambusputtock and
ecclemuchty and corriehulish and balladolly and
altnacanny and clauchanvrechan and stronachlochan and
auchenlachar and tighnacrankie and tilliebruaich and
killieharra and invervannach and achnatudlem and
machrishellach and inchtamurchan and auchterfechan and
kinlochculter and ardnawhallie and invershuggle

and what was the toast?

schiehallion! schiehallion! schiehallion!

EDWIN MORGAN

ACTIVITIES

1. Since this material does not have any logical references, you can be very inventive in your interpretation. When you are deciding on a dramatic context for this selection, let your imagination roam as freely as the author let his when he invented these new words. Determine who, where, what, when, and why as you did in Chapter 6, and explore the many ways of choral speaking in your dramatization.

2. "Gibberish," or made-up language, can be used in working with any dramatic material. Choose another script on which you have worked, and transform the lines of dialogue into gibberish. Can you still convey the meaning of the script through your manner of speaking and your physical actions? (Try using *After Liverpool*, Chapter 2, Section A, and *Us and Them*, Chapter 5, Section A.)

PLAYBILL

These two selections for choral work are thematically linked in that they are both about sacrifice and the intervention of gods in human affairs. They are also linked through their connection with the Greek story of Oedipus; the first selection is a choral passage from the middle of a play about Oedipus—*Seneca's Oedipus* (Section C, Chapter 15), and the second selection is a poem to Oedipus. The Oedipus story is explored in *Oedipus the King* (Section C, Chapter 15).

The theme of sacrifice in these selections is related to Bacchus (also known as Dionysus). He was the Greek god of wine, rebirth, and fertility, and the celebrations and rituals honoring him—processions, songs, dramatic entertainment—were the origins of Western theatre. (See Section C, Chapter 15, The Program.) As you read these selections, determine how they can be interpreted together, and what order and what choral techniques you will use to make them most effective. Also be aware of physical actions which could enhance your dramatic interpretation.

Chorus to Bacchus

OOO-AI-EE . . . KA
CHANT *3 times*
REPLY *3 times*

DANCE DEATH INTO ITS HOLE
DANCE DEATH INTO ITS HOLE
INTO ITS HOLE
ITS HOLE

ITS HOLE

ITS HOLE

HOLE

LET IT CLIMB
LET IT COME UP
LET IT COME UP
LET IT CLIMB
LET IT LIVE
OPEN THE GATE
OPEN THE GATE
LET IT LIVE
TEAR THE BLOOD
OPEN ITS MOUTH
LET IT CRY

WHILE THE WIND
CROSSES THE STONES

WHILE THE STARS TURN
WHILE THE MOON TURNS
WHILE THE SEA TURNS

WHILE THE SUN STANDS AT THE DOORWAY
YOU YOU YOU
YOU UNDER THE YOU UNDER THE
YOU UNDER THE LEAF
YOU UNDER THE STONE
YOU UNDER BLOOD UNDER THE SEA
YOU UNDER THE EARTH

UNDER THE LEAF
UNDER THE STONE
UNDER BLOOD
UNDER THE SEA
UNDER THE EARTH
} *repeat 2 times*

YOU YOU YOU YOU
YOU YOU YOU YOU

UNDER BLOOD
UNDER THE EARTH

YOU

adapted by
TED HUGHES
(from Seneca's OEDIPUS*)*

ACTIVITIES

1. Investigate ways in which you can unite these two selections into a single dramatization. Determine if there are ways of intermingling lines of speech, or of ordering the speeches, so that there is a unity to the work. Develop physical actions which are appropriate to the choral speaking and which convey the serious, ritual quality of the writing. If possible, use masks and costume pieces, such as cloaks, to add to the dramatization.

Incantation to Oedipus

Choose the darkest part o' the grove,
Such as ghosts at noon-day love.
Dig a trench, and dig it nigh
Where the bones of Laius lie;
Altars raised of turf or stone,
Will th' infernal powers have none.
Answer me, if this be done?
'Tis done.

Is the sacrifice made fit?
Draw her backward to the pit:
Draw the barren heifer back;
Barren let her be, and black.
Cut the curled hair that grows
Full betwixt her horns and brows:
And turn your faces from the sun;
Answer me, if this be done?
'Tis done.

Pour in blood, and blood-like wine,
To Mother Earth and Proserpine:
Mingle milk into the stream:
Feasts the ghosts that love the steam;
Snatch a brand from the funeral pile:
Toss it in, to make them boil:
And turn your faces from the sun;
Answer me, if this be done?
'Tis done.

JOHN DRYDEN

WORKSHOP

1. Search for other types of writing which can be dramatized through choral speaking and movement. Look at anthologies of poetry and prose, at tales and legends of native peoples, and at collections of chants and songs.

2. When working with choral speech, practise a number of vocal techniques. For example, shout the lines, whisper the lines, use a monotone for delivery, and clip each word or phrase very sharply. Find a new selection (see Activity 1, above), and try racing through it very quickly. Then do it very slowly, taking long pauses between phrases and sentences.

3. Try saying the words, phrases, and sentences of any piece to a specific metronome or drum rhythm. Vary the speed of the metronome. Include percussion instruments, such as a drum, tambourine, triangle, gong, or cymbals, in your dramatization, and find the appropriate moments for adding these percussion effects.

4. For any script selection in Section A or C transform the dialogue into choral speaking. Give the speeches the quality of a litany or ritual. How do the story, characters, and speeches change with this treatment? Experiment with physical movements and groupings to enhance the dramatization. For example, use group movement, solo movement, and freezing to create visual images.

5. Several examples of plays which use a chorus or choral dramatization were listed in The Program to Chapter 7, page 73. During your work on these plays, remember to use the knowledge you have gained in this chapter. Remember also that choral work is not just a mode of drama, but also a technique; it is a potentially useful component of any dramatic presentation. The technique of choral dramatization will be invaluable when working on "Readers Theatre" (Chapter 8), "Story Theatre" (Chapter 9), "Anthology" (Chapter 11), and "Docudrama" (Chapter 12).

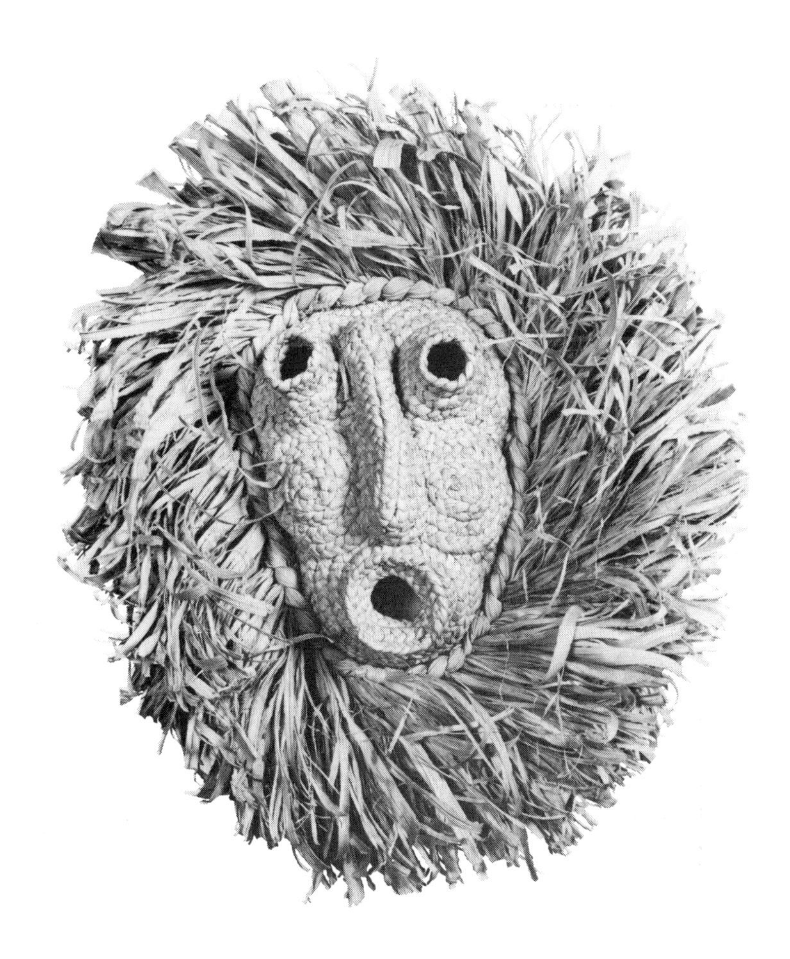

8: Readers Theatre and Chamber Theatre

THE PROGRAM

Readers Theatre

Readers Theatre is a form of dramatization that allows you to develop a script from material that was not initially written for performance. The techniques of Readers Theatre allow you to dramatize narration; you can use selections from novels, short stories, poetry, and descriptive prose. As its name implies, Readers Theatre does not require memorization. However, you should know your lines very well and use the "script" only for reference; the lines should be delivered to the audience, and your eyes should not be glued to the page.

Since the main effect of a Readers Theatre performance is in what the audience hears, you and your group must concentrate on vocal interpretation. You must work to say your lines as effectively as possible, keeping in mind timing and pacing, so that you convey the mood of the material. Choral speech, which was discussed in the previous chapter, can be very successful in Readers Theatre, and you should be ready to use choral speech wherever possible.

Readers Theatre is also visual; even though movement is kept to a minimum, your group can create a stage picture or tableau which visually enhances the material. Since you want the audience to concentrate on the words, you should use gesture and stage movement very sparingly. However, you may find moments when a particularly significant movement by one character, several characters, or by the whole group greatly enhances the dramatic impact.

Many groups decide to use a narrator for the narration and the other performers for the dialogue. This is only one solution. You can let each performer say the lines of narration which describe his or her character's thoughts and actions, or you can let several group members say the narration as a chorus—the technique used by the ancient Greeks. There are many creative ways of dramatizing narration, and you should experiment with a variety of ideas.

One problem many groups encounter is how to deal with the "she said" or "Count Dracula said" that often appears at the beginning, in the middle, or at the end of a line. Often the solution is to have one person say this narrative material while another person says only the character's dialogue. This can, however, sound somewhat artifical and tends to destroy the rhythm of the dialogue. (In comedy, on the other hand, it can be very effective.) A better solution may be to have the performer include the "she said" material in the dialogue without changing his or her tone or inflection. At first it may seem awkward, but after some practice, it will feel quite natural. This technique is invaluable in "Story Theatre," which we will look at in Chapter 9.

The staging of Readers Theatre should be simple and not require elaborate props or costumes. In this way, it is a very portable form of theatre and can be performed in many different settings. But you should be aware of opportunities to use significant props or meaningful costume pieces. Some Readers Theatre presentations are greatly enhanced by the use of masks, as long as the masks do not interfere with vocal clarity and projection.

Chamber Theatre

Chamber Theatre is a variation of Readers Theatre. The material used in Chamber Theatre should contain a great deal of narration, usually written in the first person. Novels and stories are the best source of material for this type of dramatic presentation.

Chamber Theatre requires that there be a narrator who, as the central character, delivers his or her own thoughts, feelings, and actions. The other members of the group act out what the narrator is saying, either through mime, or by saying aloud the dialogue and the narration that applies to each of their own characters, or by a combination of mime and dialogue.

Chamber Theatre can have more action and stage business than Readers Theatre. The narrator can move in and out of scenes being enacted and can assume lines of dialogue. You can also experiment by positioning the narrator apart from the actors or by having the narrator move among the actors but not being noticed by them.

Readers Theatre and Chamber Theatre presentations are exciting alternatives to traditional script presentations. They allow you to dramatize all forms of literature and can be highly rewarding. Both are limited only by your imagination and creativity.

Two of the selections in this chapter allow you to experiment with the techniques of Readers Theatre. *A Rope Against the Sun* divides the lines of dialogue among a narrator and characters in the story. *The Last Night of the World* requires that the group divide the lines appropriately, according to the group's dramatic interpretation of the selection. *I've Got A Tailor-Made Coat* can be interpreted in a Chamber Theatre style because it has a first person narrator and many possibilities for physical action.

FROM

A ROPE AGAINST THE SUN

by Al Pittman

PLAYBILL

This is a play for voices. It is set in a small town located on the coast of Newfoundland. The characters are townsfolk, children, and voices from the past. Your reading should focus on creating an atmosphere appropriate to the material.

As explored in "Choral Dramatization," more than one actor can take on the role of the narrator. The lines spoken by "Voice" can be delivered by a chorus, or several actors—portraying different characters—can divide Voice's lines among themselves. Note how the children's nursery rhymes can add a ritual quality to the reading.

Narrator: Whenever Jake Connors walks past the graveyard on the hill, which is something he does every morning of his gray-haired days, he thinks of Herb Follett and smiles to himself. Herb Follett had been a friend of Jake's. He died of gunshot wounds a few years back.

Voice: Found him dead this morning.

Voice: Dead?

Voice: In the turnip cellar.

Voice: Dead? In the turnip cellar?

Voice: Shot himself with his own twelve gauge.

Voice: Shot his ownself in the turnip cellar?

Voice: Suicide.

Voice: Suicide in the turnip cellar.

Voice: Poor old Herb.

Voice: Not a very Christian thing to do.

Voice: Poor old fellow.

Voice: Not a very Catholic thing to do.

Voice: Dead and gone.

Voice: Sure now they won't bury him in the graveyard even.

Voice: Not likely. Poor old soul.

Voice: Imagine that now.

Voice: Poor old Herb, dead.

Voice: May he rest in peace.

Voice: In the turnip cellar?

Narrator: So, in accordance with the wishes of Holy Mother Church, Herb was buried by a clump of birches just outside the barbed wire fence that marked the boundary of the consecrated soil. Then one year Father Power came, full of ambition for his new parish, and decreed that the graveyard must be expanded. And since that time Herb Follett's remains have lain smack dab centre of the holy ground, birches and all. Old Jake, as usual, takes notice of the birches waving in the wind up there on the hill and smiles to himself.

Jake: They should of knowed better than to try and keep Herb Follett out of any place he had a mind to go into

Narrator: chuckles Jake as he tips his hat in benediction to his old friend.

. . .

Narrator: The sun is higher now. The fog is farther out to sea. . . . The sheep are about the hills. The dogs have tired of teasing them and now lie sprawled about the yards or in the road. The children are about their games, scratching their strange patterns in the gravel with sticks, or skipping stones on the quiet harbor waters, or pretending to be fish-killers and skippers. . . . They see Jake making his slow easy way up the hill and greet him as they do every day.

Children: Old Jake Connors is no good
Chop him up for firewood
If the fire do not burn
Turn him into a big fat worm.

Narrator: There was a time when Jake would have chased after them and taught them something about minding their manners, but at that time there would have been no need. At that time, the children played at make-believing they were Jake Connors, skipper of the Swallow, and most renowned fish-killer in the bay. At that time, they'd try to walk like he did, and wear their caps like he wore his, perched ever so precisely on the side of his head. At that time, they wouldn't be calling him names and making so much fun of him. But now it is different, just like everything else is different. And besides, old Jake is too slowed up with age and rheumatiz to catch them, even if he cared to.

Children: Old Jake Connors is no good
Chop him up for firewood

Jake: Brazen little brats, the whole crowd of ye

Narrator: mutters Jake and goes on up the hill. The children are once more about their games. From around corners, and over hills you can hear them shouting and whispering, laughing and crying, screaming and singing.

Children: In comes the doctor
In comes the nurse
In comes the woman
With the big brown purse
Go away doctor
Go away nurse
Go away woman
With the big brown purse.

Child: Where's Peter gone to? I can't find him nowhere.

Child: Maybe he's gone home.

Child: Maybe he's hiding somewhere.

Child: Maybe the devil got him.

Child: Took him away.

Child: Et him all up.

Child: Maybe he got et up by a ghost.

Child: Old Man Follett's ghost.

Child: Ghosts don't eat people up.

Child: Protestant ghosts do.

Child: Old Man Follett wasn't no protestant.

Child: He killed he's self though. It's the same thing.

Child: Maybe he just went astray. Never got et up at all.

Child: Let's go look for him then.

Child: Where will we look?

Child: Up in the graveyard.

Child: Not me.

Child: No sir, not me neither.

Child: Scaredy cat!

Child: I ain't. I just got to go home is all.

Child: Got to go home cause you're a scaredy cat.

Children: Scaredy cat. Scaredy cat. Scaredy cat.

Narrator: There is no moon tonight to light the dark picket-fenced lanes. No moon to light the way from house to house. No moon or stars or light of any kind to break the monotony of the darkness that deepens as it stretches from hour to blacker hour. The children, who but moments ago were annoying hell out of Old Jake Connors with their noises, exhausted now by their daylong fantasies, are tucked away in the darkness of their haunted bedrooms. In the corridors and caverns of their sleep they run motionless from their private terrors. Butterflies as big as houses. Dragonflies with teeth like pitchforks. Shadows that devour childflesh. Or they fall suspended from the tops of cliffs or slip slowly into whirlpools of gnashing devils.

ACTIVITIES

1. Examine all the opportunities the script offers for choral speaking. Refer to the techniques, explained in the previous chapter, of creating effective images by the use of vocal expression and combinations of voices.

2. As mentioned in The Program to this chapter, you should develop effective visual images to enhance your reading. Look for opportunities where the "tableau" effect can be created, and be sure to see that spacing and grouping are effectively used, and that people are placed on a variety of levels. Are there opportunities in this script where the visual images can be changed?

THE LAST NIGHT OF THE WORLD

by Ray Bradbury

PLAYBILL

This is a complete short story, and it can be effectively dramatized as Readers Theatre. Unlike *A Rope Against the Sun*, the lines in this selection have not been divided for you. Where to divide the lines is the first decision your group will have to make. As you read through the story be aware of the number of voices the story will need, and how the lines can be best divided among those voices. Be aware that the lines of narrative can be dealt with in ways other than just having a narrator speak them.

"What would you do if you knew that this was the last night of the world?"

"What would I do? You mean seriously?"

"Yes, seriously."

"I don't know. I hadn't thought."

He poured some coffee. In the background the two girls were playing blocks on the parlor rug in the light of the green hurricane lamps. There was an easy, clean aroma of the brewed coffee in the evening air.

"Well, better start thinking about it," he said.

"You don't mean it!"

He nodded.

"A war?"

He shook his head.

"Not the hydrogen or atom bomb?"

"No."

"Or germ warfare?"

"None of those at all," he said, stirring his coffee slowly. "But just, let's say, the closing of a book."

"I don't think I understand."

"No, nor do I, really; it's just a feeling. Sometimes it frightens me, sometimes I'm not frightened at all but at peace." He glanced in at the girls and their yellow hair shining in the lamplight. "I didn't say anything to you. It first happened about four nights ago."

"What?"

"A dream I had. I dreamed that it was all going to be over, and a voice said it was. Not any kind of voice I can remember, but a voice anyway, and it said things would stop here on Earth. I didn't think too much about it the next day, but then I went to the office and caught Stan Willis looking out the window in the middle of the afternoon, and I said a penny for your thoughts, Stan, and he said, I had a dream last night, and before he even told me the dream I knew what it was. I could have told him, but he told me and I listened to him."

"It was the same dream?"

"The same: I told Stan I had dreamed it too. He didn't seem surprised. He relaxed, in fact. Then we started walking through the office. It wasn't planned. We didn't say, 'Let's walk around.' We just walked on our own, and everywhere we saw people looking at their desks or their hands or out windows. I talked to a few. So did Stan."

"And they all had dreamed?"

"All of them. The same dream, with no difference."

"Do you believe in it?"

"Yes. I've never been more certain."

"And when will it stop? The world, I mean."

"Sometime during the night for us, and then as the night goes on around the world, that'll go too. It'll take twenty-four hours for it all to go."

They sat awhile not touching their coffee. Then they lifted it slowly and drank, looking at each other.

"Do we deserve this?" she said.

"It's not a matter of deserving; it's just that things didn't work out. I notice you didn't even argue about this. Why not?"

"I guess I've a reason," she said.

"The same one everyone at the office had?"

She nodded slowly. "I didn't want to say anything. It happened last night. And the women on the block talked about it, among themselves, today. They dreamed. I thought it was only a coincidence." She picked up the evening paper. "There's nothing in the paper about it."

"Everyone knows, so there's no need."

He sat back in his chair, watching her. "Are you afraid?"

"No. I always thought I would be, but I'm not."

"Where's that spirit called self-preservation they talk so much about?"

"I don't know. You don't get too excited when you feel things are logical. This is logical. Nothing else but this could have happened from the way we've lived."

"We haven't been too bad, have we?"

"No, nor enormously good. I suppose that's the trouble—we haven't been very much of anything except us, while a big part of the world was busy being lots of quite awful things."

The girls were laughing in the parlor.

"I always thought people would be screaming in the streets at a time like this."

"I guess not. You don't scream about the real thing."

"Do you know, I won't miss anything but you and the girls. I never liked cities or my work or anything except you three. I won't miss a thing except perhaps the change in the weather, and a glass of ice water when it's hot, and I might miss sleeping. How can we sit here and talk this way?"

"Because there's nothing else to do."

"That's it, of course; for if there were, we'd be doing it. I suppose this is the first time in the history of the world that everyone has known just what they were going to do during the night."

"I wonder what everyone else will do now, this evening, for the next few hours."

"Go to a show, listen to the radio, watch television, play cards, put the children to bed, go to bed themselves, like always."

They sat a moment and then he poured himself another coffee. "Why do you suppose it's tonight?"

"Because."

"Why not some other night in the last century, or five centuries ago, or ten?"

"Maybe it's because it was never October 19, 1989, ever before in history, and now it is and that's it; because this date means more than any other date ever meant; because it's the year when things are as they are all over the world and that's why it's the end."

"There are bombers on their schedules both ways across the ocean tonight that'll never see land."

"That's part of the reason why."

"Well," he said, getting up, "what shall it be? Wash the dishes?"

They washed the dishes and stacked them away with special neatness. At eight thirty the girls were put to bed and kissed good night and the little lights by their beds turned on and the door left open just a trifle.

"I wonder," said the husband, coming from the bedroom and glancing back, standing there with his pipe for a moment.

"What?"

"If the door will be shut all the way, or if it'll be left just a little ajar so some light comes in."

"I wonder if the children know."

"No, of course not."

They sat and read the papers and talked and listened to some radio music and then sat together by the fireplace watching the charcoal embers as the clock struck ten thirty and eleven and eleven thirty. They thought of all the other people in the world who had spent their evening, each in his own special way.

"Well," he said at last.

He kissed his wife for a long time.

"We've been good for each other, anyway."

"Do you want to cry?" he asked.

"I don't think so."

They moved through the house and turned out the lights and went into the bedroom and stood in the night cool darkness undressing and pushing back the covers. "The sheets are so clean and nice."

"I'm tired."

"We're *all* tired."

They got into bed and lay back.

"Just a moment," she said.

He heard her get out of bed and go into the kitchen. A moment later, she returned. "I left the water running in the sink," she said.

Something about this was so very funny that he had to laugh.

She laughed with him, not knowing what it was that she had done that was funny. They stopped laughing at last and lay in their cool night bed, their hands clasped, their heads together.

"Good night," he said, after a moment.

"Good night," she said.

ACTIVITIES

1. As you make decisions about your Readers Theatre dramatization of this story, consider the following: the use of tableau to provide visual images, background music to enhance the mood, the use of masks, costume pieces and props, and the opportunities available for choral speech.

2. Using improvisation, carry this selection one scene further.

3. Investigate other science fiction stories which would lend themselves to Readers Theatre dramatizations.

I GOT A TAILOR-MADE COAT

by Alvin Lewis Curry, Jr.

PLAYBILL

As explained in The Program to this chapter, this selection can be interpreted in the Chamber Theatre style. One person can read the selection while others "act out" the scenes and characters being described. Be aware of the effect that the capitalization of the speeches has on line delivery. Also, look for opportunities to incorporate choral speaking in the dramatization.

"I GOT A TAILOR-MADE COAT". . . . i yelled to my Mother as she picked up the Dirt from the Kitchen Floor with the Dustpan.

"YOU SPEND ALL YOUR MONEY ON NUTHIN'
BUT FOOLISHNESS. . . . I GAVE YOU MY
LAST HARD-EARNED MONEY. . . TO BUY SOME CHEAP
PANTS AND SHOES. . . AND I TOLD YOU TO GET
A HAIRCUT! YOU LOOK LIKE A HIPPIE WITH
ALL THAT HAIR ON YOUR HEAD. . . BUT YOU
COME BACK HERE WITH A TAILOR-MADE COAT
. . . YOU

AIN'T WORTH THE BLANKET I BROUGHT YOU
HOME FROM THE HOSPITAL IN!!!"

yelled my mother as she washed the Dishes with a Cigarette in her Mouth.

I don't care what she says as long
as i got my TAILOR-MADE COAT.

I carefully buttoned up my TAILOR-MADE COAT and walked proudly down the Block, stopping and looking around, so i could give the Boys on the Corner enough time to look at my "TAILOR-MADE COAT." I finally got to the Store and stood in front in case anybody wanted to come up and ask me where i got my Coat from. . . . nobody came so i just went in the Store.

"GIMME A LARGE COKE."

i said as i carefully took my Coat off and held it out so he could see the Label on the inside . . . then he would know my Coat was expensive.

"WHAT KIND OF COAT IS THAT?" the man behind the counter asked me while ringing up Seventeen-Cents for the Coke.

"OH! THIS COAT . . . YOU MEAN THIS COAT? . . . IT's JUST A TAILOR-MADE COAT . . . AND IT COST ME SIXTY-NINE DOLLARS AT MACY'S . . . BUT YOU COULD GET ONE CHEAPER, MINE IS TAILOR-MADE!" i answered.

He wasn't very interested, so i just walked out the Store sipping my Coke and feeling rejected.

I love my Tailor-made Coat . . . i hope i never
have to throw it away! i can tell it
likes me too!

Me and my Coat went to the Park and we sat down and i put the Coke bottle in it to keep warm, and i counted all the Buttons on it to make sure they were still there!

When me and my Coat got home i took it off (gently so i wouldn't hurt it)

and i folded it up and put it to bed in my closet, i sung a lullabye to it before i went to sleep and i dreamed that people from all over came to see "MY TAILOR-MADE COAT" . . . and they had to pay to get in!

I woke up in the Morning and opened up the Door to my Closet to say good Morning to my Coat . . . . and it was *GONE, GONE!!* GONE! . . Somebody put their Hairy Hands in my Closet and stole my Tailor-made Coat . . . that's what they did they stole! my "TAILOR-MADE COAT" . . .

I ran downstairs and grabbed a knife, a baseballbat, a hammer and a big rusty nail and I ran out the front door . . .

I never did find my "tailor-made coat"

I cried and I stomped and I kicked and I wouldn't eat for three days.

Now I got a "Tailor-Made Hat"
Ain't nobody gettin'
their hands on that!

ACTIVITIES

1. As you develop this selection, be aware that everything happens in the eyes of the speaker. Look for opportunities to show that things may not necessarily be as he describes them. For example, the mother is presented as a stereotype: she nags, appears slovenly, and spends her time housecleaning. What if she were exactly the opposite, someone considerate, taking pride in her appearance, and who has time for others? Because you create the physical action the son is describing, you have the opportunity to interpret the action in ways that are different from his description.

2. Improvise the scene which occurs when the speaker runs outside with a knife, baseball bat, hammer, and rusty nail. (Don't use props!)

3. Improvise a scene which might occur after the speaker gets "a tailor-made hat."

4. Investigate other stories which are first person narratives and adapt them to Chamber Theatre dramatizations.

WORKSHOP

1. Projects that enhance other areas of school life can be developed using the techniques of Readers Theatre and Chamber Theatre. Some examples are:
—dramatizing sections of novels in order to encourage other students to read the novels,
—dramatizing aspects of history for other classes,
—dramatizing newspaper accounts of current events.

2. Readers Theatre can be used to dramatize the reading of poetry. Choose a number of poems on a common theme, and develop a Readers Theatre dramatization of the poems.

3. Ceremonies for special days—Remembrance Day, Thanksgiving, assembly days—can be effectively presented using Chamber Theatre or Readers Theatre. On Remembrance Day, for example, first person accounts of the First and Second World Wars could make an interesting presentation.

4. Examine scripts in other sections of this book for possible dramatization in a Readers Theatre or Chamber Theatre format. "Charlie Wilson" in *The Farm Show* (Section A, Chapter 3) is written in an appropriate style, and *The Shadow Box* (Section A, Chapter 4) has similar qualities. Experiment with various scripts.

9: Story Theatre

THE PROGRAM

Story Theatre is another technique that allows you to dramatize material other than scripts. It is similar to Readers Theatre in that the material used contains both narration and dialogue; it is different because of the physical action. In Story Theatre, all the actions and movements in the story are played out. Materials which lend themselves best to Story Theatre are simple narratives such as myth, fable, legend, folk tale, stories from the oral tradition, and children's stories.

The basic technique of Story Theatre is that a person playing a role, in addition to saying aloud any of the dialogue assigned to his or her character, says aloud the character's thoughts and feelings as described in the narration. The character also does and says aloud any actions which he or she is described as doing in the narration.

A group that is beginning a selection in Story Theatre style will first have to determine how many parts there are in the story. (Often there are more parts than there are people, so there will have to be doubling or tripling of roles.) Second, the group will have to decide who says which lines, basing this decision on each character saying all the lines which pertain to that part. This will become difficult with lines that do not seem to apply to any particular part. An example might be: "The sun was shining." If you determine who observes this fact or who is affected by it, you can assign the line to that character and avoid using a narrator.

Story Theatre uses very simple staging. Settings and properties are kept to a minimum, and capes and hats and other costume pieces are all that are needed in addition to ordinary clothing. Since the characters have the descriptive power of the narration to enhance their actions, Story Theatre can be played anywhere—a park, a gym, or a classroom.

Story Theatre can be made even more lively and energetic with the addition of songs and dances. It is also an ideal format for older students to use when performing for younger students.

The selections in this chapter will provide you with opportunities to develop the techniques of Story Theatre. *Two Crows* is an actual Story Theatre script from the Broadway production of *Story Theatre,* a play that is a collection of fables and stories; *The Wolf and the Lamb* and *The Owl Who Was God* are two fables which adapt well to Story Theatre format. *The Seven Skinny Goats* is a children's story which would be appropriate for younger audiences. (Remember that you must get the publisher's permission if you are going to perform this material for an audience.)

TWO CROWS

adapted by Paul Sills

PLAYBILL

This production script from the Broadway run of *Story Theatre* provides an example of how a simple fable is adapted to this format. Notice how each character says the dialogue and the narration which applies to his or her role. Also be aware of how much physical action each character does to elaborate the story. As you work with this script, concentrate on your actions, and attempt to create convincing crow-like characters through voice and movement.

Characters
First Crow
Second Crow

*(*FIRST CROW *enters left, crosses downstage centre, stomps on mussel.)*

First Crow: According to Aesop, there was once a crow who found a mussel on the beach. But he couldn't, for the life of him, open the shell to get at the fish.

*(*SECOND CROW *enters upstage right, crosses downstage centre, right of centre stage.)*

Second Crow: A brother crow, seeing this, said, "Caw, you're doing it all wrong."

First Crow: Oh?

Second Crow: Yes, if I were you I'd take it up to about ten thousand feet and drop it here on these rocks.

(They look from one to another, to the mussel, and up to the sky. FIRST CROW *circles counterclockwise.* FIRST CROW *picks up the mussel and starts to fly upward.)*

Higher. Higher. Higher. All right, now drop it. (FIRST CROW *drops the mussel, it cracks open.*) It worked! (SECOND CROW *quickly eats it and then flies off upstage right.* FIRST CROW *flies downstage centre.)*

ACTIVITIES

1. Since much of the material done in Story Theatre form is drawn from fables, you should concentrate on creating convincing animal characters. For this selection, explore all the ways in which you can suggest a crow. Find appropriate ways of speaking and moving which will develop the image of a crow. Use costume pieces (a peaked baseball cap?) to enhance the image.

2. It is important to remember when doing Story Theatre that you should not "drop character" when you are speaking lines of narration. Keep the character's voice and movements when you are describing your actions. The first speech of this script will give you an opportunity to practise this technique.

3. What would be an appropriate moral for this fable? Invent a moral, and have the first crow deliver it at the end of the scene.

THE WOLF AND THE LAMB

An Aesop fable retold by Ann McGovern

PLAYBILL

This selection requires that you divide the narration and dialogue between the two characters and create a script similar to *Two Crows.* After making your decisions, practise the piece, developing the animal characters through voice and action.

One day a Wolf met a Lamb who had strayed from the fold. The Wolf resolved not to kill the Lamb without a good excuse that would justify his right to eat him.

So he said, "Ah, you are the Lamb who insulted me so harshly last year."

"Indeed no," bleated the Lamb. "A year ago I was not yet born."

The Wolf tried again. "Then you must be the Lamb that feeds in my pasture."

"No, good sir," the Lamb protested, "I have not yet tasted grass."

"Well," snapped the Wolf, "then you are the Lamb who drinks from my well."

"No!" exclaimed the Lamb, "I have no need of water, for my mother's milk is both food and drink to me."

Seizing the Lamb, the Wolf snarled, "I will have my supper—even though you deny every one of my accusations!" As the Lamb struggled to be free, he thought, "*Any excuse will serve a tyrant.*"

ACTIVITIES

1. After you have divided the lines between the characters, rehearse the script you have created. Pay attention to elaborating your lines with actions that are wolf-like or lamb-like.

2. Explore a number of possible ways of delivering the moral. Do not overlook the possibility of choral speaking.

3. Experiment with the fable by changing the characters. How does the fable change if the characters are an owl and a mouse, a lion and an antelope, or two people?

THE OWL WHO WAS GOD

by James Thurber

PLAYBILL

The previous two selections provided opportunities to explore the techniques of Story Theatre. This fable will permit you to use those techniques in a longer selection with a great many characters. Examine the text for the number of roles available, remembering that sometimes you may have to play more than one role. Once the roles are set, the group must divide the lines according to which role the lines apply to. As you do this, do not overlook opportunities for choral speaking.

Once upon a starless midnight there was an owl who sat on the branch of an oak tree. Two ground moles tried to slip quietly by, unnoticed. "You!" said the owl. "Who?" they quavered, in fear and astonishment, for they could not believe it was possible for anyone to see them in that darkness. "You two!" said the owl. The moles hurried away and told the other creatures of the field and forest that the owl was the greatest and wisest of all animals because he could see in the dark and because he could answer any question. "I'll see about that," said a secretary bird, and he called on the owl one night when it was again very dark. "How many claws am I holding up?" said the secretary bird. "Two," said the owl, and that was right. "Can you give me another expression for 'that is to say' or 'namely'?" asked the secretary bird. "To wit," said the owl. "Why does a lover call on his love?" asked the secretary bird. "To woo," said the owl.

The secretary bird hastened back to the other creatures and reported that the owl was indeed the greatest and wisest animal in the world because he could see in the dark and because he could answer any question. "Can he see in the daytime, too?" asked a red fox. "Yes," echoed a dormouse and a French poodle. "Can he see in the daytime too?" All the other creatures laughed loudly at this silly question, and they set upon the red fox and his friends and drove them out of the region. Then they sent a messenger to the owl and asked him to be their leader.

When the owl appeared among the animals it was high noon and the sun was shining brightly. He walked very slowly, which gave him an appearance of great dignity, and he peered about him with large, staring eyes, which gave him an air of tremendous importance. "He's God!" screamed a Plymouth Rock hen. And the others took up the cry "He's God!" So they followed him wherever he went and when he began to bump into things they began to bump into things, too. Finally he came to a concrete highway and he started up the middle of it and all the other creatures followed him. Presently a hawk, who was acting as outrider, observed a truck coming toward them at fifty miles an hour, and he reported to the secretary bird and the secretary bird reported to the owl. "There's danger ahead," said the secretary bird. "To wit?" said the owl. The secretary bird told him. "Aren't you afraid?" he asked. "Who?" said the owl calmly, for he could not see the truck. "He's God!" cried all the creatures again, and they were still crying "He's God!" when the truck hit them and ran them down. Some of the animals were merely injured, but most of them, including the owl, were killed.

MORAL: YOU CAN FOOL TOO MANY OF THE PEOPLE TOO MUCH OF THE TIME.

ACTIVITIES

1. Once your group has determined the roles and divided the lines accordingly, you should concentrate on developing physical action to interpret the fable dramatically. These actions should enhance the story, but you must make sure that the story always remains the focus. As you rehearse the material, have one person watch the action for any activities which distract from plot development.

2. As discussed in Chapter 7, choral speaking can enhance any dramatic interpretation. Examine the script carefully for opportunities for choral work. Any narrative which describes the actions of a group of characters can be spoken chorally, and passages of narration which do not pertain to a particular character would benefit from choral speaking.

3. Use masks, costume pieces, and properties to add theatricality to your interpretation and characterizations.

THE SEVEN SKINNY GOATS

By Victor G. Ambrus

PLAYBILL

This is the text of a story taken from a children's picture book. The Story Theatre technique will

The Innkeeper was the happiest man in his town. He owned seven fine fat goats and he was very, very proud of them.

One morning a boy called Jano passed by. He was a simple lad, with nothing in his pockets but his flute, which he played for his living. Sometimes, when he was hungry, he did other jobs as well.

He asked the Innkeeper if he could mind his goats for a lump of cheese and an onion a day; and the Innkeeper agreed.

Jano took the goats to the meadow, sat down, and ate his cheese and onion. Then he took out his flute.

As soon as he started to play, the goats began to dance. They were so busy dancing they did not eat a single blade of grass.

By the time they returned home, the goats looked a sorry sight. The Innkeeper stared at them in astonishment and demanded to know what had happened. Jano explained that he had only taken them to the meadow and had even played them a tune to keep them happy.

The Innkeeper was very angry and decided to find out for himself what was happening to his goats.

So next morning, he got up early.

When Jano set out with the goats, the Innkeeper followed secretly, and waited behind a bush to see what happened.

Jano sat down and ate his cheese and onion. Then he began to play a tune. The goats immediately stood up on their hindlegs and started to dance.

Before the Innkeeper could get over his surprise, he kicked left, kicked right, and in a moment had joined the goats in their dance.

The eight of them romped around the meadow and Jano, who thought they were enjoying themselves, went on playing with all his might.

When Jano finally stopped playing, the Innkeeper, all out of breath, pounced on him and rushed him straight to the Judge.

There, he told how under Jano's care his seven fat goats had become the seven skinniest goats in town, and demanded that Jano should be punished.

The Judge looked at the goats and certainly they were the skinniest goats he had ever seen. So he sentenced Jano to be put in a barrel by the Executioner and rolled down the steepest hill out of the town.

When the townsfolk heard of this, they came flocking to the hill.

After they put Jano in the barrel, the Judge asked him, kindly: "Well, my boy, have you any last wishes?" "Just to play one tune on my flute, please, your Honor," said Jano.

"Very well," agreed the Judge.

But the Innkeeper shouted in a panic: "Don't let him play again, whatever you do! Or at least tie me to a tree, first."

But nobody took any notice of him, and Jano began to play. All the people leapt about and started dancing in earnest.

The Innkeeper kicked right, kicked left, and shouted in despair: "I knew this would happen. I knew this would happen."

And the people shouted back at him: "If you knew it, why didn't you say so!" HOP, HOP. "If you knew it, why didn't you say so!" HOP, HOP.

Jano thought they were enjoying themselves since they kept on dancing, so he went on playing until at last they all fell to the ground, exhausted.

Then the Judge pulled himself together, and gasped:

"Get out of here, young man, and never, never come back again."

Jano could see that the Judge was angry, although he had danced as hard as anyone. So he took to his heels and ran. He thought the people of this town were very odd indeed, and he was glad not to be rolled out of town in a barrel.

"No matter how hungry I am," he vowed, "I will never again go into a town where they don't appreciate good music."

allow you to dramatize the complete story, including the pictures. After determining the roles and allocating the lines, rehearse the material with a view to sharing it with an audience of young people.

ACTIVITIES

1. This story provides opportunities to utilize all the techniques of Story Theatre dramatization. You have to create human and animal characteristics, develop all the physical action described in the narration, and say aloud all the narration and dialogue. In addition, there are numerous scenes in this story in which you will have to clearly indicate the setting. Having done so, you will have to develop actions to show the transitions between these scenes. One technique for doing this transition work is to find actions that will help an audience know when a setting and scene are changing.

2. Story Theatre can be staged in many different locations. If you are going to present this story, consider staging it in a gymnasium, outdoors, on a large wagon, or in a regular classroom. How will the location affect your staging?

3. Consider developing further adventures for Jano through improvisation. Topics for you to consider are: Jano joins an orchestra, Jano goes to school, Jano rides the subway or bus.

WORKSHOP

1. If you are going to prepare presentations for children in elementary school, investigate children's literature and picture-books which can be dramatized through Story Theatre techniques. Discuss with teachers which stories children enjoy most and prepare Story Theatre presentations of that material. You should also try presenting stories with which children are not familiar, in order to see how intriguing you can make your performance.

2. When performing Story Theatre, try doing it "in-the-round"—that is, with the audience sitting all around a circular stage area. If you use this staging technique, you will have to be sure that the whole audience can hear the important dialogue and see the significant actions. You will have to re-think the blocking of the material, but you will gain the advantage of having the audience closer to you and more involved in the action.

10: Scripting

THE PROGRAM

The previous chapters of this section were explorations of ways in which other forms of writing can be dramatized. In this chapter, you will explore ways of creating your own original scripts.

Chapter 1 of this book includes this statement: "Script is the branch of literature which is the easiest to identify, since it has a shape and form which make it distinct." But this shape and form can vary greatly. Section A contains various script forms; you will see that scripts can be elaborate combinations of dialogue and stage directions (*Count Dracula* and *The Real Inspector Hound*, for example) or simply lines of dialogue on a page (*After Liverpool* and *Us and Them*). Section C contains examples of how script form has changed over the years. However, as you survey the vast range of scripts available in this book, you will find that most of them contain common elements: some form of dialogue, some indication of the character speaking, some direction as to significant actions, some sense of plot and some development in the characters.

A script usually begins by introducing the characters and indicating the plot. It advances by adding complications to the plot until these complications are resolved by a crisis or climax, and the play or scene ends in a way which settles past conflicts and indicates future directions for the characters. Of course, playwrights ignore or change this formula as often as they follow it. However, it is a good base on which to build your script.

Creating a script, or scripting, can be approached in two ways: as an opportunity for individuals to write scenes for performance, or as a group activity in which polished improvisations are scripted. You should try both approaches.

The individual method calls for one writer, but the group is still part of the process because the writer observes the group's interpretation of the script, and then edits and polishes the script on the basis of the problems that arise when the script is rehearsed. You will find that conveying ideas only through dialogue is not easy. However, not every attempt at scripting must become a polished piece of work.

As the writer, you can create any kind of script. You can be entirely original, or, by reading between the lines, you can turn the narration from a story into dialogue, or extend a story that you have read. Writing scripts requires and develops an understanding of the playwright's task and of the power of dialogue.

The group method combines spoken and written exploration, with the emphasis on oral composition. Working in groups, you can focus on a problem taken from a story, a poem, or a newspaper article, re-enact the problem, and role-play the dialogue. The selections in this chapter will provide opportunities to experiment with this method of script creation. Scripts in this book which were developed in this way are *Juve* (Section A, Chapter 1), *What Glorious Times They Had* (Section A, Chapter 1), *The Farm Show*, (Section A, Chapter 3), *1837: The Farmer's Revolt* (Section A, Chapter 4), and *The Serpent* (Section C, Chapter 16).

Here are steps you can follow for creating a script through group improvisation:

1. As a group, read and discuss the chosen selection. Determine the number of characters and the setting or settings of the story. Decide if you will write a script about the whole story, about part of the story, or about something that goes beyond the story.

2. Having chosen the roles each of you will play, improvise the story several times. Try to stay as true to the original selection as you can. After each improvisation check the story for important aspects you may have missed and for details which you may have changed.

3. When you are satisfied with your improvisation of the story, act it out again, recording it with a tape recorder. Play back the recording to be sure that it is satisfactory.

4. With everyone sharing the task, play back the tape again, stopping it to write down the dialogue as it is said. Be sure your notes indicate which character is speaking each line.

5. Write or type a good copy of the script, and make copies for each group member. Read the script aloud several times, and make any changes you feel are necessary for clarity and effectiveness.

6. Rewrite or type a final copy of the script. To test its effectiveness you can give your script to another group to perform. After this group has rehearsed, you can watch and discuss this interpretation of your script.

While the selections that follow work very well for the group method of script creation, each could also be transposed into script form by an individual playwright.

FROM

THE PIONEER YEARS

by Barry Broadfoot

PLAYBILL

Each of the following selections is a true account of events that happened to people involved in the settlement of the western prairies during the years 1900 to 1914. The selections were taken from the book *The Pioneer Years* by Barry Broadfoot. Broadfoot edited the stories from the tape recordings of his conversations with the pioneers. Another Broadfoot book about the great depression—*Ten Lost Years*—was recently the basis of a highly successful stage production.

I Wanted to Get Off That Farm

I was 16 and my father's hired man because he couldn't afford a man. So there I was, a girl of 16 doing a man's work. Or supposed to be. I hated every minute of it and the work was so heavy it was turning me into a man more than a girl. But I had to do it. There was no other way for it.

So one day we're building a stack of stooks in the field by the road and a man in a buggy comes along. He stops and asks where he can find such-and-such a girl for she'd agreed to work on his farm during the stooking and the threshing. His name was Mr. Honey and he was from Binscarth. I told him and he went down the road. Soon he came back and said the girl had left for another job the day before, and would I like the job? He said it would take a month to clean up his place, and I knew by that that he had a real big farm. I forget how many sections he and his boys farmed, but they had their own threshing outfit and crew. He said if I came he would pay me 20 dollars a month. Well, 20 dollars a month was a very fine wage in those days. Real good pay.

I knew I would have to work very hard, up before five in the morning, cooking, baking, but he said there would be a girl of 14 to help me and a boy of 16 who would do heavy work. You see, his wife was dead so I would be in charge.

I'd have given anything to get off our farm, so I thought quickly and I said to Dad that if he let me go I would give him the 20 dollars that I earned and he could hire a full-bodied man while I was away and get twice the work done. I said he might even have some money left over.

My father didn't care much for me, he just wanted the work out of me, so he said all right, if I gave him the 20 dollars I could go. You know, of course, that meant I would be working 15 hours a day, six days a week, for a month for nothing. But that's how much I wanted to get off that farm. So I ran to the house and I gathered up my few belongings and got into Mr. Honey's buggy and away we went. As we drove away I was thinking that just an hour ago I had been sweating in the field pitching those sheaves and that I had an ingrown toenail which was making me squirm and hurt and Father was yelling at me and now I was in a fine democrat and going off to a big farm and my first job.

Every Saturday afternoon Mr. Honey would come into the kitchen and he'd say, "May, come and trim my whiskers." I had to get the clippers and trim his whiskers and his hair; then he'd put on a white shirt and he'd ride away for the weekend. The first time it happened I said to his daughter, the 14-year-old, I said that her father had a woman, sure as the dickens. She said, "Don't be foolish." But that December she wrote to me and said her father was getting married. A Miss Tibbetts from Foxwarren.

Then next summer he came back for me to work for him, and I told him that I would have thought that now that he was married his wife would be doing all the work. He said, "Oh no. My wife can't make the bread and make the butter and make the meals for a bunch of men like you can." So I went with him that year again and got 20 dollars. I gave it to my father again.

ACTIVITIES

1. Part of the art of scriptwriting is finding those parts of a story which have dramatic potential. After reading this story, examine it for small scenes within it which could be improvised and then scripted using the technique outlined in The Program to this chapter. A suggestion is the negotiation between the narrator and her father over Mr. Honey's first offer of employment. Your group should focus on creating the background and atmosphere of the farm before Mr. Honey arrives.

2. Experiment with the individual method of playwriting by choosing a short segment of this story and writing the dialogue which might have occurred. Some suggestions are: Mr. Honey asking the narrator to work for him, Mr. Honey and the narrator during the buggy ride away from the farm, the narrator and Mr. Honey's daughter talking after Mr. Honey has gone out on Saturday night. As you write, keep in mind that these events occurred before the First World War, so current language usage would not be appropriate.

The Hard Way to Finish High School

It was perfectly scandalous how some of those important people in town used to take advantage of the farm girls.

We lived too far out of town to go back and forth every day, but we did want our education. We had to have it if we were going to ever get a good job in Winnipeg in an office or a business, so we had to attend high school. In those days most farmers were poor and my father just couldn't afford to pay my room and board in town, but there was one way of doing it. A family in town would take you in and you would look after their children and do a bit of work and you could go to high school.

I wanted to get the last two grades that I needed, so this family agreed to give me a place. I won't say who it was but it was in Strathclair and it could have been the home of a banker, a lawyer, doctor, a businessman. People with big homes who needed a bit of help. The woman told my mother: "Oh yes, we'll give Belle a good home and treat her like one of us."

You had to get up early and make breakfast for the family. When you came home from school at lunch you had to make lunch and there were the breakfast dishes all cold and dirty in the sink waiting for you. Back to school and home to do dinner and there were the lunch dishes in the sink. So after dinner you did the dinner dishes along with the lunch dishes and then cleaned up the baby and did some washing and some cleaning and other things and I don't know what not. You were a slave. That's what you were. All these fine people in their fine homes and they treated you like a slave. It's a wonder you could stick it out for the year, but you had to. Then next year they'd get somebody else to do their dirty work. It went on all the time.

How was a person able to do the studies? You had to do that, you know. There was always plenty of homework and nobody got out of it.

And I remember another thing about that fine house. I had beautiful hair, lovely, lovely hair. Dark brown and it used to just shine. I went home for Sunday dinner not too long after I started at this house and I was scratching my head. My mother asked me what was the matter and I said that I was itchy. Mother said, "Come over here." Lice. Just full of lice. It was that bad that Mother just took the foot of that long hair and brought it over this way and cut a huge chunk of it right off. And then we had this heater and she took that hair and shook it over that heat and those lice, you can't imagine how many, they just fell in and burned to death.

That's the kind of a house those people had. But I had to go back. I had to get that year and I had to stay someplace, but by God I worked. And I never forgot how hard those people made me work either. Them, their fancy ways.

ACTIVITIES

1. Some of the scenes in this selection which could be explored for script writing by the group or individual methods are: the scene in which Belle and her mother talk to the woman of the house about the arrangements, followed by the scene which occurs after the mother leaves and the woman of the house explains the jobs that Belle will have to do; the scene in which Belle has her hair cut.

So We Got Married

I myself did this, so it is a true story that I am telling you.

My brother came out early. We're from Parry Sound and the farming was hard there. When he bought a farm south of Russell it was just a farm. A house, a poplar pole barn, and not much more and the family had no stock. They really weren't farmers and were going to Edson, which was supposed to be a new and booming town. The man thought that his old trade of shoemaker would be good. Cobblers don't make farmers, remember that. Farmers make farmers and thank the good Lord there are enough born into this world every year.

My brother, sure, he was a crab, as we'd say. Fifteen years older than I was, but he did get himself a wife. By advertisement. Oh, it was done a lot in them years. There were newspapers in Winnipeg and he put in this advertisement and got himself a wife, and in four years they had two youngsters. She was a Polish girl. Mary. Strong and of good soul.

My brother wrote me to come out and get my roots down in this district, but he expected me to work for nothing. It was no life, so I went into town and worked at one of the livery barns. I was 22 at the time. On Saturday night of my 22nd birthday, of that week, Mary came around to the barn and left me a birthday card.

Then Dan got all tangled up in a four-horse team and a breaking plough and that killed him. When he didn't come in Mary went out and saw the horses standing in the brush and she knew what happened. It took a couple of neighbors to get him loose. He was dead anyway. Bled to death, but I think he died of other things too because that 12-inch plough, the point, was in his side.

We had the funeral and it was put on by Dan's lodge, all the men. They wore black suits. It was held on a Sunday. Mary said, after all, it was no time to take a day off for a funeral. That was something I had never thought of, making all funerals on Sunday instead of Tuesdays or Thursdays or when the time was decent.

I drove Mary home. There was no people at the house. We were too far out and the cemetery was in town. There was cows to milk so I did the barn work and then I went up to the house. I wasn't going to set out the milk pans that night. I just put the milk into the pig trough and what was left I just threw away. You see, something was on my mind.

I went to the house and I asked Mary what her plans were. She said she had an aunt in Toronto and a married cousin someplace in New York and that seemed to be about it. I asked her if she was going to leave the farm and she said, "Where would I go?" She had been a governess or lady companion or both in Winnipeg for the Stratton family, but what could she do with two little kiddies?

So we had supper that night and when the kids were in bed I said that the best thing would be if I married her. I remember her saying, "Yes, I've been thinking that myself. We're the same age. Dan was too old for me and I think we can make it work. There's no reason why not. We shouldn't let Dan's death stop us, because there's this farm to run and I'd rather have people talking about our marriage any way they want to than have them talking behind my back about you living here and working on the farm." That's not really what she said but that's what she meant.

Next morning after chores I hitched up and we drove into town and got married. Nobody said anything. Nobody to this day. I went around to the livery barn and picked up my bedroll and my rifle and my chess board and a few other things. Then we went to the store and bought some things and then back to the farm and we were married people. I think that's all I need to tell.

Accidents happened. A woman couldn't be left on a farm alone and there were a lot of weddings, quick-like. I know that today people would be shocked. It just wasn't done. Even then, in the city, it wouldn't be done, but out in the bush, you just made up another set of rules and that's the way it was. I know several cases of men marrying their brothers' widows.

ACTIVITIES

1. A scene in this story which has dramatic potential occurs when, after the funeral, the narrator asks Mary to marry him. Notice that the narrator said "That's not really what she said, but that's what she meant." Can you, in a group improvisation or as an individual, re-create the scene as you think it happened, keeping in mind the feelings and thoughts of the people involved?

WORKSHOP

1. Practise interviewing people (friends, parents, relatives) about things that have happened to them. You will need a cassette tape recorder and a list of questions. (When you ask your questions be sure your subject provides detailed answers. This may involve some impromptu questions on your part.) After the interview, transcribe the most interesting material, leaving out your questions. Work on this transcription until your subject's story flows smoothly. You now have the basis for the dramatization of a true story. This technique will be of great value when you explore "Docudrama" (Section B, Chapter 12).

2. Original scripts can be created by cutting statements, headlines, and dialogue out of newspapers, magazines, and other print sources. After examining and ordering these statements, you can glue or tape them onto a large sheet of paper. After this script has been finalized, it can be interpreted using the techniques in Section A.

3. Investigate the techniques of the script writer by analysing productions of scripts in the theatre, in motion pictures, and on television. Pay particular attention to the ways in which the characters and situations are introduced, how complications emerge until the crisis or climax is reached, and how the complications are finally resolved. Did the playwright or scriptwriter have to use contrived events to resolve the dilemmas of the major characters? Examine some of the scripts in Section A, and determine the part of the play from which these scripts have been excerpted (introduction, complication, crisis, or resolution).

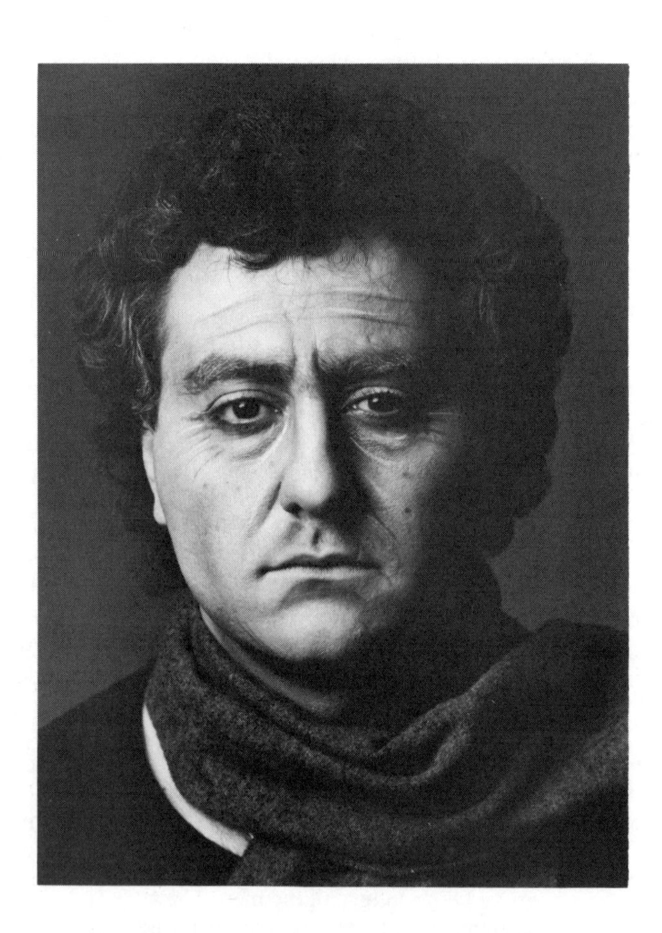

11: Anthology

THE PROGRAM

An anthology is a dramatization of several selections representing a variety of material (poems, stories, events, excerpts from novels, articles, and songs). These selections are chosen because they relate to a theme which the group wishes to explore. Other chapters in this section discuss techniques for dramatizing non-theatrical writing: "Choral Speaking," "Readers Theatre," "Chamber Theatre," "Story Theatre," and "Scripting." The first chapter in this section contains activities on how to organize selections in a dramatically effective order. Further opportunities for experimenting with the order of scenes follow *After Liverpool* (Section A, Chapter 2).

The steps generally used in creating an anthology presentation are as follows:

1. The group decides on the theme which they wish to explore dramatically. This theme can be general such as hate or love, or specific, such as why people fight. If the theme is general, it usually becomes more specific as the group decides which aspects of the theme they are most interested in. It is important to remember that choosing a theme is extremely difficult and should involve full discussion by all members of the group. There is no point in attempting to create something to which everyone is not committed.
2. After the theme is chosen, each group member is responsible for finding and bringing in material which relates to the theme in some significant way. Remember that this material can be drawn from a wide range of sources.
3. The group must next examine, discuss and analyse this material, retaining those things which it considers dramatically effective and setting aside anything which does not fit the theme. Choice of material at this point will depend on the length of the anthology, which can be anywhere from 10 minutes to a couple of hours.
4. After selecting the material, the group must decide on the order in which the material will be presented. Particular attention should be paid to a strong beginning and ending for the anthology.
5. Next, the group should begin to work with pieces of material. It is not necessary to work through the selections from beginning to end at this point. Rather, it is important to start interpreting the selections dramatically. All the techniques discussed so far in Section B work well in an anthology, and a variety of techniques should be used.
6. The next major problem is linking one selection to the next. Transitions are important because they provide continuity in the anthology. Since there will not be a plot or any main characters, the focus is on the anthology showing aspects of the theme in a way that is logical or dramatically powerful. Transitions can be effectively created through movement, song, recurring statements, improvisation, or any other means which will take the audience from one scene into the next.
7. At this point in rehearsal, some material may not be satisfactory and will have to be changed. You may want to rearrange some material. This is perfectly normal in the creative process, and analysis and discussion of these matters should be encouraged. Remember that you are involved in a group creative process, and that the perceptions of others are invaluable in helping to make the presentation the best it can be.
8. When the order of the selections has been agreed upon, pieces have been rehearsed, and transitions have been established, it is then time to work on the beginning and ending of the presentation. Remember that an effective beginning should state the theme in some way and draw the audience into the presentation. The ending should be a final statement of your group's thoughts and feelings about the theme and should leave the audience thinking about the presentation and its ideas.

The material given in this chapter is based on the theme of school-life and provides opportunities to explore the anthology concept. It is hoped that you will go on to create your own anthologies using the process outlined above.

PLAYBILL

The selections which follow are united in that they all deal with the theme of school. Other than this common theme, you will find that each piece differs from the others in style, content, genre, and attitude. There are scripts, poems, cartoons, excerpts from novels, and biographies. The theme is examined from the point of view of students and teachers in the past and in the future as well as in the present, and some selections consider the feelings of parents. Keep in mind as you examine this material that you do not have to dramatize all of a selection, nor do the selections have to follow the order in which the material is presented.

SCHOOL THIEF

by Dennis Potter

Miss Tillings: Somebody in this room is a thief!

(Silence)

Miss Tillings: Somebody—some wicked, wicked child—has stolen our lovely daffodil.

Class: Aaah!

Miss Tillings: Yes, our lovely daffodil. The one we've all watered and tended since the middle of March. Sit absolutely *still* every single one of you. Quite, quite still! I have my own ways of finding nasty little sneak-thieves.

(A long pause. MISS TILLINGS *stares hard round the class. The children try to keep their composure, scared of any movement which might be interpreted as guilt. Suddenly* NIGEL *can bear it no longer and his hands go up to his face)*

Miss Tillings: Stand up Nigel Barton!

*(*NIGEL *stands, head bowed in shame)*

Miss Tillings: Well, Nigel! Do you know anything about this? I can't believe it was you!

(At this last sentence, NIGEL *looks up, a faint hope glimmering)*

Nigel: No, Miss.

Miss Tillings: Then what do you know about it?

Nigel: I think—I think I might have had the daffodil, Miss.

Miss Tillings: (*Sharp*) *Might* have had it? What do you mean, boy! Come on, speak up.

Nigel: (*Twisting his head round*) I—I . . .

Miss Tillings: (*Menacingly*) *Well*?

Nigel: The stem was all broke, Miss. Somebody—somebody—*gave* it to me, Miss.

Miss Tillings: *Who* gave it to you?

Nigel: Um. I don't like to say, Miss . . .

Miss Tillings: You better had, Barton! And be quick about it!

Nigel: Georgie Pringle, Miss.

Class: Aaaah!

*(*GEORGIE *jerks up in indignant astonishment)*

Pringle: I never did!

Miss Tillings: Quiet Pringle! (*She advances on* NIGEL *almost cooing*) All right Nigel. Thank you. And where did Pringle give you this broken flower?

Nigel: By the bus stop, Miss. The stem was all broken. I thought I'd try to mend it.

Pringle: It's a lie! A lie!

Miss Tillings: You'd better be quiet, Pringle! Does anybody else know anything about this? Did anyone see Pringle with the flower? Anyone see him come back into the school last night?

First Boy: I saw him go back into the school, Miss.

Pringle: No, Miss no!

Miss Tillings: Quiet! Did you see him come out again?

First Boy: (*Regretfully*) N-no.

(The children sense blood and start to get nasty. There is an air of excitement. Eyes are gleaming)

Miss Tillings: *Somebody* must have seen him come out again. What about you, Bert. Or are you mixed up in it too?

Bert: (*Alarmed*) No, Miss. Not me, Miss.

Miss Tillings: Well? Was he with you? Did you see him come out?

*(*BERT *is nervous. He shoots glances at* GEORGIE*)*

Bert: Y-yes, Miss. He wasn't with *me*, Miss. I did see him come out, I mean.

*(*CLASS *lets out a deep sigh of satisfaction)*

Miss Tillings: (*Quickly*) And he had the daffodil in his hand, didn't he? Didn't he!

Bert: Yes, Miss.

Pringle: No, Bert! No!

Bert: In his left hand.

Girl: I saw him too, Miss.

Miss Tillings: Where did you see him?

Girl: (*Looking round for applause*) By the bread shop, Miss. And him had the daffodil, Miss. The stem was all broke, like Nigel says.

Miss Tillings: Come out to the front, Georgie Pringle!

Pringle: (*Tearful*) It ent true, none of it, Miss.

Miss Tillings: Come out to the front! (*Gently*) All right, Nigel, you can sit down now. Thank you for being so truthful.

Nigel: (*Smirk*) Thank you, Miss.

GOOD OLD DAYS AT SCHOOL

by Mrs. Walter M. Kiley

Talking about "Days of the Past," I started to teach school in Oxford County in Jan., 1906, after four months of training in the Woodstock Model School. My salary was $300 plus $20 to pay expenses of getting a boy to sweep and dust the school and start the fires in the winter time. The next year the Whitney government brought in a ruling of a minimum salary of $500 so our salaries went up considerably. However, our board bill was not very big.

It ranged from $1.25 to $1.50 for the five days. Cars had not appeared on the scene. I usually walked home to a little village about four miles distant from the school, returning on the Sunday evening with members of the family who had been at church.

If teachers ever get the idea their profession has seen few changes since the good old days, it might be wise for them to read this list of rules for teachers which was posted in the city of New York in 1872.

In fact, these nine regulations are good medicine for almost any one who feels down in the mouth.

Teachers each day will clean lamps, clean chimneys and trim wicks.

Each teacher will bring a bucket of water and a scuttle of coal for the day's session.

Make your pens carefully. You may whittle nibs to the individual tastes of the pupils.

Men teachers may take one evening each week for courting purposes or two evenings a week if they go to church regularly.

After ten hours in school, the teacher should spend the remaining time reading the Bible or other good books.

Women teachers who marry or engage in unseemly conduct, will be dismissed.

Each teacher should lay aside from each pay a goodly sum of his earnings for his benefit during his declining years so that he will not be a burden on society.

A teacher who smokes, uses liquor in any form, frequents pool or public halls or gets shaved in a barber shop will give good reason to suspect his worth, intentions, integrity and honesty.

The teacher who performs his labor faithfully and without fault for five years will be given an increase of 25 cents per week in his pay, providing the board of education approves.

THE CRISIS

by Ralph Connor

The new master was quick of temper, and was determined at all costs to exact full and prompt obedience. There was more flogging done those first six days than during any six months of Archie Munro's rule. Sometimes the floggings amounted to little, but sometimes they were serious, and when those fell upon the smaller boys, the girls would weep and the bigger boys would grind their teeth and swear.

The situation became so acute that Murdie Cameron and the big boys decided that they would quit the school. They were afraid the temptation to throw the master out would some day be more than they could bear, and for men who had played their part, not without credit, in the Scotch River fights, to carry out the master would have been an exploit hardly worthy of them. So, in dignified contempt of the master and his rules, they left the school after the third day.

Their absence did not help matters much; indeed, the master appeared to be relieved, and proceeded to tame the school into submission. It was little Jimmie Cameron who precipitated the crisis. Jimmie's nose, upon which he relied when struggling with his snickers, had an unpleasant trick of failing him at critical moments, and of letting out explosive snorts of the most disturbing kind. He had finally been warned that upon his next outburst punishment would fall.

It was Friday afternoon, the drowsy hour just before recess, while the master was explaining to the listless Euclid class the mysteries of the forty-seventh proposition, that suddenly a snort of unusual violence burst upon the school. Immediately every eye was upon the master, for all had heard and had noted his threat to Jimmie.

"James, was that you, sir?"

There was no answer, except such as could be gathered from Jimmie's very red and very shamed face.

"James, stand up!"

Jimmie wriggled to his feet, and stood, a heap of various angles.

"Now, James, you remember what I promised you? Come here, sir!"

Jimmie came slowly to the front, growing paler at each step, and stood with a dazed look on his face, before the master. He had never been thrashed in all his life. At home the big brothers might cuff him good-naturedly, or his mother thump him on the head with her thimble, but a serious whipping was to him an unknown horror.

The master drew forth his heavy black strap with impressive deliberation and ominous silence. The preparations for punishment itself would not amount to much. Not so Jimmie. He stood numb with fear and horrible expectation. The master lifted up the strap.

"James, hold out your hand!"

Jimmie promptly clutched his hand behind his back.

"Hold out your hand, sir, at once!"
No answer.

"James, you must do as you are told. Your punishment for disobedience will be much severer than for laughing." But Jimmie stood pale, silent, with his hands tight clasped behind his back.

The master stepped forward, and grasping the little boy's arm, tried to pull his hand to the front; but Jimmie, with a roar like that of a young bull, threw himself flat on his face on the floor and put his hands under him. The school burst into a laugh of triumph, which increased the master's embarrassment and rage.

"Silence!" he said, "or it will be a worse matter for some of you than for James."

Then turning his attention to Jimmie, he lifted him from the floor and tried to pull out his hand. But Jimmie kept his arms folded tight across his breast, roaring vigorously the while, and saying over and over, "Go away from me! Go away from me, I tell you! I'm not taking anything to do with you."

The big boys were enjoying the thing immensely. The master's rage was deepening in proportion. He felt it would never do to be beaten. His whole authority was at stake.

"Now, James," he reasoned, "you see you are only making it worse for yourself. I cannot allow any disobedience in the school. You must hold out your hand."

But Jimmie, realizing that he had come off best in the first round, stood doggedly sniffing, his arms still folded tight.

"Now, James, I shall give you one more chance. Hold out your hand."

Jimmie remained like a statue.

Whack! came the heavy strap over his shoulders. At once Jimmy set up his refrain, "Go away from me, I tell you! I'm not taking anything to do with you!"

Whack! whack! whack! fell the strap with successive blows, each heavier than the last. There was no longer any laughing in the school. The affair was growing serious. The girls were beginning to sob, and the bigger boys to grow pale.

"Now, James, will you hold out your hand? You see how much worse you are making it for yourself," said the master, who was heartily sick of the struggle, which he felt to be undignified, and the result of which he feared was dubious.

But Jimmie only kept up his cry, now punctuated with sobs, "I'm-not-taking-anything-to-do-with-you."

"Jimmie, listen to me," said the master. "You must hold out your hand. I cannot have boys refusing to obey me in this school." But Jimmie caught the entreaty in the tone, and knowing that the battle was nearly over, kept obstinately silent.

"Well, then," said the master, suddenly, "you must take it," and lifting the strap, he laid it with such sharp emphasis over Jimmie's shoulders that Jimmie's voice rose in a wilder roar than usual, and the girls burst into audible weeping.

Suddenly, above all the hubbub, rose a voice, clear and sharp.

"Stop!" It was Thomas Finch, of all people, standing with face white and tense, and regarding the master with steady eyes.

The school gazed thunderstruck at the usually slow and stolid Thomas.

"What do you mean, sir?" said the master, gladly turning from Jimmie. But Thomas stood silent, as much surprised as the master at his sudden exclamation.

He stood hesitating for a moment, and then said, "You can thrash me in his place. He's a little chap, and has never been thrashed."

The master misunderstood his hesitation for fear, pushed Jimmie aside, threw down his strap, and seized a birch rod.

"Come forward, sir! I'll put an end to your insubordination, at any rate. Hold out your hand!"

Thomas held out his hand till the master finished one birch rod.

"The other hand, sir!"

Another birch rod was used up, but Thomas neither uttered a sound nor made a move till the master had done, then he asked, in a strained voice, "Were you going to give Jimmie all that, sir?"

The master caught the biting sneer in the tone, and lost himself completely.

"Do you dare to answer me back?" he cried. He opened his desk, took out a rawhide, and without waiting to ask for his hand began to lay the rawhide about Thomas's shoulders and legs, till he was out of breath.

"Now, perhaps you will learn your place, sir," he said.

"Thank you," said Thomas, looking him steadily in the eye.

"You are welcome. And I'll give you as much more whenever you show that you need it." The slight laugh with which he closed this brutal speech made Thomas wince as he had not during his whole terrible thrashing, but still he had not a word to say.

"Now, James, come here!" said the master turning to Jimmie. "You see what happens when a boy is insubordinate." Jimmie came trembling. "Hold out your hand!" Out came Jimmie's hand at once. Whack! fell the strap.

"The other!"

"Stop it!" roared Thomas. "I took his thrashing."

With a curious savage snarl Thomas sprung at him. The master, however, was on the alert, and swinging round, met him with a straight facer between the eyes, and Thomas went to the floor.

"Aha! my boy! I'll teach you something you have yet to learn."

For answer came another cry, "Come on, boys!" It was Ranald Macdonald, coming over the seats, followed by Don Cameron, Billy Ross, and some smaller boys. The master turned to meet him.

"Come along!" he said, backing up to his desk. "But I warn you it's not a strap or a rawhide I shall use."

Ranald paid no attention to his words, but came straight toward him, and when at arm's length, sprung at him with the cry, "Horo, boys!"

But before he could lay his hands upon the master, he received a blow straight on the bridge of the nose that staggered him back, stunned and bleeding. By this time Thomas was up again, and rushing in was received in like manner, and fell back over a bench.

"How do you like it, boys?" smiled the master. "Come right along."

The boys obeyed his invitation, approaching him, but more warily, and awaiting their chance to rush. Suddenly Thomas, with a savage snarl, put his head down and rushed in beneath the master's guard, paid no attention to the heavy blow he received on the head and, locking his arms round the master's middle, buried his head close into his chest.

At once Ranald and Billy Ross threw themselves upon the struggling pair and carried them to the floor, the master underneath. There was a few moments of fierce struggling and then the master lay still, with the four boys holding him down for dear life.

It was Thomas who assumed command.

"Don't choke him so, Ranald," he said. "And clear out of the way, all you girls and little chaps."

"What are you going to do, Thomas?" asked Don, acknowledging Thomas's new-born leadership.

"Tie him up," said Thomas. "Get me a sash."

At once two or three little boys rushed to the hooks and brought one or two of the knitted sashes that hung there, and Thomas proceeded to tie the master's legs.

While he was thus busily engaged, a shadow darkened the door, and a voice exclaimed, "What is all this about?" It was the minister, who had been driving past and had come upon the terrified, weeping children rushing home.

"Is that you, Thomas? And you, Don?"

The boys let go their hold and stood up, shamed but defiant.

Immediately the master was on his feet, and with a swift, fierce blow, caught Thomas on the chin. Thomas, taken off his guard, fell with a thud on the floor.

"Stop that, young man!" said the minister, catching his arm. "That's a coward's blow."

"Hands off!" said the master, shaking himself free and squaring up to him.

"Ye would, would ye?" said the minister, gripping him by the neck and shaking him as he might a child. "Lift ye'r hand to me, would ye? I'll break ye'r back to ye, and that I will." So saying, the minister seized him by the arms and held him absolutely helpless. The master ceased to struggle, and put down his hands.

"Ay, ye'd better, my man," said the minister, giving him a fling backward.

Meantime Don had been holding snow to Thomas's head, and had brought him round.

"Now, then," said the minister to the boys, "What does all this mean?"

The boys were all silent, but the master spoke.

"It is a case of rank and impudent insubordination, sir, and I demand the expulsion of those impudent rascals."

"Well, sir," said the minister, "be sure there will be a thorough investigation, and I greatly misjudge the case if there are not faults on both sides. And for one thing, the man who can strike such a cowardly blow as you did a moment ago would not be unlikely to be guilty of injustice and cruelty."

"It is none of your business," said the master, insolently.

"You will find that I shall make it my business," said the minister. "And now, boys, be off to your homes, and be here Monday morning at nine o'clock, when this matter shall be gone into."

THE FUN THEY HAD

by Isaac Asimov

Margie even wrote about it that night in her diary. On the page headed May 17, 2155, she wrote, "Today Tommy found a real book!"

It was a very old book. Margie's grandfather once said that when he was a little boy his grandfather told him that there was a time when all stories were printed on paper.

They turned the pages, which were yellow and crinkly, and it was awfully funny to read words that stood still instead of moving the way they were supposed to—on a screen, you know. And then, when they turned back to the page before, it had the same words on it that it had when they read it the first time.

"Gee," said Tommy, "what a waste. When you're through with the book, you just throw it away, I guess. Our television screen must have had a million books on it and it's good for plenty more. I wouldn't throw it away."

"Same with mine," said Margie. She was eleven and hadn't seen as many telebooks as Tommy had. He was thirteen.

She said, "Where did you find it?"

"In my house." He pointed without looking, because he was busy reading. "In the attic."

"What's it about?"

"School."

Margie was scornful. "School? What's there to write about school? I hate school." Margie always hated school, but now she hated it more than ever. The mechanical teacher had been giving her test after test in geography and she had been doing worse and worse until her mother had shaken her head sorrowfully and sent for the County Inspector.

He was a round little man with a red face and a whole box of tools with dials and wires. He smiled at her and gave her an apple, then took the teacher apart. Margie had hoped he wouldn't know how to put it together again, but he knew how all right and after an hour or so, there it was again, large and black and ugly with a big screen on which all the lessons were shown and the questions were asked. That wasn't so bad. The part she hated most was the slot where she had to put homework and test papers. She always had to write them out in a punch code they made her learn when she was six years old, and the mechanical teacher calculated the mark in no time.

The inspector had smiled after he had finished and patted her head. He said to her mother, "It's not the little girl's fault, Mrs. Jones. I think the geography sector was geared a little too quick. These things happen sometimes. I've slowed it up to an average ten-year level. Actually, the overall pattern of her progress is quite satisfactory." And he patted Margie's head again.

Margie was disappointed. She had been hoping they would take the teacher away altogether. They had once taken Tommy's teacher away for nearly a month because the history sector had blanked out completely.

So she said to Tommy, "Why would anyone write about school?"

Tommy looked at her with very superior eyes. "Because it's not our kind of school, stupid. This is the old kind of school that they had hundreds and hundreds of years ago." He added loftily, pronouncing the word carefully, "Centuries ago."

Margie was hurt. "Well, I don't know what kind of school they had all that time ago." She read the book over his shoulder for a while, then said, "Anyway they had a teacher."

"Sure they had a teacher, but it wasn't a regular teacher. It was a man."

"A man? How could a man be a teacher?"

"Well, he just told the boys and girls things and gave them homework and asked them questions."

"A man isn't smart enough."

"Sure he is. My father knows as much as my teacher."

"He can't. A man can't know as much as a teacher."

"He knows almost as much I betcha."

Margie wasn't prepared to dispute that. She said, "I wouldn't want a strange man in my house to teach me."

Tommy screamed with laughter. "You don't know much, Margie. The teacher didn't live in the house. They had a special building and all the kids went there."

"And all the kids learned the same thing?"

"Sure, if they were the same age."

"But my mother says a teacher has to be adjusted to fit the mind of each boy and girl it teaches and that each kid has to be taught differently."

"Just the same they didn't do it that way then. If you don't like it, you don't have to read the book."

"I didn't say I didn't like it," Margie said quickly. She wanted to read about those funny schools.

They weren't even half finished when Margie's mother called "Margie! School!"

Margie looked up. "Not yet, mamma."

"Now," said Mrs. Jones. "And it's probably time for Tommy, too."

Margie said to Tommy, "Can I read the book some more with you after school?"

"Maybe," he said, nonchalantly. He walked away whistling, the dusty old book tucked beneath his arm.

Margie went into the school-room. It was right next to her bedroom, and the mechanical teacher was on and waiting for her. It was always on at the same time every day except Saturday and Sunday because her mother said little girls learned better if they learned at regular hours.

The screen was lit up, and it said: "Today's arithmetic lesson is on the addition of proper fractions. Please insert yesterday's homework in the proper slot."

Margie did so with a sigh. She was thinking about the old schools they had when her grandfather's grandfather was a little boy. All the kids from the whole neighborhood came, laughing and shouting in the schoolyard, sitting together in the classroom, going home together at the end of the day. They learned the same things so they could help one another on the homework and talk about it.

And the teachers were people.

The mechanical teacher was flashing on the screen: "When we add the fractions $\frac{1}{2}$ and $\frac{1}{4}$________"

Margie was thinking about how the kids must have loved it in the old days. She was thinking about the fun they had.

The Loser

Mama said I'd lose my head
If it wasn't fastened on.
Today I guess it wasn't
'Cause while playing with my cousin
It fell off and rolled away
And now it's gone.

And I can't look for it
'Cause my eyes are in it,
And I can't call to it
'Cause my mouth is on it
(Couldn't hear me anyway
'Cause my ears are on it),
Can't even think about it
'Cause my brain is in it.
So I guess I'll sit down
On this rock
And rest for just a minute. . . .

SHEL SILVERSTEIN

Schoolhouse

The fat sun of midday
churned our milky brains
to buttermilk
as we laughed and war whooped
through Roy Goodenow's
cornfield
on our way to toss stones
at the abandoned
one-room schoolhouse.

After the first smash
of brittle glass
we drew near to find
the chalky ghost
of old Miss Krause
writing in bat blood
15-letter words
(at least five feet high)
on the dusty blackboard.

Cicadas sang
beyond sycamore trees.
A corn wind blew red dust
in eyes that had blinked
at too much sun.
And when Jack pulled the bell
we all ran away
through Roy Goodenow's
cornfield.

DAVE ETTER

SEE MOTHER RUN!

by Joan Mills

See Mother. Mother is sleeping. "Jump up, Mother," says Father. "Jump up! Today is the first day of school!"

Oh, see Mother get out of bed! Her eyes are not open. Her slippers are on the wrong feet. She cannot find the bedroom door. Funny Mother!

"Hurry, children," says Mother. "Today is the first day of school!"

See the children go down to the kitchen. They hurry slowly on the first day of school, don't they? Mother hurries to the kitchen, too. Mother has one eye open now.

"I will give you a good breakfast," says Mother. "I will give you juice, porridge, toast, bacon, eggs, and milk from the friendly cow."

"Euchh!" says Laurie.

"Euchh!" says Bobby.

"Euchh!" says Chris.

Laurie wants cottage cheese and tea. Bobby wants Choko-Krunch Korn Krisps and cocoa with marshmallow. Chris wants three bananas.

"*Euchh!*" says Mother.

Here comes Father. He is wearing his clean white shirt and good brown suit. Father is an executive.

"I am going to work, Mother," says Father. "May I please have a dollar to put in my pocket?"

"I do not have a dollar, Father," says Mother. "Ask the children. The children have many dollars."

The children give Father a dollar. How good they are! "Good-bye! Good-bye, Father!" call Laurie, Bobby, Chris and Mother. Father waves good-bye. Father is glad he is an executive and not a mother.

"Children, children!" says Mother. "Hurry and put on your clothes. Hurry, hurry! Soon the school bus will come!"

See Laurie. Laurie is combing her hair. See Bobby. Bobby is reading about Bobby Hull. See Chris. Chris is tattooing his stomach with a ballpoint pen.

See Mother's hair stand up! What is Mother saying? Those words are not in our book, are they? *Run, children, run!*

"Mother, Mother!" says Laurie. "I have lost a shoe!"

"Mother, Mother!" says Bobby. "I think I am sick. I think I may throw up on the yellow school bus!"

"Mother, Mother!" says Chris. "My zipper is stuck, and I have a jelly bean in my ear!"

Oh, see Mother run!

"I am going mad," says Mother. "Here is Laurie's shoe on the stove. Here are other pants for Chris. Here is a thermometer for Bobby, who does not look sick to me."

Now what are the children doing?

Laurie is combing her hair. Bobby is playing the banjo. Chris is under the bed feeding jelly beans to the cat.

"Oh!" says Mother. "Hurry, hurry! It is time for the yellow school bus!"

Mother is right. (Mother is *always* right.) Here comes the yellow school bus!

See all the children on the bus jump up and down. Jump! Jump! Jump! See the pencil boxes fly out the windows! Listen to the driver of the yellow school bus. He cannot yell as loud as the children, can he? Run, Laurie! Run, Bobby! Run, Chris!

See Mother throw kisses to the children. Why do Laurie, Bobby and Chris pretend they do not know Mother?

"Good-bye! Good-bye!" calls Mother.

"*Barrooooom!*" goes the yellow bus.

How quiet it is.

Here is Chris's sweater in the boot box.

Here are Bobby's glasses under the cat.

Here is Laurie's comb in the fruit bowl.

Here is crunchy cereal all over the kitchen floor.

Here is Mother. Crunch, crunch, crunch. Mother is pouring a big cup of coffee. Mother is sitting down.

Mother does not say anything.
Mother does not do anything.
Mother just sits and smiles.
Why is Mother smiling?

Vacation Trip

The loudest thing in our car
was Mother being glum:

Little chiding valves
a surge of detergent oil
all that deep chaos
the relentless accurate fire
the drive shaft wild to arrive

And tugging along behind in its great big
balloon, that looming piece in her mind:

"I wish I hadn't come."

WILLIAM STAFFORD

What Did You Learn In School Today?

What did you learn in school today,
Dear little boy of mine?
What did you learn in school today,
Dear little boy of mine?
I learned that Washington never told a lie,
I learned that soldiers seldom die,
I learned that everybody's free,
That's what the teacher said to me,
And that's what I learned in school today,
That's what I learned in school.

What did you learn in school today,
Dear little boy of mine?
What did you learn in school today,
Dear little boy of mine?
I learned that policemen are my friends,
I learned that justice never ends,
I learned that murderers die for their crimes,
Even if we make a mistake sometimes,
And that's what I learned in school today,
That's what I learned in school.

What did you learn in school today,
Dear little boy of mine?
What did you learn in school today,
Dear little boy of mine?
I learned our government must be strong,
It's always right and never wrong,
Our leaders are the finest men,
And we elect them again and again,
And that's what I learned in school today,
That's what I learned in school.

What did you learn in school today,
Dear little boy of mine?
What did you learn in school today,
Dear little boy of mine?
I learned that war is not so bad,
I learned about the great ones we have had,
We fought in Germany and in France,
And someday I might get my chance,
And that's what I learned in school today,
That's what I learned in school.

TOM PAXTON

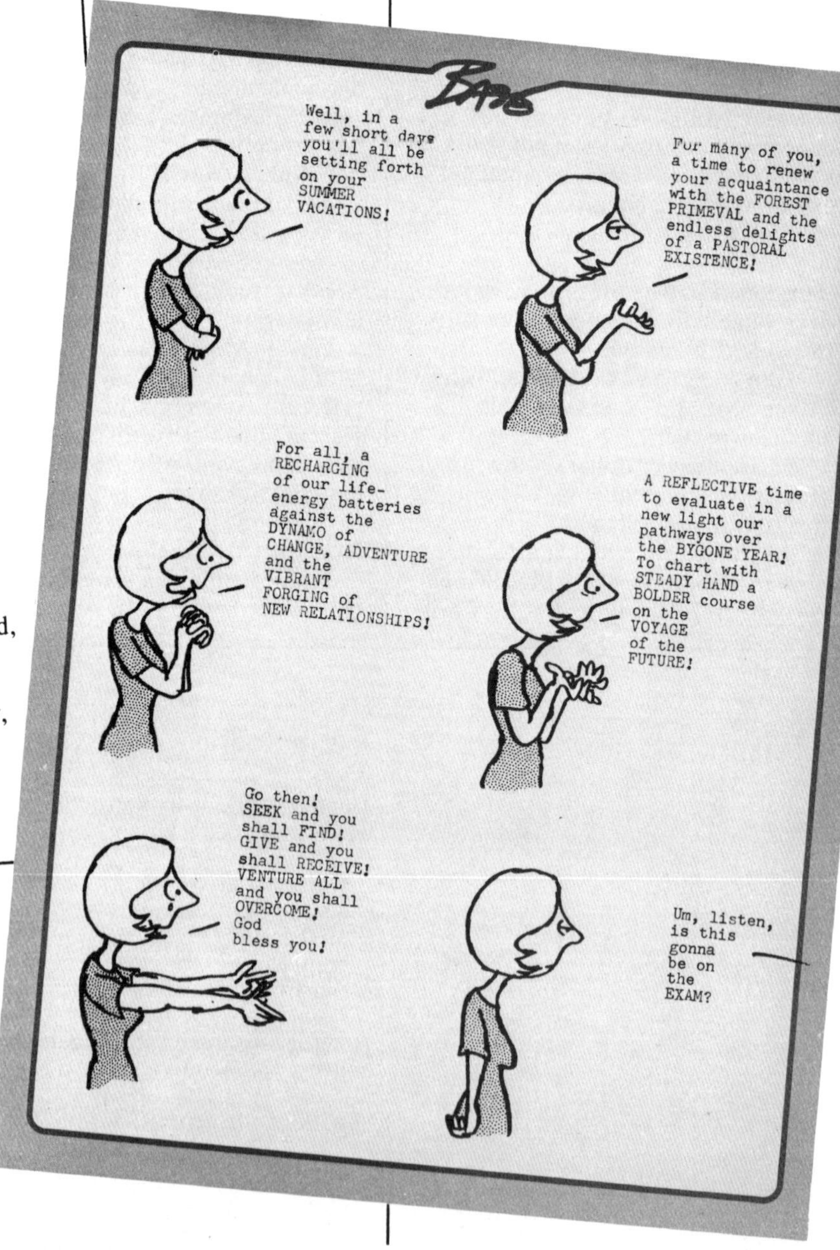

PARDON ME, YOU'RE STEPPING ON MY EYEBALL

by Paul Zindel

On Thursday, Edna and the rest of Mr. Meizner's specially selected students reported to Room 101 for the active sessions of their group-therapy-experience class—now simply known as GTE. GTE was supposed to be a code so the rest of the kids in the school wouldn't know exactly what the class was. But it was already common knowledge that GTE was for the teenage insane. It was the same kind of pretense with all the other classes that were called "Applied." Everybody knew that if they were in a class called Applied Chemistry or Applied Geometry that "Applied" simply meant that they were more stupid than the kids who were taking the real thing. But that kind of thing didn't really bother most of the kids at Curtis Lee High because almost all of them were more interested in playing poker during their study periods.

Room 101 had been a sewing room, and Edna was surprised to see Mr. Meizner had taken out all the machines and converted the room into a sort of cross between a Zen Buddhist prayer temple and a wrestling arena. The only furniture to speak of was Mr. Meizner's desk which had a phonograph on it and a swivel chair behind it. The rest of the decor was a pack of strawlike mats which covered the floor. There was one black-board and somebody had written in big letters on it "Don't be a high-school dropout. Stay and learn how to read and riot."

"Put on your blindfolds," Mr. Meizner crowed, waving a handful of black pieces of cloth. "Pick out a straw mat, stand by it and put on your blindfold. Today we're going to say hello to another face."

Edna didn't know what on earth he was talking about, but she was much too jittery to do anything but comply. She put her books down on the floor, grabbed one of the blindfolds and went to a straw mat. The last sight she saw was that of the seven other kids lined up and looking like they were going to be executed by a very plump psychologist.

"No fair peeking," Mr. Meizner instructed. "Just turn around in place until I come to get you. I want you all disoriented."

Edna heard some of the kids laughing, but her own aorta seemed like it was going to tie itself into a pretzel.

"One by one, I'm going to take you by the hand and lead you to your own special spot," Mr. Meizner droned on. "When I squeeze your hand, you just sit down and cross your legs Indian style. Don't do anything until I tell you."

"What if I have to burp?" somebody yelled out in a falsetto voice.

"Shut up!" Mr. Meizner bellowed. In a few minutes he had led the last student to his place. "You are all in position now. But let me tell you what you're going to do. Each of you is sitting, facing another person. And when I give the signal, you're going to reach out your right hand and gently touch the face of the boy or girl who's directly in front of you."

Edna felt extremely uncomfortable. Now her entire heart felt like it was tap dancing on her kidneys. She hadn't the faintest idea who she was paired with, whose fingers would be reaching out to touch her. With her luck, she figured it would be someone so obtuse they'd stick their thumb in her mouth or something. Besides, there was no one in the room she wanted to do anything like this with. The one thing Edna knew for certain was that the face she didn't want to touch most of all was the face that belonged to Louis "Marsh" Mellow. There was something about him that scared her.

Mr. Meizner sat in his swivel chair and cleared his voice. He was dead serious. "Now boys and girls, the one thing all of you have in common is that you're all socially miserable. You've all been in to see me at one time or other either on your own, or your parents dragged you in. But your common denominator is that you've got trouble expressing your emotions. The only emotion any of you seem to be able to feel is that you're depressed. And that means something is interfering with all the other emotions in life that you should have. I'm making you wear blindfolds because that way you're going to be more in touch with your feelings and not confused by what you see. Most of our prejudices come from the fact that we see too much with our minds and not enough with our gut. It will also help cover up a lot of the embarrassment that you'd feel if you didn't have the blindfolds."

"Hey, Mr, Meizner," Edna heard Snooks' voice call out. "Did you hear the one about the couple called Kelly who went around belly to belly?" Everyone laughed again until Mr. Meizner let out a sound like an ape. Then there was silence again and Mr. Meizner returned to a more civilized tone.

"All right boys and girls, let's just get on with it. Reach out and say hello to another face with your fingers."

Edna heard herself gulp.

"Come, come, come! Get those happy fingers out there! Move that right hand forward until you touch someone," Mr. Meizner continued.

Edna forced her arm to move, but now she could feel adrenalin cascading into her bloodstream. She felt ridiculous! The idea of saying hello to someone's face with her fingers was absurd. Then she felt someone touching her brow and her head jerked. But a second later her own fingers made contact with something and she froze. At first she thought it was some kind of a hairy golf ball, but then she realized her fingers were clasped around a tiny head with little teeth. She let out a scream and yanked her blindfold off. There in front of her was Marsh with a big grin holding his raccoon in his left hand. Edna had grabbed the raccoon's head.

"Keep your blindfolds in place!" Mr. Meizner demanded. He rushed toward Edna. "It's only Mr. Mellow's raccoon which I will stick in the closet for the rest of the period." He stood over Marsh yelling, "If you dare bring him in here again, I will notify the ASPCA."

Marsh looked a little frightened and handed over the raccoon. "Look, Mr. Meizner," Marsh said, "I'll tell you one thing, if you hurt Raccoon I'm going to send you up the river."

"Quiet!" Mr. Meizner insisted, putting the raccoon in the closet and slamming the door. "Do not break your concentration, boys and girls. Just keep saying hello to a face."

"Mr. Meizner, do I have to?" Edna asked softly.

"Yes, you have to!" Mr. Meizner shot back. "Put your blindfold back on immediately!"

Finally, Edna reached out her hand again, this time knowing whose face she was going to have to say hello to. She was saying hello to a face that she'd much rather say good-bye to. Marsh had started in again on her brow, kneading it like he was squeezing a grapefruit, as Edna's fingers made contact with Marsh's chin. It was very strange, Edna thought after a minute of exploration, that touching Marsh's chin was only half as revolting as the mere thought of touching it. There were a couple of little hairs growing out of it, but she knew you wouldn't call it a beard yet, it was more like slight bursts of alfalfa.

Marsh found a very strange thing happening to him as he began to creep down Edna's face. The more he touched her face, particularly her lips, the more unusual he felt. In fact, suddenly nothing was very funny to him anymore. He didn't feel he had to let out some smart-aleck falsetto remark. He didn't feel he had to honk Edna's nose like a horn which was what he had intended to do. And he was rather oblivious to Mr. Meizner's voice which was chanting, "Don't be afraid, don't be afraid. Touch each other's eyebrows and ears and hair. Realize that you are touching another human being who is very much like yourself; who has feelings like you do. Remember, even monkeys pick nits off each other."

Another couple of minutes went by and Edna felt her fingers were doing things in rhythm with Marsh's fingers. She found the two of them were feeling each other's chins at the same time, and then they'd feel their lips at the same time, and then their fingers would run up the sides of their faces at the same time. They ran their fingers gently along the bottom of the blindfolds, softly sliding the tips of their fingers under the edge of the blindfold as though trying to feel each other's eyelids. Mr. Meizner then put a record on the phonograph and the strains of a string orchestra playing "On the Sunny Side of the Street" began to play.

"Let your fingers dance on each other's faces," Mr. Meizner called out.

Crazy thoughts were galloping through Marsh's mind. He couldn't stop them. His thoughts didn't seem to make any sense to him. It seemed like his mind was turning into a short-circuited computer. Book titles, headlines, jokes, everything seemed to come pouring silently through his head. For some reason he remembered a book he once saw on a library shelf called *How to Conduct Your own Divorce and Save Lawyers' Fees*. Then he had this vision of a dozen waltzing Oscar Mayer wieners. And after that, he pictured himself smacking his mother around with a rubber duck. That led to him remembering a giant billboard he'd seen out in California with a huge girl saying "Come for the filter, you'll stay for the taste." And the memory of a bus bench came back to him with an ad for Murphy's Mortuaries. Somebody had written below it "You kill 'em, we'll chill 'em." Then he remembered some guy in one of the bars telling him that heaven was a tin box in the sky. And he remembered being with his father one time and having a pastrami sandwich at the Regina Deli. And then the thoughts went so fast they didn't seem to have any connection. Hit a shark on the head in the right spot and it'll go cross-eyed. Ordinarily Marsh knew he would blurt out such thoughts as jokes, or do something funny or idiotic, work them into a gag. But now, as he was feeling Edna Shinglebox's face, he couldn't do anything but sit still and marvel at the shape of her nose. What an interesting nose, he thought.

Edna found her mind was spinning. She couldn't think of anything except a whirlpool. It seemed she was just whirling around. Then for some silly reason she began to remember an ad she had read once in an underground newspaper. It was a personal plea that some man had published. "I'm forty-two years old, nice-looking, male, a bachelor father. My boy is fifteen years old, we enjoy tennis, golf, dancing, camping, movies, music centres and Winnebagos. Need very much to meet an honest, nongaining woman who would like to love and be loved and be mother to my son. Let's have more beautiful children together. My wife died of cancer. I offer integrity and devotion and happiness. I and my kid need you very much. Those interested, please write Box A317."

Suddenly Edna felt Marsh grab her hand. He moved it quickly away from his face, but it was too late. The first thing she felt was embarrassment. She wished it hadn't happened, but it was too late. She had felt something wet slide from Marsh's left eye, and then she heard a whisper. She thought it was Marsh, but she couldn't be sure. Again there came the whisper, and this time she heard every word.

"They've got my father in a nuthouse. Can you hear me?"

Edna didn't know what to do for a moment. Finally she heard herself whispering back, hoping that her voice couldn't be heard by anyone else.

"Yes," she said, "I heard you."

ACTIVITIES

1. One of the problems that groups face when they begin to work on anthology dramatizations is the amount of material available for any given theme. A useful way to get beyond trying to grasp the meaning of all the material and its order is to choose one selection which has potential and to dramatize that selection without considering where it will fit into the final anthology. Begin to work in the dramatic mode as soon as possible in order to experiment with the ideas which emerged from analysis and discussion. You will find that your perception of a particular selection will change as you shape it into dramatic form.

2. A dramatic anthology is unlike a conventional script in that it does not normally have unity of time, place, or characters. Often a piece of material can be followed by one which presents a completely different view of the same theme. However, an anthology is unified by the dramatic statement the group is making about the theme. This statement should be agreed upon by the group after allowing sufficient time for exploration of all the material chosen. As you develop a dramatic interpretation of each selection, can you state in a single sentence what you are saying about the theme? As you organize the order of the material and the way in which it will be presented, can you express the statement your dramatization makes about the theme? Once this dramatic statement is clarified, it will aid you in deciding how to begin and how to end your anthology.

3. Some of the selections in this chapter present people as stereotypes. Be sure that you can identify the stereotype and that your experimentation with the dramatization has explored the opposite of the stereotype and the humanity of the individual. An example is "See Mother Run!" Does your dramatization suggest that this is the way all mothers are? Have you explored the idea that this is the way some mothers sometimes see themselves? Explore the reasons why these mothers perceive themselves this way.

4. The selections in this chapter provide

you with opportunities to experiment with the dramatic form of anthology. Once the techniques have been mastered, your group can go on to create an anthology using the techniques outlined in The Program.

Remember that any theme works as anthology: the works of an author or performer, a collection of photographs on a single theme, the writings of a particular age group or type of person (handicapped people, prisoners, soldiers, etc.).

Make a list of subjects which could be anthologized, such as drawings, photographs, signs, graffiti, cartoons, posters, popular commercials, people, events from history, and so on. Be aware that these materials will have to be researched fully and arranged in some sequence. The sequence can be in chronological order, in a jumbled format (going from present day to the past, from happy to sad, from famous to obscure people), or it can be organized into "acts" by time, place, type of person, type of idea. In your group, choose a single theme and develop this theme into an anthology.

5. After a theme is selected, put together an anthology of music which might assist in the clarification of the chosen theme.

12: Docudrama

THE PROGRAM

Docudrama combines the word "documentary" with the word "drama." It is the first word which distinguishes this form of presentation from other forms. The techniques of gathering, selecting, ordering, and dramatizing material are very similar to those described in the previous chapter "Anthology"; it is the *material* which differentiates docudrama from anthology.

The word documentary implies that the material is factual and historical. It also implies that the theme or concept of the presentation is related to something that has occurred in the past (history) or something which is occurring now (current events).

Whether you choose history or current events, you and your group will have to decide on a topic for the docudrama. Some ideas are "Prisons: Past and Present," "The War of 1812," "The Changing Neighborhood," "The History of ________ Secondary School," or "Work." "Work" has been chosen as an example for this chapter.

The next step is to research material using all the resources available, including libraries, museums, galleries, records offices, kits, or rare books. You can also interview people who have knowledge of, or stories about, the relevant events. The techniques you learned in the chapter on scripting will be very valuable here.

Generally, your sources will be of two kinds: primary (eyewitness accounts of relevant events) or secondary (interpretations or re-tellings by people who were not present at the event). Your docudrama can be exclusively one or the other, or a combination of both.

Once you have collected material, the process of dramatization is very similar to that used in anthology. The major problem you will have is avoiding the distortion of factual material in your dramatic interpretation. Your aim is to stay true to the original material.

Since a great deal of the material will be narrative in style, it will be worthwhile for you to use Readers Theatre, Chamber Theatre, Story Theatre, and scripting techniques in preparing your presentation.

Docudrama is a valuable dramatic technique for you and your group. You will assemble information on important events and issues, and examine how you think and feel about these events and issues.

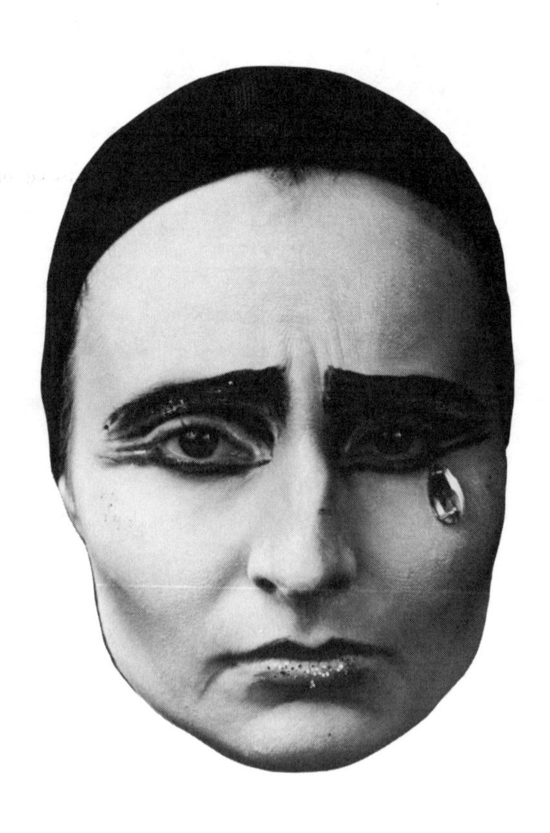

PLAYBILL

The material gathered here deals in some way with the topic of work. You will find that there are a variety of attitudes expressed: the points of view of workers, bosses, people who have only recently begun to work, people who are unemployed. Also included are lists and statistics which will test your ingenuity when you dramatize them. The order in which the material is presented here is not in any way meant to suggest the dramatic order for your group to follow in working with these selections.

WHO WORKS?

The population of Canada is 22 million, but there are 7 million over 65 years of age, leaving 15 million to do the work. People under 21 total 10 million, leaving 5 million to do the work. Two million government employees leave 3 million to do the work. Five hundred thousand in the armed forces leave 2 500 000 workers. Deduct 1 250 000 provincial, municipal, and city employees, which leaves 1 250 000 to do the work. There are 250 000 people in hospitals, asylums, etc., leaving 1 000 000 to do the work. But 700 000 of these are unemployed and 200 000 are on welfare or won't work, so that leaves 100 000 to do the work. Now it may interest you to know that there are 80 000 people out of the country at any one time and 19 998 people in jail so that leaves just two people to do all the work. And that is you and me, Brother, and I'm getting tired of doing everything by myself!

So let's get with it!

ANN LANDERS

Should teenager in ghetto quit school for work?

Dear Ann: I'm a guy and will be 16 years old in two months. I have been waiting for this birthday for quite a while because it will mean I am legally old enough to quit school and get a job.

My Pa took off six years ago and we haven't seen him since. Mom works two jobs to keep us four kids going. I'm the oldest. She refuses to go on welfare.

My grades are good, but I feel I owe it to Mom to get out and make some money. She wants me to stay in school. She told me to write to you, which is why I'm doing it. What do you have to say, Ann?—**Should Be Breadwinner.**

Dear Should Be: Education is your ticket out of the ghetto. Don't blow it. Stay in school and go on to college if possible.

What you do with the next two to six years of your life will determine what you will be doing 30 years from now. Get as much education as you can, son—you'll never regret it.

A Nursery Rhyme

Tinker,
Tailor,
Soldier,
Sailor,
Gentleman,
Apothecary,
Plough-boy,
Thief.

Soldier brave, sailor true,
Skilled physician, Oxford blue,
Learned lawyer, squire so hale,
Dashing airman, curate pale.

Army, Navy,
Medicine, Law,
Church, Nobility,
Nothing at all.

A laird, a lord,
A cooper, a thief,
A piper, a drummer,
A stealer of beef.

THE WORKPLACE

I'm very proud of my employees. I think we have a lot of winners here. I tell my employees that they don't work for me, but that we work together. We're on the same team, and I'm their captain. I hold the team together. I've always had this talent of being able to inspire the rank and file and keep the ship afloat. I have no problem with the morale of my employees. I'm on a first-name basis with all of them. The workers are very content here. Oh, sometimes I think they need a psychiatrist down there to listen to all their small talk. I have a very cheerful attitude, and I find that a little pat on the back and a friendly smile does it. We're a very happy family.

The only restrictions I impose on the employees is cleanliness, decent length of hair, not too much smoking—bad for the health; no fat or obese people, because I feel they are a bad investment—in the long run they won't last. We're not looking for people with heart failures. We're not strict here. It's a question of image and respectability. We have a presentable operation, from the top to the bottom. You won't find anybody with a beard or with long hair here. I think a large corporation should have a proper image. My employees are a reflection of me.

I respect the guy who sweeps the floor just as much as a president of another company who comes into my office. I treat them both equally. I can communicate to people at different levels. That's why all my employees love me. They have a lot of admiration for me, because they know I always bring home the bacon. I put a lot of constructive things together. They've seen what I'm capable of. I've built this empire in only nine years.

—COMPANY PRESIDENT

In order to increase the productivity of the workers, the company introduced what is known as the "Silent 90." During the first ninety minutes of the morning, you aren't allowed to talk to anyone. You're supposed to do your work in total silence. If they catch you whispering, they punish you. We are made to feel like children who are told to "go stand in the corner." To me, it represents an authoritarian, school-type atmosphere.

—SECRETARY

I was very happy when I was a bricklayer. I finished work at 4:30—no problems, no worries, no responsibilities. I went straight home. I used to relax, talk to my wife. Today, I can't talk to her anymore. I'm so tired when I get home that I just eat and go to sleep. As a bricklayer I was healthy. I was strong. It was beautiful. Today I have to push myself to work. Working with your hands—ah, that's the good life. People treat me differently now that I'm an executive. They call me "Sir" and they don't say what's on their minds. I'm the same man, but their image of me has changed.

—VICE-PRESIDENT IN A LARGE CONSTRUCTION COMPANY

When you've been pressing on the same button, you hate that button. You curse that button a million times over.

—COMPUTER OPERATOR

Children as workers

Theophile Charron, journeyman cigar-maker, aged 14, of Montreal

Q. Do you remember why you paid these fines?
A. Sometimes for talking too much, mostly for that.
Q. You were never licked?
A. Yes; not licked as any harm was done me, but sometimes they would come along, and if we happened to be cutting our leaf wrong, they would give us a crack across the head with the fist.
Q. Was it usual to beat children like that?
A. Often.
Q. Were you beaten during the first year of your apprenticeship?
A. Yes, sir.
Q. That is, you were beaten at eleven years?
A. Yes, sir.

Joseph Larkins, biscuit maker, Nova Scotia

By Mr. Heakes:—

Q. How old are you? A. I am 11 years.
Q. What is the matter with your hand? A. It got hurt in the machinery.
Q. How? A. It got caught in the rollers.
Q. What rollers? A. The rollers of a cracker machine—a biscuit machine.
Q. Did you lose any fingers? A. I lost one.
Q. Did you lose any of the joints of the others? A. I think I will lose a second finger.
Q. How long were you working in the biscuit factory? A. About seven weeks.
Q. How much wages did they give you? A. A dollar a week at first, and then a dollar and a quarter.
Q. How much do they give you now? A. Nothing at all.
Q. How long is it since you were hurt? A. Nine weeks Thursday.
Q. And they have not given you anything? A. No; except for the week I was hurt.

From the Royal Commission on Relations of Labor and Capital in Canada (1889), as reported in the Toronto *Daily Mail and Empire*, October 9, 1897

WORKERS

Society sees laborers at the bottom of the social scale. No one thinks they could possibly be happy. People are being conditioned to believe this. From early in life your parents feed it to you.

CATHY **by Cathy Guisewite**

THE ANT AND THE GRASSHOPPER

A commonwealth of Ants, having, after a busy summer, provided everything for their wants in the winter, were about shutting themselves up for that dreary season, when a Grasshopper in great distress, and in dread of perishing with cold and hunger, approached their avenues, and with great humility begged they would relieve his wants, and permit him to take shelter in any corner of their comfortable mansion. One of the Ants asked him how he had disposed of his time in summer, that he had not taken pains and laid in a stock, as they had done? Alas! my friends, says he, I passed away the time merrily and pleasantly, in drinking, singing, and dancing, and never once thought of winter. If that be the case, replied the Ant, all I have to say is this: that they who drink, sing, and dance in the summer, run a great risk of starving in the winter.

If you aren't a doctor or a lawyer, you aren't a success. You are lower class, you're no good. I grew up in a slummy area and my parents told me the same thing: "You have to work in an office. You have to hold a clean job, wear a suit." It's all a prestige trip. I make more money than a lot of white-collar workers, clerks, secretaries—and at least I enjoy what I'm doing. They are considered a class higher than the "common laborers," because they sit in offices and shuffle paper. Me, I'd rather work in my T-shirt and sandals. I smile going to work. I have chosen to do what I'm doing. I was not forced into it. That's why I am not resentful that I'm a laborer. I can say that I had the choice. The thing is that I actually enjoy working with my hands and my body, manual labor. I enjoy doing physical things, lifting things. I get a lot of satisfaction out of exerting myself.

—SHIPPER

There's an old folktale that tells the whole story of work beautifully. It's about the rich factory owner who sees an unemployed person just sitting under a tree. The owner asks the other if she wants to come to work in the factory. The woman replies "Work in the factory, and then what? What else is there for me?" The owner says, "If you work hard, you can become a supervisor in a few years." The woman says, "Yes, yes, and then what? What else is there for me?" The owner replies, "Well, then you can become the manager." The woman persists, "And then what?" The owner gets exasperated, "Well, well you can become the president of the company like me." The woman continues, "Yes, and then what?" The owner reflects, "Well, then you can relax and do nothing." The woman laughs. "Why should I work in your factory for that? I relax and do nothing now. Why wait for thirty years?"

—RESTAURANT WORKER

The Worker

My father lies black and hushed
Beneath white hospital sheets
He collapsed at work
His iron left him
Slow and quiet he sank
Meeting the wet concrete floor on his way
The wheels were still turning
They couldn't stop
Red and yellow lights flashing
Gloved hands twisting knobs
They couldn't stop
And as they carried him out
The whirling and buzzing
And humming machines
Applauded him
Lapping up his dripping iron.

RICHARD W. THOMAS

The Winnipeg Strike

by Gerry Kopelow

"That strike ruined my life. And it didn't accomplish a thing, just real hard feelings. After they used the Mounties against us it went to pieces. But we had no choice. Our children were hungry. It was a dirty deal. A raw, dirty deal."

David Simpson sits in the parlor of his house in Winnipeg's west end, a big man still, and his voice trembles as the old emotions return. He is one of the last survivors of the 1919 Winnipeg general strike. He and three other constables organized the city policemen's union, and for him the strike remains a personal experience.

"I was born June 2, 1890, in Nova Scotia. Started to work when I was 11. There was nothing in the East, so in 1909 I came to Winnipeg with my brother. There was a building boom in 1910 to '12. In '13 it died.

"Then I made my mistake. I took on with the police. I started at $75 a month, worked 10 to 12 hours a day, mostly walking a beat. We were supposed to get a $10 a month raise every year, but it was frozen during the war. Prices went wild then. The price of meat more than quadrupled. They took off $5 a month for a "Patriotic Fund." We never saw that money. In the winter of '16 the meat packers went out. They were still getting 17¢ an hour while prices rose drastically. We were ordered to break it up and we did. In the spring of '17 the teamsters went out. This time we wouldn't touch the strikers, so the CNR and CPR brought in toughs. Just a bunch of proper thugs. We arrested some for concealed weapons but they got off.

"All this time, mind you, we'd no increase in pay. By the end of the war we were pretty well done in. We went to the chief for more money. The commission told him to let go anyone who complained. A constable named Arnette tried to raise a petition. He was caught and thrown out. We talked among ourselves and decided, four of us, to go down and meet with Ernie Robertson, the secretary of the Trades and Labor Council. We came off the night shift at 11 a.m. and had our meeting with Ernie in a lumberyard behind the McLaren Hotel on Main. I remember his exact words. 'Boys,' he said, 'forming a union is no bed of roses.'

"Well, the plan was to get the firemen's union to help. They went door to door and got signatures on little cards. No lists, see? We had our first meeting down at the big hall at the Trades and Labor Offices. When we met the police commission we got our way. Our back pay came through and things looked fine.

"It turned bad again in early May of '19. The metal workers went out on May 15, and so did others, Winnipeg Electric, the streetcars, the dairies, they were all out. The town was shut down. The bosses, the big shots, formed a committee, a Committee of 1000, they called it. There was no attempt to talk, to mediate.

"We voted not to strike, but they were afraid of us. One evening in June I was walking home from work, and I saw some guys in civilian clothes directing traffic. They wore arm bands with TP on them. Temporary Police. The city had hired them.

"The next morning I reported to the station. The men were milling around. Our lockers had been broken into during the night. Guns, uniforms, even the billies were gone. The TPs were taking over, 1500 of them. They brought us down to the main station in wagons. Don McPherson, the chief, a big bear of a man, asked us to sign a paper withdrawing the union. We refused. They fired us, all 500 of us.

"We went to a meeting at the Trades and Labor Hall, and after the meeting I started to walk home with Hugh Pritchard, the assistant jailer. We walked down Main to Portage, and there was a crowd at the intersection, kind of milling around, nothing noisy. All of a sudden there's the mayor on the steps of the Bank of Montreal, reading the Riot Act. There was no riot. Next about six horses ridden by TPs came galloping north on Main. Right into the crowd. They galloped back and forth, and the people formed a kind of channel for them. Some guys broke into the restaurant and came out with eggs and tomatoes and fruit which they threw at the riders. Then the crowd broke up.

"A week later, on a Saturday afternoon, some veterans were meeting in Market Square behind City Hall. The trolleys were back on, run by scabs paid by the city. The men were demanding a meeting with the federal Minister of Labor, Gideon Robson. He was holed up in the Royal Alex Hotel. Then some damn fool scabs tried to run a streetcar right through the crowd, and it was overturned. The inside was set on fire. The Mounties charged into the crowd swinging clubs. Some of the Mounties were hauled off their horses. They reformed on Market Street and started to fire on the crowd. One man was killed. After that I never had much use for the Mounties."

History vindicated the strikers; schools and streets were named after them. A royal commission held that the strikers' goals had been collective bargaining, higher wages and social justice, not insurrection, and although several leaders were convicted of sedition, four of them were elected to the Manitoba Legislature while in prison. But David Simpson remembers no triumph.

"After the arrests the strike was bust, blown away. The police were rehired, except for 33 so-called ringleaders. I walked the streets for weeks looking for work, but I was blacklisted. I went to Saskatchewan. When I came back to Winnipeg in '23 I took work as a bailiff. It was all I could get. Collecting goods and property for bad debts. I didn't like it too much but I had no choice.

"I'm the only living member of the original police union. I was taught as a child that it's a sin to hate anybody, and I've driven that feeling out of my mind. But the men who broke the strike, those men who wouldn't listen, I hated them like the devil hates holy water."

From *Weekend Magazine*, May 12, 1979

JOB CHARACTERISTICS RANKED BY WORKERS ACCORDING TO IMPORTANCE

Rank	Characteristic
1	Work is interesting
2	Have enough information
3	Have enough authority
4	Opportunity to develop abilities
5	Receive enough help and equipment
6	See results of work
7	Responsibilities clearly defined
8	Co-workers competent
9	Supervisor is competent
10	Given a lot of freedom
11	People are friendly
12	Job security is good
13	Promotions handled fairly
14	Chance to do things I do best
15	Enough time to get job done
16	Supervisor concerned about welfare of those under him/her
17	Pay is good
18	People helpful
19	Supervisor successful in getting people to work together
20	Chances to get ahead
21	Supervisor friendly
22	Supervisor helpful
23	People helpful
24	Chances for promotion are good
25	Hours good
26	Fringe benefits good
27	Surroundings are pleasant
28	Travel is convenient
29	Problems hard enough
30	Free from conflicting demands
31	Chances to make friends are good
32	People take personal interest in me
33	Can forget personal problems
34	Not asked to do excessive amount of work

SOURCE: Statistics Canada

23 TYPICAL JOBS RATED ACCORDING TO BOREDOM

Based on interviews with 2010 workers performing 23 different jobs, the Institute for Social Research at the University of Michigan drew up "boredom factors" for each occupation. The average was considered to be 100, and the higher the rating the more boring the job.

	Job	*Boredom Rating*
1.	Assembler (work paced by machine)	207
2.	Relief worker on assembly line	175
3.	Forklift-truck driver	170
4.	Machine tender	169
5.	Assembler (working at own pace)	160
6.	Monitor of continuous flow goods	122
7.	Accountant	107
8.	Engineer	100
9.	Tool- and diemaker	96
9.	Computer programmer	96
11.	Electronic technician	87
12.	Deliver service courier	86
13.	Blue-collar supervisor	85
14.	White-collar supervisor	72
15.	Scientist	66
16.	Administrator	66
17.	Train dispatcher	64
18.	Police officer	63
19.	Air traffic controller (large airport)	59
20.	Air traffic controller (small airport)	52
21.	Professor with administrative duties	51
22.	Professor	49
23.	Physician	48

BEST-BUY DISCOUNT STORES OF CANADA LIMITED

EMPLOYMENT APPLICATION

PERSONAL INFORMATION

Date ____________ Social Insurance Number

Name ____________________ Phone No. ____________
last first middle

Present Address ____________________ How Long There ____________
no. & street city postal code

Previous Address in Canada ____________________ How Long There ____________
no. & street city postal code

Presently Employed? ____________ Date Available ____________ Referred by ____________

Ever Work for Best-Buy Discount Before ____________ If So, Where ____________

Are You Bondable ____________ Do You Have The Legal Right To Seek Employment in Canada ____________

Are Your Presently Attending School ____________ If So, At What Level ____________

Are You under The Age of 15* ____________ If So, What Age Are You ____________

*Please Note: You may be required to provide proof of age prior to hire.

AVAILABILITY

HOURS AVAILABLE	MON	TUE	WED	THU	FRI	SAT	SUN
FROM							
TO							

EMPLOYMENT BACKGROUND
List your PRESENT OR LAST position FIRST.

DATE MO. & YR.	COMPANY NAME AND ADDRESS	TELEPHONE NO. INCL. AREA CODE	NAME AND POSITION OF SUPERVISOR	YOUR POSITION	SALARY/WAGE		REASON FOR LEAVING
					START	END	
FROM TO							
FROM TO							
FROM TO							

As a condition of my application/employment, I authorize investigation of all statements contained in this application. I understand that Best-Buy Discount Stores' decision will be based solely on non-discriminatory considerations and that misrepresentation or omission of facts called for is just cause for dismissal. If hired, I agree that, due to labor shortages, promotions or training, I may be required to transfer from one store to another. I also agree that, at all times, I will follow the rules and regulations of Best-Buy Discount Stores in Canada.

Signature ____________

This application expires at the end of 30 days.

Form No. 76501
Rev. Jan./83

there is a cluster of fine young women beginning their careers now. And in between there is nothing!

External says this is partly because women don't apply. I can't argue with them on that. I meet plenty of women who are willing to assist with political compaigns but they don't see themselves as having a role in international affairs. This is the real problem which those of us concerned with the status of women must cope with.

I believe totally in telling girls exactly what they are up against. Frankly, there are still ambassadors who refuse to delegate significant tasks to women. As a result of this discrimination External has lost a number of good young women who have switched to other departments where they don't have those problems.

I am hopeful that the present generation of leaders in government is about at retirement age and that a younger generation of enlightened leaders will see things differently. I can't change the "old boys" who feel uncomfortable having a drink with a woman on equal terms but I do have confidence in the new leaders.

In Canada we've made significant strides in the status of women, but it's not yet reflected in our delegations abroad nor in the senior ranks of our public service. Changes are coming, though—for example, now CIDA has a senior woman staff member and that's important as we give assistance to the Third World.

The best group of women I've noted in my personal experience has been the fine young foreign service officers training recently at the UN mission in New York. I look to these women, who are very competent, to pioneer a new era.

Our high school girls definitely should consider careers in serving Canada abroad. But come into the battle with your eyes wide open. It is a battle which we, your predecessors, have been fighting, and we've made a few breakthroughs.

Now you should finish the job!

Some Excuses for Not Going to Work

–I live in an attic apartment and someone stole the stairs.

–My doctor is sick and I have to pay him a house call.

–I'm trying to get over a cold and both my hands are stuck to the bottle of vitamin C.

–I pricked my finger while dusting the spinning wheel and I've been overcome by an intense desire to go to sleep—

–I went to the library and they stamped my hand instead of my book and I'm due back today.

–The sparrows and the bluejays are having a hockey tournament on the birdbath and I have to referee.

–Someone has dug a moat around my house and filled it with alligators.

adapted from *Peter Gzowski's Book about This Country in the Morning*

MEMO FROM SYLVA GELBER

To: Canadian young people
re: participation in Canada's international affairs

How can I get a message to Canadian high school girls? How can I talk to young people at an age when they are very conformist? How can I tell girls that they can be ambassadors and foreign services officers?

The role of women in international affairs is still very small. In some Third World countries women have assumed senior positions, in others the women still live in serfdom and slavery. I know because I've talked with these people in their own countries. Here in Canada the record of laws to give equal rights to women is progressive, in fact quite exceptional by world standards. But this still does not mean that we share equal responsibility with men for the activities we carry out around the globe.

When I served as part of the Canadian delegation to the UN General Assembly in 1975 I was the only female delegate. I refused to allow myself to be used as a token representative. To prove myself I worked extra hard to be aware of issues far beyond what my colleagues expected me to know.

If you want to know the situation of women in international relations just look at the situation of women in External. At the senior levels only one or two women have made it to the top;

Of course every delegation thinks its women may have a seat on committees discussing human rights and social topics. Women are supposed to be compassionate. That's part of the blarney!

But why do they expect us not to be ready to discuss economic, military and political problems? Why shouldn't a woman state a country's point of view? Respect for females in international affairs is still a battle that has to be waged!

What goes on in these world debates and the role given to women there is simply a reflection of the attitude back home. The main claim of those in power is that they haven't got women with the proper kind of background for these tasks. And so they see women as lacking competence in the fields I've mentioned above.

They can't seem to think of a woman who's good at economics—but don't ask me why. If one opens the *Financial Times* on any morning one can see that half the stories are written by women. But the image of a woman in the field of economics is not yet accepted and that even goes for our leaders in External Affairs.

NOT HAVING WORK

Why did Wendy quit last week? One person said she was overworked. Another person said she was bored. Somebody else said that she didn't have a good social life. I don't know why

Wendy quit. I asked her to come and see me. She was sitting right here, and you know what? She didn't know herself! I asked her, "Wendy, why are you always sighing?" She couldn't give me a straight answer. She left, she said, "to become a receptionist, to answer phones, read magazines, and chew gum." She was competent enough to become manager someday. But she wanted a mindless, boring job.

—COMPANY PRESIDENT

The work is very satisfying. It's challenging and extremely rewarding. There's nothing more rewarding than winning a case for a worker who has been unjustly fired. You give the person back his or her pride. You make the worker feel part of the human race again. Getting fired is taken as a sign of gross irresponsibility. If you can win the case, then you prove that it's not the worker's fault, but the fault of the employer. You give pride back to the worker's children, because they see their parent back at work. It's very rewarding to solve people's problems. I guess it's like being a social worker. You go home very satisfied.

—UNION OFFICIAL

Being unemployed is hell. It's waking up each morning tired of living and ashamed to face the world. It seems that I just can't get myself together to do anything. Being unemployed really depletes your resources—mentally and financially. It's like I'm suffering from a disease. I don't really know if I can explain to you exactly what I'm going through. All I know is that a few months ago I was on top of the world—a highly paid and highly respected journalist. Then, before you know it, I'm nobody. My paper folded, and I got the sack.

Something dreadful happens to you when you lose your job. I don't know exactly why it happens. Even though you know you were good, still, your whole self-concept goes down the drain. You no longer have a place in society. You're alone. It scares you. It paralyses you. Until this happened, I never really understood what poor people go through. Once I even had to do an article on "The Horrors of Unemployment." But still I didn't understand. I just couldn't identify with the experience. I was still the unwitting victim of the myth that goes something like this: It's their own fault. They're not good enough. They don't try hard enough. They like living on handouts. They're parasites. And so on. I did not outwardly promote these ideas, but I think that deep down I felt that way. No more!

—JOURNALIST

ACTIVITIES

1. As was stated in The Program to this chapter, the process of creating a docudrama is very similar to that of creating an anthology. Refer to The Program and to the Activities section of Chapter 11 for suggestions on how to develop a docudrama on this material, particularly as regards ordering the material and developing a dramatic statement.

2. It takes inventiveness to dramatize lists such as "Job Characteristics." You might make the list into a song, create a choral reading out of it, or develop an improvisation about some of its significant features.

3. One technique for developing understanding of a situation or story to be used in a docudrama is to improvise a press conference. To do this, pick a selection from the chapter and assign the roles. The performers playing those roles must then answer questions asked by "reporters"—another group of performers—about their characters and the events they are involved in.

4. Any docudrama can benefit from the addition of the following: appropriate music, live or recorded; costumes or costume pieces which reflect the period and/or the characters; properties which are significant to the topic; or slides which recreate the time period and the setting.

5. To create your own docudramas, choose several famous people from history. Arrange a press conference wherein, after reading as much source material as possible, some members of your group question another who acts as one of the above chosen people. You may ask his or her view of current events and of events in his or her own time. Have those who are acting as reporters take on the role of other people who might have been alive at the time of the person being questioned. What kind of questions would they ask? What would be their attitudes toward the main figure? Assume the roles of others not alive at the time and continue your questions. For example, what questions might Nellie McClung wish to ask Queen Elizabeth I?

6. History has been a rich source for playwrights past and present. Samples of docudramas which have been developed into script form can be found in *The Elephant Man* (Section A, Chapter 1), *What Glorious Times They Had* (Section A, Chapter 1), *The Farm Show* (Section A, Chapter 3), and *1837: The Farmer's Revolt* (Section A, Chapter 4). Read these scripts during your work on "Docudrama."

13: Ensemble Drama

THE PROGRAM

Ensemble Drama provides an opportunity for a large group of students to participate in a dramatic presentation. The group, which can vary from 20 to 100 people, pools its artistic and creative responses and develops a unique, spontaneous dramatic event through the integration of drama, dance, music, and the visual arts.

The source material for Ensemble Drama can be drawn from many stories, including myths, legends, and folk tales, which contain timeless or universal truths. The message in the story should be as relevant to us now as it was to the people for whom the story was originally told. Ideally the story should have many characters, strong physical action, and direct, simple language.

After choosing a story, the group is divided into sub-groups. Each sub-group is assigned a specific task for the dramatization. Some of these sub-groups can be:

Storytellers—this group delivers the narrative of the story, by reading, by improvisation, or by a combination of both. Note that choral speech can be used successfully here. Rehearsal of reading and storytelling to gain dramatic power and effectiveness is very important. As in Readers Theatre, the group can also create strong visual images by the way actors are placed in the performing area.

Dancers/Movement Interpreters—this group rehearses those parts of the story which can be dramatized through dance and movement. Vocalization can be added through the use of chants where appropriate.

Musicians—this group provides percussion music (with either real or improvised instruments) for the storytelling.

Artists—this group can make masks and costumes, and design backdrops or paintings to enhance the story. During the dramatization, this group provides lighting and visual effects. The artists may even wish to be part of the setting themselves.

Each group practises on its own until called to the performance area. This area can be any large open space, inside or outdoors, which has been "dressed" by the artists during the practice time.

Performance of Ensemble Drama does not require an audience because each group of participants is the audience for the other groups. The performance begins on a given cue and unfolds spontaneously. Each group is attentive to the other parts of the story. If need be, one person can be appointed director to cue each group when to begin and when to end.

The spontaneity of Ensemble Drama, with its blending of the various arts, can lift drama into new forms of expression. Performers are provided with new insights into the power of ritualistic storytelling—one of the oldest dramatic forms known.

THE KING'S RIVAL

by Adjai Robinson
(adapted by David Booth)

PLAYBILL

This story comes from the area of Africa now known as Sierra Leone. It was spoken by storytellers and was only recently written down. In the society of the people who inhabit that area, there were secret societies exclusively for men, and others only for women. The elders are the leaders of these societies, and the oldest woman (in this story Mammy Yoko) was revered by both male and female elders. Unlike contemporary North American society, male and female roles were rigidly structured according to tasks and functions. When you read this story, be aware of the opportunities that exist for choral speaking, movement, music, and art.

King Tonko had ruled his country for a long time in peace and plenty. Like his great, great grandfather who founded their country, King Tonko was a great warrior. Like his great, great grandfather, he was a great wrestler, too. And like his great, great grandfather, he ruled wisely, was kind to his people, and honored the wise spirit, Odokoko.

But then King Tonko died. Tonkolili, his son, was a strong man like his father and his great, great, great grandfather. No one could outfight him. No one could outwrestle him. But he was not kind to his people. He made them pay twice the tax in crops, and he made all the young men spend most of their time working on his farms.

Before long the young men had less and less time to work their own farms, and it was the women who had to work harder and harder to feed their families. They had to do men's work in the fields, and when they started felling trees, their hands blistered.

The young men complained to the head wife of King Tonkolili, but the King would only listen to the old men with gray hair who sat with him. And they did not care how hard the young men worked.

Sadness was everywhere. It was in the talk of the people. It was on their faces. It was in their stories. It hung even on the trees like weeping willows on the branches.

Even Odokoko, the wise spirit whom the people never saw—seemed unhappy. Mammy Yoko, the priestess of the wise spirit, could hear only hollow rumbling sounds from Odokoko.

It got so bad that the only thing the people looked forward to was when Durosimi, the king's nephew, sneaked down to the river to sing. Then, the women forgot their blisters, and the young men forgot their griefs. Even the wise spirit seemed pleased.

Durosimi charmed the people with the daring deeds of their ancestors. He sang of the kindness of King Tonko, so that they remembered happier times. He sang of the brave hunter who killed three crocodiles with a single knife. His lullabyes were as gentle as the warmth from the soft sun's rays in May. When Durosimi sang, even the bushes seemed to sway their heads.

But even these times grew more and more rare, and the people became more and more unhappy. Finally, all the wives except the King's begged Mammy Yoko to ask the wise spirit for advice.

The following night Mammy Yoko threw her lappa over her shoulders and waited anxiously. She heard the tinniwinnie sounds of Odokoko's cricket trumpeters. When she heard the owls hooting, she approached the grove with her hands clasped over her chest. As she approached the bottomless hole of the oracle, she heard water tumbling down and down and down. Softly chanting, she began.

Odokoko
O mighty one
The father of our ancestors
The wise one of all wisdom
The great giver of all peace
The rock and defender of our tribe
Our King has taken our happiness
Give us the strength
To send the King away, away, away!

Suddenly, a star fell in the sky over a hut that Mammy Yoko knew well. Now she knew that King Tonkolili would soon be a fallen king. She poured some spirits into Odokoko's waters and returned with the answer.

At dawn the women with their water calabashes on their heads assembled at the river to hear Odokoko's advice. The men had already gone to King Tonkolili's farm outside the town. But Mammy Yoko passed the women by to sit beside Durosimi. Already he was singing. The rhythms of his songs flowed as smooth as the glassy ripples in the clear flowing river. He stopped singing when Mammy Yoko went closer to him.

"By your hand," she whispered, "shall happiness come to our people. When the moon is full, by your hand shall the great one fall."

Durosimi's surprise was seen by all.

"Me . . . me, a singer. But . . . but I am no warrior. I cannot fight . . . I cannot wrestle. How . . .?"

"The way will come to you just as surely as the hill runs down to the valley. I saw it all!" And with that, the priestess of the oracle left.

All the women, with their questions still on their faces, tried to go about their business of fetching water. Durosimi stared after Mammy Yoko. He knew she would not speak twice. But he was left with a thousand hows and five thousand whys. He was certain there was a mistake, only no one dared disobey the wise spirit.

The half moon had many full stars for her companions the next night. King Tonkolili sat in the shadow of the huge old tree with his gray-haired men and the court jester. But in the village there was silence. There were no stories and no games. The village would soon fall asleep.

Durosimi took the sack that his grandfather Tonko, the mighty warrior, had used as his hunting bag. He hastened to the King's compound and sneaked, unseen by anyone, into an empty room beside the King's room.

Before long, all became quiet in the palace. The night birds stopped chirping. The old men, with eyes heavy with sleep, returned to their huts. Even the house cricket, whose song was so shrill and long that it would deafen your ears, returned to its burrow in the earth. The half moon now halfway on its journey in the sky sent its light peeping through the window of Durosimi's hiding place.

Durosimi knew his time had come and that Tonkolili's time was up. He sprang to his feet without a sound. His left hand ransacked the hunting bag for his answer to the wise spirit. In his thoughts, he saw Mammy Yoko. He heard her say, "By your hand shall happiness come to our people."

What other way was there but by the dagger, King Tonko's dagger?

Like an elephant moving soundlessly through the open grassland, Durosimi stole quietly and silently into King Tonkolili's room. The half moon now sent its shining rays onto the King's bed. Some light rested just below his chest. If it were lightning, it would have struck him.

Durosimi began to chant.

King Tonko
Your sharp dagger
Never missed its mark
King Tonko
Your sharp dagger
Brought plenty to your country
King Tonko
Let it bring happiness
To your sad children
King Tonko
Let it take your life!!

Then, with his left hand raised and his body fully arched forward, Durosimi landed the dagger right on the King's left side. Or so he thought. Just at that moment the King shifted on his bed, and Tonko's sharp dagger only grazed the wicked Tonkolili.

The King howled his anger.

In a moment the palace was astir. The King's wives and his courtiers assembled to give thanks for the safety of the King's life, to praise his bravery, to advise him, and to blame and condemn and hurl words at the King's nephew, Durosimi.

As Durosimi was led to the prisoner's house with his wrists tied together, his head was bowed. He had failed. Then he saw the moon—it was bright, but it was still a half moon. The half moon had not turned into a full moon yet. There was time.

At the week's end, the old men listened to Durosimi defend himself. Some of them felt forced to agree that Durosimi had a sore grievance with the King. He must settle his account with the King publicly, the oldest elder decided. King and nephew would wrestle in the town square until one man fell. If Durosimi was the first to fall, he would be banished. If, on the other hand, King Tonkolili should fall, Durosimi would be allowed to bring a full petition against him. The old men were confident that Durosimi, the singer, would fail.

Mammy Yoko knew that the moon would not be full for a week. She led the women in great numbers to put their complaints before the King so that his days would be filled until the time was right. The young men went, too.

At last, the day for the great wrestling came. The whole town assembled. The women prayed in their hearts that their son Durosimi would win. The old men and the King's jester were sure King Tonkolili would win and told him so.

The wrestling started with the first light from the sun, and as they wrestled the King and Durosimi sang.

Grant me power, power, power
Let it rain
Let it rain
Grant me power
Grant me power
Let it thunder, let it roar
Mi bumi nye, nye
Mi bumi aye!
Mi bumi nye, nye
Mi bumi aye!

Only the wrestlers could sing. Indeed, the singing set their pace.

The King, heavy and strong, wrestle-sang like a lion with a heavy, strong beat. Durosimi was slow at first. The women urged him on. He remembered the wrestling tricks of his boyhood days. Gradually he gained confidence. He started to wrestle-sing as lightly as a leopard. He became quick and even.

They wrestled all day, and they wrestled all night, but neither man fell, nor lost his beat. Through his singing, Durosimi seemed to find strength he did not know he had.

Mi bumi nye, nye, nye

They wrestle-sang into the second day and the second night, but neither the lion nor the leopard fell, nor lost a beat.

Mi bumi nye, nye, nye

On the third day the sun bore into their muscled backs, the King sweating in his lion way; Durosimi wet, but springy as a leopard. Still, their wrestling was as hot as the midday sun, and not one fell that day.

Mi bumi nye, nye, nye

The fourth night thunder rolled. There was rain. Durosimi wrestled-danced in it, growing stronger in his song. But for the first time, the lion king, drenched by the rain, missed a step.

Mi . . . mi . . . bumi . . .

The court jester howled at the thunder and Mammy Yoko. The King caught his step and his song.

Mi bumi nye, nye, nye

The two men wrestled on and on through the storm, through the dawn, through the rainy day, and into the next night when the wind was fierce and cold, but the moon was full.

Odokoko, the wise spirit, was in the wind as it whistled past the thatched roofs. The wives and the young men drew closer, holding their breath. The old men and the jesters clapped and clapped.The court jester grimaced with twisted face.

The King, feeling their rhythm, seized Durosimi, but quickly let him loose when he missed a step.

Mi . . . mi . . . bumi . . . nye . . .

Out of step, he lunged again for Durosimi, but Durosimi sang-danced out of his fingers. The King rolled at his knees, but Durosimi sang-spun away.

Mi bumi nye, nye, nye

Durosimi chanted evenly, smoothly, catching the feet of the wives and young men in a swaying rhythm.

Finally, the King's voice was gone, blown away by the wind, his rhythm blown away with it. Durosimi, knowing his time had come, turned, threw his arms around the King's waist and jerked Tonkolili up, sweeping his feet off the ground. The King crashed down in defeat. The King slumped to the ground. The star had fallen.

There was a loud sigh, and then a huge cry of joy as Durosimi triumphed. Mammy Yoko stepped forward to embrace the young singer, now a great champion. The old men and the jesters bowed their heads in disappointment. Even the full moon seemed to smile as he chanted:

The star has fallen,
The hill has turned to valley
The young mountain shall bring
Joy and happiness to our country.

ACTIVITIES

1. Each of the sub-groups will be assigned a specific task to develop for the dramatization of this story. Here are some guidelines for each sub-group suggested in The Program.

Storyteller—examine the text for opportunities to use choral speaking, single voices, and groups of voices. Investigate the use of the techniques of Readers Theatre and Story Theatre. Be careful that you do not divide parts among males and females according to the roles in the story. Rather, examine the combinations of voices that most enhance the storytelling.

Dancers/Movement Interpreters—first decide which parts of the story you wish to interpret by movement/mime/dance. Do not feel you have to "do" the whole story; the storytellers will do that. Your choices should be based on those aspects of the story which will be enhanced by movement. Avoid distinguishing between male and female roles. The wrestlers can be interpreted by the whole group, and Mammy Yoko can be a group rather than an individual. Your movement work should not be an "acting out" of the story; it should convey the emotional substance of the story.

Musicians—decide which sounds (vocal and instrumental) will intensify the moods of the story. Choose moments in the story when a particular mood—sadness, happiness, anger, etc.—is predominant, and invent sounds which will complement the mood. Use instruments which you have at hand, which you make, or which you find, to create these sounds. Invent a musical opening to the story, and create appropriate sounds and rhythms for the ending.

Visual Artists—create an appropriate setting for the story. For backdrops or set pieces you can use any material that can be hung, shaped, or on which you can draw, such as garbage bags, newspapers, and large sheets of wrapping paper. The only limit is your ingenuity. Pieces of material can become cloaks and costumes for the participants, and paperbags, paper plates, or strips of cardboard can become masks. Lighting effects can be created by hand painted slides, with slide projectors as the light source. In addition, think of ways that you can become part of the setting.

2. The performance of this story, with all sub-groups involved, need not be carefully rehearsed. If each participant is attentive to the other participants' efforts, each group will recognize when it should participate and when it should allow another group to carry the story. The performance can end with a spontaneous celebration by having all the groups participate in chant, movement, and music.

14: Theatre for young people

THE PROGRAM

> As theatre for young people has matured, it has realized that children's emotions are strongly felt, and their attitudes strongly held. Their range encompasses the most universal and basic themes as well as many immediate and contemporary problems within their own world of experience.
>
> *Theatre for Young People*, Desmond Davis

It is of interest to you as a drama student that young people are enthusiastic audiences for theatre presentations. Theatre for young people consists of scripts developed especially for young audiences at various age levels. Children in the primary grades have different interests from children in the junior grades and from young adolescents, and you must be aware of the needs and interests of each particular group and of the specific theatre forms that will assist you in communicating with that group. Although your audience is young, it is not necessarily inexperienced or unsophisticated. Young people can be a very demanding audience and deserve high quality theatre.

There must always be a script of some sort for you to follow. The script may be the collective work of a group which, through exploration and rehearsal, has created a basic scenario. The script may be an anthology or a docudrama made up of shorter pieces linked together thematically. Even an improvisational performance must be pre-planned according to a theme or a form.

Today there are many scripts for young people available. James Reaney, one of Canada's foremost poets and playwrights, has created many fine plays for young audiences—*Apple Butter, Geography Match*, and *Names and Nicknames*, for example. These scripts are not meant to be read by children but to be performed for children.

Also available for dramatization are traditional stories such as fairytales, legends, myths, and fables. These can be presented in the Story Theatre format discussed in Chapter 9.

Production of these plays can be very innovative. For example, you can go to the young person's environment—a playground, a gymnasium, or a library. You can use very simple staging, since young people use their imaginations to fill out the details of a set, as well as details of costumes and properties. Performers can take on several roles in a play, or play inanimate objects and be readily accepted by the audience. Children like to participate in a play and will join in the action vocally (with chants and cheers), help the action along physically (by carrying the magic dust in their pockets), and take on roles in the play (farmers, jurors, or villagers). Sometimes the play is actually altered because children have participated fully with the actors both in the process of exploration and in the dramatization of the play.

Theatre-in-Education

Usually a presentation for young people is self-contained. That is, the play is presented and there may be a short discussion with the audience afterwards. Another concept of theatre which has more direct educational goals has begun to emerge; it is called "Theatre-in-Education" (T.I.E.). The subject matter of the play is directly related to the content of the children's school work, and the members of the T.I.E. team are both actors and educational resource people. The T.I.E. team discusses the content of the play with the children's teacher and structures the script so that it deals with certain concepts and ideas. This means that the script is usually an original creation and is created by the group or by individuals in the group. The techniques discussed in Chapter 10, "Scripting," are invaluable here.

In addition to writing the script, the T.I.E. team prepares activities for the children to do prior to the performance and follow-up work for the children to do after the performance. In this way the team works with the children and the teacher to create a comprehensive educational unit.

Theatre-in-Education projects require that the group deal with a smaller audience, usually one or two classes. The team must work closely with the teacher and the children, and should plan on several visits to the school.

First People is a play built on the curriculum of grades one, two, and three. It can be presented as a play for young audiences or it can be expanded to provide Theatre-in-Education experiences.

FIRST PEOPLE

by Faye Davis and Company

PLAYBILL

Some of the activities on pages 124-125 provide you with ideas for interaction with the children before the play is presented. Other activities give you ideas which will help the children deepen their experience after they have seen the play. As you read the script, notice the variety of techniques employed within it. You will find Readers Theatre, Story Theatre, choral dramatization, chant, and ritual, as well as conventional script forms.

CHARACTERS

Actor #1	**Sloth #2**
Actor #2	**Frog**
Actor #3	**Squirrel**
Actor #4	**Bird**
Actor #5	**Turtle**
Sun	**Rabbit**
Moon	**Snake**
Earth #1	**Sutawnee**
Earth #2	**Chief**
Earth #3	**Bonah**
Beaver #1	**Stranger**
Beaver #2	**West Wind**
Beaver #3	**Rain**
Sloth #1	

All: Long, long, long ago

Actor #1: When all was still and quiet

2: There was nothing to be heard

3: Nothing to be seen

4: Until one day

(The following sounds of life and growth are evolved through work with the groups of children prior to performance. The sounds listed are examples only.)

Actor #5: A hissing

1: Sizzling

2: Buzzing

3: Spinning

4: Thundering filled the sky.

(Obtain the assistance of the groups of children in producing these sounds during performance.)

Actor #5: And when the sun was just brand new

1: And very very hot

2: It didn't care for its shape a lot

3: It twisted and wriggled and shook bits off

(Two actors, representing SUN *and* MOON, *leave the core group of actors and stand on opposite sides of the playing area.)*

Sun: And the earth was formed.

Moon: What about me?

Earth #1: You are our moon.

Earth #2: You belong to us.

Earth #3: So stay nearby at all times.

Earth #1: And light the sky at night.

Sun: But the earth couldn't make up its mind, about its shape that is.

Moon: First it tried one shape.

Earth #1: But a square thing was much too clumsy and kept getting stuck on things.

Earth: Oops.

Sun: So Earth tried another shape.

Earth #2: A triangle! But a triangle was altogether too pointy at one end.

Sun: So Earth tried yet another shape.

Earth #3: And a long straight thing. . . .

Sun: Was much too boring.

Moon: But a round. . . .

Sun: Well, sort of round world

Earth #1: Was much more comfortable.

Sun: Yawn.

Earth #2: Why, it could fit in anywhere.

Earth #3: And could turn and roll very nicely.

Earth #1: But just when Earth was beginning to feel more comfortable. . . .

Moon: A great white thing began crawling all over it.

Earth #1: Hey, what is this?

Earth #2: It's freezing.

Earth #3: And heavy.

Earth #2: It's pressing into me and leaving a lot of bumps.

Earth #3: And hollows.

Moon: For a long time the cold winds blew.

Sun: And everything was quiet.

Moon: Except for the ice. It grew thicker and thicker. . . . (*to* SUN) Can you see what's happening down there?

Sun: (*Yawn*) Mmmmmmm?

Moon: Can't you see what's happening?

Sun: What's happening?

Moon: The earth is going to be covered with ice if you don't hurry and do something about it.

Sun: Why me?

Moon: You could use a little of that heat of yours and melt some of the ice away.

Sun: I'm too tired.

Moon: I'd gladly do it for you, but I don't have the power.

Sun: Well, of course you don't. It takes a lot of energy.

Moon: That's just what I'm saying. Use some of it and melt the ice.

Sun: Can't be bothered.

Moon: Give me some of your heat. . . . I don't mind the work.

Sun: I can't reach you, you're too far away. (*Drops off to sleep again*)

Moon: Things went on like that for quite some time.

Sun: The sun just went on sleeping.

Moon: And the moon stayed awake and worried.

Sun: The cold winds blew.

Moon: And everything was very quiet. Except for the ice. (*Ice sounds*)

Moon: (*to* SUN) Wake up, it's getting worse.

Sun: (*Yawn*) What's getting worse?

Moon: The ice.

Sun: You worry too much.

Moon: I wouldn't worry if I had your heat. I'd use some of it and melt that ice.

Sun: You would?

Moon: Yes.

Sun: I suppose you'd like to change places with me?

Moon: I'd love it. Maybe we could.

Sun: Maybe we could.

Sun & Moon: Maybe we could!

Sun: If you can arrange to send your cool rays over here. . . . I'll send my hot energy over to you.

Moon: Done.

(They arrange for two children to take their silk streamers to the opposite end and return so that MOON *now has a yellow streamer and* SUN *has a blue streamer.)*

Moon: I feel quite different.

Sun: So do I . . . now I can sleep all day.

Moon: So nice and warm . . . just what I've always wanted. Now watch me melt that ice.

Earth #1: The ice began to melt.

Earth #2: Wide deep oceans rolled onto sandy beaches.

Earth #3: Large smooth lakes looked like mirrors in the earth.

Actor #4: Rivers ran down the mountains and into the valleys.

Actor #1: Trees began to shoot up out of the hard ground.

(Celebration song to LA LA LA LA LA *as trees begin to grow.)*

Beaver #2: But then huge animals. . . .

Beaver #1: I mean really huge, began roaming through the forests looking for food.

Beaver #2: There wasn't much.

Sloth #1: I'm a giant ground Sloth.

Sloth #2: So am I, and I'm one of the biggest creatures around these parts.

Sloth #1: So am I. Why, I can pick up a whole tree if I want to. (*Tries to pick up a child.*)

Sloth #2: So can I. In fact, I'm the boss around here.

Sloth #1: So am I.

Frog: Ribet.

Beaver #1: I am a ten-foot beaver.

Beaver #2: Well, so am I.

Beaver #1: I do all the work around the creek here.

Beaver #3: So do I.

Beaver #1: I can chew through any tree I care to.

Beaver #2: Me too.

(They take a quick chomp in the direction of the children.)

Frog: Ribet. I'm just a humble frog and I drink lots of water . . . RIBET.

Sloth #1: If you're such a common humble frog. . . .

Sloth #2: Why don't you just keep quiet.

Beaver #1: Yes, drink all you want and don't bother me. I'm far too important.

Beaver #2: WE'RE far too important.

Frog: Ribet.

Sloth #2: All the smaller creatures are terrified at the sight of me.

Sloth #1: They run a mile when they see me coming.

Frog: Really? Ribet, ribet.

Beaver #1: The ground shakes when I flap my giant tail.

Beaver #3: The ground shakes when I flap my giant tail.

Beaver #2: And so does everyone else.

Frog: Oh dear. Ribet.

*(*SLOTHS *and* BEAVERS *fight, and finally make their way out of the playing area, wounded and noticeably shrinking in size.)*

Frog: Some of those really huge creatures were so busy being tough . . . they were always fighting with one another just to see who was strongest or for some other silly reason. They didn't even stop to eat. So it didn't take too long for them to disappear altogether. Ribet . . . Ribet . . . Now me . . . I just kept on drinking that water. Didn't frighten me. Ribet.

(Smaller creatures emerge)

Squirrel: Good morning, Frog.

Frog: Morning, Squirrel.

Bird: What a beautiful morning. Always like to start the day off with a drink and a splash in the old creek.

Frog: Yes, it's delicious.

Turtle: Wouldn't want to drink it all day though.

Frog: Why not, Turtle? I do.

Rabbit: If I drank as much as you do Frog I'd be too heavy to move.

Squirrel: It seems to me that this creek isn't as deep as it was yesterday.

Bird: You know why don't you?

Turtle: I've got a pretty good idea.

Rabbit: Frog just never lets up, does she?

Turtle: Never stops drinking.

*(*FROG *continues to drink water as the animals move back to their groups. Short discussion about the shrinking water level of creek.)*

Rabbit: Next morning, bright and early. . . .

Bird: We hurried back to the creek.

Rabbit: Oh, look, didn't I tell you—she's drunk the creek dry.

Squirrel: This creek used to be full to overflowing.

Bird: It's no use to me now. I can't live without water you know.

Turtle: How could such a small frog drink so much.

Frog: Ribet. It's easy.

Bird: You'd better think of some way to fill that creek up again Frog.

Frog: Oh, I'd soon give the water back if I knew how.

Squirrel: What do you mean?

Frog: I'm so uncomfortable—I'm so full I can't leap about any more.

Turtle: Yes, come to think of it I haven't seen you move for days now.

Frog: You don't suppose you could turn me upside down and tip some of the water back into the creek do you?

Rabbit: It's worth a try.

Squirrel: It'll never work if you ask me. She's much too slippery.

Rabbit: Come along, Squirrel, help us try.

*(*RABBIT *and* SQUIRREL *try to turn* FROG *over, but she slips out of their grasp.)*

Rabbit: You're right, Squirrel, she is much too slippery.

Turtle: If we could just get her mouth open really wide, I mean REALLY wide.

Bird: Yes, that should do the trick. After all, she opened it pretty wide to get all that water in there.

Squirrel: How can we do that?

Frog: Please, nothing more. No more of your bright ideas. Ribet. I haven't recovered from the last one yet.

Rabbit: Well, I suppose one more day without water won't do any harm, but we'll be needing it tomorrow.

Turtle: We'd better come up with some pretty good ideas.

Bird: Well I'm going to talk this over with my family and I suggest you should do the same.

Turtle: There's a pretty good idea already.

(Actors return to their groups with "Have you ever seen a frog open it's mouth really wide? Answers cover a wide range. Eating (flies), yawning, laughing, shock, etc. Violent suggestions dismissed immediately since FROG *is a friend and shouldn't be hurt. Each group tries their idea and with sufficient and appropriate ad-libbing all groups can participate until* FROG *begins to laugh, yawn, whatever. No jokes. When the solution is found after three or four attempts cries of "It's working!" "Here comes the water!" "Hurrah!")*

Rabbit: The water came spilling back into the creek again.

Bird: Soaking the dry hard earth.

Squirrel: The banks of the creek were covered with soft green grass.

(Celebration song: LA LA LA LA LA. ACTORS *re-group.* CHIEF, SUTAWNEE *[daughter] and* BONAH *[son] in group at one end.* BIRD *up ladder.* SNAKE *and* STRANGER *behind group.)*

Bird: Not tar from the creek where the animals had been celebrating their good fortune, there lived a tribe of people. But they did not share the happiness of the animals.

(The celebration song is played mournfully on a recorder by BIRD.*)*

Sutawnee: Father, our people are sick and dying—what are we to do?

Chief: It's the mighty water snake from the river. It robs the land of its goodness and comes among the people and makes them sick.

Bonah: Why don't we chase it away, Father?

Chief: The snake is too powerful. We have tried many times, but the snake keeps coming back.

Sutawnee: Why don't we leave here then?

Bonah: And leave our homes?

Sutawnee: It seems the only thing left to do.

Chief: It will be hard for the people to leave their homes.

Sutawnee: Why don't we ask them father?

Chief: Very well. Call a meeting of the people and we'll decide the best thing to do.

Bonah: THE CHIEF WILL SPEAK TO US TONIGHT. THE CHIEF WILL SPEAK TO US TONIGHT.

Bird: That night the people gathered for the meeting.

Chief: My people—the home that we love has become unsafe to live in because of the sickness the great water snake brings. It would be wise for us to move on to another place where the snake cannot follow.

Bonah: Father, how can we be sure the snake won't follow us?

Chief: The snake cannot be too long away from water. When we move we will keep to the woods—he cannot follow us too far.

Sutawnee: I hope not.

Chief: Who is ready to move with me tonight?

(Response from GROUPS*)*

Chief: Very well. These are our plans. The snake will come again tonight, but we will pretend to be asleep. As soon as the snake leaves we will creep off as quietly as we can.

Bonah: And we must each take a branch and cover our footprints as we go.

*(*ACTORS *prepare their individual groups for sleep.)*

Bird: That night, the people huddled together in their longhouses and pretended to sleep. The Great Snake came slithering into the village, (ACTOR *moves into Playing area as* SNAKE) but no one moved. The Snake thought the people were asleep.

Snake: Hmmph!

Bird: And went sliding off back to the river.

Chief: We have tricked the snake. Now is the time to leave. Let us go quietly.

Bonah: Make sure to cover your tracks. (*They move out and into another area.*)

Chief: Rest now. You've done well. The snake has not followed us and we are now too far from the river.

(Everyone rests and the STRANGER *appears.)*

Bonah: Look! A Stranger. Who is he, Father?

Stranger: You are the strangers here, not I.

Bonah: Who are you?

Chief: Wait! We mean no harm. We will not be here long. We are looking for a new home.

Bonah: We come from Oniagara.

Sutawnee: The Great Water Snake has forced us to leave.

Stranger: No one passes this way without my permission. Are you the leader of these people?

Chief: I am.

Stranger: Then it is you who must wrestle with me for the right to pass.

Chief: And if I lose?

Stranger: Then you must all return to Oniagara.

Bonah: Let me wrestle him, Father.

Chief: No, Bonah. This is something I must do myself.

*(*CHIEF *and* STRANGER *wrestle. It is a draw.)*

Stranger: You are indeed a strong leader of your people. You have won for your people the right to pass this way as often as they like. And as a token of our friendship and your great courage, I have a gift for you. It is an ear of corn. When you reach your new land, split it into many parts and scatter the seeds near to your new homes. Then, in a month, it will grow. You will never want for food again.

Chief: To never want for food again. This is indeed a great reward. You do me and my people an honor.

Stranger: When it is full grown take it and grind it into flour. In the months of the year when the hunting and fishing cannot be done you will have flour from the corn to make bread.

Chief: Thank you. My people thank you also. (*The* ACTORS *and* GROUPS *make the thank you sign.) But we must now continue our search for a new home.*

Stranger: I know of someone who may be able to help you in your search. She sees farther than our eyes can see. Would you be able to guide these people, Bird, my good friend?

Bird: It will be a pleasure. I know of a creek that has clear running water, the greenest grass you've ever seen and the tallest trees in the woods.

Sutawnee: It sounds wonderful.

Stranger: Go then. I wish you well. (*He leaves.*)

Bonah: Can we follow you there now?

Bird: Indeed, you can, but you must promise not to harm those creatures already living there.

Bonah: Every creature has its home and we are the newcomers. We will not harm them.

Bird: Let's go then.

Chief: Gather your belongings my people. It is time for us to continue our journey.

(The GROUPS *sing to* LA LA LA LA LA *as they move into the new area.)*

Bird: Here we are. This is the creek I told you about. It runs into the mighty Lake Ontario.

Sutawnee: What a beautiful place this is.

Chief: We are here. This is our new home. I know we will be happy here.

Bird: And so the people found their new home far from the Great Water Snake. Here they settled. And then the Chief remembered the gift of the

Stranger. And he called for the ceremony of the growing of the corn.

Chief: We must now use our sounds of life and growth.

Sutawnee: My people will call upon the Earth to receive the corn.

Chief: My people will call upon the Sun to warm the Earth.

Bonah: My people will call upon the Rain to water the corn.

West Wind: My people will call upon the Wind to bring the Rain.

Bird: And my people will call upon the Earth to help the seeds to grow.

(All GROUPS *make their sounds of life and growth and then* BIRD *leads the singing of the ceremonial song.)*

Help our corn to grow
Help our corn to grow
Bring the sun and bring the rain
Please help our corn to grow.

(Sung three times. SUTAWNEE *has been planting the corn.* STRANGER *now becomes* WEST WIND *and* BONAH *becomes* RAIN.*)*

Sutawnee: It is done, Father. In a month, the corn will be growing.

Bird: But soon after Sutawnee and her friends had scattered the corn, clouds gathered in the sky, rushing ahead of the wild West Wind as he came out of the West. With him was his friend Rain who was never far behind him. West Wind was a mischievous wind, and the corn on the ground was a great temptation to him.

*(*WEST WIND *begins to blow the corn around, laughing, pointing and inviting* RAIN *to share the fun.)*

Bird: Don't do that, West Wind. How can the corn grow if you blow it away?

West Wind: We don't have anything better to do, do we, Rain?

Rain: I don't have much choice, do I?

West Wind: Poor Rain, he can't see very well. I lead him everywhere.

Rain: And mostly into trouble.

*(*WEST WIND *continues to blow the corn about.)*

Bird: I don't think the people will be very happy about this, West Wind. They're going to be back in a month to see if the corn has grown.

West Wind: Oh, Bird. We're just having a bit of fun. Aren't we, Rain?

Rain: Fun? If you say so, West Wind. Fun.

West Wind: Rain?

Rain: Huh?

West Wind: Let's go into the village and blow on a few people.

Rain: Which way?

West Wind: Hang on, Rain. I'll lead the way.

Bird: You're asking for trouble, West Wind. Don't say I didn't warn you.

West Wind: Don't ruffle your feathers Bird. We won't do any harm.

Bird: (*To* GROUPS) I know he doesn't mean any harm, he just doesn't know his own strength.

West Wind: Let's blow some leaves on these people. (*They do.*) Rain, give me a little water and I'll blow a few drops on these people.

*(*CHIEF *and* SUTAWNEE *appear.)*

West Wind: Is that the Chief over there?

Rain: I can't see.

West Wind: Well, I'm going to play a trick on him anyway.

Rain: Do you think you should?

West Wind: It's all in fun, Rain.

Rain: I hope the Chief thinks so.

*(*WEST WIND *with* RAIN *behind him manoeuvres his way around the* CHIEF *and* SUTAWNEE *so as not to be seen. He blows them around and finally blows them over completely.)*

Chief: West Wind. I know it's you. Where are you? (CHIEF *stands up and is blown down again.*) Stop that. This is your last warning.

Rain: Did you hear that West Wind? Last warning.

West Wind: He doesn't mean it. He's only joking.

Rain: I don't think so West Wind. I didn't hear him laughing.

*(*WEST WIND *blows* SUTAWNEE *off her feet.)*

Sutawnee: Father. Do something.

Rain: Oh, no.

Chief: Look what you've done, West Wind.

Sutawnee: I'm covered in mud.

West Wind: Oh, I beg your pardon. I didn't mean to hurt her. It was just a little blow.

Rain: He gets carried away.

Chief: I'm going to see that he is carried away.

*(*CHIEF *asks for assistance.)*

West Wind: What are you going to do with me?

Chief: Take West Wind to the edge of the Village and point him toward the West. That is where you belong.

West Wind: But. . . .

Chief: Not another word West Wind. I'm very fond of you but you can't come back in the Village till you learn to behave yourself.

West Wind: But. . . . (*He blows away.*)

Bird: Off he blew. Rain, of course, who could not see without West Wind had to go along as well. In one month the Chief and his daughter came to see if the corn had grown.

Chief: Is this where you scattered the seeds of corn?

Sutawnee: Yes, father. But nothing has grown.

Chief: The earth is bone dry. The corn will never grow, till the rain comes.

Bird: Excuse me, Chief, but when you sent West Wind away, Rain went away too.

Chief: But I didn't mean for rain to go as well . . . only West Wind.

Bird: Rain doesn't see too well. West Wind leads him everywhere.

Chief: But we have to have rain. How will anything grow?

Bird: If you want the rain, you'll have to have the West Wind too.

Chief: What shall we do?

Sutawnee: Perhaps Bird can help us again. She can travel fast and see far.

Chief: Bird, will you go and bring them back? Search the West till you find West Wind and Rain.

Bird: Very well I'll do my best. (BIRD *may take a couple of her group along with her, or even the whole group, depending on its size.*) Bird (and her friends) flew for many days looking for West Wind and Rain. It seemed as if they had disappeared completely. Then on the last day she (they) happened to see some long grass gently blowing back and forth. She knew then that West Wind had to be close by.

*(*BIRD *lands near the group where* WEST WIND *and* RAIN *are hiding.)*

Bird: Oh, there you are West Wind.

West Wind: Oh Bird. Good to see you.

Rain: That you Bird?

Bird: Yes it is Rain. The Chief has sent us to find you. He needs you very much.

West Wind: He does?

Rain: Why?

Bird: The corn is not growing. The people need to have food before the winter comes.

West Wind: What has that got to do with me?

Bird: Well, it's not so much you, West Wind. It's Rain we need at the moment to make the corn grow quickly.

Rain: That's right, West Wind. You'll have to get me back as quickly as you can.

West Wind: If I'm not wanted, I don't think I'll bother to go.

Bird: You know you're welcome West Wind, just so long as you don't play tricks on people.

Rain: Oh, he's changed. Haven't you, West Wind?

Bird: The Chief will be pleased to hear that.

Rain: And he'll be even more pleased to hear what West Wind has to tell him about the Great Water Snake.

Bird: Snake? Snake? What snake?

Rain: On our way here we passed Oniagara and West Wind saw something important about the Great Water Snake.

Bird: You know how the people feel about the Great Water Snake. If you have any news of it they will thank you for bringing it. You will be made very welcome.

Rain: (*pleading*) West Wind.

West Wind: Oh, all right. Come along, Rain. Here we go.

Bird: Just a minute . . . we'll never be able to keep up with you.

West Wind: No problem, Bird. You (and your friends) keep just ahead of me and I'll blow you along.

Bird: Oh boy. A free ride. Let's go.

(CHIEF *and* SUTAWNEE *are waiting.*)

Sutawnee: Father. Here they come.

Rain: Take me over the corn, West Wind.

West Wind: There you go, Rain. Rain away.

(*He does—they come back to* CHIEF *and* SUTAWNEE.)

Chief: My people thank you. You've been very helpful, West Wind. I wish to welcome you both back to the Village.

West Wind: Thank you.

Rain: West Wind has news of the Great Water Snake.

Chief: The Great Water Snake?

Sutawnee: It's not following us here, is it?

Rain: Tell them.

West Wind: Well. . . . You remember the Great Water Snake?

Chief: Very well indeed.

(WEST WIND *blows them gently out of the playing area and begins narration.* SNAKE *comes on stage.*)

After you left your old village the snake returned. It found no one—not even a track to follow. It was so angry
it snorted
and growled
and slithered back into the river.

Down the river swam the Great Snake, lashing its tail against the sides of the river till it reached a narrow bend and there it stuck.

(*The* SNAKE *growls in frustration.*)

West Wind: It growled and it roared, but it couldn't move.

Rain: The water rushed over the top of the snake and tumbled down the other side.

Chief: The water is still falling.

Sutawnee: And the snake growls underneath.

Bird: But it will never be able to harm anyone again.

West Wind: And often the people return to the river.

Bird: And watch the great falls.

Chief: And celebrate their escape from the Snake.

(*Celebration dance and song.*)

O—NI —A— GA — RA

Oniagara
Oniagara
Here we live and here we grow
Oniagara

O—NI —A— GA — RA

ACTIVITIES

1. In order to investigate the structure of this play, develop a synopsis of it according to scenes and describe each scene in a short statement. In order to aid your analysis, here is how the play is described by the originating group:

The theme of the play is the search for harmony and meaning in the natural environment and the celebration of the complexities and interdependence of life forms: elements, plants, animals, and people.

Stories told in the play explain such things as: how lakes and hills were formed; how ice retreated after the ice age; how prehistoric animals lived; why the first people moved inland away from the great bodies of water; and why corn is regarded as a symbol of friendship.

The style of the play is transformation. By small changes in voice, movement, and costume, the performers become elements, animals, or people. By seeing the performers do this with minimal props or costumes, the children can transform themselves into the First People, animal families, and elements to help in the unfolding of the stories.

2. If you decide to present the play as a Theatre for Young People performance, prepare the play using the techniques discussed in this section, and refer to the techniques for analysing and rehearsing scripts contained in Section A.

3. If you decide to develop this script as a Theatre-in-Education project, here are some guidelines and suggestions:

a) **Activities for the children before they see the play:** After discussing your plans thoroughly with the children's teacher, arrange to meet the children before you do the play. You and the children should become familiar with each other. This also provides you with time to explore some of the concepts of the play.

First discuss and explore the concept of celebration with the children. You might begin by asking why we have celebrations such as Thanksgiving and birthdays. Some of the answers the children might give are: to remember an important event in our lives; to pass on beliefs that are important; to honor someone's special achievement; and to celebrate being alive after some particularly hard time.

Next have the children consider some of the celebrations they participate in, such as birthdays, religious events, anniversaries, vacations, etc. Then, with the children, you can explore some of the components of many celebrations, such as giving and receiving of gifts; singing of songs; dressing up in special clothes; putting decorations around the house; sharing food with others; telling stories; and playing games. Rather than just talking about these components, let the children act them out through mime and movement.

It is important that your group members also become involved in these activities.

The next stage of the pre-play activities is an examination of stories and myths which explain natural phenomena. Because the play is about how certain things occurred according to mythology, the group can research and prepare a reading of stories and myths from other lands and cultures. For example, Greek myths of the creation of the world can be told. The stories should be kept simple and short, and, after you have read or told the story, the children can dramatize the story through movement and sound. Members of your group can take part.

b) **Activities for the children after the play:** The children can re-enact the ceremony of planting. They can create new chants, calling on the rain, the sun, and the earth to nourish the seeds.

The children can be read other stories about seeds and growth. They might want to write a story themselves about the summer.

There can be a discussion of the problems the people faced in the play and of the qualities these people had to have in order to solve these problems. Some examples might be: the courage of the chief as he wrestled with the stranger; the perseverance of Bird as she flew in search of West Wind and Blind Rain; and the trust the people placed in their leaders.

The children or the group can suggest other problems which faced the people, such as floods, fire, or wild animals, and the children can be asked to invent ways of solving these problems. They can express their answers through drama, writing, or painting.

The children can explore some of the transformation concepts presented in the play and find their own ways of expressing these concepts. Some examples might be: the earth trying to find its shape; the giant sloths; and the water snake.

The children can go on to do drawings, paintings and writing activities under the guidance of the classroom teacher. Perhaps the children will send your group their art work and writing so you can see their responses to the project.

Solving riddles based on some aspects of the play is another activity which encourages response. Try using the following riddles.

Riddles for Kindergarten to Grade Two

1. I am everywhere, but you cannot see me. Sometimes I am very strong, but other times, I can be so still that not a leaf moves. What am I? (Air)
2. I am very hard and come in many shapes and sizes. Most of my family is gray. Some of my family wear bright colors. You like to climb on me sometimes. What am I? (Rock)
3. I can be happy in a sandbox or in a garden. I am great fun when I am mixed with water. What am I? (Earth)
4. Without me, swimming and bathing would be difficult. You drink me, although I have no taste to speak of. What am I? (Water)
5. I am too hot to touch, but lovely to look at. I often use smoke as my messenger. What am I? (Fire)

Riddles for Grades Two and Three

6. I am everywhere except where I am not. I am always light, but some days I seem very heavy. I am invisible, but, if angered, I can take the town apart. What am I? (Air)
7. I am rugged, hard, and unfeeling. I can rise to great heights and reach to the bottoms of oceans as well. Some of my kind are worth much money and considered precious, while others are lucky to see the inside of a cement mixer. What am I? (Rock)
8. I am friend to every living thing, and not a day goes by that you do not use me. Spring, mineral, sea, and fresh are a few words that describe me at different times. What am I? (Water)
9. I am beautiful to look at, but terrible to touch. All the colors of the rainbow are mine. But stand back! I strike those who come too close! What am I? (Fire)

SECTION C: The Cycle of Theatre

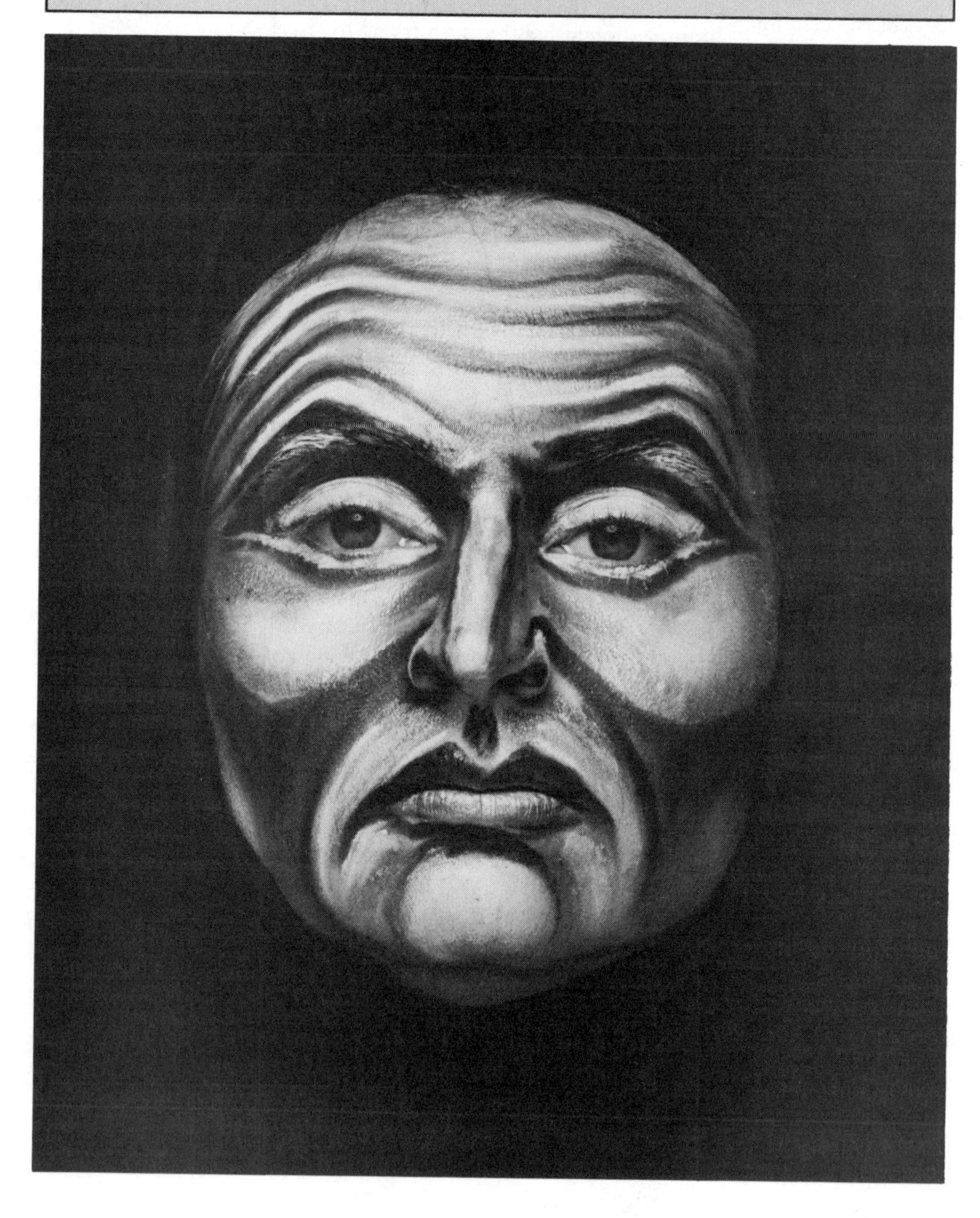

Introduction

> Like everything else, the drama has a beginning. The *first* drama is, however, also the *last* drama. It is, in a sense, contemporary drama. It is still being practised by the primitive races that have survived into our own century; it still exists in the basic instincts and responses of modern man; and its cardinal elements still prevail, and will undoubtedly always prevail, in the theatre.
>
> John Gassner,
> *Masters of the Drama*

Section A introduces you to various types of scripts. Section B examines the nature of scripting. Section C looks at scripts through the perspective of history. In Section C, scripts from the important periods of theatre are presented alongside recent plays. This format not only gives you a sense of the development of the theatre, from the earliest ritual to the most contemporary creation, it also gives you a sense of the cycle of theatre—those concepts, themes, and ideas which recur in theatre as we attempt to understand ourselves.

From its beginning, theatre has expressed humanity's need to communicate ideas and feelings. A play, through the use of language, characters, action, and the visual effects of setting, costume, makeup, and mask, is a symbolic representation of complex, varied, and important meanings. That these meanings are important is evidenced by the fact that playwrights separated by time and culture examine similar themes. Every playwright sheds new light on the theme he or she has chosen to explore. The universal power and mystery of these themes is demonstrated by the fact that no playwright can provide the final, definitive explanation of the issues a theme raises; there will always be a playwright in the future who interprets the theme afresh. The cycle of theatre, viewed from the perspective of the present world, offers us insights into these universal themes.

As you work through this section, examine what the scripts say about life and about the human condition by considering the following: the language and kind of language used by the playwright; what the characters think of themselves and of each other; the audience that each play was written for; the effect that the play would have had on this audience; and what the scene means to you and to your group.

Each of the chapters in this section is preceded by a short scene from David Mamet's play *A Life in the Theatre*, a play which examines the actor's life, on- and off-stage. These scenes will give you the flavor of the material to be explored in each chapter, and will give some insight into the lives of those who give life to the script—the actors.

THE DEVELOPMENT OF THE THEATRE IN THE WESTERN WORLD

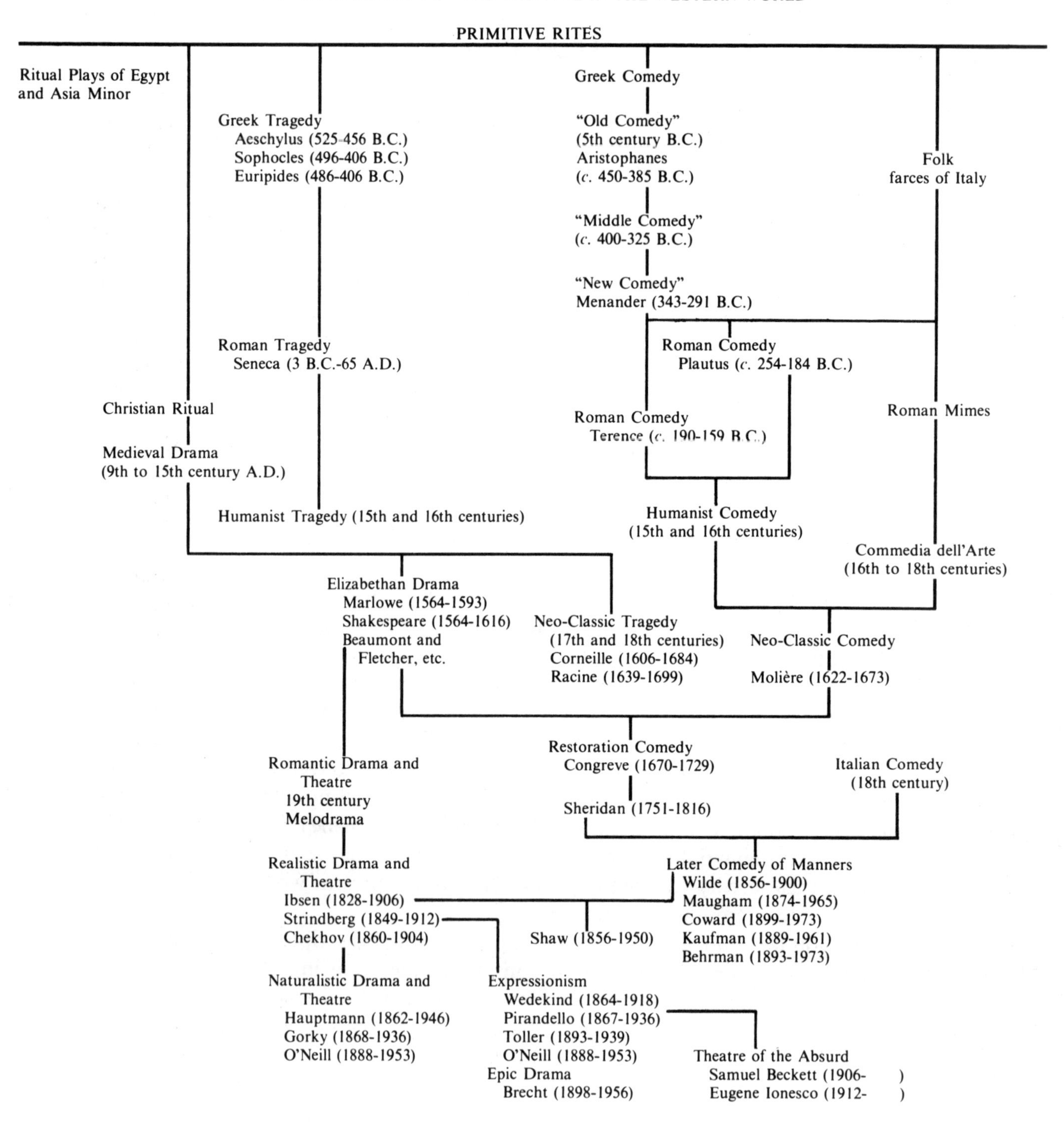

15: Early People

THE PROGRAM

Primitive Origin: There are many theories about the origins of theatre; the common element in most theories is the role that primitive ritual played in the development of drama.

Primitive societies which did not have written languages used ritual enactment to embody their understanding of the human condition and of the world around them. Ritual was also a way of communicating this knowledge to others. Furthermore, it was believed that ritual could be used to influence or control natural phenomena such as rainfall, the growth of crops, and recovery from disease.

Ritual had a religious purpose in society. Ritual was used to glorify supernatural powers and to invoke these powers to intercede on behalf of the society. In addition, rituals were a form of entertainment because of the spectacle of the performance and the skill of the performers. For example, because hunting was the main source of food for many tribes, performers became particularly skilled in creating animal characters through movement and sound.

Rituals had common elements regardless of the society they served. There was music or rhythmic accompaniment, dancing and elaborate movement, masks, makeup, and costume. In addition, highly skilled performers presented the rituals to a knowledgeable audience, in an acting area defined for the performance.

Over the centuries, as humanity's confidence in its own skill and power increased and less reliance was placed on supernatural powers, theatre as a non-religious activity emerged. Ritual still served its religious function, but theatre fulfilled humanity's need to entertain, enlighten, and communicate.

Egyptian Ritual: The hieroglyphics of ancient Egypt provide us with the first written record of ritual and dramatic performance. One of the most important Egyptian rituals took place at the time of the death of a reigning pharaoh and the coronation of his successor. As in the example given in this chapter, the characters in the drama were not the people involved in the real-life event, but rather the gods of Egyptian mythology. Osiris was the god whose story was most frequently enacted.

Osiris, it was believed, was born of the union of earth and sky. He came to Egypt to save the Egyptian people from savagery by giving them laws to govern themselves. He married a goddess, Isis, and together they taught the people to survive by growing crops.

Osiris was killed by his brother Set who was jealous of his popularity. The remains of Osiris' body were hidden throughout Egypt by Set. Isis and her son, Horus, searched for and found the remains of the body. The remains were reassembled, and Osiris was brought back to life. Osiris became king of the underworld.

In *Coronation Event and Drama* the new pharaoh of Egypt is represented by the god Horus who, at one time, succeeded his own father, Osiris. The roles of Isis and Set are as they were in the myth. Since there is no account of how the ritual was enacted, your exploration of the text will involve a great deal of experimentation.

The second selection in this chapter is from *Savages*, a contemporary retelling of a South American Indian myth. It provides another opportunity for ritual enactment. Since the play deals with the present day genocide of an Indian tribe, the ritual can have great power on both the primitive and contemporary levels of meaning.

Greek Drama: There is much evidence to suggest that Greek mythology was strongly influenced by earlier Egyptian mythology. But, while Egyptian theatre never evolved beyond ritual performance where the same ceremonies were repeated yearly for centuries, Greek performance evolved from ritual to a highly sophisticated theatrical form. Greek theatre was the foundation of all Western Theatre.

One of the earliest Greek rituals paid homage to Dionysus, the Greek god of wine and fertility. The form which the ritual took was called a dithyramb, a hymn that was both sung and danced by a chorus. An improvised story was sung by the chorus leader and a refrain was sung by the chorus. (This technique is explored in "Choral Dramatization," Section B, Chapter 7.) These stories were originally about Dionysus, but gradually other stories were added to the dithyramb. For example, stories about Greek heroes—good and bad—and their wars, feuds, marriages, and the destinies of their children (who often suffered for the sins of their parents) were always popular. During the ritual of the dithyramb, a goat, the animal sacred to Dionysus, was sacrificed, and the chorus members wore costumes made of goat skins.

Theatre emerged from ritual when Thespis (*c.* 560 B.C.), spoke independently of the chorus and assumed the role—usually performed by a priest—of the god or hero of the story. Thespis engaged in dialogue with the chorus and is regarded as the first actor. While these innovations in performance were taking place, the acting area itself was also undergoing change. The stage was raised above ground level, and it was separated from the audience. Public interest in performances increased, and writers emerged to define and organize the structure of the original improvised stories. Eventually, theatre festivals were organized to display the works of the writers.

Greek playwrights based all their work on Greek myths or history, and plays remain today of the three major writers: Aeschylus, Sophocles, and Euripides (see Chart). Each of their plays has a similar structure, because Greek playwrights developed the concept of the unity of place, time, and action, sometimes known as the "three unities." This meant that the play occurred in a single setting, that time was continuous, and that the action proceeded without interruption towards an inevitable conclusion. For example, when a play begins, most of the action has occurred and only the final part of the story is dramatized. Consequently, earlier events are explained by the chorus or by the main characters while the climax of the action is unfolding on-stage. Scenes of death and violence occur off-stage and are retold by messengers and servants. Therefore, the action occurs (or is told) in one place, at one time. The characters in a Greek drama are usually broadly drawn, that is, we learn about the characters' psychological and ethical characteristics, but not much about personal details. The major characters were of noble heritage or descended from the gods.

As Greek drama flourished in the festivals, each major writer added innovations. Aeschylus, the earliest playwright, introduced a second actor, the "antagonist," to counter the "protagonist" that Thespis had created. Later, Sophocles added a third actor. Euripides developed more realistic characters and dialogue.

In his *Poetics* (330 B.C.), the Greek philosopher Aristotle examined and defined the major dramatic mode in which plays were written at this time. The mode is called tragedy, which literally means "goat song." According to Aristotle, the six elements of tragedy are plot, character, thought, diction, song, and spectacle. Aristotle defined tragedy as "the imitation of an action that is serious," and noted that the protagonist often suffered because of a tragic flaw of character (such as excessive pride) which led to a downfall as he or she struggled with moral or ethical problems.

Oedipus the King, by Sophocles, is regarded as an example of the Greek well-made play. There is unity of time and place, and the action unfolds relentlessly until the powerful conclusion. The second Oedipus play in this chapter, *Seneca's Oedipus* by Ted Hughes, is a modern adaptation of the Roman writer Seneca's rewrite of Sophocles' original *Oedipus*. It was very common for Roman dramatists to copy the plays of the Greeks, whose work they greatly admired. Seneca's plays were not written for performance but for dramatic readings in the homes of Roman nobles. Both the Sophocles and the Hughes selections are the concluding scenes of the plays. Although the action is the same, the language is significantly different and the style of presentation varies.

It is important to remember that tragedy was not the only theatrical form developing at this time. Comedy was also a major force in Greek theatre, and was presented in the drama festivals to balance the "seriousness" of the tragedies. Comedy generally involved satirizing domestic situations and making fun of myths. It also commented on contemporary society, politics, and literature. Aristophanes' *The Birds*, another selection, is an example of early Greek comedy. This play mocks Athenian life by contrasting Athens and the utopia "Cloudcuckooland." *The Birds* demonstrates the use of comic action and extreme characterizations, two techniques which still survive in contemporary comedy.

The Cycle: Finally, *Murder in the Cathedral* fully demonstrates the cycle of theatre. This play, written by the twentieth-century poet T.S. Eliot, uses the conventions of Greek tragedy in order to relate a story based on the conflict between religious and secular authority in England during the middle ages. The play bridges the five hundred year gap (often referred to as the "Dark Ages") between the flourishing theatre of Ancient Greece and Rome and the theatre which emerged in the later Middle Ages in Christian religious festivals.

As you read these plays, focus on those features which are similar, such as the use of a chorus, the nobility of the characters, and the human dilemmas each character explores. As well, notice how each play is a unique and individual expression of the author.

FROM
A LIFE IN THE THEATRE
by David Mamet

SCENE 7

(A short scene in which JOHN *and* ROBERT *encounter each other coming into the theatre for an early-morning rehearsal.)*

Robert: Good morning.

John: Morning.

Robert: 'Nother day, eh?

John: Yes.

Robert: Another day. (*He sighs.*) Another day.

CORONATION EVENT AND DRAMA

PLAYBILL

Although this selection is from a papyrus document dated around 1970 B.C., the ritual it describes may have been performed as early as 3300 B.C. The text gives an account of the traditional ceremonies which occurred at the installation of a new king. The characters are drawn from the Osiris myth and represent the real participants in the coronation. The use of ritual can be seen in this selection in chants, movement, and incantations. The purpose of this ritual appears to be to ensure the orderly accession to power of the new monarch and to provide an organized way of dealing with the loss of the deceased monarch. Notice the dramatic element of conflict which is present between Horus and Set.

CHARACTERS

Horus, the new king
Corpse of Osiris, a mummy representing the old king
Thoth, the chief officiant
Isis, the wife of Osiris
Followers of Horus, princes, embalmers, morticians, etc.
Set and Henchmen, temple and sacral personnel

SCENE I

(ACTION): THE CEREMONIAL BARGE IS EQUIPPED.

HORUS *requests his* FOLLOWERS *to equip him with the Eye of power.*

(ACTION): THE LAUNCHING OF THE BARGE MARKS THE OPENING UP OF THE NILE & INAUGURATES THE CEREMONY OF INSTALLING OR RECONFIRMING THE KING.

Horus: (*to his* FOLLOWERS)
Bring me the EYE
whose spell
opens this river.

HORUS *also instructs his* FOLLOWERS *to bring upon the scene the god* THOTH, *who is to act as master of ceremonies, & the corpse of his father,* OSIRIS.

(ACTION): BEER IS PROFFERED.

SCENE II

(ACTION): THE ROYAL PRINCES LOAD EIGHT JARS INTO THE BOW OF THE BARGE.

THOTH *loads the corpse of* OSIRIS *upon the back of* SET, *so that it may be carried up to heaven.*

Thoth: (*to* SET)
See, you cannot
match this
god, the stronger.
(*to* OSIRIS)
As your Heart masters his Cold.

(ACTION): THE ELDERS OF THE COURT ARE MUSTERED.

SCENE III

(ACTION): A RAM IS SENT RUSHING FROM THE PEN, TO SERVE AS A SACRIFICE IN BEHALF OF THE KING. MEANWHILE—AS AT ALL SUCH SACRIFICES—THE EYE OF HORUS IS DISPLAYED TO THE ASSEMBLY.

Isis appears on the scene.

Isis: (*to* THOTH)
That your
lips
may open
that the Word may
come
may give the EYE
to Horus.

(ACTION): THE ANIMAL IS SLAUGHTERED. ITS MOUTH FALLS OPEN UNDER THE KNIFE.

Isis: (*to* THOTH)
Open thy mouth—
the Word!

SCENE IV

(ACTION): PRIESTS SLAUGHTER THE RAM. THE CHIEF OFFICIANT HANDS A PORTION TO THE KING & FORMALLY PROCLAIMS HIS ACCESSION.

THOTH *conveys the Eye to* HORUS.

Thoth: (*to* HORUS)
Son takes his
father's
place: the Prince
is Lord.

(ACTION): THE KING IS ACCLAIMED BY THE ASSEMBLY.

SCENE V

(ACTION): GRAIN IS STREWN UPON THE THRESHING FLOOR.

HORUS *requests his* FOLLOWERS *to convey to him the Eye which survived the combat with* SET.

Horus: (*to his* FOLLOWERS)
Bringing your wheat
to the barn
or bringing me
THE EYE
wrenched from Set's
clutches.

SCENE VI

(ACTION): THE CHIEF OFFICIANT HANDS TWO LOAVES TO THE KING.

The two loaves symbolize the two eyes of HORUS*: the one retained by* SET, *& the one restored to* HORUS *by* THOTH.

Thoth: (to HORUS)
See, this is THE EYE
I bring you:
EYE-YOU-WILL-NEVER-LOSE.

(ACTION): DANCERS ARE INTRODUCED.

Horus: (to THOTH)
My EYE that dances for joy before
you.

SCENE VII

(ACTION): A FRAGRANT BOUGH IS HOISTED ABOARD THE BARGE.

The Corpse of OSIRIS *is hoisted onto the back of* SET, *his vanquished assailant.*

The Gods: (to SET)
O Set! who never will escape
The-one-who-masters-masters-thee.

Horus: (gazing on the corpse of OSIRIS)
O this noble
body, this
lovely beautiful
body.

(ACTION): THE WORKMEN STAGGER UNDER THE WEIGHT OF THE BOUGH.

Horus: (to SET)
You bend under him, you plot no
more against him!

ACTIVITIES

1. All ritualistic enactments require the following:
—solemnity
—processional movement
—choral chanting, speaking, or singing.
Obviously, you cannot authentically recreate this ritual because we do not have enough information about it. However, you can examine the various scenes, and, using the above-listed elements, develop a dramatization which conveys the quality of the event.

2. Using mime and movement, take each of the lines which indicate complex actions—"the ceremonial barge is equipped," for example—and develop these actions dramatically using a minimum of props.

3. Examine the opportunities for choral speaking and group movement in the script. Develop each of these techniques for maximum dramatic effect. Techniques for developing choral dramatization can be found in Section B, Chapter 7; this selection can be treated in the manner described in "Ensemble Drama," Section B, Chapter 13.

4. To understand the concept of ritual more fully, take an event from everyday life, such as the evening meal or a club meeting, and dramatize it in a ritualistic manner using the elements in Activity 1.

FROM
SAVAGES
by Christopher Hampton

CHARACTERS
Alan West
Boy
Brother-in-law
Jaguar
Jaguar's wife
Village people

PLAYBILL

This play was written as a protest against the widespread killing of native Indians by the government of Brazil. Alan West, the narrator in the selection, is a British diplomat who has been kidnapped by guerrillas opposed to Brazil's military government. In this

(Bare stage. In the centre, five or six blazing torches inclined towards each other to form a pyramid with a single head of flame. The theatre is entirely lit by this. Indian music, flutes, drums, chanting. Shadowy forms.

After a time, WEST *appears. As he speaks,* INDIANS *enter, one by one, from the wings, through the auditorium. Each takes a torch and returns with it the way he came.)*

West:
Origin of fire.
In the old days men ate raw flesh
And had no knowledge of fire.
Also they had no weapons

And hunted the game with their bare hands.

A boy went hunting one day with his brother-in-law.
They saw a macaw's nest perched up on a cliff-ledge.
They built a ladder and the boy climbed up to the ledge.
In the nest were two eggs.
The boy took them and threw them down to his brother-in-law
But in the air they turned into jagged stones
Which as he went to catch them cut his hands.
He was very angry.
He thought the boy was trying to kill him.
He took the ladder down broke it and went away.

The boy was on the ledge for many days and nights
Dying slowly of hunger
Eating his own excrement
Until one day the jaguar passed by
With his bows and arrows
And seeing a shadow cast ahead of him on the ground
Looked up and saw the boy.
The jaguar mended the ladder helped the boy down
Took him back to his home and revived him
Feeding him cooked meat.

The jaguar loved the boy and treated him as his son
Calling him the foundling
But the jaguar's wife was very jealous of him
And when the jaguar was away she never missed a chance
To scratch him or to knock him over.
The boy complained to the jaguar that he was always frightened
So the jaguar gave him a bow and arrow
And taught him how to use them.
The next time the jaguar's wife attacked him
He shot an arrow at her and killed her.

scene, West relates the Xingu Indian ritual of the origin of fire. This ritual (which is authentic) is part of a ceremony known as the *Quarup*, which the Xingu perform to mark the death of a high ranking member of the tribe. Like so many funeral rituals, such as the preceding Egyptian *Coronation Event and Drama*, this ritual is not only a lament for the dead, but also a celebration of rebirth.

Christopher Hampton has placed scenes of Indian rituals, such as the one that follows, throughout the play. In this way he contrasts the dignity of the natives with the fruitless efforts of the guerrillas to stop the massacres. As you read, consider the dramatic techniques you might use to give this myth all the ritualistic power possible.

The boy was terrified by what he had done.
He took his bow and a large piece of cooked meat
And escaped into the jungle.
After many days wandering he reached his own village
And told his people all the things that had happened to him
Showing them the meat and the bow.
The men were very excited by his discoveries
And they set off on an expedition to the jaguar's home
To steal his weapons
And to steal his fire.

What you take from people
They will never find again.
Now the jaguar has no weapons
Except his hatred for man.
He eats no cooked meat
But swallows the raw flesh of his victims.
And only the reflection and the memory of fire
Burn in his eyes.

(Silence. The last torch has vanished. Embers. A strange cry in the darkness.)

BLACKOUT

ACTIVITIES

1. A dramatization of this material would benefit from the techniques of "Ensemble Drama" (Section B, Chapter 13). Following are some ideas for your dramatization.

a) The single speaker of the text (West) can be replaced by a chorus. Have one group practise speaking the lines chorally.
b) Another group can enact the story through movement/mime. Be sure that everyone in the group is involved in a significant way even when there are only one or two major characters.
c) Another group can become a percussion/rhythm group which will provide sound effects, chanting, and music to enhance the enactment.

After practising separately, the three groups can come together and re-enact the story.

2. This ritual involves an animal character with human qualities. Since primitive societies were so dependent on animals for food, they knew the qualities of each animal intimately. Experiment with ways of creating the character of the jaguar in movement and in sound so that you convey the qualities of this cat. You may have to research the particular features of this animal. Perhaps a mask or makeup would enhance the characterization.

The creation of other animal characters is explored in "Story Theatre" (Section B, Chapter 9), and cats of a different kind will be encountered in Chapter 21.

FROM

OEDIPUS THE KING

by Sophocles

PLAYBILL

In this selection, Oedipus, king of the city of Thebes, is confronted by the Chorus, which represents the people of Thebes. The city is suffering from a terrible plague, and Oedipus assures the Thebans that he will find its cause. An oracle is consulted and reveals that the plague will vanish when the murderer of Laius, the former king, is found and expelled from the city.

Oedipus consults the prophet Tiresias, who tells him that he, Oedipus, is the murderer. Oedipus is outraged but must pursue the truth. He discovers that, when he was an infant, his mother, Jocasta, learned of a prophecy that Oedipus would kill his own father and marry her. Horrified, she gave her son to a shepherd who was to leave the infant on Mount Cithaeron to die. The shepherd, however, took pity on the child and gave him to a couple in a neighboring country. Oedipus grew to manhood, and, learning of the prophecy about himself and believing that he would kill his adoptive parents, he fled to Thebes. On his way he argued with and killed an old man who, unknown to Oedipus, was Laius, king of Thebes and Oedipus' real father. On arriving in the city, Oedipus outwitted the Sphinx, a creature who had been the cause of another plague. The people proclaimed him king, and he married the newly widowed queen, Jocasta, his real mother. In this final scene, Oedipus has discovered these facts through relentless questioning and investigation, and, off-stage, has blinded himself as punishment. Jocasta

CHARACTERS

Oedipus, King of Thebes
Chorus, people of Thebes
Servant

(Enter OEDIPUS.*)*

Chorus: This suffering turns a face of terror to the world.
There is no story told, no knowledge born
That tells of greater sorrow.
Madness came striding upon you, Oedipus,
The black, annihilating power that broods
And waits in the hand of time. . . .
I cannot look!
We have much to ask and learn and see.
But you blind us with an icy sword of terror.

Oedipus: Where will you send this wreckage and despair of man?
Where will my voice be heard, like the wind drifting emptily
On the air. Oh you powers, why do you drive me on?

Chorus: They drive you to the place of horror,
That only the blind may see,
And only the dead hear of.

Oedipus: Here in my cloud of darkness there is no escape,
A cloud, thick in my soul, and there it dumbly clings;
That cloud is my own spirit
That now wins its fiercest battle and turns back
To trample me. . . . The memory of evil can tear
Like goads of molten fire, and go deep,
Infinity could not be so deep.

Chorus: More than mortal in your acts of evil.
More than mortal in your suffering, Oedipus.

Oedipus: You are my last friend, my only help; you have
Waited for me, and will care for the eyeless body
Of Oedipus. I know you are there . . . I know . . .
Through this darkness I can hear your voice.

Chorus: Oedipus, all that you do
Makes us draw back in fear. How could you take
Such vivid vengeance on your eyes?
What power lashed you on?

Oedipus: Apollo, my lords, Apollo sent this evil on me.
I was the murderer; I struck the blow. Why should I
Keep my sight? If I had eyes, what could delight them?

Chorus: It is so; it is as you say.

Oedipus: No, I can look on nothing. . . .
And I can love nothing—for love has lost
Its sweetness, I can hear no voice—for words
Are sour with hate. . . . Take stones and beat me
From your country. I am the living curse, the source
Of sickness and death!

Chorus: Your own mind, reaching after the secrets
Of the gods, condemned you to your fate.
If only you had never come to Thebes . . .

Oedipus: But when my feet were ground by iron teeth
That bolted me in the meadow grass,
A man set me free and ransomed me from death.
May hell curse him for that murderous kindness!
I should have died then
And never drawn this sorrow on those I love
And on myself . . .

Chorus: Our prayers echo yours.

Oedipus: Nor killed my father,
Nor led my mother to the room where she gave me life.
But now the gods desert me, for I am
Born of impurity, and my blood
Mingles with those who gave me birth.
If evil can grow with time to be a giant
That masters and usurps our world,
That evil lords its way through Oedipus.

Chorus: How can we say that you have acted wisely?
Is death not better than a life in blindness?

Oedipus: Do not teach me that this punishment is wrong—
I will have no advisers to tell me it is wrong!

Why choke my breath and go
among the dead
If I keep my eyes? For there I know
I could not
Look upon my father or my poor
mother. . . .
My crimes have been too great for
such a death.
Or should I love my sight because it
let me
See my children? No, for then I
would
Remember who their father was. My
eyes
Would never let me love them, nor
my city,
Nor my towers, nor the sacred
images
Of gods. I was the noblest lord in
Thebes,
But I have stripped myself of
Thebes, and become
The owner of all miseries. For I
commanded
My people to drive out the unclean
thing, the man
Heaven had shown to be impure in
the house
Of Laius.
I found such corruption in me—
could I see
My people and not turn blind for
shame? . . .
My ears are a spring, and send a
river
Of sound through me; if I could
have damned that river
I would have made my poor body
into a bolted prison
In which there would be neither light
nor sound.
Peace can only come if we shut the
mind
Away from the sorrow in the world
outside.

has killed herself. As you read this scene, observe the action and function of the chorus and how it interacts with Oedipus.

Cithaeron, why did you let me live?
Why
Did you not kill me as I lay there? I
would
Have been forgotten, and never
revealed the secret
Of my birth. Polybus, Corinth, the
palace
They told me was my father's, you
watched over
My youth, but beneath that youth's
nobility lay
Corruption—you see it in my acts, in
my blood!
There are three roads, a hidden
valley, trees,
And a narrow place where the roads
meet—they
Drink my blood, the blood I draw
from my father—
Do they remember me, do they
remember what I did?
Do they know what next I did? . . .
The room, the marriage
Room—it was there I was given life,
and now
It is there I give the same life to my
children.
The blood of brothers, fathers, sons,
the race
Of daughters, wives, mothers, all the
blackest
Shame a man may commit. . . . But I
must not name
Such ugly crimes. Oh, you heavens,
take me
From the world and hide me, drown
me in oceans
Where I can be seen no more!
Come, do not fear
To touch a single unhappy man.
Yes, a man,
No more. Be brave, for my
sufferings can fall to no one
But myself to bear!

ACTIVITIES

1. In groups of two (one person reading the part of the chorus) read the selection aloud. Stop and discuss any lines which are unclear. Re-read the scene several times. Put the script down and improvise the scene staying as true to the original as you can.

2. In Greek tragedy, the chorus was made up of 12 to 15 people. It moved in a stately, co-ordinated manner, and it could be subdivided into smaller groups, among whom the lines would get divided. Examine the choral speeches, and decide on ways of presenting the material. Techniques for choral dramatization are found in Section B, Chapter 7.

3. If you have worked on *Antigone* in Section A, Chapter 3, compare the qualities of the chorus in that play with the chorus in *Oedipus the King*. Can you change the chorus in *Oedipus* to one similar to that in *Antigone*? In what ways can you make *Oedipus* as contemporary as *Antigone*?

4. Actors of Greek tragedy used masks. Design and make character masks for the main characters and the chorus of this play. You can also make robes to enhance your presentation. As you rehearse the scene, be aware of how the interpretation is affected by these additions.

FROM

SENECA'S OEDIPUS

adapted by Ted Hughes

PLAYBILL

Lucius Annaeus Seneca (3 B.C.-65 A.D.) was a Roman poet who adapted a number of Greek plays for dramatic reading, though not for acting. Seneca's writings show a concern with the evils of unrestrained emotion and a preoccupation with the intermixing, through magic and death, of the natural and supernatural worlds.

Seneca's rarely produced *Oedipus* was adapted in 1974 by British poet Ted Hughes, who focused on the mythic, primitive, and ritualistc elements in Seneca's work. This approach contrasts starkly with Sophocles' more civilized and moral treatment of the Oedipus legend. As you read this selection, note how the language is different from the language of the previous selection. (The point at which this selection begins is the same at which the Sophocles selection began; Oedipus has learned all and blinded himself off-stage.)

CHARACTERS

Chorus
Slave
Oedipus
Jocasta

Chorus: Fate is the master of everything it is vain to fight against fate
from the beginning to the end the road is laid down human
scheming is futile worries are futile prayers are futile
sometimes a man wins sometimes he loses
who decides whether he loses or wins
it has all been decided long ago elsewhere
it is destiny
not a single man can alter it
all he can do is let it happen
the good luck the bad luck everything that happens
everything that seems to toss our days up and down
it is all there from the first moment
it is all there tangled in the knotted mesh of causes
helpless to change itself
even the great god lies there entangled
helpless in the mesh of causes
and the last day lies there tangled with the first
a man's life is a pattern on the floor like a maze
it is all fixed he wanders in the pattern
no prayer can alter it
or help him to escape it nothing
then fear can be the end of him
a man's fear of his fate is often his fate
leaping to avoid it he meets it

(Enter OEDIPUS*)*

Oedipus: all is well I have corrected all the mistakes and
my father has been payed what he was owed I like
this darkness I wonder which god it is that I've
finally pleased which of them has forgiven me for all
that I did he's given me this dark veil for my head
pleasant
the light that awful eye that never let me rest
and followed me everywhere peering through every
crack at last you've escaped it you haven't driven
it away you haven't killed that as you killed your
father it's abandoned you left you to yourself
simply it's left you to your new face the true face
of Oedipus

Chorus: Look Jocasta coming out of the palace demented
look at Jocasta why has she stopped look at her
she's staring at her son she hardly knows what's
happening darkness is nearly swamping her
there he stands blasted his blind mask turned to
the sky she wants to speak she's afraid of him
she comes closer her grief stronger than everything
she's stepping towards him

Jocasta: what can I call you now what shall I call you
you're my son shall I call you my son
are you ashamed
you are my son I lost you
you're alive I've found you
speak to me
show me your face
turn your head towards me show me your face

Oedipus: you are making all my pains useless you are spoiling
my comfortable darkness forcing me to see again
go away we must not meet the salt bottomless
ocean should be washing between our bodies not to
cleanse them nothing can cleanse them if another
world hangs somewhere under some other sun
and lost away among other stars one of us should be
there

Jocasta: you were my husband you are my son you
killed my husband I bore your sons nothing
can be blamed everything that has happened is here
there is no road away from it

Oedipus: no more words mother I beg you by all that in our
names is right and wrong let there be no more words
between us two

Jocasta: nothing in me moves can I not feel I shared the
wrong how do I share the punishment it's me
I'm at the root of it I am the root my blood is
the dark twisted root this womb darkness
swallowing all order and distinction so die let
out this hell that lives in you nothing would be

enough to punish it if god
smashed his whole
universe on to me it wouldn't be
enough a mother
a morass all I want is
death find it you
killed your father finish it the
same hand
your mother finish it is this
the sword that
killed him is this it that killed my
husband and my
husband's father with a single
stab where shall I
have the second stab this point
under my breast
or this long edge across my
throat don't you know
the place it's here this the
place the gods
hate where everything began the
son the husband
up here

Chorus: look her hand slackens
from the hilt the whelm
of blood squeezes the blade out

Oedipus: you god of the oracle you
deceived me lied to me it
has not turned out as you
said only my father's
death was required it was
enough it has been
doubled and the blame has been
doubled my mother
is dead and her death comes from
me both my
father and my mother are dead
under my fate it is
more than I was promised now
go the dark
road quickly quickly be-
gin do not stumble
on the body of your mother you
people of Thebes
crushed under this plague your
spirits broken look I
am going away I am taking my
curse off you
now you can hope again lift your
faces now you
will see the skies alter and the
sun and the grass
everything will change now all
you stretched out
hoping only for death your faces
pressed to your graves
look up if you can move
now if you can breathe
suck in this new air it will cure
all the sickness
go and bury your dead now without
fear because
the contagion is leaving your land I
am taking it with
me I am taking it
away fate remorseless
my enemy you are the friend I
choose come with
me
pestilence ulcerous
agony blasting consumption
plague terror plague blackness despair
welcome come with me you
are my guides
lead me

(The CHORUS *celebrate the departure of* OEDIPUS *with a dance.)*

ACTIVITIES

1. Develop a dramatization which stresses the ritualistic qualities of this selection. Pay particular attention to the form and structure of the language. Use masks and costumes to enhance your work, and concentrate on finding appropriate actions and movements for the characters.

2. Another group can prepare a dramatization of Sophocles' *Oedipus*, while a third group works on "Incantation to Oedipus" and "Chorus to Bacchus" found in "Choral Dramatization," Section B, Chapter 7. Can the four pieces of material be organized into an anthology presentation as described in Section B, Chapter 11?

FROM
THE BIRDS
by Aristophanes

PLAYBILL

The main characters, Pisthetairos, and his friend, Euelpides, leave Athens to find a quiet, uncomplicated life among the birds. They hate the "busyness" of Athens with its law givers, busybodies, gossips, malcontents, and meddlers. They convince the birds to create a utopian place called Cloudcuckooland, which Pisthetairos then begins to turn into an exact copy of Athens. (Aristophanes believed that character is destiny; Pisthetairos is Athenian and cannot escape his origins.) With the help of the birds, Pis-

CHARACTERS
Chorus
Meton, the surveyor
Pisthetairos
Inspector
Legislator
Acolyte
Slaves

Chorus:
Again we raise
the hymn of praise
and pour the sacred wine.
With solemn rite
we now invite
the blessèd gods to dine.
But don't *all* come—
perhaps just one,
and maybe then again,
there's not enough
(besides, it's tough),
so stay away. Amen.

(From the side enters the geometrician and surveyor METON, *his arms loaded with surveying instruments.)*

Meton: The occasion that hath hied me hither—

Pisthetairos: Not another! State your business, stranger. What's your racket? What tragic error brings you here?

Meton: My purpose here is a geodetic survey of the atmosphere of Cloudcuckooland and the immediate allocation of all this aerial area into cubic acres.

Pisthetairos: Who are *you*?

Meton: Who am *I*? Why, Meton, of course. Who else could *I* be? Geometer to Hellas by special appointment.

Pisthetairos: And those tools?

Meton: Celestial rules, of course. Now attend, sir. Taken *in extenso*, our welkin resembles a cosmical charcoal oven or potbellied stove worked by the convection principle, though vaster. Now then, with the flue as my base, and twirling the calipers thus, I obtain the azimuth, whence, by calibrating the arc or radial sine—you follow me, friend?

Pisthetairos: No, I don't follow you.

Meton: No matter. Now then, by training the theodolite here on the vectored zenith tangent to the Apex A, I deftly square the circle, whose conflux, or C, I designate as the centre or axial hub of Cloudcuckooland, whence, like global spokes or astral radii, broad boulevards diverge centrifugally, forming, as it were—

Pisthetairos: Why, this man's a regular Thales! (*Whispering confidentially*) Pssst. Meton.

Meton: Sir?

Pisthetairos: I've taken quite a shine to you. Take my advice, friend, and decamp while there's still time.

Meton: You anticipate danger, you mean?

Pisthetairos: The kind of danger one meets in Sparta. You know, nasty little riots, a few foreigners beaten up or murdered, knifings, fighting in the streets and so on.

Meton: Dear me, you mean there might actually be revolution?

Pisthetairos: I certainly hope not.

Meton: Then what *is* the trouble?

Pisthetairos: The new law. You see, attempted fraud is now punishable by thrashing.

Meton: Er, perhaps I'd best be going.

Pisthetairos: I'm half afraid you're just a bit too late. Yes! Look out! Here comes your thrashing! (*He batters* METON *with a surveying rod.*)

Meton: HALP! MURDER!

Pisthetairos: I warned you. Go survey some other place, will you?

(Exit METON. *From the other side enters an* INSPECTOR, *dressed in a magnificent military uniform and swaggering imperiously.)*

Inspector: Fetch me the Mayor, yokel.

Pisthetairos: Who's this popinjay?

Inspector: Inspector-general of Cloudcuckooland County, sir, invested, I might add, with plenary powers—

Pisthetairos: Invested? On whose authority?

thetairos plans to become rich by having both gods and men pay money to Cloudcuckooland to allow smoke from incense and sacrificial offerings to pass through to the gods. As this scene opens, Pisthetairos is attempting to prepare a sacrificial offering to the gods to ensure the success of his venture, but he is being hounded by officials similar to the ones he tried to escape when he left Athens. As you read, note those comic actions which, although in a play written over 2000 years ago, appear familiar to you.

Inspector: Why, the powers vested in me by virtue of this piddling piece of paper here signed by one Teleas of Athens.

Pisthetairos: Look. Let me propose a little deal, friend. I'll pay you off right now, provided you leave the city.

Inspector: A capital suggestion. As it so happens, my presence is urgently required at home. They're having one of their Great Debates. The Persian crisis, you know.

Pisthetairos: Really? Splendid. I'll pay you off right now. (*Violently beating the* INSPECTOR) Take that! And that!

Inspector: What does this outrage mean?

Pisthetairos: The payoff. Round One of the Great Debate.

Inspector: But this is mutiny! Insubordination! (*To the* CHORUS) Gentlemen, I call on you Birds to bear me witness that this man wilfully assaulted an Inspector.

Pisthetairos: Shoo, fellow, and take your ballot-boxes with you when you go. (*Exit* INSPECTOR) What confounded gall! Sending us one of their Inspectors before we've even finished the Inaugural Service.

(Enter an itinerant LEGISLATOR *reading from a huge volume of laws.)*

Legislator: BE IT HEREBY PROVIDED
THAT IF ANY CLOUDCUCKOOLANDER
SHALL WILFULLY INJURE OR WRONG
ANY CITIZEN OF ATHENS—

Pisthetairos: Gods, what now? Not *another* bore with a book?

Legislator: A seller of laws and statutes, sir, at your service. Fresh shipment of by-laws on special sale for only—

Pisthetairos: Perhaps you'd better demonstrate your wares.

Legislator: (*Reading*)
BE IT HEREBY PROVIDED BY LAW
THAT FROM THE DATE SPECIFIED BELOW
THE WEIGHTS AND MEASURES OF
THE CLOUDCUCKOOLANDERS ARE TO BE ADJUSTED
TO THOSE IN EFFECT AMONG THE OLOPHYXIANS—

Pisthetairos: (*Pummelling him*) By god, I'll Olo-phyx you!

Legislator: Hey, mister, stop!

Pisthetairos: Get lost, you and your laws, or I'll carve mine on the skin of your tail.

(Exit LEGISLATOR. *Enter* INSPECTOR*)*

Inspector: I summon the defendant Pisthetairos to stand trial in court on charges of assault and battery not later than April.

Pisthetairos: Good gods, are *you* back too? (*He thrashes* INSPECTOR *who runs off. Re-enter* LEGISLATOR)

Legislator:
IF ANY MAN, EITHER BY WORD OR ACTION, DO IMPEDE OR RESIST
A MAGISTRATE IN THE PROSECUTION OF HIS OFFICIAL DUTIES, OR REFUSE
TO WELCOME HIM WITH THE COURTESY PRESCRIBED BY LAW—

Pisthetairos: Great thundery Zeus, are *you* back here too? (*He drives the* LEGISLATOR *away. Re-enter* INSPECTOR)

Inspector: I'll have you sacked. What's more, I'm suing you for a fat two thousand.

Pisthetairos: By Zeus, I'll fix you and your blasted ballot boxes once and for all!

(Exit INSPECTOR *under a barrage of blows. Re-enter* LEGISLATOR*)*

Legislator: Remember that evening when you lied in court?

Pisthetairos: Dammit! Someone arrest that pest! (*Exit* LEGISLATOR) And this time stay away! But enough's enough. We'll take our goat inside and finish this sacrifice in peace and privacy.

(Exit PISTHETAIROS *into house, followed by* ACOLYTE *with basket and* SLAVES *with the sacrifice.)*

Chorus: (*Wheeling sharply and facing the audience*)

Praise Ye the Birds, O Mankind!
Our sway is over all.
The eyes of the Birds observe you:
we see if any fall.

We watch and guard all growing green,
protecting underwing
this lavish lovely life of earth,
its birth and harvesting.

We smite the mite, we slay the pest,
all ravagers that seize
the good that burgeons in your buds
or ripens on your trees.

Whatever makes contagion come,
whatever blights or seeks
to raven in this green shall die,
devoured by our beaks.

ACTIVITIES

1. Although it has only two speeches in this scene, the chorus is present throughout the action. As in *Oedipus the King*, the chorus in this scene should comment on and add to events. The group playing the chorus can invent comic actions and reactions in movement and mime to enhance and complement the events that occur. It would be helpful to create masks and costume pieces to develop your bird-character.

2. As you can see from this scene, comic action has not changed substantially since 414 B.C., when this play was first performed. Concentrate on developing physical actions to heighten the comic effect of Pisthetairos "beating" and "pummelling" the officials. Remember, it will be these actions, which in another context could be frightening, that will convey the comic quality. (It is very important that these actions be carefully choreographed to prevent injury.)

3. Examine other examples of comedy in this book, and note any similarities to *The Birds*. In Section A, you can look at *Barefoot in the Park*, *The Real Inspector Hound*, *Jitters*, and *Count Dracula*. Chapter 17 examines comedy in detail; there is a startling resemblance between this scene from *The Birds* and *Love and Marriage Lazzi Style*.

FROM

MURDER IN THE CATHEDRAL

by T.S. Eliot

PLAYBILL

T.S. Eliot's verse play about the martyrdom, in the 12th century, of the Archbishop of Canterbury, Thomas à Becket, was written in 1935 and had its first performance in Canterbury Cathedral. Becket, who was accused of disloyalty to the King, and who was seen by the ruling class as a threat to the King's power, was believed to have turned the Pope against the King. *Murder in the Cathedral* begins with Becket returning to Canterbury after seven years absence. The chorus (the women of Canterbury) fear that his return will cause upset in their lives. The three priests fear for his safety and urge Becket to protect himself from harm. (Prior to this excerpt from the second act, Becket was accused of disloyalty by four knights who left in a rage, vowing to return.) The Archbishop has considered his position carefully and has accepted his fate.

CHARACTERS

Three Priests of the Cathedral
Archbishop Thomas Becket
Four Knights
Chorus of Women of Canterbury

Priests: The door is barred.
We are safe. We are safe.
The enemy may rage outside, he will tire
In vain. They cannot break in.
They dare not break in.
They cannot break in. They have not the force.
We are safe. We are safe.

Thom: Unbar the doors! throw open the doors!
I will not have the house of prayer, the church of Christ,
The sanctuary, turned into a fortress.
The Church shall protect her own, in her own way, not
As oak and stone; stone and oak decay,
Give no stay, but the Church shall endure.
The Church shall be open, even to our enemies. Open the door!

Priests: My Lord! these are not men, these come not as men come, but
Like maddened beasts. They come not like men, who
Respect the sanctuary, who kneel to the Body of Christ,
But like beasts. You would bar the door
Against the lion, the leopard, the wolf or the boar,
Why not more
Against beasts with the souls of damned men, against men
Who would damn themselves to beasts. My Lord! My Lord!

Thom: Unbar the door!
You think me reckless, desperate and mad.
You argue by results, as this world does,
To settle if an act be good or bad.
You defer to the fact. For every life and every act
Consequence of good and evil can be shown.
And as in time results of many deeds are blended
So good and evil in the end become confounded.
It is not in time that my death shall be known;
It is out of time that my decision is taken
If you call that decision
To which my whole being gives entire consent.
I give my life
To the Law of God above the Law of Man.
Those who do not the same
How should they know what I do?
How should you know what I do?
Yet how much more
Should you know than these madmen beating on the door.
Unbar the door! unbar the door!

We are not here to triumph by fighting, by stratagem, or by resistance,
Not to fight with beasts as men. We have fought the beast
And have conquered. We have only to conquer
Now, by suffering. This is the easier victory.
Now is the triumph of the Cross, now
Open the door! I command it. OPEN THE DOOR!

(The door is opened. The KNIGHTS *enter, slightly tipsy.)*

Priests: This way, my Lord! Quick. Up the stair. To the roof. To the crypt. Quick. Come. Force him.

Knights: *(one line each)*
Where is Becket, the traitor to the King?
Where is Becket, the meddling priest?
Come down Daniel to the lions' den,
Come down Daniel for the mark of the beast.

Are you washed in the blood of the Lamb?
Are you marked with the mark of the beast?
Come down Daniel to the lions' den,
Come down Daniel and join in the feast.

Where is Becket the Cheapside brat?
Where is Becket the faithless priest?
Come down Daniel to the lions' den,
Come down Daniel and join the feast.

Thom: It is the just man who
Like a bold lion, should be without fear.
I am here.
No traitor to the King. I am a priest,
A Christian, saved by the blood of Christ,
Ready to suffer with my blood.
This is the sign of the Church always,
The sign of blood. Blood for blood.
His blood given to buy my life,
My blood given to pay for His death,
My death for His death.

Knights: Absolve all those you have excommunicated.
Resign the powers you have arrogated.
Restore to the King the money you appropriated.
Renew the obedience you have violated.

As you read this play, note its similarities to Greek tragedy. The use of the chorus as direct participants in and observers of the action is one similarity, as is the nobility and resoluteness of the protagonist. The play is also tied directly to medieval religious drama, which is examined in the next chapter.

Thom: For my Lord I am now ready to die,
That His Church may have peace and liberty.
Do with me as you will, to your hurt and shame;
But none of my people, in God's name,
Whether layman or clerk, shall you touch.
This I forbid.

Knights: Traitor! traitor! traitor! traitor!

Thom: You, Reginald, three times traitor you:
Traitor to me as my temporal vassal,
Traitor to me as your spiritual lord,
Traitor to God in desecrating His Church.

1st Kni: No faith do I owe to a renegade,
And what I owe shall now be paid.

Thom: Now to Almighty God, to the Blessed Mary ever Virgin, to the blessed John the Baptist, the holy apostles Peter and Paul, to the blessed martyr Denys, and to all the Saints, I commend my cause and that of the Church.

(While the KNIGHTS *kill him, we hear the* CHORUS.*)*

Chor: Clear the air! clean the sky! wash the wind! take stone from stone and wash them.
The land is foul, the water is foul, our beasts and ourselves defiled with blood.
A rain of blood has blinded my eyes. Where is England? where is Kent? where is Canterbury?
O far far far far in the past; and I wander in a land of barren boughs: if I break them, they bleed; I wander in a land of dry stones: if I touch them they bleed.
How how can I ever return, to the soft quiet seasons?
Night stay with us, stop sun, hold season, let the day not come, let the spring not come.
Can I look again at the day and its common things, and see them all smeared with blood, through a curtain of falling blood?
We did not wish anything to happen.
We understood the private catastrophe,
The personal loss, the general misery,
Living and partly living;
The terror by night that ends in daily action,
The terror by day that ends in sleep;
But the talk in the market-place, the hand on the broom,
The nighttime heaping of the ashes,
The fuel laid on the fire at daybreak,
These acts marked a limit to our suffering.
Every horror had its definition,
Every sorrow had a kind of end:
In life there is not time to grieve long.
But this, this is out of life, this is out of time,
An instant eternity of evil and wrong.
We are soiled by a filth that we cannot clean, united to supernatural vermin,
It is not we alone, it is not the house, it is not the city that is defiled,
But the world that is wholly foul.
Clear the air! clean the sky! wash the wind! take the stone from the stone, take the skin from the arm, take the muscle from the bone, and wash them. Wash the stone, wash the bone, wash the brain, wash the soul, wash them wash them!

(The KNIGHTS, *having completed the murder, advance to the front of the stage and address the audience.)*

1st Kni: We beg you to give us your attention for a few moments. We know that you may be disposed to judge unfavorably of our action. You are Englishmen, and therefore you believe in fair play: and when you see one man being set upon by four, then your sympathies are all with the underdog. I respect such feelings, I share them. Nevertheless, I appeal to your sense of honor. You are Englishmen, and therefore will not judge anybody without hearing both sides of the case. That is in accordance with our long established principle of Trial by Jury. I am not myself qualified to put our case to you. I am a man of action and not of words. For that reason I shall do no more than introduce the other speakers, who, with their various abilities, and different points of view, will be able to lay before you the merits of this extremely complex problem. I shall call upon our youngest member to speak first. William de Traci.

ACTIVITIES

1. Unlike Greek drama, the violent climax of this play is presented on-stage. You will notice that the playwright gives no explicit directions on how the killing of Becket is staged. In groups, experiment with ways, appropriate to the mood and setting of the play, of depicting this action. Keep in mind that the killing should have a ritual and symbolic power. It may help to know that one of the central images throughout the play is a wheel. At one point Becket says, "For good or ill, let the wheel turn."

2. Many of the speeches in this play are delivered chorally. For techniques of and approaches to choral dramatization, see Section B, Chapter 7. Develop ways of delivering the speeches of the priests, the knights, and the chorus so that they enhance the power of the scene. Add appropriate physical action to these choral passages.

3. Note the speeches of the knights when they enter. These speeches are significantly different from previous speeches. What quality should the knights convey while saying these lines? And why are they indicated as being "slightly tipsy"?

4. After the chorus has finished speaking, the knights step forward and address the audience directly to explain why they murdered Becket. Decide on, and then improvise, the reasons that the knights might give for their actions. Why has the playwright suddenly switched to contemporary speech?

WORKSHOP

1. Look through books, magazines, and newspapers to find examples of primitive forms of theatre. From your findings develop a scene which represents that primitive form. Attempt to find music, masks, and costumes which would fit the mood and theme.

2. Examine legends and myths from the Norse, North American Indian, Oriental, or African tradition, and dramatize one of these myths as it might be (or have been) presented in the original culture. Then adapt the legend or myth to contemporary society.

3. Find a myth from Greek civilization and examine the myth for dramatic potential. What action would you dramatize, and how would you use a chorus in the scene? Find out if the myth was used by a Greek playwright as subject material for a play.

4. Research the audience of a particular culture (for example, Greek, Roman, West African). What demands would it have made about a performance? Choose a script which is appropriate to the culture chosen, and dramatize the script in such a way that the demands of the audience are met. Is the presentation different than it would be for a contemporary audience?

5. Examine the differences between comedy and tragedy. In comedy, does the audience laugh *at* or *with* the characters? In tragedy, how does the audience become concerned about the ethical dilemma of a play? To test your understanding of these genres, introduce inappropriate elements into a scene. For example, what happens to *Oedipus the King* if the chorus performs in comic ways, and how does *The Birds* change if the characters have a philosophical discussion about violence?

6. Ritual and ceremony are as important today as they were in the past. Determine what rituals, such as marriage and funerals, exist in society today. Using a contemporary ritual, present a scene in the Greek style of theatre. That is, add a chorus and use masks, costume, and stylized movement to provide dramatic effect. How might this same ritual be presented in a primitive society?

7. The themes and concepts examined in this chapter recur in other chapters. Ritual is examined in scripts based on religion in Chapter 16, "Religious People," and in scripts based on "manners" in Chapter 19, "Well-mannered People." Tragedy is explored in Chapter 18, "Shakespeare's People," and Chapter 20, "Real and Unreal People." Comedy occurs again in Chapter 17, "Funny People," and in Chapter 19. Examine the scripts in Section A and the material in Section B and decide if the concepts of ritual, tragedy, and/or comedy fit any aspects of these selections.

16: Religious People

THE PROGRAM

After the fall of Rome, theatre entered a "dark age" which lasted from the fifth to the tenth century. During this time, although no important drama emerged from western Europe, theatrical activity still took place; itinerant players, troupes of mimes, and acrobats went from town to town. There were also mummer groups, formed of townsfolk, performing crude dramas on festive occasions.

Since most of life in the Dark Ages was organized around the church, it was natural that dramatic forms began to appear in church services. Such "drama" was a practical way to communicate the Bible and religious rites and ceremonies to a populace which could neither read nor write. Religious drama began in the service with the choir (chorus) and priest (protagonist) telling a story and evolved to more complicated dialogue and storytelling.

Gradually, these performances moved out of the church to involve more people and a larger space. On important religious occasions, scenes and stories from the Bible, from the creation of the world to the second judgement, were mounted on wagons. Each trade guild (Carpenters' Guild, Shipbuilders' Guild, etc.) assumed responsibility for a single story or play. Over several days the wagons, called pageant wagons, were drawn from place to place in the town so that the people could see each play.

It was usual for a guild to undertake a play appropriate to that guild's function. For example, the Plasterers' Guild would do "Creation of the World," the Bakers' Guild would do "The Last Supper," and the Shipbuilders' Guild would do "Noah's Ark." The actors in these plays were usually amateurs from the guilds, and the writing of the play was a group effort. The plays, crude in structure and with limited action, might not have great dramatic merit. However, each play was part of a larger whole which was relevant and effective theatre.

In England, these cycles of plays were named after the town in which they were staged. The selection, *The Creation of Man*, in this chapter is from the Chester Cycle which consisted of twenty-five plays.

The second selection, *The Serpent*, is a modern retelling of the same story and provides an example of how innovative staging and dialogue can enhance and expand a story.

FROM

A LIFE IN THE THEATRE

by David Mamet

SCENE 20

(Backstage. JOHN *is dressing.* ROBERT *enters, speaking slowly to himself.)*

Robert: Oh God, oh God, oh God, oh God, oh God. (*He sees* JOHN. *Pause.*) New sweater?

John: Yes.

Robert: Nice.

John: Mmm.

Robert: What is it?

John: What?

Robert: What is it? Cashmere?

John: I don't know.

Robert: Looks good on you.

John: Thanks.

Robert: Mmm.

FROM

THE CREATION OF MAN

from *The Chester Cycle of Mystery Plays*

PLAYBILL

The plays from which the following selection is taken were first performed around the year 1375 in the English city of Chester. The twenty-five pageants or plays in the cycle were presented over a three-day period, on the Monday, Tuesday, and Wednesday following Pentecost. In Chester *The Creation of Man* was performed by the Guild of Drapers. As this selection begins, God has created the earth and is about to create man and woman. As you read this scene, keep in mind how the staging would be affected by the confined space of a pageant wagon.

CHARACTERS

God
Adam
Devil
Eve

God: Now Heaven and earth are made express,
Make we man to our likeness:
Fish, fowl, beasts, greater and less
To master shall he have the right.

In our shape now make I thee,
Man and woman I will there be,
Grow and multiply also shall ye
And fulfil earth with might.

Now this is done, I see aright
And all things made through my might
The sixth day now, here in my sight
Is made all of the best.

Heaven and earth is wrought with peace
And all that needs to be therein;
Tomorrow the seventh day, I will cease
And from my work take rest.

But now this man that I have made
With spirit of life fully arrayed,
Rise up, Adam, rise, be not afraid,
A man full of soul and life.

And come with me to Paradise
A place packed with dainty device,
It is good that thou shouldst be wise
Bring not thyself into strife.

Here Adam I give thee this place
Thee to comfort and to solace;
Keep to it, and thy whole race,
And do as I thee say.

(Takes ADAM *to Paradise)*

Of all the trees that be herein
Shalt thou eat and nothing sin,
But of this tree for good therein
Thou shalt eat in no way.

If thou eatest of this tree,
Death will come, believe thou me,
Therefore this fruit, I tell thee, flee
And be thou not so bold.

Beasts and fowls that thou may see
To thee obedient shall ever be.
What name they be given by thee
That name they shall ever hold.

*(*GOD *causes him to lie down)*

It is not good man alone to be
Help for him now make we;
But to cause sleep behoveth me
Anon in this man here.

*(*ADAM *sleeps)*

Asleep thou art now, well I see;
Therefore a bone I take of thee,
And flesh also with heart free
To make thee a mate.

Adam: O lord, where have I so long been?
For since I slept much have I seen
That all have truly wonders been
Hereafter to be known.

God: Hear, Adam, rise and wake.
Behold a wife made for thy sake,
And her to thee now shalt thou take
And name her as thine own.

*(*ADAM *rises)*

Adam: I see well, Lord, through thy grace,
Bone of my bone in her I trace
And flesh of my flesh I see in her face,
Of my shape through thy word.

Therefore shall she be called, I wis,
Woman, and nothing amiss
For out of man she taken is
And to man is she bound.

Therefore man shall kindly forsake
Father and mother a wife him to take,
Two in one flesh, as Thou canst make
Each other to make glad.

(They stand together)

Devil: Out, out! what sorrow is this?
That I have lost so much bliss.
For once I think I did amiss
Out of heaven I fell.

The brightest angels I was ere this
That ever was or yet is,
But pride cast me down, I wis,
From heaven right down to hell.

Spiritual paradise was I in
But thence I fell through my sin;
Of earthly paradise now, as I have seen
A man is given mastery.

Should such a caitiff, made of clay,
Have such bliss? No, by this day.
For I shall teach his wife a play
If I may have a while.

Her to deceive I hope I may
And through her bring both away
For she will do whatever I say.
Her I hope to beguile.

Disguise me I will that I can see
And offer her of that tree
So shall they both for their disloyalty
Be banished forever from bliss.

A manner of an adder is in this place
With wings like a bird around her to lace,
Feet like an adder, but a maiden's face;
Her form I will take.

And of that tree of Paradise
Shall she eat through my subtle advice
For women are caught with a dainty device
And she shall not deny,

And eat of it she will full greedily.
They both shall fare as did I,
Be banished both from this valley
With their offspring for aye.

Woman, why was God so nice
To bid desert your dainty device
And of each tree of paradise
To forsake the meat?

Eve: Nay, of the fruit of each tree
For to eat good leave have we,
Save the fruit of one we must flee
And of it we must not eat.

This tree here in midst now is
If we eat of it we do amiss.
God said we should die, I wis,
If we touch that tree.

Devil: Woman, I say: leave not this.
It can lose you no bliss
Nor no joy that is His
But be as wise as He.

Take of this fruit and taste this day.
It is good food, I will lay,
And if thou find'st that thou must pay
Say that I am all false.

Eat thou one apple and no more
And you shall know both weal and woe,
And be like Gods wherever you go,
Thou and thy husband also.

Eve: Ah, lord, this tree is fair and bright
Green and seemly in my sight,
The fruit sweet and full of might
That gods it can us make.

An apple of it I will eat,
To see the taste of its fine meat
And my husband I will meet
To take a morsel too.

Adam, husband; my life so dear,
Eat some of this apple here;
It is sweet, now have no fear,
You will enjoy it without mistake.

*(*ADAM *eats)*

Adam: That is true, Eve, I have no fear;
The fruit is sweet and fair, my dear.
Therefore I will do thy prayer
And one morsel will I take.

ACTIVITIES

1. It is important to remember that these mystery plays were created by groups of working people, and not by playwrights. It was important for these people to elevate language into the poetic, with the result that the rhyme scheme seems a little forced at times. It is important that you do not stress the rhyme, however. Instead, treat the script with the same seriousness and devotion that the originators would have had for the story it tells. Develop a dramatization of this scene based on your understanding of the story and on the importance the story would have had for a medieval audience.

2. Recreate the original task that the guilds had when developing a play for a pageant. Choose a story to dramatize from the Old Testament. Determine the dramatic elements, and create dialogue to convey the story clearly. If possible, attempt to use poetic language. The techniques discussed in "Scripting," Chapter 10, will be valuable.

3. If a number of groups create short plays from the Bible, develop a pageant wagon procession. If this is not possible, use the alternative method of "stations." With this method, the audience moves in sequence from scene to scene (station to station) while the performing groups stay in their places.

FROM

THE SERPENT

by Jean-Claude Van Itallie

CHARACTERS

Chorus of Four Women
Creatures in the Garden of Eden
Heron
The Serpent (Composed of five people)
Eve
Adam (non-speaking)

THE GARDEN

(Everyone's breath comes short and heavy and rhythmically, as if in surprise. The four CHORUS WOMEN *dressed in black detach themselves from the rest of the group and in short spurts of movement and speech go to the downstage right area, facing the audience.)*

PLAYBILL

The playwright describes his intentions in this play as follows:

> Theatre is not electronic. Unlike movies and unlike television, it does require the live presence of both audience and actors in a single space. This is the theatre's uniquely important advantage and function, its original religious

First woman of the chorus: I no longer live in the beginning.

Second woman of the chorus: I've lost the beginning.

Third woman of the chorus: I'm in the middle,
Knowing.

Third and fourth women of the chorus: Neither the end
Nor the beginning.

First woman: I'm in the middle.

Second woman: Coming from the beginning.

Third and fourth women: And going toward the end.

(In the meantime, others are forming the creatures in the garden of Eden. They, too, emanate from the same communal "first breath." Many of the creatures are personal, previously selected by each actor as expressing an otherwise inexpressible part of himself or herself. For the audience, perhaps the HERON *has the most identifiable reality. It moves about gently, tall, proud, in slow spurts; it stands on one foot, moves its wings slightly, occasionally, and makes a soft "brrring" noise. Other creatures become distinguishable. The* SERPENT *is formed by five (male) actors all writhing together in a group, their arms, legs, hands, tongues, all moving.*

The CHORUS WOMEN *have repeated their "in the beginning" lines from above. They speak these lines as a secret to the audience.*

* * *

There is a sense of awe about the whole creation of the garden. The two human creatures also become discernible. As EVE *sits up and sees the world, she screams in amazement. The sound of her scream is actually made by one of the four* CHORUS WOMEN. *They are also* EVE. *They think of themselves as one person, and any one of them at this moment might reflect* EVE.

ADAM *falls asleep. The* HERON *and the* SERPENT *are now more clearly discernible from the other creatures. The creatures play with themselves and each other quietly, in awe. The* SERPENT *is feeling out the environment with hands and mouths and fingers. There is nothing orgiastic about the garden—on the contrary, there is the restraint of curious animals in a strange environment.)*

function of bringing people together in a community ceremony where the actors are in some sense priests or celebrants, and the audience is drawn to participate with the actors in a kind of Eucharist.

When other acting groups want to perform *The Serpent*, I hope that they will use the words and movements only as a skeleton on which they will put their own flesh. Because *The Serpent* is a ceremony reflecting the minds and lives of the people performing it. What I would like to think is that we have gone deep enough into ourselves to find and express some notions, some images, some feelings which will bring the actors together with the audience, and that these images, these ideas, these feelings, will be found to be held in common.

As you read, note the ceremonial quality of this script. Also be aware of how the actors create animals, and of the function of the chorus. Many of the qualities of this script relate directly to the primitive origins of theatre.

EVE AND THE SERPENT

Serpent 1: Is it true?

Serpent 2: Is it true

Serpent 3: That you and he,

Serpent 4: You and he

Serpent 4 and 5: May do anything?

Serpent 2: Anything in the garden you want to do?

Serpent 1: Is that true?

Eve: We may do anything
Except one thing

First woman of the chorus: We may do anything
Except one thing.

(In the dialogue between EVE *and the* SERPENT *the first of the* CHORUS WOMEN *echoes* EVE*'s lines, but with the emphasis placed on different words. The four* CHORUS WOMEN *look at the audience as if it were the* SERPENT *in front of them. The* SERPENT *speaks and hisses to* EVE *with all his five mouths. Care must be taken by the actors playing the* SERPENT *that all the words are heard distinctly, despite overlap in speaking.* EVE *is almost in a state of tremor at being alive. The* SERPENT *is seducing her with his even greater aliveness, as well as with the intellectual argument. As* EVE *comes closer to being in the state the* SERPENT *is in, her movements begin to imitate the* SERPENT*'s, and she, finally, is seducing him, too. Some of the other actors are now seated on a bench facing the audience, at the back of the stage where they sit, and rest, and pay attention to the action. This is where those who are not playing a particular scene will always go—none of the actors will ever actually leave the stage. During* EVE*'s dialogue with the* SERPENT, *only the* HERON *and one or two other animals in the garden are upright, but they do not distract our attention. The* SERPENT *is not only the* SERPENT, *he is also the* TREE, *and he holds apples.)*

Serpent 2: What one thing?

Eve: We are not allowed to eat from the tree.

First woman: We are not allowed
To eat from the tree.

Serpent 3: Not allowed to eat?

Eve: We may not even touch it.

Woman: We may not even touch it.

Serpent 1: Not even touch?

Serpent 4 and 5: Not touch?

Serpent 5: Why not even touch?

Eve: Adam said I would die.

Woman: Adam said I would die.

(The SERPENT *is gently surrounding her until she has touched him without her realizing it.)*

Serpent 3: If you—

Serpent 4: If you touch—

Serpent 4 and 5: If you touch the tree—

Serpent 1: Adam said

Serpent 2: If you touch the tree

Serpent 4 and 5: If you even touch the tree
You will die—

Serpent 1: But—

Serpent 2: But—

Serpent 3: But—

*(*EVE *realizes her back is against the tree.)*

Serpent 5: Have you died?

Serpent 4: (*Whispering*) Have you died?

Eve: I don't know.

Woman: I don't know.

Serpent 2: You touched the tree.

Serpent 2 and 3: And you haven't died.

Serpent 4: You haven't died.

Eve: But Adam said—

Woman: But Adam said—

Serpent 1: Oh, Adam said

Serpent 2: Adam said, Adam said . . .

Serpent 1 and 2: Listen.

Serpent 2 and 3: Answer me this.

Serpent 5: (*overlapping the others*)
This.
Serpent 4: Could it?
Serpent 3: Could it hurt more
To eat than to touch?
Serpent 5: To eat than to touch?
Serpent 1: Could it?

Eve: It is forbidden.
Woman: It is forbidden.

Serpent 2: Who has forbidden it?
Serpent 1: Who?

Eve: God.
Woman: God.

Serpent 4: And why?
Serpent 5: Why has he forbidden it?
Serpent 4: Why?
Serpent 3: Why does he set limits
Serpent 2 and 3: Against you and Adam?
Serpent 1: Think.
Serpent 2: Is the fruit God's property?
Serpent 3: Is it?
Serpent 1: He says Adam and Eve may not eat.
But are Adam and Eve
Guests in this garden?
Serpent 2: Are they guests?
Serpent 1: Don't they live here?
Serpent 3: May they not eat where they want?

Eve: (*Turning away*) I don't know.
Woman: I don't know.

Serpent 5: Also, also haven't you
Serpent 4 and 5: Haven't you noticed
Serpent 4: That the younger always have rule
Over the elder creation?
Serpent 2: Haven't you noticed,
and aren't you afraid?
Serpent 1: Aren't you afraid
And hadn't you better hurry
Serpent 1 and 2: And eat the fruit now
Before the next comes to rule
Over you?

Eve: I'm not afraid.
Woman: I'm not afraid.

Serpent (*to itselves*) **1:** She's not afraid.
Serpent 2: Why should she be?
Serpent 3: How could she be?
Serpent 4: How?
Serpent 5: She couldn't be,
She doesn't know.
Serpent 4: Doesn't know what?
Serpent 3: Doesn't know she exists.
Serpent 4: Why doesn't she know it?
Serpent 3: Because she hasn't eaten.
Serpent 2: If she'd eaten, she'd know.
Serpent 1: Know what?
Serpent 4: What worlds she would know
If she ate.
Serpent 5: What worlds?
Serpent 1: If she ate she would know
Serpent 1 and 2: And if she knew
Serpent 1 and 2 and 3: She could—

Eve: What?
Woman: What?

Serpent 4: You don't know
Serpent 5: Because you haven't eaten.

Eve: Do you know?
Woman: Do you know?

Serpent 2: I don't know.
Serpent 1: I don't.
Serpent 3: But I can imagine.
Serpent 4: Imagine.
Serpent 5: Imagine.

Eve: But, is what you can imagine
What will be?
Woman: But, is what you can imagine
What will be?
Serpent 1 and 2: How can you know
Until you eat?
Serpent 5: How can I know?
Serpent 4: How can I know until you eat?
Serpent 1: This garden
Serpent 2: All these animals and these plants
Serpent 2 and 3: Were once only imagined.

Eve: Shall I risk losing all these?
Woman: Shall I risk losing all these?

Serpent 1: It may be.
Serpent 2: It may be that no garden
Serpent 4: Is better than this one.
Serpent 5: This garden.
Serpent 4: It may be.
Serpent 2: But you won't know,
Serpent 1: You can't know
Until you eat.
Serpent 2: How could you know?

Eve: If I eat
And if I die
Will you die too?
Woman: If I eat
And if I die
Will you die too?

Serpent 1: If you die
I will die too.

Eve: Why do you want me to eat?
Woman: Why do you want me to eat?

Serpent 5: Because I want
Serpent 4: I want to
Serpent 3: I want to know.

Eve: Know what?
Woman: Know what?
Serpent 2: Know what you will know.
Serpent 1: Know what will happen.

Eve: I might.
I might do it.
I might do it if God didn't know.
Woman: I might.
I might do it.
I might do it if God didn't know.
Serpent 3: You might
Serpent 4: Might do it if God didn't know?
Serpent 2: But you want to.
Serpent 1: And he knows you want to.
Serpent 5: Is a crime
Serpent 4: Only a crime
Serpent 5: When you're caught?

Eve: Shall I do what I want to then?
Woman: Shall I do what I want to then?

Serpent 1 and 2 and 3 and 4 and 5: Yes!

Eve: Even if what I want is to listen
To God and not to you?
Woman: Even if what I want is to listen
To God and not to you?

Serpent 1: Yes.
Serpent 2: If you want.
Serpent 3 and 4: If you want.
Serpent 5: Yes.

Eve: Then I will eat.
Woman: Then I will eat.

(She bites into one of the apples held by the many hands of the SERPENT.*)*

Eve: Because I want to.
Woman: Because I want to.

ACTIVITIES

1. Develop an improvisation which explores the central conflict in this scene. Perhaps several people could convince one person to do something that that person does not want to do. Those playing the temptors should try several techniques such as logical argument, intense feeling, ridicule, and group power

to convince the tempted person. Decide which techniques have the greatest effect. **2.** This scene provides opportunities for exploration through movement and sound in creating animal characters.	Regard the stage directions as useful guides but not as prescriptive rules. Find alternative ways of developing the serpent and the animals of the garden. Do not overlook the possibility of using masks.	**3.** Investigate how the scene changes if the character who echoes Eve's lines changes to a chorus of women or to a chorus of men and women. Also find ways of integrating the animal characters into the scene so that they react to and focus on the action.

WORKSHOP

1. Read about medieval theatre and find out when plays were performed, where they were performed, who made up the audience, and how this audience reacted to the plays. Pay particular attention to the transition of theatre from a popular entertainment serving religious functions to a private performance for the nobility. Discuss how the plays changed according to their audience; for example, what qualities would a play need for a largely illiterate, uneducated audience, and what qualities would have been present for a knowledgeable audience?

2. Choose a story from the Bible, and dramatize the story in the style of *The Serpent*. Stress ritual qualities, ceremony, and the use of choral speaking and elaborate movement.

17: Funny People

THE PROGRAM

Comedy began with making fun of or burlesquing the seriousness of rituals. It has been suggested, therefore, that comedy was the dramatic form which enabled theatre to emerge from ritual. Certainly, humanity has always wanted and needed to laugh, and comic plays were one of the earliest expressions of that need.

Theatrical comedy arose in Greece with such plays as *The Birds*, by Aristophanes. His and other writers' plays were an integral part of the drama festivals. In the early Middle Ages, comic mimes took place even when there was no other theatrical activity. In the later Middle Ages, in Italy, a comic theatre arose that became the foundation of comic characters and actions which exist up to the present.

"Commedia dell'Arte" (literally meaning "comedy of professional players") had great popularity in Italy around 1550 and was a development from the travelling bands of mimes, acrobats, and players of earlier days. The troupes of Commedia dell'Arte performers usually consisted of seven or eight men and three or four women. They travelled from town to town performing indoors in large halls or outdoors on raised platforms. The main characteristics of Commedia dell'Arte are the use of improvisation and the presence of stock characters or stereotypes in the plays. The dialogue and action of the plays are not written in any detailed way. Rather, there is a plot outline or "scenario" from which the dialogue and action are improvised. Each player in the company had one stock character which he or she always played.

As the action of the play unfolds, there are standard bits of comic action or "lazzi" which are inserted when appropriate, such as the "lazzo of comic woe"—exaggerated weeping and wailing with facial expressions and gestures to match. The stories of the plays are generally based on love, intrigue, disguises, and people working at cross-purposes.

The characters are divided into two types: the straight characters, and the exaggerated characters. The straight characters are the young lovers, who are witty, handsome, and fashionable. The young man, "innamorato," is usually opposed in his love for the young woman, "innamorata," by an older man, one of the exaggerated characters.

The exaggerated characters are either masters or servants. Usually, the masters are of three stock types. The Capitano is a braggart and a coward. He usually boasts of his great prowess in love and war and is usually discredited in both. He wears a mask, sword, and cape to identify the character. Pantalone is usually an elderly merchant and a miser. He believes that everyone wants his money, and he pretends to be poor. He will do anything he can to avoid paying, even if it is payment for the marriage of his children. Pantalone's costume is usually red with a black coat, and his mask has a long hooked nose. He also has a straggly grey beard. Il Dottore is the third "master" character. He pretends to be very learned, but talks a great deal of nonsense. He always has the wrong answer for everything, and he believes everything that he is told. He wears a mask and dresses in black.

The stock servant characters, called "zanni," are usually the main characters in the plays. Arlecchino (or Harlequin) is a faithful servant to one of the young lovers and is usually smarter than his employer. He is a trickster, but he is not malicious. He takes joy in his cunning and loves intrigues, but in an innocent way. His costume is usually patches of diamond-shaped colors, and he wears a black mask (sometimes with a carbuncle). He carries a slapstick—a paddle made with two thin flat pieces of wood. When a part of the body is struck, there is a lot of noise as the slats strike each other, but no pain for the person hit. Brighella is the opposite of Arlecchino in that he is crafty, unscrupulous, and out only for himself. If he hurts someone in his quest for money, he never repents. He is a comic villain. He is masked, with a moustache, and wears military type clothes. Columbina (Franceschina, or Fantesca) is a female servant who is good-hearted, friendly, energetic, and who has great common sense. She aids Arlecchino and is frequently romantically interested in him. Often this character does not wear a mask. There are many variations of these characters, but the qualities of the characters do not change much.

Commedia dell'Arte had an indelible effect on comic drama. Moliere, writing in France in the 17th Century, used commedia characters as the basis for *Scapin* and other plays. Today, these stock characters can easily be spotted in contemporary comedy.

The Commedia dell'Arte selection in this chapter is *Love and Marriage Lazzi Style*. The following selection, *Lucy's Fake Illness*, shows how commedia characters and style are present in contemporary comedy. *A Day at the Races* demonstrates how comic characters can be adapted and changed yet still retain the elements of the original commedia stereotypes. The final selection, *Archie in the Hospital*, gives an example of a stereotypical character who regards everyone as a stereotype. The immense popularity of the Archie character is witness to the enduring qualities of commedia characters.

All the selections in this chapter have a common theme, illness. This demonstrates that comedy has an underlying element of seriousness, and that comic treatment of a serious issue springs from a deep emotional base within us. If we laugh at illness, it is to still our fears about being ill. As you read the following selections, be aware of any scenes that might easily be converted from comedy to tragedy.

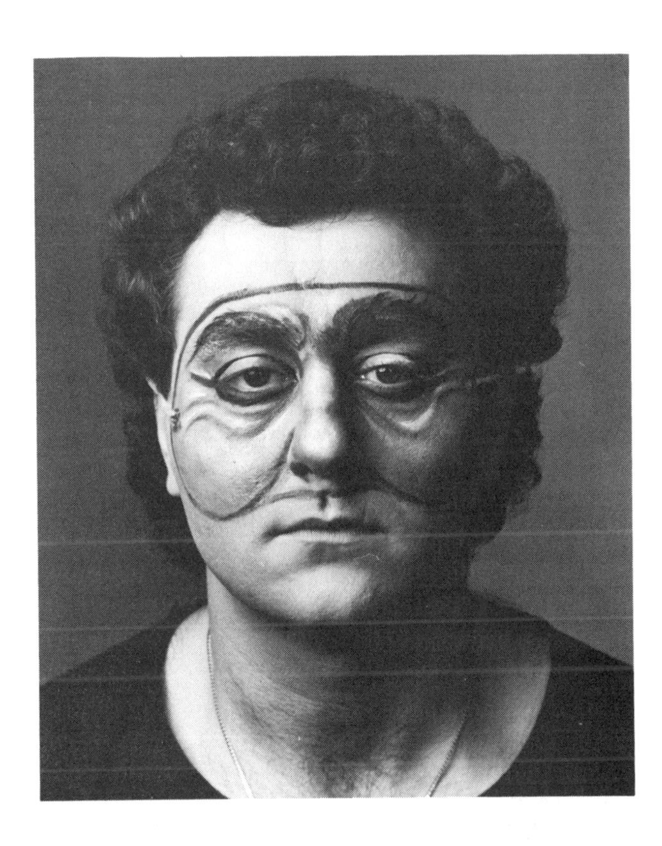

FROM

A LIFE IN THE THEATRE

by David Mamet

SCENE 24

(On-stage. ROBERT and JOHN are dressed in surgical smocks, and stand behind a form on an operating table.)

Robert: Give me some suction there, doctor, will you . . . that's good.

John: What I wouldn't give for a cigarette.

Robert: Waaal, just a few more minutes and I think I'll join you in one. (*Pause.*) Nervous, Jimmy?

John: No. Yes.

Robert: No need to be. A few years, you'll be doing these in your sleep. Suction. Retractor. (*Business.*) No, the *large* retractor.

John: Sorry.

Robert: It's all right. Give me another one, will you?

(Business.)

John: (*pointing*) What's that?

(Pause. ROBERT shakes his head minutely. JOHN nods his head.)

What's that?

(ROBERT minutely but emphatically shakes his head.)

(Pause.)

(JOHN mumbles something to ROBERT. ROBERT mumbles something to JOHN.)

(Pause.)

Robert: Would you, uh, can you give me some sort of reading on the, uh, electro . . . um . . . on the. . . . Would you get me one, please? (*motioning JOHN off-stage*) No . . . on the, uh . . . would you get me a reading on this man?

John: (*pointing*) What's *that!!!?*

Robert: What is what? Eh?

John: What's that near his spleen? (*Pause.*) A curious growth near his spleen?

Robert: What?

John: A Curious Growth Near His Spleen? (*Pause.*) Is that one, there?

Robert: No, I think not. I think you cannot see a growth near his spleen for some *time* yet. So would you (as this man's in shock) . . . would you get me, please, give me a reading on his vital statements. Uh, *Functions*. .? Would you do that one thing for me, please?

FROM

LOVE AND MARRIAGE LAZZI STYLE

by T.G. Kottke

PLAYBILL

This text is an adaptation of several commedia scripts, and it contains some of the commedia characters and events presented to audiences over three hundred years ago. The script is written in the form of a scenario, and it requires that you improvise both action and dialogues for comic effect. You will notice that much of the comic action is similar to that in *The Birds*. This shows that comedy as a theatre form has had a long, continuous history.

CHARACTERS

Flavio, An *innamorato:* a young and handsome man, deeply in love with Silvia. He is the son of Pantalone; he wears contemporary clothes of a stylish nature.

Silvia, An *innamorata*: a young and beautiful girl who loves Flavio as much as he loves her; she is the daughter of Dottore; she wears contemporary and stylish clothes.

Pantalone, A masked old man. Pantalone would like to marry Silvia himself, despite the fact that he is the father of Flavio. He is mean, garrulous, and stingy; wears red clothes with an ankle length black coat, turkish-type shoes, and a soft black cap. He wears a brown mask, fashioned with a large hooked nose and gray beard.

Dottore, the comic doctor and father of Silvia. He is hypocritical, a tyrant who is awed by simple things. He is laughed at, either openly or often behind his back. He wears black clothes with a doctor's cap and gown. A black mask covers his nose and eyes.

Fantesca, A servant girl who is bright and witty in a coarse way: servant to Silvia and always ready to assist in a trick or intrigue. She wears servant clothes and may or may not wear a mask.

Arlecchino, One of the masked *zanni.* He is foolish, clumsy and dull, but very acrobatic. He carries a slapstick. His costume has a pattern of red, blue, and green triangles; a black mask covers his face. On the mask is a carbuncle.

THE SETTING

A city street in front of Dottore's House. There is a long bench.

THE SCENARIO AND THE *LAZZI*

SCENE ONE

Silvia and her father, Dottore, talk. Dottore tells Silvia she must marry old Pantalone. Silvia refuses and says she is in love with Flavio, Pantalone's son. Fantesca, Silvia's servant girl, weeps and wails . . .

[***Lazzo* of comic woe: *exaggerated weeping and wailing.***]

. . . as Silvia and Dottore have a comic argument.

[*Lazzo* of comic argument: ***very heated and exaggerated in gesture and mood.***]
Arlecchino walks by and Silvia takes his slapstick and beats her father, Dottore.

[*Lazzo* of the slapstick: ***A comic beating with the prop. The extreme reaction of the person being hit is humorous—not the beating itself.***]

Dottore takes the slapstick from Silvia, and begins beating Arlecchino, saying "It's your slapstick."

[*Lazzo* of the slapstick: ***Repeated.***]

Silvia and Dottore leave, while Arlecchino and Fantesca stay and fall in love.

[*Lazzo* of exaggerated politeness: ***Arlecchino falls on his face trying to impress Fantesca with his manners.***]
Immediately followed by. . . .

[*Lazzo* of comic love: ***Arlecchino tries to hug and kiss Fantesca as she holds him off.***]

SCENE TWO

While Fantesca and Arlecchino are on stage, Silvia and Flavio enter and talk of love.

[*Lazzo* of comic love: ***Arlecchino and Fantesca "copy" Silvia and Flavio, in an exaggerated and comic manner.***]

Pantalone enters and catches them and tells Flavio, his son, he will disinherit him if he continues to see Silvia. Silvia leaves with Fantesca and Pantalone leaves to settle the marriage contract with Silvia's father, Dottore.

Flavio tells Arlecchino his troubles. Arlecchino promises to help if Flavio will hire him and feed him, and let him marry Silvia's servant girl, Fantesca. Flavio agrees and exits.

SCENE THREE

Pantalone and Dottore enter and talk about the problem of Silvia's dislike for Pantalone. Arlecchino overhears their conversation . . .

[*Lazzo* of the fly: ***While this scene is going on, Arlecchino catches and eats a fly. He tears off the wings, then munches on the fly's corpse with evident enjoyment.***]

. . . and introduces himself as once having had the same problem. They listen and take ARLECCHINO*'s suggestion that* PANTALONE *should feign illness. In this way he may get the love and sympathy of* SILVIA.

ARLECCHINO, *after* DOTTORE *and* PANTALONE *exit, tells the audience that he will pretend that he is a doctor and will go to* PANTALONE*'s bedside.*

[*Lazzo* of suicide: ***Arlecchino decides his plan is too stupid and he can't help Flavio. He does the LAZZO of weeping and wailing, followed by the LAZZO of comic suicide. He first holds his mouth closed with one hand and his nose by the other, so that he can no longer breathe. This fails in a vast explosion and inhalation of air. He then tries to tickle himself to death. This fails and he resolves to go through with his plan.***]

SCENE FOUR

PANTALONE *enters and gets into bed. He is very "sick."* DOTTORE *enters with* SILVIA, FLAVIO *and* FANTESCA. FLAVIO *leaves to get a doctor.* FLAVIO *enters with* ARLECCHINO *disguised as a doctor.* ARLECCHINO *examines* PANTALONE . . .

[*Lazzo* of the fake medico: ***In Arlecchino's examination of Pantalone he makes Pantalone stick out his tongue, wiggle his ears, touch his toes, carry him on his back, and on. After the examination, he gives Pantalone "medicine" with a very large spoon.***]

[*Lazzo* of comic love: ***Simultaneously, during the lazzo described above, Arlecchino stops everything once in a while and goes to Fantesca to attempt to hug and kiss her.***]

. . . and tells him he will die in twenty-four hours.

[*Lazzo* of Pantomime: ***All are gathered around Pantalone and he whispers into the ear of the person next to him about the "doctor's" prognosis. "I have twenty-four hours to live." This is passed around the circle with weeping and wailing. Pantalone is told again by the last person in the chain. The news is news to Pantalone.***]

DOTTORE *and* PANTALONE *agree to let* SILVIA *and* FLAVIO *marry and to sign over* PANTALONE*'s fortune to his son,* FLAVIO. PANTALONE *has the marriage contract and will which are signed by all.* ARLECCHINO *is discovered as the fake doctor and the play ends with* PANTALONE *and* DOTTORE *chasing and beating* ARLECCHINO.

[*Lazzo* of slapstick: ***Again.***]

FANTESCA *is also beating* PANTALONE *and* DOTTORE *in order to protect* ARLECCHINO *as* SILVIA *and* FLAVIO *laugh.*
CURTAIN

ACTIVITIES

1. Examine the script closely for those characters and comic actions which have contemporary equivalents in theatre, television, and movies. Discuss the similarities and differences between commedia and contemporary styles of comedy. Decide what comic qualities have enduring appeal to people.

2. Develop an improvisation based on a contemporary situation and insert commedia characters and actions into this situation. The contemporary characters can play their parts "straight," and the commedia characters can do all the comic actions and dialogue. Some suggestions are: commedia characters in a classroom; commedia characters in a business meeting; or commedia characters on a bus, subway, or airplane. What have you discovered from these improvisations about the nature of comedy?

3. Prepare your own scenario in the commedia style on topics of your own choosing. Some topics might be: Dottore runs a hospital; Pantalone has to give money away; or Fantesca has two jobs—one with Dottore, one with Pantalone.

LUCY'S FAKE ILLNESS

A scenario from *I Love Lucy*

PLAYBILL

This scenario is from one of the earliest and most popular of television's situation comedies, *I Love Lucy*. Although *I Love Lucy* was produced in the 1950's, many television stations still show re-runs of the program. Even if you are not familiar with the *I Love Lucy* characters, you will be able to improvise the following scenario by basing your characterizations on commedia stereotypes. Lucy is the equivalent of Arlecchino; Ricky is a combination of an innamorato and Pantalone; and Fred, the neighbor, is similar to a commedia servant.

CHARACTERS

Lucy
Ricky, Lucy's husband
Fred, a neighbor
Hal March, a friend of Ricky

"Lucy's Fake Illness"; January 28, 1952.

Contemplating a nervous breakdown because Ricky won't hire her for his new act, Lucy consults a book, *Abnormal Psychology*, for a solution. Three symptoms of her frustration are likely to appear, according to the text: She will assume the identity of a celebrity, develop a hopeless case of amnesia, and revert to her childhood. When Ricky arrives home, he is bombarded with not just one complex, but all three: Lucy impersonates Tallulah Bankhead, can't recognize herself in the mirror, and recklessly rides a tricycle around the living room. Ricky wants to call in psychiatrist Dr. Stevenson to help Lucy, but Fred first warns him that Lucy is faking. Therefore, Ricky decides to enlist the aid of an actor friend, Hal March, to play a phony physician. Doctor: "Just as I feared ... You've contracted ... the gobloots.... It came into the country on the hind legs of the boo shoo bird.... We may have to operate.... We'll have to go in and take out your zorch." Lucy believes him and prepares for her death. Ricky finally spills the beans whereupon Lucy insists on being in the nightclub act. Now Ricky is the one feigning amnesia.

ACTIVITIES

1. Divide up into groups of four and assign roles. Practise the roles individually, deciding what you want to say and do, and then return to your group. Without practising as a group, present the *Lucy* scenario. How smooth is your dramatization? As a group, discuss what did and did not work, and present the scenario again, incorporating any changes.

2. After dramatizing this scenario, develop an original scenario based on an incident which could occur in family life. Base your incident on reality, but extend the actions and characters with comic exaggeration.

3. View a contemporary television "situation comedy" and make notes on the characters and plot development. Write the story as a scenario in the style of commedia. Do the TV characters relate to the commedia characters? Can any of the actions in the television show be described as lazzi?

FROM

A DAY AT THE RACES

(a Marx Brothers comedy)

PLAYBILL

During the 1930's, the Marx Brothers made movies which are still popular today. They began their careers in Vaudeville, a form of theatre which emphasized "slapstick" humor and "zany" characters. (As you can see, even the words to describe humor are drawn from Commedia dell'Arte.) The following movie script is typical of the kind of comic action and word play which became the Marx Brothers' trademark.

CHARACTERS

Whitmore, the business manager
Morgan, Whitmore's cohort, who wants to turn the sanitarium into a casino
Judy Standish, the sanitarium owner
Dr. Hackenbush, (Groucho Marx) the new head of the sanitarium
Telephone Operator
Stuffy, (Harpo Marx) friend of Dr. Hackenbush
Tony, (Chico Marx) friend of Dr. Hackenbush
Dr. Wilmerding, a staff doctor
Intern
Secretary
Nurse
Orderly
Patients

Interior, Whitmore's Office
Medium Shot—Whitmore and Morgan

(WHITMORE *is on the phone.* MORGAN *listens.)*

Whitmore: (*into phone*) What about that call to the Florida Medical Board? What? Well, keep on trying. Call me the moment you get it. (*He hangs up and sits on the desk.)*

Morgan: That's great. You can't even get any action from your own telephone operator.

Whitmore: Don't worry, I'll get the dope on that Florida quack.

Morgan: Now listen, Whitmore. I want to turn this place into a gambling casino before the season ends. With my race track and my night club and this, I'll have every sucker in America flocking here. But every day counts.

Whitmore: I'll let you know the moment I get the call.

Morgan: I'll be waiting. (*He turns to leave.*)

Interior, Lobby
Two Shot—Judy and Hackenbush

(*He is wearing a white doctor's coat.* PATIENTS *lounge about in the background.*)

Judy: Doctor, may I have one of your photographs?

Hackenbush: Why, I haven't one. I can let you have my footprints, but they're upstairs in my socks.

Judy: No. I want to announce your association with the sanitarium. We'll send your picture to all the papers. (*They move across the room;* JUDY *sits down.*)

Hackenbush: The Florida papers?

Judy: Yes, it'll be wonderful publicity.

Hackenbush: Publicity? Oh, we mustn't have any of that, Miss Standish. You know, the ethics of my profession. (*He sits next to her.*)

Judy: But—we have to get new patients.

Hackenbush: Well after all, the old patients were good enough for your father. Besides, who wants to see my picture—I'm not a famous man. I'm just a simple country doctor with horse sense.

Judy: Oh, you're too modest. Never mind, we'll forget about the pictures. And Doctor, remember—I'm counting on you. The success of the sanitarium is in your hands.

Hackenbush: Ummm . . . Look, Miss Standish . . . Suppose, suppose that I were to tell you that . . . that I'm not the doctor you think I am.

Judy: Well, you're the only one that can help me. (*She stands.*) And do be nice to Mrs. Upjohn,[1] won't you?

Medium Close Shot—Hackenbush

(*Shooting over* JUDY'*s shoulder.*)

Hackenbush: Well she's not exactly my type, but for you, I'd make love to a crocodile.

Judy: Silly. (*She giggles and leaves.*)

[1]the woman who recommended Dr. Hackenbush for the job.

Groucho Marx, as Dr. Hackenbush (actually a horse doctor), has been appointed head of the financially troubled Standish Sanitarium by its owner, Judy Standish. Whitmore, the business manager, is scheming to sell the sanitarium so that it can be turned into a gambling casino. Chico Marx, as Tony, and Harpo Marx, as Stuffy, are Dr. Hackenbush's friends and are trying to help him prevent the sale.

The Marx Brothers always played the same kinds of characters. Groucho was fast-talking and wisecracking, walked in a crouch, and smoked cigars. Chico spoke with an Italian accent. Harpo, a marvellous mime artist, never uttered a word in all the movies he made.

You will note that the structure of this script is unlike conventional theatre scripts since it contains directions for the camera shots. As you read, keep in mind how you will adapt the script for the stage.

Medium Shot—Hackenbush and Operator

(*He moves quickly over to the telephone* OPERATOR.)

Hackenbush: Have the florist send some roses to Mrs. Upjohn, and write "Emily, I love you" on the back of the bill.

Operator: Oh, just a moment, Dr. Hackenbush.

Medium Close Shot—Operator

Operator: Yes, Mr. Whitmore. No, I haven't been able to get that call through to the Florida Medical Board.

Medium Shot—Operator and Hackenbush

(*He reacts to her saying "call through to the Florida Medical Board."*)

Operator: Well, I'm doing the best I can! It ought to be here any minute.

Hackenbush: If that call's what I think it is, she can cancel those roses and make it lilies for me!

(*Camera pans* HACKENBUSH *as he hurries away from the* OPERATOR.)

Interior, Office
Medium Shot—Hackenbush

(*He hurries in, sits at the desk and grabs the telephone.*)

Hackenbush: (*into the phone*) Get me Mr. Whitmore.

Medium Long Shot—Hackenbush

(*The screen splits diagonally:* HACKENBUSH *on the phone in his office on the left, and* WHITMORE *in his office picking up the ringing phone on the right.* HACKENBUSH *holds his nose and talks like an operator.*)

Whitmore: Hello.

Hackenbush: (OPERATOR'*s voice*) Here's your Florida call, Mr. Whitmore.

Whitmore: All right. Hello.

Hackenbush: (*he changes to a Southern woman's voice*) Florida Medical Board. Good morning.

Whitmore: I'd like to talk to the man in charge of the records, please.

Medium Close-up—Hackenbush

Hackenbush: (*Southern woman's voice*) Record department? Just a moment, sugar.

Medium Close-up—Whitmore
Medium Close-up—Hackenbush

Hackenbush: (*putting on his Southern-colonel voice*) Record department. Colonel Hawkins talking.

Medium Close-up—Whitmore

Whitmore: (*into phone*) Colonel Hawkins, did you get a wire from me regarding Dr. Hackenbush?

Medium Close-up—Hackenbush

(*He turns on a small table fan next to the telephone.*)

Hackenbush: I'm sorry, sir, but there's a hurricane blowing down here (*He puts paper into it to make more noise.*) and you'll have to talk a little louder. Whew—it certainly is the windiest day we ever did have!

Medium Close-up—Whitmore

(*He looks at his phone receiver, trying to figure out what's going on.*)

Hackenbush: (*offscreen*) Whew! It certainly is windy!

Whitmore: I want to know about Doctor . . .

Medium Close-up—Hackenbush

(*He leans back in his chair and lifts his leg.*)

Whitmore: (*offscreen*) . . . Hackenbush.

Close-up—Hackenbush's Foot

(*He buzzes* WHITMORE'*s intercom,*

pushing the button with his foot.)

Medium Close-up—Whitmore
(He hears the intercom, gets up, walks over to it.)

Whitmore: (*into the intercom*) Yes.

Medium Close-up—Hackenbush
Hackenbush: (*in his own voice*) Whitmore, you'll have to cut out that squawkin'. The patients are all complaining.

Medium Close-up—Whitmore
(He turns off the intercom and hurries back to the telephone.)

Hackenbush: (*offscreen, back to his Colonel Hawkins' voice*) And I hope sir, that is the information that you require.

Whitmore: (*seated*) I'm sorry, Colonel, I didn't hear it. I was called to the Dictograph.

Medium Close-up—Hackenbush
Hackenbush: (*as Colonel Hawkins*) What was that you said, sir?

Close Shot—Whitmore
Whitmore: I was called to the Dictograph.

Close Shot—Hackenbush
(He moves his foot to the intercom and buzzes.)

Medium Close-up—Whitmore
(He moves to the intercom and clicks it on.)

Medium Close-up—Hackenbush
Hackenbush: (*into the intercom in his own voice*) Whitmore, one more yelp out of you and I'll have you bounced out of here.

Close Shot—Whitmore
(He goes back to his desk and the phone.)

Hackenbush: (*offscreen, Colonel Hawkins' voice*) And I trust, suh, that that answers your question.

Whitmore: I'm terribly sorry, Colonel, I didn't hear you.

Close Shot—Hackenbush
Hackenbush: (*Colonel Hawkins' voice*) I can't hear you. You'll have to talk a little louder.

Medium Close Shot—Whitmore
Whitmore: I want to find out something about Hackenbush! (*The intercom buzzes*) Well, what is it now? *(Furious, he rushes to the intercom.)*

Medium Close-up—Hackenbush
Hackenbush: (*leans back in his chair with his foot on the intercom button; in his own voice*) Whitmore, that's the last time I'm going to warn you about that yowling!

Medium Close-up—Whitmore
(He goes back to his desk.)

Hackenbush: (*offscreen, Colonel Hawkins' voice*) And in conclusion, let me say—

Whitmore: I'm sorry, Colonel. What was that you said about Hackenbush?

Close Shot—Hackenbush
Hackenbush: (*into the phone, Colonel Hawkins' voice*) Hacken—You mean Dr. Hackenbush? Oh, no . . .

Close Shot—Whitmore
Hackenbush: (*offscreen*) . . . he's not here.

Whitmore: (*into phone*) I know he's not there. He's here.

Close Shot—Hackenbush
Hackenbush: (*Colonel Hawkins' voice*) Then what are you bothering me for, Yankee?

Close Shot—Whitmore
Whitmore: But I want to know something about his Florida record!

Close Shot—Hackenbush:

Hackenbush: (*holds his nose; the operator's voice again*) Here's your Florida call, Mr. Whitmore.

Close Shot—Whitmore
Whitmore: Operator, will you get off the line! Hello. Hello, Colonel.

Hackenbush: (*offscreen, Colonel Hawkins' voice*) Yes?

Whitmore: Are you sure you're speaking of Doctor . . .

Close Shot—Hackenbush
Whitmore: (*offscreen*) Hugo Z. Hackenbush?

Hackenbush: (*Colonel Hawkins' voice*) Who?

Close Shot—Whitmore
Whitmore: Hugo Z. Hackenbush.

Close Shot—Hackenbush
Hackenbush: (*Colonel Hawkins' voice*) Who's calling him?

Close Shot—Whitmore
Whitmore: The Standish Sanitarium.

Close Shot—Hackenbush
Hackenbush: (*Colonel Hawkins' voice*) Yes, that's where he works. Say I understand he's doing a mighty fine job up there.

Close Shot—Whitmore
Whitmore: I . . . I want some information regarding his qualifications for the job.

Close Shot—Hackenbush
Hackenbush: (*Colonel Hawkins' voice*) What job?

Close Shot—Whitmore
Whitmore: As head of the sanitarium.

Close Shot—Hackenbush
Hackenbush: (*Colonel Hawkins' voice*) Who?

Close Shot—Whitmore
Whitmore: Hackenbush.

Medium Close-up—Hackenbush
(He buzzes the intercom.)

Medium Close-up—Whitmore
(He turns to the buzzing intercom.)

Close Shot—Hackenbush
Hackenbush: (*in his own voice*) Whitmore, you calling me?

Medium Shot—Whitmore
Whitmore: (*into intercom*) No, you sap! (*Into phone*) Hello . . .

Close Shot—Hackenbush

Hackenbush: (*Colonel Hawkins' voice*) Yes, now . . . now what was that name?

Medium Close-up—Whitmore
Whitmore: Hackenbush! Hackenbush!

Close Shot—Hackenbush
Hackenbush: (*Colonel Hawkins' voice*) Uh, huh, well as soon as he comes in I'll have him get in touch with you.

Medium Close-up—Whitmore
Whitmore: Bah! (*He slams the receiver down.*)

Medium Shot—Whitmore
(The windows behind him open slightly and someone peers in as WHITMORE *storms out of the room.)*

Medium Shot—Stuffy and Tony
Tony: (*through the open window*) You see that sourpuss? Thatsa Whitmore, the man you gotta watch. Hesa no good. He's ina with Morgan and I think they're trying to get the sanitarium away from Miss Judy.

(That angers STUFFY *and he jumps into the room head first.* TONY *follows him.* STUFFY *moves toward the*

door as though he's going to find WHITMORE *and kill him.)*

Tony: (*stopping him*) Hey, hey, hey! No! No! You no wanna fight him. You're gonna watch 'im. You gotta watch him like a hawk. (STUFFY *nods "yes" and tries to run to the door anyway.* TONY *stops him.*) Not so fast. No! Not so fast. Now look, first I gotta get you in here as a patient or elsa Whitmore is gonna get wise to you. Come on, I take you to the doctor. (STUFFY *doesn't like that and makes a dash for the window.*)

Wider Shot—Stuffy and Tony

(STUFFY *goes out the window head first.* TONY *grabs him and pulls him back into the room.*)

Tony: Hey Stuffy, Stuffy, hey, come here! Hey, he won't hurt you. (STUFFY *mimes his arm being cut off.*) No, no, come here. This fellow's a nice doc. You're hungry, eh? (STUFFY *nods his head "yes".*) You wanna some ice cream? (STUFFY *again nods "yes".*) You wanna a nice big steak? (STUFFY *nods "yes".*) With spinach? (STUFFY *turns to dive out the window;* TONY *pulls him back.*) All righta, all right, no spinach, no spinach. Apple pie? Anda beautiful nurses? (TONY *shows how curvy the nurses are and* STUFFY *begins to grin.*) Oh, baby, come on, you're gonna get a nurse. (TONY *leads* STUFFY *to the door.*)

Interior, Sanitarium Examination Room

Long Shot—Wilmerding and Intern

Wilmerding: Have you seen Doctor Hackenbush?

Intern: No, I haven't, Doctor.

Wilmerding: Well, go and find him right away. Mrs. Upjohn wants him.

(The door opens and a SECRETARY *followed by a* NURSE *enters. Another* NURSE *moves quickly across the room in the background.)*

Intern: What's the matter with Mrs. Upjohn?

Wilmerding: Nothing. In its most violent form.

Medium Shot—the Doorway

(The door opens and DR. HACKENBUSH, *in a wheelchair pushed by an* ORDERLY, *is rolled to the centre of the room. He rises, puffs on his cigar.)*

Hackenbush: (*to the* ORDERLY) Ah, pick me up at five.

Orderly: Yes, sir.

(HACKENBUSH *goes to his desk, hangs his head reflector on a clothes tree and sits.)*

Two Shot—Secretary and Hackenbush

Secretary: (*she hands him a note*) Doctor, may I have an okay on this, please?

Hackenbush: Ummm, I'm too busy right now. I'll tell you what. I'll put the "O" on now and come back later for the "K."

ACTIVITIES

1. Examine the characters in this script and compare them to the stock characters in commedia. Find ways to play the scene in commedia style by changing the characters to their commedia equivalents. Change the script to a scenario and find where you can insert lazzi. Discuss how the script changes when it is done as commedia.

2. This script provides opportunities to investigate comic pacing and timing. As you rehearse it, vary the speed at which lines are delivered. Do the script very fast and then very slowly. How does the scene change? To find the funny lines, have someone with a drum deliver a sharp drum beat or "rim shot" after every line which should get a laugh. Freeze for three seconds after the line is delivered before going on to the rest of the dialogue. How can facial expression and gesture enhance the comic lines?

ARCHIE IN THE HOSPITAL

an episode from
All In The Family

PLAYBILL

Archie Bunker, a character on the television program *All In The Family*, is well known to most people in North America. Although Archie is a bigot, a braggart, and an illiterate, he is a very popular TV character. This is a comment on the nature of comedy. We like Archie not because of his failings, but because his failings allow us to see our own. When we laugh or get angry at Archie, we are laughing or getting

CHARACTERS

Mike, Archie's son-in-law
Gloria, Archie's daughter
Edith, Archie's wife
Archie
Dr. Spence

SCENE 1

Interior Living Room—Night.

(*At Rise:* MIKE *enters from kitchen with apple. He's reading Bobby Fisher's book.* EDITH *watching T.V. intently.* GLORIA *reading a magazine.)*

Archie: (*Voice off-stage.*) Edith! Edith! Edith! My back is killing me!

Mike: There he goes again. (MIKE *sits on sofa. Sound of hammering on floor, Off* R.*)*

(Sound: Tense dramatic background music on the T.V. EDITH *and* GLORIA *as before.* MIKE *is playing chess by himself on sofa.)*

Gloria: Ma—daddy's calling again. (*Looks at* EDITH *who is lost in the T.V. drama.*) Ma? Hey—why've they stopped talking on the T.V.?

Edith: They're getting ready to operate on the little boy.

Gloria: What's wrong with him?

Edith: Well, the world famous surgeon thinks it's a burst appendix, but Marcus Welby says it's nothin' but a green apple belly-ache.

Mike: What do you think it is, ma?

Edith: Well, I gotta go along with Doctor Welby.

Mike: Ma, I was talking about Archie.

Edith: Oh no, Archie never eats apples unless they're cooked. (*Sound: More heavy banging from the bedroom.*)

Gloria: Ma, do you want me to go this time?

Edith: Would you, Gloria? Thank you!

(*EDITH's concentrating on her T.V. show.* MIKE *goes back to his chess as* GLORIA *starts out. Halfway she meets* ARCHIE *in his robe coming in.*)

Archie: Edith! Edith! Edith!

Gloria: I'm coming, daddy!

Archie: You ain't Edith! Why didn't your mother come when I called!

Edith: (*Reacts to* ARCHIE*'s appearance.*) Archie! What're you doing out of bed??

Archie: I feel like I'm shipwrecked on a desert island, in there! Geez, even Robinson Crusoe had company on Fridays! (*Wincing from pain,* ARCHIE *hangs on the door jam.*)

Gloria: Well ma can't be running in every time you bang on the floor! She's tired.

Archie: She's tired? I'm the one who's been layin' in bed all week!!

Edith: I'm sorry, Archie. Is your back gettin' worse?

Archie: All the time, Edith, all the time! Did Stretch Cunningham call me back?

Gloria: No, he didn't.

Archie: Well, he must be in awful trouble down there on the job without me. Are you sure our phone is working okay?

Edith: I'm sure the plant can get along fine without you.

Archie: (*Snapping.*) What do you mean by that?

Gloria: Ma just means nobody's indispensable.

Archie: Well, you're wrong. I happen to be the most dispensable guy down there!

Edith: What did you want me for this time, Archie?

Archie: I want my back rubbed! And next time I call for you I don't want the second team sent in there!

Gloria: (*Hurt.*) Thanks a lot, daddy, it's real nice to be appreciated!

Edith: (*Getting liniment from sideboard.*) Oh, he don't mean nothing, Gloria. It's just the pain talking!

Archie: You're the only pain that's talking!

Edith: Do you want to lie down?

angry at ourselves. As you read this selection you will recognize a number of Commedia dell'Arte features in it.

Archie: I'll never make it to the sofa! Do it here! (*He steadies himself against the door jam and* EDITH *lifts his pajama jacket to rub his back.*) Oh! Edith!! Your fingers are as cold as tricycles. (*Sound: Telephone rings.*)

Gloria: I'll get it. (*She answers phone.*) Hello? Oh hello, Mr. Cunningham.

Archie: Is that Stretch?? Gimme the phone . . .

Gloria: (*On phone.*) Oh, that's good, daddy will be glad to hear that.

Archie: Hear what? Gimme the phone, gimme the phone!

Gloria: (*To* ARCHIE.) He says don't worry about the job—stay in bed.

Archie: Gimme that!! (*He snatches phone from* GLORIA.) Hiya Stretch. Well, I just wanted to know how everything was down at work—Fine, huh. How's the new guy Chuck Matthews, yeah, I know he's as strong as an ox. I just wanted to say, I'll be well in a couple of days and I'll come down and straighten everything out. Everything's all straightened out, eh? Oh, well all right, Stretch. Thanks for calling me back! (*He hangs up.*) You lousy crum!

Edith: Wasn't that nice of Mr. Cunningham to call you and put your mind at rest?

Archie: Edith, don't talk; it makes the pain worse. Help me over to my chair. (*Going to his chair.*)

Edith: Ain't you goin' back to bed?

Archie: No, I ain't. (*To* GLORIA.) Will you get your little keester out of my chair.

Edith: Archie, you don't want the doctor to come and find you up! It makes a better impression if you ain't walking around.

Archie: Oh, them doctors don't care if you're up or down. Doctors, you could be hangin' in a closet for all they care—all you are to them is a side of beef! (*Groans.*) Ah gee, the pain goes through me like a knife!

Mike: You probably aggravated it when you came down. What was so important about it, anyway??

Archie: (*Feigns surprise.*) It talks! I thought that was a dummy outta the Wax Museum! Look at him gawkin' over his checkers.

Mike: It's not checkers. It's chess.

Archie: Aw, tell me somethin' I don't know. I know it's chess. I'll tell you somethin' that you don't know. That there's a Commie game.

Mike: Chess is a Commie game??

Archie: See. You didn't know that. Certainly, them Russians force that game on the kids in kindergarten instead of learnin' them hand ball. Edith, I wonder what Stretch Cunningham meant when he said they was doin' good without me. (*Groans.*) Ahhh!! Ohhh!! (ARCHIE *groans louder than before.*)

Mike: Look at that. Every time you mention work your back gets worse. You know I think your illness is psychosomatic.

Edith: Psychosomatic?

Archie: What's that?

Edith: Oh, my, I hope it ain't as bad as the heartbreak of psoriasis.

Archie: Well, is it?

Mike: Psychosomatic means your problem is all in your mind. You see, sometimes worry can bring on all the symptoms of a physical illness.

Gloria: Daddy, have you been worried about your job?

Archie: I ain't worried about my job.

Edith: Archie, I didn't know you was worried about your job.

Archie: Stifle yourself, hah!

Mike: It's that new guy, right? Chuck Matthews, sure! He's young, he's strong and you're worried about him taking over down there!

Archie: That's a lie! (*He jumps to his feet.*) Ahh! Ohhh! (*He yells with agony as he clutches his back and sits down.* MIKE, GLORIA *and* EDITH *all jump up to help him. He can't get his feet down.*) Get away from me. Get away from me. Edith, get the feet down. Get the feet down. (*As* EDITH *puts his feet down, he groans loud.*) Ahhhhh!!! You're hurting me. You're hurtin' me.

(*Sound: Doorbell.* GLORIA *opens the door to a rumpled-looking man with a cigarette drooping from his lips. He removes the cigarette to say "Hello" but goes, instead, into a violent fit of coughing.* GLORIA *waits for it to subside.*)

Dr. Spence: (*Enters.*) Hello, Gloria. (*Coughing fit.*)

Gloria: Come on in, Doctor.

Edith: (*Going to meet him.*) Hello, Doctor Spence. Thank you for coming. Archie's been in a lot of pain. He's complaining about his back. I think it might be lumbago.

Dr. Spence: Lumbago? You really think so? (DR. SPENCE *comes over to* ARCHIE.) She thinks it might be lumbago.

Archie: If I believed her I wouldn't send for you. Let's go to the bedroom. Come on, doc'. (DR. SPENCE *coughs.*)

Edith: Oh, doctor, that cough don't sound too good.

(As they exit ARCHIE *is groaning and* SPENCE *is coughing. Doctor coughs off-stage.)*

Archie: (*Off-stage.*) Geez—Doc, you're germinatin' all over me here!

Edith: (*To* MIKE *and* GLORIA.) Oh, my, I hope he can help Archie.

Gloria: Don't worry, ma, daddy will be okay.

Edith: I hope so—'cause Archie ain't too good at feeling bad!

Gloria: It's like having a wounded bear around the house all day!

Edith: It ain't so good at night neither—Archie keeps waking me up to turn him over! And sometimes he rolls back again before I can get out of the way!

Gloria: Oh, no!

Edith: Yeah—my arm was the only part of me that went to sleep all night! I better go and see what's going on. (*Doctor enters.*) Oh, doctor—how is Archie? Will he have to stay home much longer?

Dr. Spence: No—just today, Mrs. Bunker.

Edith: Oh, good.

Dr. Spence: Tomorrow I want him to go into the hospital!

CURTAIN

ACTIVITIES

1. To investigate the fragile nature of comedy, play this scene without any comic overtones. Do not make any attempt to make lines funny, and develop actions and reactions which work against comic interpretation. How does the scene change? Does it become clear from your presentation that comedy is based on the serious things in life?

2. Do this scene as a commedia scenario, and use commedia characters and lazzi.

WORKSHOP

1. Prepare an anthology of comic theatre forms. (See "Anthology," Section B, Chapter 11.) Use selections from this chapter (17), as well as other comedy script selections found throughout this book. Also include examples of comedy from movies and television and consider the material of stand-up comedians. Focus your anthology on discovering what it is that makes people laugh and how that laughter is elicited by writers and performers.

2. Develop jokes into theatrical form by dramatizing them. How does the joke change when it is acted out?

3. Investigate the nature of theatrical comedy in other cultures. What qualities seem to have universal appeal? What comedy is unique to a particular culture? Are there examples of things that are not funny to one group but very funny to another?

18: Shakespeare's People

THE PROGRAM

In the sixteenth century, England became a political force in Europe, and the English people wanted to read and see plays about their own history. During the reign of Elizabeth I, 1552-1602, theatre activity grew tremendously as playwrights wrote and produced plays that reflected English life, attitudes, and beliefs. Most of these plays were based on stories from Greece, Italy, Spain, France, and Denmark, and were influenced by the classical theatre of Greece and Rome and the theatrical traditions of the Middle Ages. Some of the major playwrights of this period were Thomas Kyd, John Lyly, Ben Jonson, and Christopher Marlowe. (An excerpt from Marlowe's *Tragedy of Dr. Faustus* is in Chapter 3 of this book.) The greatest playwright of this time, however, is perhaps the greatest playwright of all time— William Shakespeare. While it is not possible to discuss Shakespeare's life and plays in detail in this book, some general points can be made.

Shakespeare wrote 38 plays during his life, and these plays have characteristics in common. They are based on stories from many sources including history, mythology, and legends, and were reworked until they became Shakespeare's own. For example, the play *Hamlet*, which seems to be about Denmark, is really about court life in England and is based, in part, on an ancient Danish legend and a French story.

Shakespeare's plays have large casts, and the characters range from the young to the old, from the innocent to the corrupt, and from the heroic and noble to the ridiculous and inept. Shakespeare created living characters, and not one-dimensional stage figures; his characters' motivations are based on universal emotions such as love, fear, greed, and revenge, and the characters have qualities which we can recognize within ourselves. We can identify with their psychological and emotional states.

The characters and situations are established at the beginning of the plays. Since there are very few stage directions, it is usually the opening speeches which set the scene, establish the mood, and give us insight into the thoughts and emotions of the characters. The series of plots which run throughout the plays are also established at the beginning. Often these plots appear to unfold independently. They tie in together towards the end of the play as the resolution of one plot line leads to the resolution of others. In this way, what originally appeared to be a diversity of plots is, in the end, a total unity.

The action of Shakespeare's plays ranges widely in space and time. Scenes may occur in many different settings and may be separated by a time span of months and even years. The language of Shakespeare's plays is equally rich and complex. The more deeply you examine the language, the more intricate the network of associations the language releases.

The plays were performed in London in theatres and in the courtyards of inns and were very popular. Generally, the actors were divided into those who played "straight" roles and those who played comic roles. All the actors were male, and young boys played the female roles. Each of the major theatres, such as the Globe, had resident acting companies, and the actors were professionals who also had to possess skills as dancers and singers. The playwright was actively involved in the mounting of the production and would, at times, act in his own play. The actors were known to contribute dialogue and acting when the play was in rehearsal, although there was less improvisation than in earlier medieval theatre. Shakespeare had definite views on how a play should be performed, as you can see by examining Hamlet's speech to the players in the Introduction to Section A of this book.

Although London was the centre of theatrical activity, there were many companies that toured the country. The group of actors in *Rosencrantz and Guildenstern are Dead* is representative of such companies, and Hamlet's scheme to put on a play for Claudius is made possible because of the existence of such companies.

As you will see, this chapter focusses on Shakespeare's *Hamlet*. The cycle of theatre can be seen in the continued popularity of this play and in the way in which contemporary playwrights are drawn to reexamine the play. The *Hamlet* scene presented here is presented again in Tom Stoppard's *Rosencrantz and Guildenstern are Dead* but from a completely different viewpoint: that of two characters who are of minor importance in Shakespeare's play.

Charles Marowitz's *Hamlet*, the third selection, is a complete reworking of Shakespeare's lines and is an entirely new interpretation of the text. You may not agree with Marowitz's concept of *Hamlet*, but the experience of working with the Marowitz script can nevertheless provide fresh insights into the original text. When you consider that *Hamlet* was first produced around 1600, it is a tribute to the power of the play that we are still exploring it.

FROM
A LIFE IN THE THEATRE
by David Mamet

SCENE 4

*(*ROBERT *and* JOHN *have just completed a curtain call for an Elizabethan piece.)*

Robert: Say, keep your point up, will you?

John: When?

Robert: When we're down left, eh, right before the head cut. You've been getting lower every night.

John: I'm sorry.

Robert: That's all right. Just make sure that you're never in line with my face. I'll show you. Look:

*(*ROBERT *begins to demonstrate the fencing combination.)*

You *parry ... parry ... THRUST*, but, see, you're thrusting high ... aaaand *head cut.*

May we try it one more time?

*(*JOHN *nods.)*

Robert: Good.

(They strike a pose and prepare to engage. They mime the routine as ROBERT *speaks lines.)*

And: "But *fly* my *liege* and *think* no *more* of *me*." Aaaaand *head cut.*

Eh? You're never in line with my face. We don't want any blood upon the stage.

*(*ROBERT *knocks wood.)*

John: No.

(Pause.)

Robert: Please knock on wood.

(Pause.)

*(*JOHN *knocks.)*

Good. Thank you.

FROM
HAMLET
by William Shakespeare

PLAYBILL

Before the play begins, Hamlet's father, the king of Denmark has died, and Claudius, the brother of the king, has ascended the throne and married Hamlet's mother, Queen Gertrude. In the beginning of the play Hamlet meets his father's ghost, who accuses Claudius of pouring poison in his ear while he was sleeping. Hamlet swears to avenge his father's death. In order to get Claudius to reveal his guilt, Hamlet decides to have a group of travelling players put on a play which will duplicate the murder of Hamlet's father. In the scene which you will study, Claudius decides to spy on Hamlet to see why Hamlet is behaving so strangely.

There are many problems to consider as you work with this scene. Is Hamlet's madness in this scene real or pretended? Why does Hamlet treat Ophelia, whom he says he loves, so badly? Does

CHARACTERS

King Claudius, Hamlet's uncle
Queen Gertrude, Hamlet's mother
Rosencrantz
Guildenstern friends of Hamlet
Polonius, Lord Chamberlain and father of Ophelia
Ophelia
Hamlet

ACT 3, SCENE 1

(The lobby of the audience chamber, the walls hung with arras; a table in the midst; to one side a faldstool with a crucifix.

The KING *and the* QUEEN *enter with* POLONIUS, ROSENCRANTZ, *and* GUILDENSTERN; OPHELIA *follows a little behind.)*

King: And can you by no drift of conference
Get from him why he puts on this confusion,
Grating so harshly all his days of quiet
With turbulent and dangerous lunacy?

Rosencrantz: He does confess he feels himself distracted,
But from what cause a' will by no means speak.

Guildenstern: Nor do we find him forward to be sounded,
But with a crafty madness keeps aloof
When we would bring him on to some confession
Of his true state.

Queen: Did he receive you well?

Rosencrantz: Most like a gentleman.

Guildenstern: But with much forcing of his disposition.

Rosencrantz: Niggard of question, but of our demands
Most free in his reply.

Queen: Did you assay him
To any pastime?

Rosencrantz: Madam, it so fell out that certain players
We o'er-raught on the way. Of these we told him,
And there did seem in him a kind of joy
To hear of it: they are here about the court,
And as I think, they have already order
This night to play before him.

Polonius: 'Tis most true,
And he beseeched me to entreat your majesties
To hear and see the matter.

King: With all my heart, and it doth

much content me
To hear him so inclined.
Good gentlemen, give him a further edge,
And drive his purpose into these delights.

Rosencrantz: We shall, my lord.

(ROSENCRANTZ and GUILDENSTERN go out.)

King: Sweet Gertrude, leave us too,
For we have closely sent for Hamlet hither,
That he, as 'twere by accident, may here
Affront Ophelia;
Her father and myself, lawful espials,
Will so bestow ourselves, that seeing unseen,
We may of their encounter frankly judge,
And gather by him as he is behaved,
If't be th'affliction of his love or no
That thus he suffers for.

Queen: I shall obey you—
And for your part, Ophelia, I do wish
That your good beauties be the happy cause
Of Hamlet's wildness, so shall I hope your virtues
Will bring him to his wonted way again,
To both your honors.

Ophelia: Madam, I wish it may.

(the QUEEN goes)

Polonius: Ophelia, walk you here. Gracious, so please you,
We will bestow ourselves . . . Read on this book,

(he takes a book from the faldstool)

That show of such an exercise may color
Your loneliness; we are oft to blame in this,
'Tis too much proved, that with devotion's visage
And pious action we do sugar o'er
The devil himself.

King: O, 'tis too true,
How smart a lash that speech doth give my conscience.
The harlot's cheek, beautied with plast'ring art,
Is not more ugly to the thing that helps it,
Than is my deed to my most painted word:
O heavy burden!

Polonius: I hear him coming, let's withdraw, my lord.

Hamlet know that the king and Polonius are spying on him? Why does Hamlet have so much difficulty deciding on a course of action to avenge his father's death? The decisions you make will influence your interpretation of the scene.

(They bestow themselves behind the arras; OPHELIA kneels at the faldstool.)

(HAMLET enters, in deep dejection.)

Hamlet: To be, or not to be, that is the question,
Whether 'tis nobler in the mind to suffer
The slings and arrows of outrageous fortune,
Or to take arms against a sea of troubles,
And by opposing, end them. To die, to sleep—
No more, and by a sleep to say we end
The heart-ache, and the thousand natural shocks
That flesh is heir to; 'tis a consummation
Devoutly to be wished to die to sleep!
To sleep, perchance to dream, ay there's the rub,
For in that sleep of death what dreams may come
When we have shuffled off this mortal coil
Must give us pause—there's the respect
That makes calamity of so long life:
For who would bear the whips and scorns of time,
Th'oppressor's wrong, the proud man's contumely,
The pangs of disprized love, the law's delay,
The insolence of office, and the spurns
That patient merit of th'unworthy takes,
When he himself might his quietus make
With a bare bodkin; who would fardels bear,
To grunt and sweat under a weary life,
But that the dread of something after death,
The undiscovered country, from whose bourn
No traveller returns, puzzles the will,
And makes us rather bear those ills we have,
Than fly to others that we know not of?
Thus conscience does make cowards of us all,
And thus the native hue of resolution
Is sicklied o'er with the pale cast of thought,
And enterprises of great pitch and moment
With this regard their currents turn awry,
And lose the name of action. . . . Soft you now,
The fair Ophelia—Nymph, in thy orisons
Be all my sins remembered.

Ophelia: (*rises*) Good my lord,
How does your honor for this many a day?

Hamlet: I humbly thank you, well, well, well.

Ophelia: My lord, I have remembrances of yours,
That I have longed long to re-deliver.
I pray you now receive them.

Hamlet: No, not I,
I never gave you aught.

Ophelia: My honored lord, you know right well you did,
And with them words of so sweet breath composed
As made the things more rich. Their perfume lost,
Take these again, for to the noble mind
Rich gifts wax poor when givers prove unkind.
There, my lord. (*She takes jewels from her bosom and places them on the table before him.*)

Hamlet: (*remembers the plot*) Ha, ha! are you honest?

Ophelia: My lord?

Hamlet: Are you fair?

Ophelia: What means your lordship?

Hamlet: That if you be honest and fair, your honesty should admit no discourse to your beauty.

Ophelia: Could beauty, my lord, have better commerce than with honesty?

Hamlet: Ay truly, for the power of beauty will sooner transform honesty from what it is to a bawd, than the force of honesty can translate beauty into his likeness. This was sometime a paradox, but now the time gives it proof. I did love you once.

Ophelia: Indeed, my lord, you made me believe so.

Hamlet: You should not have believed me, for virtue cannot so inoculate our old stock, but we shall relish of it—I loved you not.

Ophelia: I was the more deceived.

Hamlet: (*points to the faldstool*) Get thee to a nunnery, why wouldst thou be a breeder of sinners? I am myself indifferent honest, but yet I could accuse me of such things, that it were better my mother had not borne me: I am very proud, revengeful, ambitious, with more offences at my beck, than I have thoughts to put them in, imagination to give them shape, or time to act them in: what should such fellows as I do crawling between earth and heaven? We are arrant knaves all, believe none of us—go thy ways to a nunnery. . . . (*suddenly*) Where's your father?

Ophelia: At home, my lord.

Hamlet: Let the doors be shut upon him, that he may play the fool no where but in's own house. Farewell. *(he goes out)*

Ophelia: (*kneels before the crucifix*) O help him, you sweet heavens!

Hamlet: (*returns, distraught*) If thou dost marry, I'll give thee this plague for thy dowry—be thou as chaste as ice, as pure as snow, thou shalt not escape calumny; get thee to a nunnery, go, farewell. . . . (*he paces to and fro*) Or if thou wilt needs marry, marry a fool, for wise men know well enough what monsters you make of them: to a nunnery, go, and quickly too, farewell. *(he rushes out)*

Ophelia: O heavenly powers, restore him!

Hamlet: (*once more returning*) I have heard of your paintings too, well enough. God hath given you one face and you make yourselves another, you jig, you amble, and you lisp, you nickname God's creatures, and make your wantonness your ignorance; go to, I'll no more on't, it hath made me mad. I say we will have no mo marriage—those that are married already, all but one, shall live, the rest shall keep as they are: to a nunnery, go. *(he departs again)*

Ophelia: O, what a noble mind is here o'erthrown!
The courtier's, soldier's, scholar's, eye, tongue, sword,
Th'expectancy and rose of the fair state,
The glass of fashion, and the mould of form,
Th'observed of all observers, quite quite down,
And I of ladies most deject and wretched,
That sucked the honey of his music vows,
Now see that noble and most sovereign reason
Like sweet bells jangled, out of tune and harsh,
That unmatched form and feature of blown youth,
Blasted with ecstasy! O, woe is me!
T'have seen what I have seen, see what I see! (*she prays*)

(The KING *and* POLONIUS *steal forth from behind the arras.)*

King: Love! his affections do not that way tend,
Nor what he spake, though it lacked form a little,
Was not like madness—there's something in his soul,
O'er which his melancholy sits on brood,
And I do doubt the hatch and the disclose
Will be some danger; which for to prevent,
I have in quick determination
Thus set it down: he shall with speed to England,
For the demand of our neglected tribute.
Haply the seas, and countries different,
With variable objects, shall expel
This something-settled matter in his heart,
Whereon his brains still beating puts him thus
From fashion of himself. What think you on't?

(Ophelia comes forward)

Polonius: It shall do well. But yet do I believe
The origin and commencement of his grief
Sprung from neglected love. . .. How now, Ophelia?
You need not tell us what Lord Hamlet said,
We heard it all . . . My lord, do as you please,
But if you hold it fit, after the play,
Let his queen-mother all alone entreat him
To show his grief, let her be round with him,
And I'll be placed (so please you) in the ear
Of all their conference. If she find him not,
To England send him; or confine him where
Your wisdom best shall think.

King: It shall be so,
Madness in great ones must not unwatched go.

(they depart)

ACTIVITIES

1. After reading this script aloud, decide which of your lines you do not fully understand. In the next reading, leave those lines out. Does the meaning of the scene change? Which lines have to be put back in for the full meaning of the scene to be clear?

2. Read in two ways the part of Hamlet in the scene with Ophelia:

1) as a person who is insane; and
2) as a person who knows that the King is watching and therefore pretends to be insane.

Examine the difference between the two approaches.

3. To help you discover the actions and intentions of each character, improvise the scene after you have read it aloud several times. Use contemporary dialogue, and focus your improvisation on discovering the meaning of the scene. After the improvisation, go back to the text to find those speeches and actions you left out. Examine what it is in those speeches which you do not yet understand. Chapter 4, "Rehearsing the Script," gives a number of other useful rehearsal techniques for developing an interpretation of a scene.

FROM

ROSENCRANTZ AND GUILDENSTERN ARE DEAD

by Tom Stoppard

PLAYBILL

Rosencrantz and Guildenstern, two minor characters in Shakespeare's play, are fellow students of Hamlet. They are sent for and charged by King Claudius to find out what is wrong with Hamlet. The playwright has cleverly woven scenes from the original play into the scene presented here. As you will see, Rosencrantz and Guildenstern participate in and comment on all that is going on about them. They also get involved with the travelling players, the same players who were given the instructions quoted in the Introduction to Section A. The players are present to give the performance of the play which Hamlet hopes will cause Claudius to reveal himself as the murderer of Hamlet's father. As you work with the scene, be aware of how little control Rosencrantz and Guildenstern seem to have over what happens to them.

CHARACTERS

King Claudius
Queen Gertrude
Polonius
Ophelia
Rosencrantz
Guildenstern
Hamlet
Travelling Players
- **Lead Player** (director)
- **Alfred** (playing the Queen)
- **Player** (King)
- **Player** (poisoner)
- **Two other cloaked players**

(A grand procession enters, principally CLAUDIUS, GERTRUDE, POLONIUS, *and* OPHELIA. CLAUDIUS *takes* ROS*'s elbow as he passes and is immediately deep in conversation: the context is Shakespeare Act III, Scene i.* GUIL *still faces front as* CLAUDIUS, ROS *etc., Upstage and turn.)*

Guil: Death followed by eternity . . . the worst of both worlds. It *is* a terrible thought.

(He turns Upstage in time to take over the conversation with CLAUDIUS. GERTRUDE *and* ROS *head Downstage.)*

Gertrude: Did he receive you well?

Ros: Most like a gentleman.

Guil: (*Returning in time to take it up.*) But with much forcing of his disposition.

Ros: (*A flat lie and he knows it and shows it, perhaps catching* GUIL*'s eye.*) Niggard of question, but of our demands most free in his reply.

Gertrude: Did you assay him to any pastime?

Ros:
Madam, it so fell out that certain players
We o'erraught on the way: of these we told him
And there did seem in him a kind of joy
To hear of it. They are here about the court,
And, as I think, they have already order
This night to play before him.

Polonius:
'Tis most true
And he beseeched me to entreat your Majesties
To hear and see the matter.

Claudius:
With all my heart, and it doth content me
To hear him so inclined.
Good gentlemen, give him a further edge
And drive his purpose into these delights.

Ros: We shall, my lord.

Claudius: (*Leading out procession.*)
Sweet Gertrude, leave us, too,
For we have closely sent for Hamlet hither,
That he, as t'were by accident, may here
Affront Ophelia. . . .

(Exeunt CLAUDIUS *and* GERTRUDE.*)*

Ros: (*Peevish.*) Never a moment's peace! In and out, on and off, they're coming at us from all sides.

Guil: You're never satisfied.

Ros: Catching us on the trot. . . . Why can't *we* go by *them*?

Guil: What's the difference?

Ros: I'm going. (ROS *pulls his cloak round him.* GUIL *ignores him. Without confidence* ROS *heads Upstage. He looks out and comes back quickly.*) He's coming.

Guil: What's he doing?

Ros: Nothing.

Guil: He must be doing something.

Ros: Walking.

Guil: On his hands?

Ros: No, on his feet.

Guil: Stark naked?

Ros: Fully dressed.

Guil: Selling toffee apples?

Ros: Not that I noticed.

Guil: You could be wrong?

Ros: I don't think so.

(Pause.)

Guil: I can't for the life of me see how we're going to get into conversation.

*(*HAMLET *enters Upstage, and pauses, weighing up the pros and cons of making his quietus.* ROS *and* GUIL *watch him.)*

Ros: Nevertheless, I suppose one might say that this was a chance. . . . One might well . . . accost him. . . . Yes, it definitely looks like a chance to me. . . . Something on the lines of a direct informal approach . . . man to man . . . straight from the shoulder. . . . Now look here, what's it all about . . . sort of thing. Yes. Yes, this looks like one to be grabbed with both hands, I should say . . . if I were asked. . . . No point in looking at a gift horse till you see the whites of its eyes, etcetera. (*He has moved towards* HAMLET *but his nerve fails. He returns.*) We're overawed, that's our trouble. When it comes to the point we succumb to their personality. . . .

(OPHELIA enters, with prayerbook, a religious procession of one.)

Hamlet: Nymph, in thy orisons be all my sins remembered.

(At his voice she has stopped for him, he catches her up.)

Ophelia: Good my lord, how does your honor for this many a day?

Hamlet: I humbly thank you—well, well, well.

(They disappear talking into the Wing.)

Ros: It's like living in a public park!

Guil: Very impressive. Yes, I thought your direct informal approach was going to stop this thing dead in its tracks there. If I might make a suggestion—shut up and sit down. Stop being perverse.

Ros: (*Near tears.*) I'm not going to stand for it! (*A FEMALE FIGURE, ostensibly the QUEEN, enters. ROS marches up behind her, puts his hands over her eyes and says with a desperate frivolity.*) Guess who?!

Player: (*Having appeared in a Downstage corner.*) Alfred!

(ROS lets go, spins around. He has been holding ALFRED, in his robe and blond wig. He makes a break for an exit. A TRAGEDIAN dressed as a KING enters. ROS recoils, breaks for the opposite Wing. Two cloaked TRAGEDIANS enter. ROS tries again but another TRAGEDIAN enters, and ROS retires to Midstage. The PLAYER claps his hands matter-of-factly.)

Player: Right! We haven't got much time.

Guil: What are you doing?

Player: Dress rehearsal. Now if you two wouldn't mind just moving back . . . there . . . good. . . . (*To TRAGEDIANS:*) Everyone ready? And for goodness' sake, remember what we're doing. (*To ROS and GUIL.*) We always use the same costumes more or less, and they forget what they are supposed to be *in* you see. . . . Stop picking your nose, Alfred. When Queens have to they do it by a cerebral process passed down in the blood. . . . Good. Silence! Off we go!

Player-King: Full thirty times hath Phoebus' cart—

Player: (*He jumps up angrily.*) No, no, no! Dumbshow first, your confounded majesty! (*To ROS and GUIL.*) They're a bit out of practice, but they always pick up wonderfully for the deaths—it brings out the poetry in them.

Guil: How nice.

Player: There's nothing more unconvincing than an unconvincing death.

Guil: I'm sure.

(PLAYER claps his hands.)

Player: Act One—moves now.

(The mime. Soft music from a recorder. PLAYER-KING and PLAYER-QUEEN embrace. She kneels and makes a show of protestation to him. He takes her up, declining his head upon her neck. He lies down. She, seeing him asleep, leaves him.)

Guil: What is the dumbshow for?

Player: Well, it's a device, really—it makes the action that follows more or less comprehensible; you understand, we are tied down to a language which makes up in obscurity what it lacks in style.

(The mime (continued)—enter POISONER. He takes off the SLEEPER's crown, kisses it. He has brought in a small bottle of liquid. He pours the poison in the SLEEPER's ear, and leaves him. The SLEEPER convulses heroically, dying.)

Ros: Who was that?

Player: The King's brother and uncle to the Prince.

Guil: Not exactly fraternal.

Player: Not exactly avuncular, as time goes on.

(The QUEEN returns, makes passionate action, finding the KING dead. The POISONER comes in again, attended by TWO OTHERS (the two in cloaks). The POISONER seems to console with her. The dead BODY is carried away. The POISONER woos the QUEEN with gifts. She seems harsh awhile but in the end accepts his love. End of mime, at which point, the wail of a woman in torment and OPHELIA appears, wailing, closely followed by HAMLET in a hysterical state, shouting at her, circling her, both Midstage.)

Hamlet: Go to, I'll no more on't; it hath made me mad! (*She falls on her knees weeping.*) I say we will have no more marriage! (*His voice drops to include the TRAGEDIANS, who have frozen.*) Those that are married already—(*He leans close to the PLAYER-QUEEN and POISONER, speaking with quiet edge.*) all but one shall live. (*He smiles briefly at them without mirth, and starts to back out, his parting shot rising again.*) The rest shall keep as they are. (*As he leaves, OPHELIA tottering Upstage, he speaks into her ear a quick clipped sentence.*) To a nunnery, go.

(He goes out. OPHELIA falls on to her knees Upstage, her sobs barely audible. A slight silence.)

Player-King: Full thirty times hath Phoebus' cart—

(CLAUDIUS enters with POLONIUS and goes over to OPHELIA and lifts her to her feet. The TRAGEDIANS jump back with heads inclined.)

Claudius:

Love? His affections do not that way tend,
Or what he spake, though it lacked form a little,
Was not like madness. There's something
In his soul o'er which his melancholy sits on
Brood, and I do doubt the hatch and the
Disclose will be some danger; which for to
Prevent I have in quick determination thus set
It down: he shall with speed to England . . .

(Which carries the three of them—CLAUDIUS, POLONIUS, OPHELIA—out of sight. The PLAYER moves, clapping his hands for attention.)

Player: Gentle*men!* (*They look at him.*) It doesn't seem to be coming. We are not getting it at all. (*To GUIL.*) What did you think?

Guil: What was I supposed to think?

Player: (*To TRAGEDIANS.*) You're not getting across!

(ROS had gone halfway up to OPHELIA; he returns.)

Ros: That didn't look like love to me.

Guil: Starting from scratch again . . .

Player: Act Two! Positions!

Guil: Wasn't that the end?

Player: Do you call that an ending?—

with practically everyone on his feet? My goodness no—over your dead body. (*He laughs briefly and in a second seems never to have laughed in his life.*) There's a design at work in all art—surely you know that? Events must play themselves out to aesthetic, moral and logical conclusion.

Guil: And what's that, in this case?

Player: It never varies—we aim at the point where everyone who is marked for death dies.

Guil: Marked?

Player: Between "just deserts" and "tragic irony" we are given quite a lot of scope for our particular talent. Generally speaking, things have gone about as far as they can possibly go when things have got about as bad as they reasonably get. (*He switches on a smile.*)

Guil: Who decides?

Player: (*Switching off his smile.*) *Decides?* It is *written.* (*He turns away.* GUIL *grabs him and spins him back violently. Unflustered.*) We're tragedians, you see. We follow directions—there is no *choice* involved. The bad end unhappily, the good unluckily. That is what tragedy means. (*Calling.*) Positions!

ACTIVITIES

1. Examine the scene carefully to determine where you think lines from the original *Hamlet* have been put into Stoppard's play. When you do the scene, try to make the transitions between the two types of speech as smooth as possible so that it appears to be "natural."

2. When you run through this scene, concentrate on the complex physical actions which must be worked out to do this scene successfully. (Refer to blocking techniques in *A Midsummer Night's Dream*, Section A, Chapter 4.) Close attention should be paid to the intricate dialogue in order to discover all the possible meanings that exist.

3. Concentrate on the "dumb show" or mime play which the players are rehearsing. Decide what the effect of their rehearsal should be and rehearse this scene doing only the physical actions and eliminating the dialogue around it. A thorough understanding of this action will provide background for Hamlet's dilemma.

4. Compare the Lead Player's definition of tragedy with that of the chorus in *Antigone*, Chapter 3. Which definition do you prefer? Why?

5. This scene provides an elaboration of the theatrical convention of a play-within-a-play. Other examples are found in Section A: *What Glorious Times They Had* (Chapter 1), *The Real Inspector Hound* (Chapter 2), *Jitters* (Chapter 2), and *A Midsummer Night's Dream* (Chapter 4). How has Stoppard changed this convention?

FROM
HAMLET
adapted by Charles Marowitz

PLAYBILL

In this extreme reshaping of Shakespeare's *Hamlet*, Charles Marowitz has chosen speeches at random from the play and completely restructured their order. Marowitz has also changed some characters. For example, a minor character like Fortinbras, who appears only at the end of Shakespeare's play to restore order in Denmark, has a major role in Marowitz's adaptation. Marowitz describes his reworking of *Hamlet* in the following way:

> In my view, radical theatrical experiments need to be justified, if at all, only when they fail. The Hamlet collage was, on the whole, successful, and earned a certain credibility of its own. But if one were hard-pressed for justification, I would say that the re-structur-

CHARACTERS

Hamlet
Fortinbras, Prince of Norway, who conquers Denmark
Queen Gertrude
King Claudius
Ophelia
Laertes, Ophelia's brother, Polonius' son
Clown
Rosencrantz
Guildenstern
Ghost of Hamlet's Father
Others of the court (as chorus)

All: Judgement! Judgement! Judgement!

(*A trial is swiftly arranged:* HAMLET *placed in the dock by* FORTINBRAS, *who acts as counsel. The* KING *acts as Judge.*
All are seated behind a long tribunal table.)

Queen: Hamlet, thou hast thy father much offended.

Hamlet: Mother, you have my father much offended.

King: (*As Judge*) Come, come, you answer with an idle tongue.

Hamlet: Go, go, you question with an idle tongue.

King: Ophelia, prithee speak.

Ophelia: (*Soberly giving testimony*)
My Lord, as I was sewing in my chamber,
Lord Hamlet with his doublet all unbrac'd,
No hat upon his head, his stockings foul'd
Ungarter'd and down-gyved to his ankle,
Pale as his shirt, his knees knocking each other,
And with a look so piteous in purport,
As if he had been loosed out of hell,
To speak of horrors, he comes before me.

Fortinbras: (*Explaining*) Mad for thy love.

Ophelia: My Lord, I do not know.

King: What said he?

Ophelia: He took me by the wrist and held me hard;
Then goes he to the length of all his arm,
And with his other hand thus o'er his brow,

He falls to such perusal of my face
As he would draw it. Long stay'd he so.
At last, a little shaking of mine arm;
And thrice his head thus waving up and down,
He rais'd a sigh so piteous and profound
As it did seem to shatter all his bulk
And end his being. That done, he lets me go,
And with his head over his shoulder turn'd,
He seemed to find his way without his eyes
For out a doors he went without their help,
And to the last bended their light on me.

Fortinbras: (*to Court*)
This is the very ecstasy of love
Whose violent property fordoes itself,
And leads the will to desperate undertakings
As oft as any passion under Heaven
That does afflict our natures.

Ophelia: (*Slowly turning mad*) I hope all will be well. We must be patient, but I cannot choose but weep to think they should lay him in the cold ground: my brother shall know of it, and so I thank you for your good counsel. Come, my coach: good night Ladies, good night sweet Ladies, good night, good night.

(Exits as if in the seat of a coach and six.)

Laertes: (*Of* OPHELIA)
O treble woe,
Fall ten times treble on that cursed head
Whose wicked deed thy most ingenious sense
Depriv'd thee of.

(Makes for HAMLET.*)*

Hamlet: Away thy hand!

King: Pluck them asunder.

Fortinbras: (*Aside, to* HAMLET)
Good my Lord, be quiet.

(To Court)

Was't Hamlet wrong'd Laertes? Never Hamlet.
If Hamlet from himself be ta'en away
And when he's not himself does wrong Laertes,
Then Hamlet does it not. Hamlet denies it.
Who does it then?

ing of a work, the characters and situations of which are widely known, is an indirect way of making contact with that work's essence. Just as the human organism is understood differently when its metabolism is scrutinized in isolation, so certain "classical" works are understood differently when their components are reformed. This different understanding is not only the result of a new vantage-point (although this advantage should not be under-estimated), but the consequence of changing the play's time-signature. A collage form bequeaths speed, and when you have the advantage of speed in the theatre (without, one must add, the loss of definition), not only do you change the nature of what is being said, you also change the purpose for saying it.

As you read this selection, try to find lines of dialogue that you encountered in the previous two selections. How has Marowitz changed their meaning by changing their context?

Clown: (*Impulsively*) His madness.

Fortinbras: If't be so, Hamlet is of the faction that is wrong'd. His madness is poor Hamlet's enemy.

Clown: (*To others behind table*)
That he is mad, 'tis true;
'tis true, 'tis pity, and pity 'tis, 'tis true.

Guildenstern: My Lord, the Queen would speak.

Queen: (*Rising*) Hamlet in madness hath Polonius slain.

All: (*Suddenly thumping table*) Vengeance!

Queen: In his lawless fit,
Behind the arras, hearing something stir,
He whips out his rapier and cries, A rat, a rat,
And in this brainish apprehension kills
The unseen good old man.

(The CLOWN, *as* POLONIUS, *rises and bows his head. All at the table bow their heads in condolence.)*

King: It had been so with us had we been there.

Fortinbras: Of that I shall have also cause to speak, Wherein . . .

Queen: His liberty is full of threats to all; To you yourself, to us, to everyone.

(All thump table vengefully, as before.)

Hamlet: (*Rising to defend himself;* FORTINBRAS *struggles to keep him seated.*) Indeed my lord, I am very proud, revengeful, ambitious, with more offences at my beck than I have thoughts to put them in, imagination to give them shape, or time to act them in. What should such fellows as I do, crawling between heaven and earth? We are arrant knaves all, believe none of us.

(The Court bristles with contempt and all agitatedly consult the KING. FORTINBRAS *talks urgently to* HAMLET *and forces a paper into his hands.)*

Fortinbras: (*Trying to undo* HAMLET*'s harm*) My lord, will the King hear this.

Hamlet: (*Rises, under sufferance, and reads prepared statement*) "This presence knows,
And you must needs have heard how I am punish'd
With sore distraction. What I have done
That might your nature, honor and exception
Roughly awake, I here proclaim was madness."

Laertes: Madness!
And so have I a noble father lost,
A sister driven into desperate terms.
Whose worth (if praises may go back again)
Stood challenger on the mount of all the age
For her perfections. But my revenge will come.

Hamlet: Hear you, sir:
What is the reason that you use me thus?
I lov'd you ever.

Laertes: (*Bristling with anger*)
You mock me, sir.

Hamlet: Not by this hand.

Laertes: (*Springing on* HAMLET)
The devil take your soul.

(Others part LAERTES *and* HAMLET. *General scuffle stopped suddenly by the* GHOST*'s entrance.)*

Ghost: Mark me.

Hamlet: Alas, poor ghost.

King: Speak.

Hamlet: Do not come your tardy son to chide
That laps'd in time and passion lets go by
Th' important acting of your dread command.

King: I charge thee, speak.

Ghost: (*Directly to* KING)
In the corrupted currents of this world,
Offence's golden hand may shove by justice,
And oft 'tis seen the wicked prize itself
Buys out the Law; but 'tis not so above,
There is no shuffling, there the action lies
In his true nature, and we ourselves compell'd
Even to the teeth and forehead of our faults,
To give in evidence.

(Suddenly turns to HAMLET, *who averts his gaze.)*

Hamlet: (*To himself*) How all occasions do inform . . .

Ghost: Eyes without feeling, feeling without sight,
Ears without hands, or eyes, smelling, sans all
Or but a sickly part of one true sense
Could not so mope.

Hamlet: (*Swearing to himself*)
Thy commandment all alone shall live . . .

Ghost: Let . . . not . . . the royal bed . . . of Denmark . . . be . . . a Couch . . . for luxury and damned . . . incest.

Hamlet: (*Kneeling before* FATHER)
Thy commandment all alone shall live,
Within the book and volume of my brain,
Unmix'd with baser matter; yes, yes, by Heaven.
I have sworn't.

Queen: (*Rising*)
And thus awhile the fit will work on him:
Anon as patient as the female dove,
When that her golden couplets are disclosed,
His silence will sit drooping.

(All rise for verdict.)

King: Confine him.
Madness in great ones must not unwatch'd go.

(As Court moves off in all directions, HAMLET *tries to stop them with the next speech.)*

Hamlet: Let me speak to th' yet unknowing world,
How these things came about. So shall you hear
Of carnal, bloody and unnatural acts,
Of accidental judgements, casual slaughters,
Of deaths put on by cunning, and forc'd cause,
And in the upshot, purposes mistook,
Fall'n on the inventors' heads. All this can I
Truly deliver.

(By the time HAMLET *has finished his speech, he is ranting to the empty air as the Court have all disappeared.* FORTINBRAS, *sitting alone, looks up at him.* HAMLET *sinks down exhausted at his side.)*

Fortinbras: So oft it chances in particular men
That for some vicious mole of nature in them
As in their birth—wherein they are not guilty,
Since nature cannot choose his origin,—
By the o'ergrowth of some complexion,
Oft breaking down the pales and forts of reason;
Or by some habit that too much o'er-leavens
The form of plausive manners; that these men,
Carrying, I say, the stamp of one defect,
Being nature's livery or Fortune's star,
Their virtues else, be they as pure as grace,
As infinite as man may undergo,
Shall in the general censure take corruption
From that particular fault.

Hamlet: (*As if not understanding the implication*)
Does it not, think'st thee, stand me now upon?
He that hath kill'd my King, and whor'd my mother,
Popped in between the' election and my hopes,
Thrown out his angle for my proper life,
And with such cozenage: is't not perfect conscience,
To quit him with this arm? and is't not to be damn'd
To let this canker of our nature come
In further evil?

Fortinbras: (*Patronizing*) Ay, marry is't.

Hamlet: (*Acting*) Now could I drink hot blood,
And do such bitter business as the day
Would quake to look on.

Fortinbras: (*trying another tack*)
Rightly to be great
Is not to stir without great argument
But greatly to find quarrel in a straw
When honor's at the stake.

Hamlet: (*Hearing it for the first time*)
How stand I then,
That have a father kill'd, a mother stain'd,
Excitements of my reason and my blood,
And let all sleep.

Fortinbras: (*Urging direct action*)
Then trip him that his heels may kick at Heaven
And that his soul may be as damn'd and black
As Hell, whereto it goes.

(Pause.)

Hamlet: No.
When he is drunk asleep, or in his rage,
Or in the incestuous pleasure of his bed . . .

Fortinbras: (*He's heard it all before*)
Ay sure, this is most brave.

Hamlet: (*On the defensive*) The spirit that I have seen
May be the devil . . . the devil hath power
To assume a pleasing shape.

*(*FORTINBRAS, *unmoved by this ruse, regards* HAMLET *knowingly.)*

Do not look upon me,
Lest with this piteous action you convert
My stern effects; then what I have to do
Will want true color.

Fortinbras: That we would do
We should do when we would; for this "would" changes,
And hath abatements and delays, as many
As there are tongues, are hands, are accidents,
And this "should" is like a spendthrift sigh
That hurts by easing.

Hamlet: (*Seeking escape hatch*)
How all occasions . . .

Fortinbras: (*Taking him by the shoulders*)
What would you undertake
To show yourself your father's son in deed
More than in words?

Hamlet: (*Squirming*)
I'll . . . observe his looks; I'll . . . tempt him to the quick,
I'll have grounds more relative than this.

Fortinbras: (*Washing his hands of him completely*)
Thus conscience does make cowards of us all,
And thus the native hue of resolution
Is sicklied o'er with the pale cast of thought
And enterprises of great pith and moment
With this regard their currents turn awry
And lose the name of action. (*Exits*)

(Long pause.)

Hamlet: (*Bid to audience*)
Had *he* the motive and the cue for passion
That I have, he would drown the stage with tears
And cleave the general ear with horrid speech,
Make mad the guilty and appal the free,
Confound the ignorant and amaze indeed
The very faculty of eyes and ears.
Yet I
A dull and muddy-mettled rascal . . .
Peak like . . .
John a' Dreams . . . and
can do nothing.

(Before the end of this speech, the GHOST *and all the other characters have walked on very slowly. They form a semi-circle around the bent figure of* HAMLET. *Eventually, the* GHOST *comes forward. He is holding* HAMLET*'s toy sword.)*

Ghost: (*Mock frightened*)
Angels and ministers of grace defend us:
Be thou a spirit of health, or a goblin damn'd,
Bring with thee airs from Heaven or blasts from Hell?
Be thy intents wicked or charitable,
Thou comest in such a questionable shape
That I will speak to thee. I'll call thee Hamlet.

(Puts toy sword under HAMLET*'s arm, like a crutch. The Cast, now fully assembled, expresses its delight over the* GHOST*'s send-up.)*

Clown: (*Acknowledging its wit*)
A hit, a very palpable hit.

Ghost: (*Still playing it up like mad*)
Speak, I am bound to hear.

(A long pause, during which everyone's sarcastic laughter gradually mounts.)

Hamlet: (*Weakly*)
To be or not to be that is the question.

(All laugh.)

(*Weakly*) The play's the thing wherein I'll catch the conscience of the King.

(All laugh again.)

(*Vainly trying to find the right words*) There is something rotten in the state of Denmark.

(The laughter sharply cuts out. A powerful, stark silence issues from everyone. No one moves. Slowly HAMLET*'s frame begins to bend, gradually his knees sag and his back arches until he slumps down on to his knees. Then his head slowly rolls forward on to his chest and he sinks even further, on to his haunches. He leans on his toy sword for support. This descent takes a good deal of time, and occurs in total silence.)*

Fortinbras: (*Coming out of semi-circle, sarcastically*)
What a piece of work is man.

(*Chants*)

How noble in reason.

All: (*Chanting*) Noble in reason.

Fortinbras: (*Chants*) How infinite in faculty.

All: (*Chanting*) Infinite in faculty.

Fortinbras: (*Chanting*)
In form and moving, how express and admirable.

All: (*Chanting*) Express and admirable.

Fortinbras: (*Chanting*) In action, how like an angel.

All: (*Chanting*) How like an angel.

Fortinbras: (*Chanting*) In apprehension, how like a god.

All: (*Chanting*) How like a god.

(After this choral send-up led by FORTINBRAS, *all look again to* HAMLET, *who has not stirred.)*

Ophelia: (*Like old-time tragedienne, dashing forward*)
O what a noble mind is here o'erthrown.

All: (*Make a cry of being aghast.*)

Ophelia: The courtier's, soldier's, scholar's eye, tongue, sword.

All: (*Make a sound of great mock anguish*)

Ophelia: The expectancy and rose of the fair State.

All: (*Make a sound of mock pity*)

Ophelia: And I of ladies most deject and wretched
That suck'd the honey of his music vows.

All: (*Make a sound commiserating with the girl's wretchedness*)

Ophelia: Now see that noble, and most sovereign reason,
Like sweet bells jangled out of tune, and harsh,
That unmatch'd form and feature of blown youth,
Blasted with ecstasy. O woe is me . . .

All: (*Wailing*) Woe is meeeeee . . .

Ophelia: T' have seen what I have seen.

(Looks disgustedly at the slouched HAMLET*)*

See what I see.

(There is another stony silence, during which all watch the motionless HAMLET.*)*

Ghost: (*Coming forward; the father of old*)
If . . . thou . . . hast . . . Nature . . . in . . . thee . . . bear . . . it . . . not!

Hamlet: (*Still slumped, making a vow*)
Thy commandment all alone shall live
Within the book and volume of my brain.

Ghost: Swear.

Hamlet: All saws of books . . .

Ghost: Swear . . .

Hamlet: All forms . . .

Ghost: Swear . . .

Hamlet: All pressures past . . .

Ghost: Swear!

Hamlet: (*rising*)
Thy commandment all alone shall live.

(As he has struggled to his feet, ROSENCRANTZ *and* GUILDENSTERN *come up to him—and at that moment, he collapses into their arms and is borne—like a dead soldier—to the pedestal.)*

Fortinbras: Bear Hamlet like a soldier to the stage

For he was likely (had he been put on)
To have prov'd most royally.

(HAMLET, slumped on circular pedestal, summons up one last burst of energy.)

Hamlet: O Vengeance!

(Thrusts his toy sword into host of imaginary victims. After each thrust, a character falls to the ground, truly slain, until the corpses of all the characters lie strewn around HAMLET like a set of downed ninepins.)

From . . . this . . . time . . . forth

(The corpses, still stretched out, begin derisive laughter.)

My thoughts be bloody or be nothing worth.

(Corpses, laughing hysterically, mock HAMLET with jeers, whistles, stamping and catcalls, till final fade out.)

CURTAIN

ACTIVITIES

1. After reading this scene, have a discussion about the merits and the faults of the script. How do you feel about Marowitz's right to alter Shakespeare's original? Can you find other examples of re-interpretations of Shakespeare's work? How were they received? Are there instances in other art forms, such as music and the visual arts, where original work has been radically altered? Summarize the major points made in your discussion.

2. In the text of this script notice what has happened to Hamlet's soliloquy, "What a piece of work is man." Conduct a similar experiment with Hamlet's soliloquy, "To be or not to be" presented in the selection from Shakespeare's *Hamlet*. Re-interpret it as a piece of choral speaking, or as a scene involving a number of people. How does the meaning change?

3. Examine the entire text of *Hamlet* for famous lines such as "To thine own self be true." Extract as many of these lines as you can, and arrange them as dialogue to create a scene involving a number of characters. You will also have to invent a context and a dramatic structure.

WORKSHOP

1. Many of Shakespeare's plays have been made into movies and television shows. If possible, attempt to see one or more of these works, and discuss the interpretation of the text. Is it a radical or conventional dramatization of the text? Can you determine what parts of the text have been left out? What has been added in order to translate the play into another medium?

2. Using the techniques in *Rosencrantz and Guildenstern are Dead*, choose another of Shakespeare's plays from which you can extract minor characters. Build a scene in which these characters comment on and are affected by the action going on around them.

3. Choose another scene from this book and experiment with it in the same manner as Marowitz experimented with *Hamlet*. Change the order of the lines and the importance of the characters. Put the play in a different context. If the play is comic, make it tragic, or, if tragic, make it comic. Use choral speaking in your re-interpretation.

19: Well-mannered People

THE PROGRAM

Theatres in England were shut down from 1642 to 1660, the time of the English Civil War and the rule of Oliver Cromwell. They were reopened after 1660 when, with the reign of Charles II, the monarchy was restored. Consequently, the drama produced in this period, from 1600 to the late 1700's, is called Restoration Theatre.

At this time, there was a renewed interest in the drama of ancient Greece and Rome, and the Restoration plays were modelled on examples from this period. Its major characteristics were the observation of the three unities; the *time* of the play was a 24-hour period, the *action* was continuous within this time (with related subplots occurring simultaneously), and the *places* in which the various scenes occurred were related in some way. These "rules" changed the types of drama being written.

The most important form of theatre in the Restoration period was the "comedy of manners." It had the following characteristics: the characters were members of the aristocracy and the upper classes; the plots revolved around intrigues of love, arranged marriages, mistaken identity, and the loss or acquisition of large fortunes; gossip about fashion, appearance, and dress formed a large part of the dialogue; an aptitude for witty repartee and clever statements was regarded as an important social quality; and most plays advanced the conventional moral viewpoint of the period—that the wise and virtuous are rewarded and the foolish are ridiculed.

The Restoration period also resulted in several significant changes in the production of professional plays. Acting companies which were attached to specific London Theatres were created, and several of these companies had acting schools to train young apprentices. Women became members of the acting companies, and many leading actresses became major attractions of productions. Writers created parts for women knowing that these parts would be played by women rather than by young boys, as had been the case in Elizabethan Theatre.

Actors generally played a limited number of character types, and once an actor established a role as his or her own, he or she always played that role. An actor would be categorized as a player of serious roles, or as a player of comic secondary roles. Less established actors would have "walk-ons" or play "general-utility" roles. The Restoration period was the beginning of the "star" system; audiences would go to the theatre as much to see a particular actor as to see a particular play.

Most theatre companies presented a series of plays in repertory; that is, the play would change every few nights, and an actor had to be ready to play a different role at twenty-four hour's notice. Rehearsal periods for plays were brief—two weeks—and the playwright usually directed the first three rehearsals. After that, the lead player would direct the production according to his interpretation. This led to the evolution of the actor-manager, the precursor of the present day director.

Acting style was usually non-realistic. Most scenes were played downstage, and lines were delivered to the audience with no attempt made to create the effect of conversation. Because lines were not memorized until the last moment, there was much improvisation, and a leading actor would not divulge any innovative business he or she had invented until the first performance, much to the surprise of the audience and fellow actors. Lines were delivered in an oratorical manner (which sometimes sank to bombast); some Restoration acting rules show this clearly: never turn your back on the audience; seldom stand in profile; exchange stage positions after each speech; and (since there was no curtain call) accept the applause of the audience when you have made a good "point" during a scene.

Going to the theatre was a major event, and a performance could last from three to five hours. First on the bill would be a half-hour of music. Then the prologue to the play would be delivered, followed by the performance of the play. Between acts (there were usually five) various entertainments were presented. This could be singers, dancers, acrobats, or trained animal acts. After the main play, there was a short "after piece" in the form of a comic opera or farce, and then the evening would conclude with singing and dancing.

The first selection in this chapter is from Sheridan's *The Rivals*, a play from the later Restoration period. This play is typical of the period, and presents Mrs. Malaprop, one of the most famous characters in British stage history. Following *The Rivals* is *Black-Ey'd Susan*, an example of nineteenth-century melodrama, which is a direct descendant of Restoration Theatre. However, while the Restoration period had excellent playwrights, and the quality of the writing has sustained the plays, the nineteenth-century theatre was a truly "popular" entertainment; the playwrights "gave the public what it wanted." Consequently, the drama was exaggerated and highly sentimental, the characters were one-dimensional, and the lines between good and evil were clearly drawn. Nineteenth-century melodrama can in this way be compared to contemporary television programs, particularly to soap opera.

Towards the end of the nineteenth century, the popularity of melodrama waned, and the music hall became the popular source of entertainment. Oscar Wilde's play, *The Importance of Being Earnest*, written in 1895, catered to an exclusive privileged class and signalled a return to the style of Restoration Theatre. Theatre once again concerned itself with presenting high society to high society, and dialogue was full of biting wit and sophistication.

The last selection in this chapter, *The Nearlyweds*, is an example of contemporary comedy/melodrama and owes a good deal of its plot to *The Rivals*. But although it is a direct descendant of the comedy of manners, it also contains elements of popular appeal—many of which can be found in *Black-Ey'd Susan*.

After working with these scripts, you may wish to view television situation-comedies and soap operas as contemporary equivalents of these plays.

FROM

A LIFE IN THE THEATRE

by David Mamet

SCENE 17

(At the makeup table.)

Robert: A makeup table. Artificial light. The scent of powder. Tools. Sticks. Brushes. Tissues. (*Pause.*) Cold *cream.* (*Pause.*) Greasepaint. (*Pause.*) Greasepaint! What is it? Some cream base, some coloring . . . texture, smell, color . . . analyse it and what have you? Meaningless component parts, though one could likely say the same for anything. . . . *But* mix and package it, affix a label, set it on a makeup table . . . a brush or two . . .

John: Would you please shut up?

(Pause.)

Robert: Am I disturbing you?

John: You are.

(Pause.)

Robert: Enough to justify this breach of etiquette?

John: What breach? What etiquette?

Robert: John . . .

John: Yes?

Robert: When one's been in the theatre as long as I . . .

John: Can we do this later?

Robert: I feel that there is something here of worth to you.

John: You do?

Robert: Yes.

John: (*sighs*) Let us hear it then.

Robert: All right. You know your attitude, John, is not of the best. It isn't. It just isn't.

John: (*Pause*) It isn't?

Robert: Forms. The Theatre's a closed society. Constantly abutting thoughts, the feelings, the emotions of our colleagues. Sensibilities (*pause*) bodies . . . *forms* evolve. An etiquette, eh? In our personal relations with each other. Eh, John? In our personal relationships.

(Pause.)

John: Mmm.

Robert: One generation sows the seeds. It instructs the preceding . . . that is to say, the *following* generation . . . from the quality of its actions. Not from its discourse, John, no, but organically. (*Pause.*) You can learn a lot from keeping your mouth shut.

John: You can.

Robert: Yes. And perhaps this is not the place to speak of attitudes.

John: Before we go on.

Robert: Yes. But what is "life on stage" but attitudes?

John: (*Pause*) What?

Robert: Damn little.

(Pause.)

John: May I use your brush?

Robert: Yes. (*Hands* JOHN *brush.*) One must speak of these things, John, or we will go the way of all society.

John: Which is what?

Robert: Take too much for granted, fall away and die. (*Pause.*) On the boards, or in society at large. There must be law, there must be a reason, there must be tradition.

(Pause.)

John: I'm sorry that I told you to shut up.

Robert: No, you can't buy me off that cheaply.

John: No?

Robert: No.

(Pause.)

John: Would you pass me the cream, please?

Robert: Certainly. (*Passes the cream.*) Here is the cream.

John: Thank you.

FROM

THE RIVALS

by Richard Sheridan

CHARACTERS

Mrs. Malaprop, Lydia's guardian aunt
Captain Jack Absolute, Lydia's suitor (also known as Ensign Beverley)

SCENE III

MRS. MALAPROP'S LODGINGS.

*(*MRS. MALAPROP, *with a letter in her hand, and* CAPTAIN ABSOLUTE.*)*

Mrs. Mal: Your being Sir Anthony's son, captain, would itself be a sufficient accommodation; but from the ingenuity of your appearance, I am convinced you deserve the character here given of you.

Abs: Permit me to say, madam, that as I never yet have had the pleasure of seeing Miss Languish, my principal inducement in this affair at present is the honor of being allied to Mrs. Malaprop; of whose intellectual accomplishments, elegant manners, and unaffected learning, no tongue is silent.

Mrs. Mal: Sir, you do me infinite honor! I beg, captain, you'll be seated.—(*They sit.*) Ah! few gentlemen, now-a-days, know how to value the ineffectual qualities in a

PLAYBILL

Lydia Languish, the heroine, is wealthy, but her fortune is controlled by her aunt, Mrs. Malaprop. Captain Jack Absolute, pretending to be the impoverished Ensign Beverley, has won Lydia's heart; at the same time, Mrs. Malaprop has promised Sir Anthony Absolute that his son Jack can marry Lydia. Consequently, Captain Jack Absolute is his own rival.

woman!—few think how a little knowledge becomes a gentlewoman.—Men have no sense now but for the worthless flower of beauty!

Abs: It is but too true, indeed, ma'am;—yet I fear our ladies should share the blame—they think our admiration of beauty so great, that knowledge in them would be superfluous. Thus, like garden-trees, they seldom show fruit, till time has robbed them of more specious blossom.—Few, like Mrs. Malaprop and the orange-tree, are rich in both at once!

Mrs. Mal: Sir, you overpower me with good-breeding.—He is the very pineapple of politeness!—You are not ignorant, captain, that this giddy girl has somehow contrived to fix her affections on a beggarly, strolling, eaves-dropping ensign, whom none of us have seen, and nobody knows anything of.

Abs: Oh, I have heard the silly affair before.—I'm not at all prejudiced against her on that account.

Mrs. Mal: You are very good and very considerate, captain. I am sure I have done everything in my power since I exploded the affair; long ago I laid my positive conjunctions on her, never to think on the fellow again;—I have since laid Sir Anthony's preposition before her; but, I am sorry to say, she seems resolved to decline every particle that I enjoin her.

Abs: It must be very distressing, indeed, ma'am.

Mrs. Mal: Oh! it gives me the hydrostatics to such a degree.—I thought she had persisted from corresponding with him; but, behold, this very day, I have interceded another letter from the fellow; I believe I have it in my pocket.

Abs: Oh, the devil; my last note. (*Aside.*)

Mrs. Mal: Ay, here it is.

Abs: Ay, my note indeed! Oh, the little traitress Lucy.[1] (*Aside.*)

Mrs. Mal: There, perhaps you may know the writing. (*Gives him the letter.*)

Abs: I think I have seen the hand before—yes, I certainly must have seen this hand before—

Mrs. Mal: Nay, but read it, captain.

[1] Lydia's servant

Mrs. Malaprop's famous misuse of the English language has made her one of the best known characters in English theatre. This scene is an example of Mrs. Malaprop at her best and has comic effect because she does not realize that Captain Jack and Ensign Beverley are the same person.

Abs: (*Reads.*) *My soul's idol, my adored Lydia!*—Very tender, indeed!

Mrs. Mal: Tender, ay, and profane too, o' my conscience.

Abs: (*Reads.*) *I am excessively alarmed at the intelligence you send me, the more so as my new rival—*

Mrs. Mal: That's you, sir.

Abs: (*Reads.*) *Has universally the character of being an accomplished gentleman and a man of honor.*—Well, that's handsome enough.

Mrs. Mal: Oh, the fellow has some design in writing so.

Abs: That he had, I'll answer for him, ma'am.

Mrs. Mal: But go on, sir—you'll see presently.

Abs: (*Reads.*) *As for the old weather-beaten she-dragon who guards you.*—Who can he mean by that?

Mrs. Mal: Me, sir!—me!—he means me!—There—what do you think now?—but go on a little further.

Abs: Impudent scoundrel!—(*Reads.*) *it shall go hard but I will elude her vigilance, as I am told that the same ridiculous vanity, which makes her dress up her coarse features, and deck her dull chat with hard words which she don't understand—*

Mrs. Mal: There, sir, an attack upon my language! what do you think of that?—an aspersion upon my parts of speech! was ever such a brute! Sure, if I reprehend any thing in this world it is the use of my oracular tongue, and a nice derangement of epitaphs!

Abs: He deserves to be hanged and quartered! let me see—(*Reads.*) *same ridiculous vanity—*

Mrs. Mal: You need not read it again, sir.

Abs: I beg pardon, ma'am.—(*Reads.*) *does also lay her open to the grossest deceptions from flattery and pretended admiration*—an impudent coxcomb!—*so that I have a scheme to see you shortly with the old harridan's consent, and even to make her a go-between in our interview.*—Was ever such assurance!

Mrs. Mal: Did you ever hear anything like it?—he'll elude my vigilance, will he?—Yes, yes! ha! ha! he's very likely to enter these doors;—we'll try who can plot best!

Abs: So we will, ma'am—so we will! Ha! ha! ha! a conceited puppy, ha! ha! ha!—Well, but, Mrs. Malaprop, as the girl seems so infatuated by this fellow, suppose you were to wink at her corresponding with him for a little time—let her even plot an elopement with him—then do you connive at her escape—while I, just in the nick, will have the fellow laid by the heels, and fairly contrive to carry her off in his stead.

Mrs. Mal: I am delighted with the scheme; never was anything better perpetrated!

Abs: But, pray, could not I see the lady for a few minutes now?—I should like to try her temper a little.

Mrs. Mal: Why, I don't know—I doubt she is not prepared for a visit of this kind. There is a decorum in these matters.

Abs: O Lord! she won't mind me—only tell her Beverley—

Mrs. Mal: Sir!

Abs: Gently, good tongue. (*Aside.*)

Mrs. Mal: What did you say of Beverley?

Abs: Oh, I was going to propose that you should tell her, by way of jest, that it was Beverley who was below; she'd come down fast enough then—ha! ha! ha!

Mrs. Mal: 'Twould be a trick she well deserves; besides, you know the fellow tells her he'll get my consent to see her—ha! ha! Let him if he can, I say again. Lydia, come down here!—(*Calling.*) He'll make me a go-between in their interviews!—ha! ha! ha! Come down, I say, Lydia! I don't wonder at your laughing, ha! ha! ha! his impudence is truly ridiculous.

Abs: 'Tis very ridiculous, upon my soul, ma'am, ha! ha! ha!

Mrs. Mal: The little hussy won't hear. Well, I'll go and tell her at once who it is—she shall know that Captain Absolute is come to wait on her. And I'll make her behave as becomes a young woman.

Abs: As you please, madam.

Mrs. Mal: For the present, captain, your servant. Ah! you've not done laughing yet, I see—elude my vigilance; yes, yes; ha! ha! ha! (*Exit.*)

ACTIVITIES

1. Examine the errors Mrs. Malaprop makes in word usage ("malapropisms"), and be sure you know which words she intended to use. The person playing Mrs. Malaprop must not emphasize the misused word. Refer back to *Archie In The Hospital* (Chapter 17); Archie's use of malapropisms is one of the "signatures" of his character.

2. The use of the "aside" is a convention not much used today. It provides a problem for those actors onstage who are not supposed to hear it. Find instances in this scene where many asides occur and practise maintaining the continuity of the dialogue.

FROM

BLACK-EY'D SUSAN

by Douglas Jerrold

PLAYBILL

This play was written in 1829 and was immensely popular with audiences up to the beginning of the twentieth century. It is a dramatization of a ballad by the poet John Gay. Doggrass, Susan's uncle and heartless landlord, has convinced William, Susan's husband, to become a sailor. Unknown to Susan, William has just been reported as lost at sea. This next scene is the precursor to that stock melodramatic scene—"I've come for the rent." As you read the scene, which occurs early in Act I, think about the stereotypes the characters represent and the genuine emotions that are, here, burlesqued.

CHARACTERS

Susan

Gnatbrain

Doggrass, Susan's uncle and landlord

SCENE III

Dame Hatley's Cottage; door in flat (practical) and a lattice window in L. *flat; another door,* R. 2 E.

(SUSAN *is heard without, singing a verse of "Black-Ey'd Susan." Enter* SUSAN, R.)

Susan: Twelve long tedious months have passed, and no tidings of William. Shame upon the unkind hearts that parted us—that sent my dear husband to dare the perils of the ocean, and made me a pining, miserable creature. Oh! the pangs, the dreadful pangs that tear the sailor's wife, as wakeful on her tear-wet pillow, she lists and trembles at the roaring sea.

(*Enter* GNATBRAIN, *at the cottage door in flat.*)

Gnatbrain: There she is, like a caged nightingale, singing her heart out against her prison bars—for this cottage is little better than a gaol to her. Susan!

Susan: Gnatbrain!

Gnatbrain: In faith, Susan, if sorrow makes such sweet music, may I never turn skylark, but always remain a goose.

Susan: Have you seen my uncle?

Gnatbrain: Oh, yes!

Susan: Will he show any kindness?

Gnatbrain: I cannot tell. You have flowers from an aloe tree if you wait a hundred years.

Susan: He has threatened to distress the good dame.

Gnatbrain: Ay, for the rent. Oh, Susan, I would I were your landlord. I should think myself well paid if you would allow me every quarter-day to put my ear to the key-hole, and listen to one of your prettiest ditties. Why, for such payment, were I your landlord, I'd find you in board, washing, and lodging, and the use of a gig on Sundays. I wish I—But, la! what's the use of my wishing? I'm nobody but half gardener, half waterman—a kind of alligator, that gets his breakfast from the shore, and his dinner from the sea—a—

(DOGGRASS *passes window,* L. *to* R.)

Susan: Oh! begone! I see Mr. Doggrass; if he find you here—

Gnatbrain: He must not; here's a cupboard—I'm afraid there's plenty of room in it.

Susan: No, no, I would not for the world—there is no occasion—meet him.

Gnatbrain: Not I, for quiet's sake. We never meet but, like gunpowder and fire, there is an explosion. This will do. (*Goes into closet,* R. 2 E.)

(*Enter* DOGGRASS, *door in flat*)

Doggrass: Now, Susan, you know my business—I say, you know my business. I come for money.

Susan: I have none, sir.

Doggrass: A pretty answer, truly. Are people to let their houses to beggars?

Susan: Beggars! Sir, I am your brother's orphan child.

Doggrass: I am sorry for it. I wish he were alive to pay for you. And where is your husband?

Susan: Do you ask where he is? I am poor, sir—poor and unprotected; do not, as you have children of your own, do not insult me. (*Weeps*)

Doggrass: Ay, this is to let houses to women; if the taxgatherers were to be paid with crying, why nobody would roar more lustily than myself; let a man ask for his rent, and you pull out your pocket handkerchief. Where's Dame Hatley?

Susan: In the next room—ill, very ill.

Doggrass: An excuse to avoid me; she shall not. (*Going,* R.)

Susan: You will not enter.

Doggrass: Who shall stop me?

Susan: If heaven give me power, I! Uncle, the old woman is sick—I fear dangerously. Her spirit, weakened by late misfortune, flickers like a dying light—your sudden appearance might make all dark. Uncle—landlord! would you have murder on your soul?

Doggrass: Murder?

Susan: Yes; though such may not be the common word, hearts are daily crushed, spirits broken—whilst he who slays, destroys in safety.

Doggrass: Can Dame Hatley pay me the money?

Susan: No.

Doggrass: Then she shall go to prison.

Susan: She will die there.

Doggrass: Well?

Susan: Would you make the old woman close her eyes in a gaol?

Doggrass: I have no time to hear sentiment. Mrs. Hatley has no money—you have none. Well, though she doesn't merit lenity of me, I'll not be harsh with her.

Susan: I thought you could not.

Doggrass: I'll just take whatever may be in the house, and put up with the rest of the loss.

ACTIVITIES

1. Examine the stereotype characters in the script. Write a description of each stereotype, and then do the scene in such a way as to exaggerate the stereotype. Next, go through the scene playing against the stereotyped characteristics and emphasizing other qualities the characters possess. Discuss the differences this makes to your dramatization, and consider what it is about stereotype characters that makes them appealing to an audience.

2. View an episode of a television soap-opera, and observe the melodramatic content in terms of plot and characters. Improvise the scene from *Black-Ey'd Susan* in the style of a contemporary soap opera. What qualities of the script remain the same?

3. In the style of melodrama, improvise a continuation of *Black-Ey'd Susan*. Consider having William appear to "save the day." Improvise a scene where Susan stands up to her uncle and takes charge of events.

4. Compare this scene with *Count Dracula* (Section A, Chapter 4). *Count Dracula* is a form of melodrama labelled "Gothic"; that is, it has supernatural elements, exotic locations, and unusual events. Try introducing *Dracula*-type elements into an improvised scene from *Black-Ey'd Susan*.

FROM

THE IMPORTANCE OF BEING EARNEST

by Oscar Wilde

PLAYBILL

This play revives the qualities of Restoration Theatre: upper-class characters, witty repartee, love intrigues, gossip, and morality. Jack Worthing has invented a younger brother called "Ernest" to justify his frequent visits to London from his country estate. Gwendolen, Lady Bracknell's daughter, has just been proposed to by Jack whom she thinks *is* Ernest, a name that she loves. In this scene, Lady Bracknell is examining Jack to determine his eligibility as a husband for Gwendolen. As you read, pay attention to the speech of Lady Bracknell and her use of epigrams; for example, "Ignorance is like a delicate, exotic fruit; touch it and the bloom is gone."

CHARACTERS

Lady Bracknell, mother of Gwendolen
Jack Worthing, Gwendolen's suitor

Lady B: (*Sitting down*) You can take a seat, Mr. Worthing. (*Looks in her pocket for note-book and pencil*)

Jack: Thank you, Lady Bracknell, I prefer standing.

Lady B: (*Pencil and note-book in hand*) I feel bound to tell you that you are not down on my list of eligible young men, although I have the same list as the dear Duchess of Bolton has. We work together, in fact. However, I am quite ready to enter your name, should your answers be what a really affectionate mother requires. Do you smoke?

Jack: Well, yes, I must admit I smoke.

Lady B: I am glad to hear it. A man should always have an occupation of some kind. There are far too many idle men in London as it is. How old are you?

Jack: Twenty-nine.

Lady B: A very good age to be married at. I have always been of opinion that a man who desires to get married should know either everything or nothing. Which do you know?

Jack: (*After some hesitation*) I know nothing, Lady Bracknell.

Lady B: I am pleased to hear it. I do not approve of anything that tampers with natural ignorance. Ignorance is like a delicate exotic fruit; touch it and the bloom is gone. The whole theory of modern education is radically unsound. Fortunately in England, at any rate, education produces no effect whatsoever. If it did, it would prove a serious danger to the upper classes, and probably lead to acts of violence in Grosvenor Square. What is your income?

Jack: Between seven and eight thousand a year.

Lady B: (*Makes a note in her book*) In land, or in investments?

Jack: In investments chiefly.

Lady B: That is satisfactory. What between the duties expected of one during one's lifetime, and the duties exacted from one after one's death, land has ceased to be either a profit or a pleasure. It gives one position, and prevents one from keeping it up. That's all that can be said about land.

Jack: I have a country house with some land, of course, attached to it, about fifteen hundred acres, I believe; but I don't depend on that for my real income. In fact, as far as I can make out, the poachers are the only people who make anything out of it.

Lady B: A country house! How many bedrooms? Well, that point can be cleared up afterwards. You have a town house, I hope? A girl with a simple, unspoiled nature, like Gwendolen, could hardly be expected to reside in the country.

Jack: Well, I own a house in Belgrave Square, but it is let by the year to Lady Bloxham. Of course, I can get it back whenever I like, at six months' notice.

Lady B: Lady Bloxham? I don't know her.

Jack: Oh, she goes about very little. She is a lady considerably advanced in years.

Lady B: Ah, nowadays that is no guarantee of respectability of character. What number in Belgrave Square?

Jack: 149.

Lady B: (*Shaking her head*) The unfashionable side. I thought there was something. However, that could easily be altered.

Jack: Do you mean the fashion, or the side?

Lady B: (*Sternly*) Both, if necessary, I presume. What are your politics?

Jack: Well, I am afraid I really have none. I am a Liberal Unionist.

Lady B: Oh, they count as Tories. They dine with us. Or come in the evening, at any rate. Now to minor matters. Are your parents living?

Jack: I have lost both my parents.

Lady B: To lose one parent, Mr. Worthing, may be regarded as a misfortune; to lose both looks like carelessness. Who was your father? He was evidently a man of some wealth. Was he born in what the Radical papers call the purple of commerce, or did he rise from the ranks of the aristocracy?

Jack: I am afraid I really don't know. The fact is, Lady Bracknell, I said I had lost my parents. It would be nearer the truth to say that my parents seem to have lost me.... I don't actually know who I am by birth. I was ... well, I was found.

Lady B: Found!

Jack: The late Mr. Thomas Cardew, an old gentleman of a very charitable and kindly disposition, found me, and gave me the name of Worthing, because he happened to have a first-class ticket for Worthing in his pocket at the time. Worthing is a place in Sussex. It is a seaside resort.

Lady B: Where did the charitable gentleman who had a first-class ticket for this seaside resort find you?

Jack: (*Gravely*) In a hand-bag.

Lady B: A hand-bag?

Jack: (*Very seriously*) Yes, Lady Bracknell. I was in a hand-bag—a somewhat large, black leather hand-bag, with handles to it—an ordinary hand-bag in fact.

Lady B: In what locality did this Mr. James, or Thomas, Cardew come across this ordinary hand-bag?

Jack: In the cloak-room at Victoria Station. It was given to him in mistake for his own.

Lady B: The cloak-room at Victoria Station?

Jack: Yes. The Brighton line.

Lady B: The line is immaterial. Mr. Worthing, I confess I feel somewhat bewildered by what you have just told me. To be born, or at any rate bred, in a hand-bag, whether it had handles or not, seems to me to display a contempt for the ordinary decencies of family life that reminds one of the worst excesses of the French Revolution. And I presume you know what that unfortunate movement led to? As for the particular locality in which the hand-bag was found, a cloak-room at a railway station might serve to conceal a social indiscretion—has probably, indeed, been used for that purpose before now—but it could hardly be regarded as an assured basis for a recognized position in good society.

Jack: May I ask you then what you would advise me to do? I need hardly say I would do anything in the world to ensure Gwendolen's happiness.

Lady B: I would strongly advise you, Mr. Worthing, to try and acquire some relations as soon as possible, and to make a definite effort to produce at any rate one parent, of either sex, before the season is quite over.

Jack: Well, I don't see how I could possibly manage to do that. I can produce the hand-bag at any moment. It is in my dressing-room at home. I really think that should satisfy you, Lady Bracknell.

Lady B: Me, sir! What has it to do with me? You can hardly imagine that I and Lord Bracknell would dream of allowing our only daughter—a girl brought up with the utmost care—to marry into a cloak-room, and form an alliance with a parcel. Good morning, Mr. Worthing!

ACTIVITIES

1. One of the problems with playing comedy is that, while the *actor* has to know what is funny in a line, scene, or situation, the actor must not give the audience any indication that the *character* he or she is playing knows what is funny. Read the scene aloud, and note any lines which give you problems because of the humor. Improvise scenes around these lines; for example, improvise a "sad" scene when Jack states that he has no parents. When working with the "seriousness" of this comedy, it might help you to keep in mind the title of this play.

2. Examine how the selection changes if you put it in a contemporary setting with contemporary characters.

3. Compare Lady Bracknell and Mrs. Malaprop. Improvise a scene in which they discuss the difficulty of finding a suitable young man.

FROM

THE NEARLYWEDS

by Lloyd J. Schwartz and Wendell Burton

PLAYBILL

Before this scene begins, Doug has attempted to abduct Marcy, at Helen's urging, to prevent Marcy from marrying Leonard. Marcy, however, is in love with Doug and the abduction is not necessary. Helen then receives a telephone call informing her that Leonard has crashed his car into a Baskin-Robbins store—Leonard's "life cut short in thirty-one flavors." As the scene opens, Marcy is just returning from a visit to the neighbors. You will note that this play has thematic connections (the reference to the navy, the search for a suitable partner, and mistaken identity) with the previous selections.

CHARACTERS

Helen, Marcy's mother
Marcy
Doug
Leonard

Marcy: (*She opens the door with her key.*) I'm home! Is it all over?

(DOUG *and* HELEN *look at each other.* MARCY *doesn't know the sad double meaning of her question.)*

Helen: Dear, come in and sit down for a minute. Mother would like to talk to you.

Marcy: (*She crosses the room with solemn curiosity.*) This sounds serious.

Helen: It is. The most serious.

Marcy: (*She sits down next to her mother on the couch.* DOUG *crosses to her immediately and reassuringly puts his arm around her.*) Mother, what is it?

Helen: I don't know how to tell you this. (*A deep breath.*) There's been an accident. Leonard is . . .

Marcy: Is he hurt?

Helen: Worse. I'm afraid it's anchors aweigh.

Marcy: (*Starting to cry.*) Oh, no. It can't be true.

Helen: It is. Leonard is no longer with us.

Marcy: How did it happen?

Helen: Leonard was in his official navy car coming over here. I'm sure he must have been terribly distraught. He probably had tears in his eyes. And you—above all—know how unaccustomed he was to driving on land. He was speeding to save his future happiness and couldn't negotiate the turn. There was a crash. His last words were: "Tell Marcy and her mother that I love them." Considerate to the end.

Marcy: That was the kind of guy Leonard was.

Doug: He sounds like he was one hell of a man. I'm just sorry it all had to end this way.

Helen: Doug, it's too bad you never knew Leonard. Whenever you needed him, he was there.

Marcy: It's just not fair.

Helen: He was on his way to becoming the youngest Secretary of the Navy.

Marcy: But now his career has ended. Cut short in thirty-one flavors. It's so sad.

Helen: But, Marcy, your life must go on. You and Doug must get married. Leonard would have wanted it that way. No one wants you to forget Leonard, but you and Doug have a life . . .

Doug: (*Interrupting; to* HELEN.) Excuse me. (*To* MARCY.) I have a question. Did you say "Cut-short in thirty-one flavors"?

Marcy: Yes. That's where Mother said poor Leonard crashed.

Doug: But that's not what Mother said.

Helen: I didn't?

Doug: That's what you told me. You didn't say anything to Marcy about thirty-one flavors.

Marcy: I just assumed . . .

Helen: I must have left that part out.

Doug: Wait a minute. I hate to nitpick at a time like this, but it doesn't seem sensible that you could know where Leonard crashed if no one told you. How could you know?

Marcy: (*Weakly.*) E.S.P.?

Doug: (*He now paces in the manner of a detective putting the clues together.*) No. Things are suddenly becoming clear. Of course. How could I have been so stupid?!

Marcy: (*Angrily to* HELEN.) I told you it wouldn't work!

Doug: You two have been deceiving me! But I'm too sharp for you. Marcy just made that call from the Gallaghers, right?

Marcy: (*Sheepishly.*) Right.

Doug: And I know why. Because there was no accident, right?

Marcy: Right.

Doug: Because Leonard isn't dead. That's it, isn't it? Am I right?

Marcy: Well . . .

Helen: (*Quickly.*) Right. You're too sharp for us.

Doug: But why?

Helen: Why what?

Doug: Why would you tell me Leonard is dead if he isn't?

Marcy: (*To* HELEN *sotto voce.*) Why?

Doug: I know why!!!

Marcy: You do?

Doug: (*To* MARCY.) Because you were afraid that if Leonard came here, we would fight. And you knew what could happen. You were trying to protect me. (*A new idea.*) Or you were trying to protect Leonard . . . (DOUG *studies his own frail frame.*) You were trying to protect me. Marcy, you're wonderful.

Helen: (*To* DOUG.) And you're too sharp for us.

Doug: Thank you for trying.

(DOUG *and* MARCY *kiss. FREEZE. "BOING."* HELEN *turns to the audience.)*

Helen: Close. Very close. When this is all over, I'm going to go away for a while or be put away for a while. (*Then to* DOUG.) We're sorry. (*The apology marks the END OF FREEZE. "BOING."*)

Doug: (*To* MARCY.) You ought to know better. You never should have told me Leonard is dead. Whatever the consequences of his coming over, this sort of trickery is no way to start a marriage.

Marcy: How true.

Helen: You're absolutely right, but it's not Marcy's fault. It was my idea to say Leonard was dead. I should have known you'd see through it. Blame me.

Doug: I'm not blaming anybody, but sometimes in your desire to see everybody happy, you overdo it and get things all mixed up. We're just lucky that your abduction plan worked.

Helen: At least now everything is open and above-board.

Marcy: Excuse me. I have a question. (*To* DOUG.) Did you just say, "Her" abduction plan?

Doug: Yes.

Helen: (*Quickly to* DOUG.) Loose lips sink ships.

Marcy: You mean to say that tying my mother up and dragging me off was my mother's idea?

Doug: Yes, but I bought the panty hose.

Marcy: You mean it wasn't your plan to be a hero and carry me away?

Doug: You know me, Marcy. I'm not exactly the Tarzan type.

Marcy: You're not even Cheetah! Here I thought you were finally taking things into your own hands and all you were doing was following orders.

Doug: I'm sorry I can't be a gladiator or a conquistador or an admiral. I'm only an almanac researcher, and if that's not enough, too bad. If you can't take me the way I am, let's call the whole thing off.

Marcy: That's fine with me. And to tell the truth, I'm glad it's over.

Doug: I'm gladder.

Marcy: If I can't have an honest relationship with someone who cares enough to do what's in his heart and not what's in my mother's head, then I don't want any relationship at all.

(During the ensuing argument, HELEN *senses where it will end and tries to be as inconspicuous as possible.)*

Doug: You're really the one to talk about honest relationships. All this time you've wanted me to be something I'm not. If anything's not honest, that's not honest.

Marcy: Now look who's talking about honest! You certainly weren't honest with that phoney abduction plot.

Doug: That was a lot more honest than saying Leonard is dead. That's the least honest.

Marcy: If you think that's not honest, just listen to this . . . (HELEN *looks to the audience with a look of "It's all over now."*) Leonard doesn't exist!

Doug: Honest?

Marcy: Honest.

Doug: (*Dumbfounded.*) Leonard doesn't exist?

Marcy: Never has.

Doug: Wait a minute. You mean that. . .

Marcy: Yes. But only because . . .

Doug: But surely, that's no reason . . .

Marcy: Did you leave me any choice?

Doug: Certainly not that.

Marcy: No. I wouldn't have if you . . .

Doug: I can't, but you—you're the one who had to go and . . .

Marcy: Does it make a difference now that . . .

Doug: Not that it matters.

Marcy: Right.

Doug: Right is right, but I . . .

Marcy: No, he was . . .

Doug: No, you . . .

Marcy: Me?

Doug: You.

Marcy: Me. But, she . . .

Doug: She?

Marcy: She.

Marcy and Doug: (*Now agreeing and slowly turning to* HELEN.) She!!!

Helen: (*Meekly.*) Me?

Marcy and Doug: You!

Helen: Listen, kids, you probably think that I have been less than honest when I sort of got you to go along with some cute little ideas I had to bring you two youngsters closer together. Now, I know it may appear that I've overdone it a hair. To tell the truth, maybe I have. But you must admit my motives were good and concerned only with your future happiness. Is that any reason for you to be upset with me? (MARCY *and* DOUG *shake their heads in unison, "Yes."*) Will you forgive me? (MARCY *and* DOUG *shake their heads in unison, "No."*) That's what I thought . . . (HELEN, *throughout the remainder of this speech, collects her coat, looks through her purse to see if she has her key, and backs out of the room.*) I have an idea. It's such a pretty night. I think I'll go for a nice long walk. That will give each of us a chance to reflect upon the events of this evening. And perhaps give us a new perspective and let us set aside these temporary emotional responses for a clearer approach. Who knows? With a little luck, I might even be mugged.

(She has backed out of the door. DOUG *turns to* MARCY.)

Doug: Well, what do you think?

Marcy: I don't know. What do you think?

Doug: I think I love you.

Marcy: I think I love you, too. (*They kiss, but as they individually begin to think about the intrigue that* HELEN *put them through, they begin to laugh.*) It's amazing how deceptive my mother actually is.

Doug: She went through that whole complicated scheme—taking into account all those possibilities, just so you and I would get married tomorrow.

Marcy: And you know what bothers me?

Doug: What?

Marcy: It worked.

Doug: It sure did, and I'm glad.

Marcy: I'm gladder.

Doug: But from now on, let's make a pact. No matter how good your mother's intentions are, it's up to us when and how we do things.

Marcy: When and how we do what things?

Doug: A lot of things. (*They are interrupted by the doorbell.*) Your mother doesn't believe in surrendering.

Marcy: (*She gets up to answer the door.*) Remind me later. (*She opens the door.*) Yes?

(An attractive man in his late twenties steps into the room. He wears the navy coat and braided hat of a full admiral. It is confusing but obvious that he is LEONARD T. APPLEBRIGHT. DOUG *sees him and quickly crosses to the door.)*

Doug: Who are you?

Leonard: (*Militarily.*) Who are you, Sir?!

Doug: (*Taken aback.*) Who are you, Sir?

Leonard: (*Saluting.*) Applebright, Leonard T. Rear Admiral, United States Navy.

CURTAIN

ACTIVITIES

1. Compare this scene to the scene from *The Rivals* to find similarities in characters and dramatic action. Note the variation in the use of the aside in this scene. Experiment with portraying Helen as a Mrs. Malaprop.

2. As you run through this scene, use the convention of the dramatic freeze throughout and have each character speak his or her thoughts and feelings while the other characters are frozen.

WORKSHOP

1. To develop an understanding of the characters and to make them more than stereotypes, improvise a scene in which Mrs. Malaprop, (black-ey'd) Susan, Lady Bracknell, and Helen discuss their problems. Include in the scene a discussion of how each character sees the others. Perhaps you can make use of the format of *Come and Go* (Section A, Chapter 1).

2. Examine *Barefoot in the Park* (Section A, Chapter 1) and *Count Dracula* (Section A, Chapter 4) as examples of plays which developed out of Restoration Theatre and melodrama. What qualities in these two plays are similar to and what qualities are different from those in the scripts in this chapter?

3. Experiment with doing the "Archie Bunker" script in Chapter 17 in the style of *The Rivals* or *The Importance of Being Earnest*. What qualities do Edith Bunker, Mrs. Malaprop, and Lady Bracknell have in common?

20: Real and Unreal People

THE PROGRAM

With a few exceptions, theatre in the nineteenth century made the worst features of Restoration Theatre the mainstay of popular entertainment. People went to see undistinguished melodramas, light comedies, burlesques, and musical dramas. Most of the presentations were based on spectacle, sentimentalism, and romanticism. Music hall variety shows were very popular, and the best musical theatre of the period was that of Gilbert and Sullivan.

The first playwright to attack effectively the sentimentality of the nineteenth century was a Norwegian—Henrik Ibsen (1828-1906). Because he sought to write realistic drama, Ibsen discarded soliloquies, asides to the audience, and any other device which detracted from the illusion of reality. Ibsen wanted drama to be a source of insight for an audience; a play should generate discussion because of the ideas it conveys. Ibsen's usual themes were the main character's struggle for integrity, and the attempt to reconcile the duty one has to oneself with the duty one has to others. Ibsen believed that any character has a psychological makeup which is affected by heredity and environment. Based on the belief that dramatic action has to be motivated by human behavior, Ibsen demonstrated that the action of a play unfolds in a logical way, the action of one scene affecting the action of another. Ibsen was regarded as a radical thinker in his time, and his plays created great controversy. His work was a model for realistic playwrights who followed. In fact, Arthur Miller, a well-known modern playwright, adapted *An Enemy of the People*, a selection in this chapter, to a twentieth century setting.

By the beginning of the twentieth century, stage design had also changed as stage settings attempted to create the illusion of reality. Improved lighting, brought about by the advent of gas lamps (and later electricity), enhanced this new realism.

At the same time, the art of acting was undergoing radical change, mostly through the work and writings of Constantin Stanislavsky (1863-1938), a Russian actor and director. He believed that actors must study the play for a long time before production and that they must pay careful attention to each detail in the text. In order to communicate without artificiality, actors were urged to become skilled observers of reality and to find an inner motivation for every action and speech.

Stanislavsky developed the "magic if" question discussed in Section A, Chapter 3, and insisted that actors must understand a script in order to work effectively. Each character in a play has an objective, and in seeking to accomplish that objective, that character affects the other characters and events in the play. Actors must concentrate totally on the action of the play as it unfolds during performance so that they can create the illusion that the events are happening for the first time. Stanislavski's theories changed acting and allowed for the convincing performance of realistic plays.

Realism was a reaction to the romanticism of the nineteenth century and, in its turn, realism engendered another reaction. Anti-illusionist drama, which flourished during the 1920's and 1930's, challenged and negated realistic dramatic values. It encouraged illogical and non-sequential action. Characters did things without apparent motivating psychology and said things without using rationally comprehensible language. Anti-illusionism rejected the concept that theatre must mirror the surface reality of life.

One of the most influential exponents of these theories was Antonin Artaud (1896-1948), a French poet and playwright. He was influenced by North American Indian rituals and Eastern dance theatre and claimed that words are not effective symbols of the objects or ideas they are supposed to represent. Consequently, other forms of symbolic expression have to be found. Artaud felt that an audience recognizes these symbols with a part of the consciousness that is beyond the intellectual. If the audience is brought to focus on ritualistic enactment and mythology, it experiences trance and inspiration. Once again, the cycle of theatre recurs.

Some of Artaud's theories are taken up in what has been called "theatre of the absurd," of which *The Bald Soprano* (Eugene Ionesco, b. 1912) is an example. Absurdist drama seeks neither to please an audience nor to instruct it; rather, reality is presented as an image in a shattered mirror—fragments of meaning. As you will see in *The Bald Soprano*, absurdism offers an audience suggestions and images that puzzle and tease but which elude logical interpretation. Such is the absurdist's view of the human condition. Absurdist drama is often both comic and tragic; these elements, absurdists say, are two aspects of the same situation.

Another theatrical form which developed as a reaction to realism is *expressionism*. It flourished in Europe during and after the First World War and was based on the belief that to find truth, drama must investigate people's spiritual qualities rather than their external appearances. In order to do so, new artistic means were needed to express the subjective nature of expressionist drama. Unusual settings were created with distorted lines, exaggerated shapes, and abnormal coloring. Actors used mechanical movement and unusual speech patterns to help the audience get beyond surface appearances.

Expressionism had a political bias; it sought to transform those social and political conditions which were regarded as distorting people's spirits and preventing people from attaining happiness.

Bertolt Brecht (1891-1956), a German director and playwright, was greatly influenced by expressionism and used many of its concepts in the development of his "Epic Theatre." By "epic," he meant that his theatre covered a broad sweep of history and characters and combined the use of storytelling techniques with conventional dramatic techniques. Brecht sought to destroy the illusion of reality and created the concept of "alienation" to achieve this aim. Because he wanted the audience to watch his plays in an active rather than a passive manner, he made the stage events sufficiently strange that the spectator would question them. To emphasize the way in which "surface" is an illusion, Brecht revealed the mechanics of the theatre; lighting bars were visible, musicians were seen; and scenery changes were done in full view of the audience. Songs and narrative passages occurred between scenes, and masks, signs, and slogans were often used. Actors addressed the audience directly and the scenery was non-representational. Brecht thought that in understanding the mechanics of the theatrical experience, the audience would also be able to understand the mechanics of social and economic conditions outside the theatre and would become equipped to change those conditions.

Many qualities of Epic Theatre are evident in the excerpt in this chapter from *The Good Person of Szechwan.* In this play the world is so arranged that the good person cannot win. Brecht seems to be saying that goodness and success are mutually exclusive and that this conflict cannot be resolved. At the end of the play, the audience is invited to consider the dilemma.

The last selection in this chapter combines both realism and anti-realism. *Six Characters in Search of an Author* (Luigi Pirandello, 1867-1936), presents actions and characters which are logical in development, but the situation is absurd; a play rehearsal is interrupted by characters who are seeking a script in which they can play parts. This play takes the dramatic convention of the play-within-a-play to absurdist extremes, and in so doing it explores a very real human issue; for many of us, fate has not yet written the script in which we might play a part.

The debate between proponents of realism and adherents of anti-illusionist drama continues to this day. As you read scripts you will see that, as playwrights continue to search for meaning in events and people, plays range from the realistic to the absurd, the poetic to the mundane. You are part of that search as you examine and experiment with scripts and try to discover what each script can tell us about the world, other people, and ourselves. The father in *Six Characters in Search of an Author* speaks for every person when he says: "The drama is in us."

FROM

A LIFE IN THE THEATRE

by David Mamet

SCENE 2

(ROBERT *and* JOHN *in the Wardrobe area.)*

Robert: Your hat.

(Pause.)

John: Thank you.

Robert: Like an oven in here.

John: Yes.

Robert: Got no space to *breathe.*

John: No? (*Pause.*) Am I in your way?

Robert: No. Not at all. (*Pause.*) Quite the contrary.

John: (*handing* ROBERT *his hat*) Your hat.

Robert: I thank you. (*Pause.*) (*Soliloquizing.*) My hat, my hat, my hat. (*Pause.*) Eh?

John: *Mmm.*

FROM

AN ENEMY OF THE PEOPLE

by Henrik Ibsen
(adapted by Arthur Miller)

CHARACTERS

Dr. Thomas Stockmann
Mrs. Catherine Stockmann, his wife
Petra, his daughter
Peter Stockmann, his brother and Mayor of the town
Dr. Stockmann's two sons (one speaking and one non-speaking part)

PLAYBILL

Dr. Stockmann, a medical doctor and scientist, discovered that the water in his town was useful for health baths, and as a result the town became a popular tourist centre. (Health baths, or spas, were very popular at the end of the nineteenth century because it was believed that the minerals and chemicals in the water could cure or alleviate illness.) At the beginning of this play, Dr. Stockmann has discovered that the water is contaminated and can, in fact, *cause* illness. He is determined to release this information and has invited his brother, Peter, who is mayor of the town and director of the corporation which runs the baths, to discuss the matter. *An Enemy of the People* was written in 1882 and still has relevance for us today.

Dr. Stockmann: (*goes to dining-room and looks in*) Catherine! Oh, you're home already, Petra!

Petra: (*coming in*) I just got back from school.

Mrs. Stockmann: (*entering*) Hasn't he been here yet?

Dr. Stockmann: Peter? No, but I just had a long chat with Hovstad. He's really fascinated with my discovery, and you know, it has more implications than I thought at first. Do you know what I have backing me up?

Mrs. Stockmann: What in heaven's name have you got backing you up?

Dr. Stockmann: The solid majority.

Mrs. Stockmann: Is that good?

Dr. Stockmann: Good? It's wonderful. You can't imagine the feeling, Catherine, to know that your own town feels like a brother to you. I have never felt so at home in this town since I was a boy. (*A noise is heard.*)

Mrs. Stockmann: That must be the front door.

Dr. Stockmann: Oh, it's Peter then. Come in.

Peter Stockmann: (*entering from the hall*) Good morning!

Dr. Stockmann: It's nice to see you, Peter.

Mrs. Stockmann: Good morning. How are you today?

Peter Stockmann: Well, so so. (*To* DR. STOCKMANN.) I received your thesis about the condition of the springs yesterday.

Dr. Stockmann: I got your note. Did you read it?

Peter Stockmann: I read it.

Dr. Stockmann: Well, what do you have to say?

(PETER STOCKMANN *clears his throat and glances at the women.)*

Mrs. Stockmann: Come on, Petra. (*She and* PETRA *leave the room at the left.*)

Peter Stockmann: (*after a moment*) Thomas, was it really necessary to go into this investigation behind my back?

Dr. Stockmann: Yes. Until I was convinced myself, there was no point in—

Peter Stockmann: And now you are convinced?

Dr. Stockmann: Well, certainly. Aren't you too, Peter? (*Pause.*) The University chemists corroborated . . .

Peter Stockmann: You intend to present this document to the Board of Directors, officially, as the medical officer of the springs?

Dr. Stockmann: Of course, something's got to be done, and quick.

Peter Stockmann: You always use such strong expressions, Thomas. Among other things, in your report you say that we *guarantee* our guests and visitors a permanent case of poisoning.

Dr. Stockmann: But, Peter, how can you describe it any other way? Imagine! Poisoned internally and externally!

Peter Stockmann: So you merrily conclude that we must build a waste-disposal plant—and reconstruct a brand-new water system from the bottom up!

Dr. Stockmann: Well, do you know some other way out? I don't.

Peter Stockmann: I took a little walk over to the city engineer this morning and in the course of conversation I sort of jokingly mentioned these changes—as something we might consider for the future, you know.

Dr. Stockmann: The future won't be soon enough, Peter.

Peter Stockmann: The engineer just smiled at my extravagance and gave me a few facts. I don't suppose you have taken the trouble to consider what your proposed changes would cost?

Dr. Stockmann: No, I never thought of that.

Peter Stockmann: Naturally. Your little project would come to at least three hundred thousand crowns.

Dr. Stockmann: (*astonished*) That expensive!

Peter Stockmann: Oh, don't look so upset—it's only money. The worst thing is that it would take some two years.

Dr. Stockmann: Two years?

Peter Stockmann: At the least. And what do you propose we do about the springs in the meantime? Shut them up, no doubt! Because we would have to, you know. As soon as the rumor gets around that the water is dangerous, we won't have a visitor left. So that's the picture, Thomas. You have it in your power literally to ruin your own town.

Dr. Stockmann: Now look, Peter! I don't want to ruin anything.

Peter Stockmann: Kirsten Springs are the blood supply of this town, Thomas—the only future we've got here. Now will you stop and think?

Dr. Stockmann: Good God! Well, what do you think we ought to do?

Peter Stockmann: Your report has not convinced me that the conditions are as dangerous as you try to make them.

Dr. Stockmann: Now listen; they are even worse than the report makes them out to be. Remember, summer is coming, and the warm weather!

Peter Stockmann: I think you're exaggerating. A capable physician ought to know what precautions to take.

Dr. Stockmann: And what then?

Peter Stockmann: The existing water supply for the springs is a fact, Thomas, and has got to be treated as a fact. If you are reasonable and act with discretion, the directors of the Institute will be inclined to take under consideration any means to make possible improvements, reasonably and without financial sacrifices.

Dr. Stockmann: Peter, do you imagine that I would ever agree to such trickery?

Peter Stockmann: Trickery?

Dr. Stockmann: Yes, a trick, a fraud, a lie! A treachery, a downright crime, against the public and against the whole community!

Peter Stockmann: I said before that I am not convinced that there is any actual danger.

Dr. Stockmann: Oh, you aren't? Anything else is impossible! My report is an absolute fact. The only trouble is that you and your administration were the ones who insisted that the water supply be built where it is, and now you're afraid to admit the blunder you committed. Damn it! Don't you think I can see through it all?

Peter Stockmann: All right, let's suppose that's true. Maybe I do care a little about my reputation. I still say I do it for the good of the town—without moral authority there can be no government. And that is why, Thomas, it is my duty to prevent your report from reaching the Board. Some time later I will bring up the matter for discussion. In the meantime, not a single word is to reach the public.

Dr. Stockmann: Oh, my dear Peter, do you imagine you can prevent that!

Peter Stockmann: It will be prevented.

Dr. Stockmann: It can't be. There are too many people who already know about it.

Peter Stockmann: (*angered*) Who? It can't possibly be those people from the *Daily Messenger* who—

Dr. Stockmann: Exactly. The liberal, free, and independent press will stand up and do its duty!

Peter Stockmann: You are an unbelievably irresponsible man, Thomas! Can't you imagine what consequences that is going to have for you?

Dr. Stockmann: For me?

Peter Stockmann: Yes, for you and your family.

Dr. Stockmann: What the hell are you saying now?

Peter Stockmann: I believe I have the right to think of myself as a helpful brother, Thomas.

Dr. Stockmann: You have been, and I thank you deeply for it.

Peter Stockmann: Don't mention it. I often couldn't help myself. I had hoped that by improving your finances I would be able to keep you from running completely hog wild.

Dr. Stockmann: You mean it was only for your own sake?

Peter Stockmann: Partly, yes. What do you imagine people think of an official whose closest relatives get themselves into trouble time and time again?

Dr. Stockmann: And that's what I have done?

Peter Stockmann: You do it without knowing it. You're like a man with an automatic brain—as soon as an idea breaks into your head, no matter how idiotic it may be, you get up like a sleep-walker and start writing a pamphlet about it.

Dr. Stockmann: Peter, don't you think it's a citizen's duty to share a new idea with the public?

Peter Stockmann: The public doesn't need new ideas—the public is much better off with old ideas.

Dr. Stockmann: You're not even embarrassed to say that?

Peter Stockmann: Now look, I'm going to lay this out once and for all. You're always barking about authority. If a man gives you an order he's persecuting you. Nothing is important enough to respect once you decide to revolt against your superiors. All right then, I give up. I'm not going to try to change you any more. I told you the stakes you are playing for here, and now I am going to give you an order. And I warn you, you had better obey it if you value your career.

Dr. Stockmann: What kind of an order?

Peter Stockmann: You are going to deny these rumors officially.

Dr. Stockmann: How?

Peter Stockmann: You simply say that you went into the examination of the water more thoroughly and you find that you overestimated the danger.

Dr. Stockmann: I see.

Peter Stockmann: And that you have complete confidence that whatever improvements are needed, the management will certainly take care of them.

Dr. Stockmann: (*after a pause*) My convictions come from the condition of the water. My convictions will change when the water changes, and for no other reason.

Peter Stockmann: What are you talking about convictions? You're an official, you keep your convictions to yourself!

Dr. Stockmann: To myself?

Peter Stockmann: As an official, I said. God knows, as a private person that's something else, but as a subordinate employee of the Institute, you have no right to express any convictions or personal opinions about anything connected with policy.

Dr. Stockmann: Now you listen to me. I am a doctor and a scientist—

Peter Stockmann: This has nothing to do with science!

Dr. Stockmann: Peter, I have the right to express my opinion on anything in the world!

Peter Stockmann: Not about the Institute—that I forbid.

Dr. Stockmann: You forbid!

Peter Stockmann: I forbid you as your superior, and when I give orders you obey.

Dr. Stockmann: Peter, if you weren't my brother—

Petra: (*throwing the door at the left open*) Father! You aren't going to stand for this! (*She enters.*)

Mrs. Stockmann: (*coming in after her*) Petra, Petra!

Peter Stockmann: What have you two been doing, eavesdropping?

Mrs. Stockmann: You were talking so loud we couldn't help . . .

Petra: Yes, I was eavesdropping!

Peter Stockmann: That makes me very happy.

Dr. Stockmann: (*approaching his brother*) You said something to me about forbidding—

Peter Stockmann: You forced me to.

Dr. Stockmann: So you want me to spit in my own face officially—is that it?

Peter Stockmann: Why must you always be so colorful?

Dr. Stockmann: And if I don't obey?

Peter Stockmann: Then we will publish our own statement, to calm the public.

Dr. Stockmann: Good enough! And I will write against you. I will stick to what I said, and I will prove that I am right and that you are wrong, and what will you do then?

Peter Stockmann: Then I simply won't be able to prevent your dismissal.

Dr. Stockmann: What!

Petra: Father!

Peter Stockmann: Dismissed from the Institute is what I said. If you want to make war on Kirsten Springs, you have no right to be on the Board of Directors.

Dr. Stockmann: (*after a pause*) You'd dare to do that?

Peter Stockmann: Oh, no, you're the daring man.

Petra: Uncle, this is a rotten way to treat a man like Father!

Mrs. Stockmann: Will you be quiet, Petra!

Peter Stockmann: So young and you've got opinions already—but that's natural. (*To* MRS. STOCKMANN.) Catherine dear, you're probably the only sane person in this house. Knock some sense into his head, will you? Make him realize what he's driving his whole family into.

Dr. Stockmann: My family concerns nobody but myself.

Peter Stockmann: His family and his own town.

Dr. Stockmann: I'm going to show you who loves this town. The people are going to get the full stink of this corruption, Peter, and then we will see who loves his town!

Peter Stockmann: You love your town when you blindly, spitefully, stubbornly go ahead trying to cut off our most important industry?

Dr. Stockmann: That source is poisoned, man. We are getting fat by peddling filth and corruption to innocent people!

Peter Stockmann: I think this has gone beyond opinions and convictions, Thomas. A man who can throw that kind of insinuation around is nothing but a traitor to society!

Dr. Stockmann: (*starting toward his brother in a fury*) How dare you to—

Mrs. Stockmann: (*stepping between them*) Tom!

Petra: (*grabbing her father's arm*) Be careful, Father!

Peter Stockmann: (*with dignity*) I won't expose myself to violence. You have been warned. Consider what you owe yourself and your family! Good day! (*He exits.*)

Dr. Stockmann: (*walking up and down*) He's insulted. *He's* insulted!

Mrs. Stockmann: It's shameful, Tom.

Petra: Oh, I would love to give him a piece of my mind!

Dr. Stockmann: It was my own fault! I should have shown my teeth right from the beginning. He called me a traitor to society. Me! Damn it all, that's not going to stick!

Mrs. Stockmann: Please, think! He's got all the power on his side.

Dr. Stockmann: Yes, but I have the truth on mine.

Mrs. Stockmann: Without power, what good is the truth?

Petra: Mother, how can you say such a thing?

Dr. Stockmann: That's ridiculous, Catherine. I have the liberal press with me, and the majority. If that isn't power, what is?

Mrs. Stockmann: But, for heaven's sake, Tom, you aren't going to—

Dr. Stockmann: What am I not going to do?

Mrs. Stockmann: You aren't going to fight it out in public with your brother!

Dr. Stockmann: What else do you want me to do?

Mrs. Stockmann: But it won't do you any earthly good. If they won't do it, they won't. All you'll get out of it is a notice that you're fired.

Dr. Stockmann: I am going to do my duty, Catherine. Me, the man he calls a traitor to society!

Mrs. Stockmann: And how about your duty toward your family—the people you're supposed to provide for?

Petra: Don't always think of us first, Mother.

Mrs. Stockmann: (*to* PETRA) You can talk! If worst comes to worst, you can manage for yourself. But what about the boys, Tom, and you and me?

Dr. Stockmann: What about you? You want me to be the miserable animal who'd crawl up the boots of that damn gang? Will you be happy if I can't face myself for the rest of my life?

Mrs. Stockmann: Tom, Tom, there's so much injustice in the world! You've simply got to learn to live with it. If you go on this way, God help us, we'll have no money again. Is it so long since the north that you've forgotten what it was to live as we lived? Haven't we had enough of that for one lifetime? (*The boys enter.*) What will happen to them? We've got nothing if you're fired!

Dr. Stockmann: Stop it! (*He looks at the boys.*) Well, boys, did you learn anything in school today?

Morten: (*looking at them, puzzled*) We learned what an insect is.

Dr. Stockmann: You don't say!

Morten: What happened here? Why is everybody—

Dr. Stockmann: Nothing, nothing. You know what I'm going to do, boys? From now on I'm going to teach you what a man is. (*He looks at* MRS. STOCKMANN. *She cries as*)

THE CURTAIN FALLS

ACTIVITIES

1. Examine closely the positions of Dr. Stockmann and Peter Stockmann and determine the merits of each stance. Take turns playing both parts, and make sure that in each part you act with complete conviction that you are right. (This same situation arises in *Antigone*, Section A, Chapter 3.)

2. Look at the dilemma Mrs. Stockmann is in at the end of the scene. How would you express the thoughts and feelings she has about the events in the scene? Improvise a scene in which she discusses her problem with a good friend.

3. With your group, invent some possible solutions to the problem this play poses. Improvise scenes in which each solution is proposed to the people of the town. Those who play the townsfolk must remember that these people are worried about protecting their livelihoods and incomes.

4. Many of the scripts in this book are written in a realistic manner. Some examples are *The Elephant Man* in Chapter 1, *Whose Life is it Anyway?* in Chapter 3, and *The Shadow Box* in Chapter 4. Compare these scripts to *An Enemy of the People*.

FROM

THE BALD SOPRANO

by Eugene Ionesco

PLAYBILL

During an evening at home, Mr. and Mrs. Smith are visited by Mr. and Mrs. Martin. That is the extent of the plot. However, as you read the script, you will find that the playwright is making observations about people in contemporary society and about how people interact.

CHARACTERS

Mrs. Smith
Mr. Smith
Mrs. Martin
Mr. Martin

(MR. *and* MRS. SMITH *enter from the right.*)

Mrs. Smith: Good evening, dear friends! Please forgive us for having made you wait so long. We thought that we should extend you the courtesy to which you are entitled and as soon as we learned that you had been kind enough to give us the pleasure of coming to see us without prior notice we hurried to dress for the occasion.

Mr. Smith: (*furious*) We've had nothing to eat all day. And we've been waiting four whole hours for you. Why have you come so late?

(MR. *and* MRS. SMITH *sit facing their guests. The striking of the clock underlines the speeches, more or less strongly, according to the case. The* MARTINS, *particularly* MRS. MARTIN, *seem embarrassed and timid. For this reason the conversation begins with difficulty and the words are uttered, at the beginning, awkwardly. A long embarrassed silence at first, then other silences and hesitations follow.*)

Mr. Smith: Hm. (*Silence*)

Mrs. Smith: Hm, hm. (*Silence*)

Mrs. Martin: Hm, hm, hm. (*Silence*)

Mr. Martin: Hm, hm, hm, hm. (*Silence*)

Mrs. Martin: Oh, but definitely. (*Silence*)

Mr. Martin: We all have colds. (*Silence*)

Mr. Smith: Nevertheless, it's not chilly. (*Silence*)

Mrs. Smith: There's no draft. (*Silence*)

Mr. Martin: Oh no, fortunately. (*Silence*)

Mr. Smith: Oh dear, oh dear, oh dear. (*Silence*)

Mr. Martin: Don't you feel well? (*Silence*)

Mrs. Smith: No, he's wet his pants. (*Silence*)

Mrs. Martin: Oh, sir, at your age, you shouldn't. (*Silence*)

Mr. Smith: The heart is ageless. (*Silence*)

Mr. Martin: That's true. (*Silence*)

Mrs. Smith: So they say. (*Silence*)

Mrs. Martin: They also say the opposite. (*Silence*)

Mr. Smith: The truth lies somewhere between the two. (*Silence*)

Mr. Martin: That's true. (*Silence*)

Mrs. Smith: (*to the* MARTINS) Since you travel so much, you must have many interesting things to tell us.

Mr. Martin: (*to his wife*) My dear, tell us what you've seen today.

Mrs. Martin: It's scarcely worth the trouble, for no one would believe me.

Mr. Smith: We're not going to question your sincerity!

Mrs. Smith: You will offend us if you think that.

Mr. Martin: (*to his wife*) You will offend them, my dear, if you think that . . .

Mrs. Martin: (*graciously*) Oh well, today I witnessed something extraordinary. Something really incredible.

Mr. Martin: Tell us quickly, my dear.

Mr. Smith: Oh, this is going to be amusing.

Mrs. Smith: At last.

Mrs. Martin: Well, today, when I went shopping to buy some vegetables, which are getting to be dearer and dearer . . .

Mrs. Smith: Where is it all going to end!

Mr. Smith: You shouldn't interrupt, my dear, it's very rude.

Mrs. Martin: In the street, near a café, I saw a man, properly dressed, about fifty years old, or not even that, who . . .

Mr. Smith: Who, what?

Mrs. Smith: Who, what?

Mr. Smith: (*to his wife*) Don't interrupt, my dear, you're disgusting.

Mrs. Smith: My dear, it is you who interrupted first, you boor.

Mr. Smith: (*to his wife*) Hush. (*To* MRS. MARTIN) What was this man doing?

Mrs. Martin: Well, I'm sure you'll say that I'm making it up—he was down on one knee and he was bent over.

Mr. Martin, Mr. Smith, Mrs. Smith: Oh!

Mrs. Martin: Yes, bent over.

Mr. Smith: Not possible.

Mrs. Martin: Yes, bent over. I went near him to see what he was doing . .

Mr. Smith: And?

Mrs. Martin: He was tying his shoe lace which had come undone.

Mr. Martin, Mr. Smith, Mrs. Smith: Fantastic!

Mr. Smith: If someone else had told me this, I'd not believe it.

Mr. Martin: Why not? One sees things even more extraordinary every day, when one walks around. For instance, today in the Underground I myself saw a man, quietly sitting on a seat, reading his newspaper.

Mrs. Smith: What a character!

Mr. Smith: Perhaps it was the same man!

(The doorbell rings.)

Mr. Smith: Goodness, someone is ringing.

Mrs. Smith: There must be somebody there. I'll go and see. (*She goes to see, she opens the door and closes it, and comes back.*) Nobody. (*She sits down again.*)

Mr. Martin: I'm going to give you another example . . . (*Doorbell rings again.*)

Mr. Smith: Goodness, someone is ringing.

Mrs. Smith: There must be somebody there. I'll go and see. (*She goes to see, opens the door, and comes back.*) No one. (*She sits down again.*)

Mr. Martin: (*who has forgotten where he was*) Uh . . .

Mrs. Martin: You were saying that you were going to give us another example.

Mr. Martin: Oh, yes . . .

(Doorbell rings again.)

Mr. Smith: Goodness, someone is ringing.

Mrs. Smith: I'm not going to open the door again.

Mr. Smith: Yes, but there must be someone there!

Mrs. Smith: The first time there was no one. The second time, no one. Why do you think that there is someone there now?

Mr. Smith: Because someone has rung!

Mrs. Martin: That's no reason.

Mr. Martin: What? When one hears the doorbell ring, that means someone is at the door ringing to have the door opened.

Mrs. Martin: Not always. You've just seen otherwise!

Mr. Martin: In most cases, yes.

Mr. Smith: As for me, when I go to visit someone, I ring in order to be admitted. I think that everyone does the same thing and that each time there is a ring there must be someone there.

Mrs. Smith: That is true in theory. But in reality things happen differently. You have just seen otherwise.

Mrs. Martin: Your wife is right.

Mr. Martin: Oh! You women! You always stand up for each other.

Mrs. Smith: Well, I'll go and see. You can't say that I am obstinate, but you will see that there's no one there! (*She goes to look, opens the door and closes it.*) You see, there's no one there. (*She returns to her seat.*)

Mrs. Smith: Oh, these men who always think they're right and who're always wrong!

(The doorbell rings again.)

Mr. Smith: Goodness, someone is ringing. There must be someone there.

Mrs. Smith: (*in a fit of anger*) Don't send me to open the door again. You've seen that it was useless. Experience teaches us that when one hears the doorbell ring it is because there is never anyone there.

Mrs. Martin: Never.

Mr. Martin: That's not entirely accurate.

Mr. Smith: In fact it's false. When one hears the doorbell ring it is because there is someone there.

Mrs. Smith: He won't admit he's wrong.

Mrs. Martin: My husband is very obstinate, too.

Mr. Smith: There's someone there.

Mr. Martin: That's not impossible.

Mrs. Smith: (*to her husband*) No.

Mr. Smith: Yes.

Mrs. Smith: I tell you *no*. In any case you are not going to disturb me again for nothing. If you wish to know, go and look yourself!

Mr. Smith: I'll go.

*(*MRS. SMITH *shrugs her shoulders.* MRS. MARTIN *tosses her head.)*

Mr. Smith: (*opening the door*) Oh! how do you do. (*He glances at* MRS. SMITH *and the* MARTINS, *who are all surprise.*) It's the Fire Chief!

ACTIVITIES

1. Experiment with playing the characters in a variety of different ways to see how the interpretation of the play changes. Play them as absolutely realistic characters for whom everything which happens is logical, and play them as exaggerated, illogical people. You might also consider using *After Liverpool* (Section A, Chapter 2) for other possible character clues.

2. As was pointed out in The Program to this chapter, one of the key qualities of absurdism is its suggestiveness. Reality is fragments; meaning is what we make of these fragments. Play around with this scene, using as many variations of pace, inflection, and emotion as you can come up with.

3. Improvise a continuation of the scene after the entrance of the fire chief. Retain the same quality of dialogue.

FROM

THE GOOD PERSON OF SZECHWAN

by Bertolt Brecht

PLAYBILL

At the beginning of the play, three gods have come to earth to find a person who is truly good. Shen Teh, a young woman, gives them lodging, and they determine that she is a virtuous person and reward her with a bag of gold. Shen Teh uses the money to buy a tobacco shop, but she soon becomes the victim of people who seek to live off her riches. Since Shen Teh cannot refuse to help others less fortunate than she, she assumes the identity of an imaginary cousin, Shui Ta, a harsh, ruthless businessman who manages through cruel means to keep the business alive. Shen Teh's disappearance, however, raises questions among the townspeople, and at the end of the play Shui Ta is put on trial for the murder of Shen Teh. In this scene, the three gods, acting as judges, have just dismissed the witnesses from the courtroom. Think about the effect that the final speech might have on an audience.

CHARACTERS

Shen Teh, the "good person", is disguised as **Shui Ta**, her male cousin
The First God
The Second God
The Third God dressed as judges
Wang, the water seller
Witnesses

Shui Ta: Are they gone? All of them? I can't keep silent any longer. I have recognized you, Enlightened Ones!

The Second God: What have you done with our good person of Szechwan?

Shui Ta: Let me confess the awful truth, I am your good person! (*He removes his mask and tears off his outer garments.* SHEN TEH *stands before the judges*)

The Second God: Shen Teh!

Shen Teh: Yes, it is I. Shui Ta and Shen Teh, I am both of them.
Your order long ago
To be good and yet to live
Tore me like lightning into two halves. I
Don't know how it happened: I could not
Be good at once to others and myself.
To help myself and others was too hard for me.
Ah, your world is hard. Too much poverty, too much despair!
The hand that is held out to the wretched
Is soon wrenched off! He who helps the lost
Is himself lost! For who can
Long refuse to be wicked when starvation kills?
Where was I to take all that was needed? Only
From myself! But then I would die.
Good intentions
Crushed me to the ground. But when I did wrong
I strode in power and ate good meat!
There must be something wrong with your world. Why
Is wickedness so richly rewarded and why does such hard punishment
Await the good? Oh, there was in me
Such eagerness to indulge myself. And I had also
A secret knowledge, for my foster-mother
Washed me in gutter water! That gave me
A sharp eye. Yet pity
Brought me such pain that ferocious rage overcame me
At the sight of misery. Then
I felt a change come over me.
My teeth turned to fangs. A kind word
Was bitter as ashes in my mouth. And yet
I wished to be an angel to the slums. To give
Was a passion with me. A happy face
And I walked on clouds.
Condemn me: all my crimes
Were committed to help my neighbors
To love my beloved and
Save my little son from want.
O gods, for your great projects
I, poor mortal, was too small.

The First God: (*with every indication of horror*) Speak no more, unhappy creature! We were so glad to have found you again, and now what are we to think?

Shen Teh: I'm only trying to tell you that I am the wicked man who committed the crimes they have all been telling you about!

The First God: The good person of whom all had only good to say!

Shen Teh: No, the bad person too!

The First God: A misunderstanding! A few unfortunate incidents! A few heartless neighbors! A little too much zeal!

The Second God: But how is she to go on living?

The First God: She will manage. She is strong and strapping, she can endure a good deal.

The Second God: But didn't you hear what she said?

The First God: (*violently*) Muddled, extremely muddled! What she says is inconceivable, absolutely inconceivable. Are we to admit that our commandments are fatal? Are we to give up our commandments? (*Stubbornly*) Never! Is the world to be changed? How? By whom? No, everything is in order. (*He strikes the desk quickly with his gavel*) And now . . . (*At a sign from him, music rings out; a rosy glow is seen*)
Let us go home. This little world
Has moved us deeply. Its joys and sorrows
Have greatly cheered and grieved us. Yet
Up there beyond the stars we shall be glad
To think of you, Shen Teh, the good person
Who here below bears witness to our spirit
And holds the little lamp in the cold darkness.
Farewell! Good luck!

(At a sign from him the ceiling opens. A pink cloud descends. On it the three gods rise very slowly)

Shen Teh: Oh no, Enlightened Ones! Don't go away! Don't leave me! How am I going to face those two good old people who have lost their shop, and the water seller with his stiff hand? How am I going to defend myself against the barber whom I don't love and Sun whom I do love? And I'm with child, soon my little son will be here, wanting to eat. I can't stay here! (*She looks frantically toward the door through which her tormentors will enter*)

The First God: You'll manage. Just be good and everything will turn out all right!

(Enter the WITNESSES. *They look with amazement at the* JUDGES *hovering on their pink cloud)*

Wang: Show your veneration! The gods have appeared among us! Three of the highest gods have come to Szechwan, looking for a good person. They found one, but . . .

The First God: No buts! Here she is!

All: Shen Teh!

The First God: She wasn't dead, she was only hidden. She will remain in your midst, a good person!

Shen Teh: But I need my cousin!

The First God: Not too often!

Shen Teh: At least once a week!

The First God: Once a month: that will do!

Shen Teh: Oh, don't go away, Enlightened Ones! I haven't told you everything. I need you terribly!

The Gods:

All too long on earth we've lingered
Swiftly drops the fleeting day:
Shrewdly studied, closely fingered
Precious treasures melt away.
Now the golden flood is dying
While your shadows onward press
Time that we too started flying
Homeward to our nothingness.

Shen Teh: Help!

The Gods:

The search is over, therefore we
Must really hurry on
So glory be and glory be
To good Shen Teh of Szechwan!

(As SHEN TEH *desperately holds out her arms toward them, they vanish, smiling and waving.)*

EPILOGUE

(One of the players steps before the curtain and, addressing the audience apologetically, speaks the epilogue.)

Ladies and gentlemen, don't be annoyed
We know this ending leaves you in the void.
A golden legend we set out to tell
But then somehow the ending went to hell.
We're disappointed too, struck with dismay
All questions open though we've closed our play.
Especially since we live by your enjoyment.
Disgruntled spectators mean unemployment.
It's sad but true, the heavens defend us
We're ruined unless you recommend us.
Fear may well have blocked *our* inspiration
But what's *your* answer to the situation?
For love nor money we could find no out:
Refashion man? Or change the world about?
Or turn to different gods? Or don't we need
Any? Our bewilderment is great indeed.
There's only one solution comes to mind:
That you yourselves should ponder till you find
The ways and means and measures tending
To help good people to a happy ending.
Ladies and gentlemen, in you we trust:
The ending must be happy, must, must, must!

ACTIVITIES

1. Examine the moral dilemma this play raises. How would you express this dilemma? Invent a series of improvisations based on situations in which a person would encounter this dilemma in contemporary life.

2. Have a chorus speak the epilogue. Others in the class can be members of the audience and advise the chorus on how the play can end happily. Go on to improvise these happy endings. How satisfactory are they? Compare this epilogue to the 1st Knight's last speech in *Murder in the Cathedral.* What similarities can you find?

3. Imagine that the gods are visitors from a more advanced civilization, and that they demand that your group produce one good person from contemporary society or they will destroy the earth. Who will your group advance as this good person and what qualities and deeds will you point to as examples of goodness? Improvise a scene in which this confrontation occurs.

FROM

SIX CHARACTERS IN SEARCH OF AN AUTHOR

by Luigi Pirandello

PLAYBILL

This play, written in 1921, combines both absurdism and realism. The six Characters, who are presented as real people who conduct themselves in a realistic manner, enter a theatre and interrupt a play rehearsal. As you read, remember that there are people other than the Characters in the scene, and that these people must be clearly distinguishable from the Characters.

CHARACTERS

Commissionaire, the door-keeper
Director
Actors, (nine or ten, including Leading Man, Leading Lady, Juvenile Lead)
Six Characters:
Father, about 50
Mother
Stepdaughter, about 18
Son, about 22
Boy, about 14
Child, a sister, about 4
Stage-Manager

*(*COMMISSIONAIRE *enters followed by* SIX CHARACTERS*)*

Commissionaire: (*cap in hand*) Excuse me, sir.

Director: (*snapping at him rudely*) Now what's the matter?

Commissionaire: There are some people here, sir, asking for you.

(The DIRECTOR *and the* ACTORS *turn in astonishment and look out into the auditorium.)*

Director: (*furiously*) But I've got a rehearsal on at the moment! And you know quite well that no one's allowed in here while a rehearsal's going on. (*Then addressing the* CHARACTERS.) Who are you? What do you want?

Father: (*he steps forward, followed by the others, and comes to the foot of one of the flights of steps*) We are here in search of an author.

Director: (*caught between anger and utter astonishment*) In search of an author? Which author?

Father: Any author, sir.

Director: But there's no author here.... We're not rehearsing a new play.

Stepdaughter: (*vivaciously, as she rushes up the steps*) So much the better! Then so much the better, sir! *We* can be your new play.

One of the Actors: (*amidst the lively comments and laughter of the others*) Oh, just listen to her! *Listen* to her!

Father: (*following the* STEPDAUGHTER *on to the stage*) Yes, but if there isn't any author.... (*To the* DIRECTOR.) Unless *you'd* like to be the author....

(Holding the LITTLE GIRL *by the hand, the* MOTHER, *followed by the* BOY, *climbs up the first few steps leading to the stage and stands there expectantly. The* SON *remains morosely below.)*

Director: Are you people trying to be funny?

Father: No.... How can you suggest such a thing? On the contrary, we are bringing you a terrible and grievous drama.

Stepdaughter: And we might make your fortune for you.

Director: Perhaps you'll do me the kindness of getting out of this theatre! We've got no time to waste on lunatics!

Father: (*he is wounded by this, but replies in a gentle tone*) Oh.... But you know very well, don't you, that life is full of things that are infinitely absurd, things that, for all their impudent absurdity, have no need to masquerade as truth, because they are true.

Director: What the devil are you talking about?

Father: What I'm saying is that reversing the usual order of things, forcing oneself to a contrary way of action, may well be construed as madness. As, for instance, when we create things which have all the appearance of reality in order that they shall look like the realities themselves. But allow me to observe that if this indeed be madness, it is, nonetheless, the sole *raison d'être* of your profession.

(The ACTORS *stir indignantly at this.)*

Director: (*getting up and looking him up and down*) Oh, yes? So you think ours is a profession of lunatics, do you?

Father: Yes, making what isn't true *seem* true ... without having to ... for fun.... Isn't it your function to give life on the stage to imaginary characters?

Director: (*immediately, making himself spokesman for the growing anger of his actors*) I should like you to know, my dear sir, that the actor's profession is a most noble one. And although nowadays, with things in the state they are, our playwrights give us stupid comedies to act, and puppets to represent instead of men, I'd have you know that it is our boast that we have given life, here on these very boards, to immortal works!

(The ACTORS *satisfiedly murmur their approval and applaud the* DIRECTOR.*)*

Father: (*breaking in and following hard on his argument*) There you are! Oh, that's it exactly! To living beings ... to beings who are more alive than those who breathe and wear clothes! Less real, perhaps, but truer! We're in complete agreement!

(The ACTORS *look at each other in utter astonishment.)*

Director: But.... What on earth! ... But you said just now ...

Father: No, I said that because of your ... because you shouted at us that you had no time to waste on lunatics ... while nobody can know better than you that nature makes use of the instrument of human fantasy to pursue her work of creation on a higher level.

Director: True enough! True enough! But where does all this get us?

Father: Nowhere. I only wish to show you that one is born into life in so many ways, in so many forms.... As a tree, or as a stone; as water or as a butterfly.... Or as a woman. And that one can be born a character.

Director: (*ironically, feigning amazement*) And you, together with these other people, were born a character?

Father: Exactly. And alive, as you see. (*The* DIRECTOR *and the* ACTORS *burst out laughing as if at some huge joke. Hurt.*) I'm sorry that you laugh like that because, I repeat, we carry within ourselves a terrible and grievous drama, as you can deduce for yourselves from this woman veiled in black.

(And so saying, he holds out his hand to the MOTHER *and helps her up the last few steps and, continuing to hold her hand, leads her with a certain tragic solemnity to the other side of the stage, which immediately lights up with a fantastic kind of light. The* LITTLE GIRL *and the* BOY *follow their* MOTHER. *Next the* SON *comes up and goes and stands to one side, in the background. Then the* STEPDAUGHTER *follows him on to the stage; she stands downstage, leaning against the proscenium arch. The* ACTORS *are at first completely taken-aback and then, caught in admiration at this development, they burst into applause—just as if they had had a show put on for their benefit.)*

Director: (*at first utterly astonished and then indignant*) Shut up! What the ...! (*Then turning to the* CHARACTERS.) And you get out of here! Clear out of here! (*To the* STAGE-MANAGER.) For God's sake, clear them out!

Stage-Manager: (*coming forward, but then stopping as if held back by some strange dismay*) Go away! Go away!

Father: (*to the Director*) No, no! Listen.... We....

Director: (*shouting*) I tell you, we've got work to do!

Leading Man: You can't go about playing practical jokes like this....

Father: (*resolutely coming forward*) I wonder at your incredulity. Is it perhaps that you're not accustomed to seeing the characters created by an author leaping to life up here on the stage, when they come face to face with each other? Or is it, perhaps, that there's no script there (*he points to the prompt box*) that contains us?

Stepdaughter: (*smiling, she steps towards the* DIRECTOR*; then, in a wheedling voice*) Believe me, sir, we really are six characters ... and very, very interesting! But we've been cut adrift.

Father: (*brushing her aside*) Yes, that's it, we've been cut adrift. (*And then immediately to the* DIRECTOR.) In the sense, you understand, that the author who created us as living beings, either couldn't or wouldn't put us materially into the world of art. And it was truly a crime ... because he who has the good fortune to be born a living character may snap his fingers at Death even. He will never die! Man ... The writer ... The instrument of creation ... Will die.... But what is created by him will never die. And in order to live eternally he has not the slightest need of extraordinary gifts or of accomplishing prodigies. Who was Sancho Panza? Who was Don Abbondio? And yet they live eternally because—living seeds—they had the good fortune to find a fruitful womb—a fantasy which knew how to raise and nourish them, and to make them live through all eternity.

Director: All this is very, very fine indeed.... But what do you want here?

Father: We wish to live, sir!

Director: (*ironically*) Through all eternity?

Father: No, sir; just for a moment ... in you.

An Actor: Listen to him! ... listen to him!

Leading Lady: They want to live in us!

Juvenile Lead: (*pointing to the* STEPDAUGHTER) I've no objection ... so long as I get her.

Father: Listen! Listen! The play is in the making. (*To the* DIRECTOR) But if you and your actors are willing, we can settle it all between us without further delay.

Director: (*annoyed*) But what do you want to settle? We don't go in for that sort of concoction here! We put on comedies and dramas here.

Father: Exactly! That's the very reason why we came to you.

Director: And where's the script?

Father: It is in us, sir. (*The* ACTORS *laugh.*) The drama is in us. *We* are the drama and we are impatient to act it—so fiercely does our inner passion urge us on.

ACTIVITIES

1. Pirandello has suggested that the Characters wear masks which free the mouth, nose, and eyes, and which symbolize the dominant feelings of each Character: "remorse" for Father, "sorrow" for Mother, "contempt" for Son, "revenge" for Stepdaughter, "timidity" for Boy, and "innocence" for Child. If you are able, construct, decorate, and use masks for the Characters. How does the interpretation change when the Characters have masks compared to when they do not have masks?

2. Invent a scene in which each of the six Characters is given a role based on the emotions his or her mask conveys.

3. Investigate how the scene changes if the Director and Actors all wear neutral masks and the Characters do not wear any masks.

4. Find other scripts in this book into which the Characters can intrude. For example, what would happen if the six Characters appeared on the set of *The Care and Treatment of Roses*, the play-within-a-play in *Jitters* (Section A, Chapter 2).

WORKSHOP

1. Choose a current controversial issue, such as disarmament or acid rain, which can be argued about from two points of view. Research the arguments for each side by reading newspapers and magazines. When the arguments are fully understood, develop an improvisation in which there is a confrontation. You may want to use *An Enemy of the People* as an example for your improvisation.

In your work, experiment with the effect the character that you play has on the argument. For example, if you adopt the role of a mild-mannered person, how effective are your arguments? This improvisation can be developed into a script using the techniques outlined in chapter 10, "Scripting."

2. Using *The Bald Soprano* as a model, choose an ordinary action, such as buying a newspaper or eating dinner, and improvise dialogue and action that develop in illogical ways.

3. Examine scenes from *Monty Python's Flying Circus*, *SCTV*, or *Saturday Night Live* for qualities which indicate that these shows are related to theatre of the absurd.

4. Examine other scripts in this book which present a moral dilemma similar to the one found in *The Good Person of Szechwan*. Some suggestions are *The Tragedy of Dr. Faustus*, *Whose Life Is It Anyway*? and *Us and Them*. Choose one script and compare the playwright's approach to the dilemma with Brecht's approach. Next, improvise the chosen script in a manner similar to *The Good Person of Szechwan*.

5. Using the technique demonstrated in *Six Characters in Search of an Author*, have the characters in any script in this book step out of the script to talk about the play, their roles, their feelings about the situation, and the other characters. Improvise scenes where characters from one script talk to characters in another script. For example, the husband and wife in *The Last Night of the World*, drinking their last cups of coffee, might talk to the husband and wife drinking their tea in *Countdown*.

6. Create an improvisation based on "An Author Searches for Characters." One person, in the role of a playwright, interviews other people playing roles drawn from any script in this book. Try to create a play which will accommodate all of the characters.

Epilogue: Tomorrow's People

This final chapter revolves around three poems from T.S. Eliot's *Old Possum's Book of Practical Cats*. This book was used as the basis of an extremely popular musical, *Cats*, which opened on Broadway in 1982. *Cats* is not only representative of much of the work you have done in *Interpretation*, but is also an indication of how theatre will continue to develop in the future.

Cats was the inspiration of composer Andrew Lloyd Weber. After reading *Old Possum's Book*, Weber had several ideas about how the poems could be made into a script. Just as you did in Section B, Alternative Scripts, Weber used material not thought of as script and explored techniques for transposing this material into dramatic form. When this task was accomplished, Weber had a "conventional" script which then had to be explored, interpreted, and communicated by actors, the work you did in Section A, Theatre Scripts. As you saw in Section C, The Cycle of Theatre, every script is a new interpretation of a universal theme; *Cats* is no different. Just as primitive people used animal characters in their rituals to deepen their understanding of life, so too *Cats*, a highly technical, modern production, explores, through animal persona, the human condition.

We have included here three of the poems used by Weber in *Cats*, so that you can examine the material that he found so promising. However, we caution you that in the normal course of events the publishers of T.S. Eliot's work do not give permission for any dramatic use to be made of his verse, even in the classroom. In the case of *Cats*, it was only through the wishes of Valerie Eliot, T.S. Eliot's widow, that an exception to this rule was permitted.

Your task, therefore, after reading Eliot's poems, will be to create *your own* script for "tomorrow," using material you find yourselves. As you work with some of the ideas presented in Workshop, remember that the most unlikely material can be transformed, through creativity and energy, into theatrical form. If you are willing to risk, to experiment, and to challenge conventional thinking, perhaps you will be one of "tomorrow's people."

"On the fourth floor of a renovated factory off Union Square in lower Manhattan, early on a sweltering August day, romantical cats and pedantical cats, allegorical cats and metaphorical cats are assembling. They may be masquerading as Broadway performers—the nearly anonymous acting-singing-dancing dynamos who pump the American musical machine—but for as long as their stamina and luck hold out, they are the American *Cats*."

Time, September 27, 1982

The Old Gumbie Cat

I have a Gumbie Cat in mind,
her name is Jennyanydots;
Her coat is of the tabby kind, with tiger stripes and leopard spots.
All day she sits upon the stair or on the steps or on the mat:
She sits and sits and sits and sits—and that's what makes a Gumbie Cat!

But when the day's hustle and bustle is done,
Then the Gumbie Cat's work is but hardly begun.
And when all the family's in bed and asleep,
She tucks up her skirts to the basement to creep.
She is deeply concerned with the ways of the mice—
Their behavior's not good and their manners not nice;
So when she has got them lined up on the matting,
She teaches them music, crocheting and tatting.

I have a Gumbie Cat in mind, her name is Jennyanydots;
Her equal would be hard to find, she likes the warm and sunny spots.
All day she sits beside the hearth or in the sun or on my hat:
She sits and sits and sits and sits—and that's what makes a Gumbie Cat!

But when the day's hustle and bustle is done,
Then the Gumbie Cat's work is but hardly begun.
As she finds that the mice will not ever keep quiet,
She is sure it is due to irregular diet
And believing that nothing is done without trying,
She sets right to work with her baking and frying.
She makes them a mouse-cake of bread and dried peas,
And a *beautiful* fry of lean bacon and cheese.

I have a Gumbie Cat in mind, her name is Jennyanydots;
The curtain-cord she likes to wind, and tie it into sailor-knots.
She sits upon the window-sill, or anything that's smooth and flat:
She sits and sits and sits and sits—and that's what makes a Gumbie Cat!

But when the day's hustle and bustle is done,
Then the Gumbie Cat's work is but hardly begun.
She thinks that the cockroaches just need employment
To prevent them from idle and wanton destroyment.
So she's formed, from that lot of disorderly louts,
A troop of well-disciplined helpful boy-scouts,
With a purpose in life and a good deed to do—
And she's even created a Beetle's Tattoo.

So for Old Gumbie Cats let us now give three cheers—
On whom well-ordered households depend, it appears.

"In their second week of rehearsal, the chosen Shubert Alley cats are getting down to business learning to feel feline. Says Steven Gelfer, 33, one of the eight acrobat-dancers in the troupe: 'We spent hours on our hands and knees—moving about, resting, cleaning ourselves. Now we have to take what we learned from being on all fours and transfer it to two legs. Just when we were getting comfortable on our knees.'"

Time, Sept. 27, 1982

Mungojerrie and Rumpelteazer

Mungojerrie and Rumpelteazer were a very notorious couple of cats.
As knockabout clowns, quick-change comedians, tight-rope walkers and acrobats
They had an extensive reputation. They made their home in Victoria Grove—
That was merely their centre of operation, for they were incurably given to rove.
They were very well known in Cornwall Gardens, in Launceston Place and in Kensington Square—
They had really a little more reputation than a couple of cats can very well bear.

If the area window was found ajar
And the basement looked like a field of war,
If a tile or two came loose on the roof,
Which presently ceased to be waterproof,
If the drawers were pulled out from the bedroom chests,
And you couldn't find one of your winter vests,
Or after supper one of the girls
Suddenly missed her Woolworth pearls:
Then the family would say: 'It's that horrible cat!
It was Mungojerrie—or Rumpelteazer!'—And most of the time they left it at that.

Mungojerrie and Rumpelteazer had a very unusual gift of the gab.
They were highly efficient cat-burglars as well, and remarkably smart at a smash-and-grab.
They made their home in Victoria Grove. They had no regular occupation.
They were plausible fellows, and liked to engage a friendly policeman in conversation.

When the family assembled for Sunday dinner,
With their minds made up that they wouldn't get thinner
On Argentine joint, potatoes and greens,
And the cook would appear from behind the scenes
And say in a voice that was broken with sorrow:
'I'm afraid you must wait and have dinner *tomorrow*!
For the joint has gone from the oven—like that!'
Then the family would say: 'It's that horrible cat!
It was Mungojerrie—or Rumpelteazer!'—And most of the time they left it at that.

Mungojerrie and Rumpelteazer had a wonderful way of working together.
And some of the time you would say it was luck, and some of the time you would say it was weather.
They would go through the house like a hurricane, and no sober person

could take his oath
Was it Mungojerrie—or Rumpelteazer?
or could you have sworn that it mightn't be both?

And when you heard a dining-room smash
Or up from the pantry there came a loud crash
Or down from the library came a loud *ping*
From a vase which was commonly said to be Ming—
Then the family would say: 'Now which was which cat?
It was Mungojerrie! AND Rumpelteazer!'—And there's nothing at all to be done about that!

"The setting of *Cats*, at the Winter Garden, is a city dump of superlative squalid disorder, and it is there that the assortment of singing and dancing cats who make up the entire cast of this peculiar musical forgather by night to boast of their exploits, to contemplate old age and death, and, in one lucky instance, to be translated into cat heaven, where cats await without impatience rebirth into one or another of the nine lives to which, by common cat calculation, they are said to be entitled."

New Yorker, October 18, 1982

FROM Gus: the Theatre Cat

Gus is the Cat at the Theatre Door.
His name, as I ought to have told you before,
Is really Asparagus. That's such a fuss
To pronounce, that we usually call him just Gus.
His coat's very shabby, he's thin as a rake,
And he suffers from palsy that makes his paw shake.
Yet he was, in his youth, quite the smartest of Cats—
But no longer a terror to mice and to rats.
For he isn't the Cat that he was in his prime;
Though his name was quite famous, he says, in its time.
And whenever he joins his friends at their club
(Which takes place at the back of the neighboring pub)
He loves to regale them, if someone else pays,
With anecdotes drawn from his palmiest days.
For he once was a Star of the highest degree—
He has acted with Irving, he's acted with Tree.
And he likes to relate his success on the Halls,
Where the Gallery once gave him seven cat-calls.
But his grandest creation, as he loves to tell,
Was Firefrorefiddle, the Fiend of the Fell.

'I have played', so he says, 'every possible part,
And I used to know seventy speeches by heart.
I'd extemporize back-chat, I knew how to gag,
And I knew how to let the cat out of the bag.

Then, if someone will give him a toothful of gin,
He will tell how he once played a part in *East Lynne*.
At a Shakespeare performance he once walked on pat,
When some actor suggested the need for a cat.
And he says: 'Now, these kittens, they do not get trained
As we did in the days when Victoria reigned.
They never get drilled in a regular troupe,
And they think they are smart, just to jump through a hoop.'
And he'll say, as he scratches himself with his claws,
'Well, the Theatre's certainly not what it was.
These modern productions are all very well,
But there's nothing to equal, from what I hear tell,
That moment of mystery
When I made history
As Firefrorefiddle, the Fiend of the Fell.'

WORKSHOP

1. Look through poetry anthologies to find five or six poems about one subject. Birds, for example, might make a good choice because of the number of poems available, and the visual potential of the subject.

2. After selecting your poems, decide on a theme or themes that will tie the poems together. You will also have to decide on a setting for the poems. (A pet shop, forest, or zoo might be a good setting for the bird poems.) What theme would tie this setting into a statement about the human condition: life in prison? loss of freedom?

3. Begin work on the individual poems.
—The poems can be a basis for creating characters. Examine each poem carefully to discover the qualities of its character(s). Use makeup, masks, and costumes to enhance the characterizations.
—Use the techniques of choral dramatization (Chapter 7), Readers Theatre (Chapter 8), and Story Theatre (Chapter 9) to polish your vocal presentation of the poems.

4. Begin pulling the poems together into a story.
—Use the techniques of anthology (Chapter 11) to enhance the poems with additional written material.
—Each poem provides opportunities for extended improvisation and creation of additional dialogue. Develop these scenes using the techniques of scripting (Chapter 10).
—Find music that works with the poems, and develop a movement/dance interpretation.

5. Use all the rehearsal techniques given in Chapter 4, "Rehearsing the script," as you prepare for a presentation.

6. Sometime before the performance of your script, read the rest of this chapter, including the final scene from *A Life in the Theatre*. Keep the thoughts expressed in this material in mind as you deliver your presentation.

> As a means of expression and communication, drama—quite apart from telling stories or providing models of social situations in action—is to a very considerable extent concerned with the recreation of human states of emotion.
>
> The play which communicates to us important lessons about social behavior, which tells us a gripping story, may also open up unknown areas of emotional experience through powerful poetic images.
>
> Drama is as multifaceted in its images, as ambivalent in its meanings, as the world it mirrors. That is its main strength, its characteristic as a mode of expression—and its greatness.
>
> Martin Esslin,
> *An Anatomy of Drama*

This book has been about using the power of theatre to enhance artistic growth and understanding. Every script is a vehicle for exploration; we hope that through this exploration you have acquired a sense of the people involved in the art of interpretation over the centuries. If you have been willing to risk taking on roles, taking on other "lives," then you have discovered more about yourself and about your place in tomorrow's world. We hope that you will continue to see in script interpretation a medium for learning and a means of using that learning in your life.

FROM

A LIFE IN THE THEATRE

by David Mamet

SCENE 26

(Backstage, after a show.)

Robert: I loved the staircase scene tonight.

John: You did?

Robert: Just like a poem.

(Pause.)

John: I thought the execution scene worked beautifully.

Robert: No. You *didn't.*

John: Yes. I did.

(Pause.)

Robert: *Thank* you. Getting cold, eh?

John: Yes.

Robert: (*to himself*) It's getting cold. (*Aloud*) You know, my father always wanted me to be an actor.

John: Yes?

Robert: Always wanted me to be . . .

(Pause.)

John: Well! (*Crosses and picks up umbrella.*)

Robert: It's raining?

John: I think it will. You got a fag?

Robert: Yes. Always wanted me to be.

*(*ROBERT *hands* JOHN *a cigarette.)*

John: Thank you.

Robert: Mmm.

John: Got a match?

Robert: You going out?

John: Yes.

Robert: Where? A party?

John: No. I'm going with some people.

Robert: Ah.

John: You have a match?

Robert: No.

*(*JOHN *hunts for a match on the makeup table.)*

John: Are you going out tonight?

Robert: I don't know; I suppose so.

John: Mmm.

Robert: I'm not eating too well these days.

John: No, eh?

Robert: No.

John: Why?

Robert: Not hungry.

*(*JOHN *picks up matchbook, struggles to light match.)*

I'll get it.

John: Do you mind?

Robert: No.

*(*ROBERT *takes matchbook and lights* JOHN*'s cigarette.)*

John: Thank you.

(Pause.)

Robert: A life spent in the theatre.

John: Mmm.

Robert: Backstage.

John: Yes.

Robert: The bars, the house, the drafty halls. The pencilled scripts . . .

John: Yes.

Robert: Stories. Ah, the stories that you hear.

John: I know.

Robert: It all goes so fast. It goes so quickly.

(Long pause.)

John: You think that I might borrow twenty 'til tomorrow?

Robert: What, you're short on cash?

John: Yes.

Robert: Oh. Oh. (*Pause.*) Of course. (*He digs in his pocket. Finds money and hands it to* JOHN.)

John: You're sure you won't need it?

Robert: No. No, not at all. No. If I don't know how it is, who does?

(Pause.)

John: Thank you.

Robert: Mmm. Goodnight.

John: Goodnight.

Robert: You have a nice night.

John: I will.

Robert: Goodnight.

*(*JOHN *exits. Pause.)*

Ephemeris, ephemeris. (*Pause.*) "An actor's life for me."

*(*ROBERT *composes himself and addresses the empty house. He raises his hand to stop imaginary applause.)*

You've been so kind . . . Thank you, you've really been so kind. You know, and I speak, I am sure, not for myself alone, but on behalf of all of us . . . (*composes himself*) . . . All of us here, when I say that these . . . *these* moments make it all . . . they make it all worthwhile.

(Pause. JOHN *quietly reappears.)*

You know . . .

*(*ROBERT *sees* JOHN.*)*

John: They're locking up. They'd like us all to leave.

Robert: I was just leaving.

John: Yes, I know. (*Pause.*) I'll tell them.

Robert: Would you?

John: Yes.

(Pause.)

Robert: Thank you.

John: Goodnight.

Robert: Goodnight.

(Pause.)

*(*JOHN *exits.)*

Robert: (*to himself*) The lights dim. Each to his own home. Goodnight. Goodnight. Goodnight.

Glossary

The words listed in this Glossary are words which are used in this book, but which were not fully explained at the time of their use. The definitions you are given in this Glossary pertain to theatre and drama only; each word may have many other definitions which are not explained here. Some of the words in this Glossary are in italics. This indicates that there is a separate Glossary entry for the italicized word.

Above: to be or to go *up-stage* of an object or person.

Ad Lib: to add or *improvise* words and/or gestures.

Alarum: used in Elizabethan drama, an *off-stage* sound effect of trumpets, drums, or guns.

Antagonist: the *character* who is directly opposed to the *hero* or *protagonist* and tries to prevent the hero from reaching his or her goal.

Antecedent Events: actions which have occurred before a play begins, and which are often described in introductory stage notes or in the *exposition* of a play.

Aside: a dramatic *convention* by which an actor directly and audibly addresses the audience but is not supposed to be heard by other actors on the stage.

Backdrop: the *curtain* at the back of a stage. It usually forms part of the scenery or setting.

Backgrounding: a process used by an actor to supply more information about his or her *character* than is given in the script, in order that the actor can understand the character more fully. (See *motivation*.)

Below: to be or to go *downstage* of an object or person.

Blackout: the sudden extinguishing of all stage lighting.

Blocking: the working out of the physical movements of actors in a play. Blocking should be organic—that is, arising from the *motivations* of the characters—rather than imposed.

Bombast: insincere, extravagant language that is disproportionate to the matter it expresses.

Build: to increase the emotion, tension, and/or energy of a speech or scene.

Burlesque: a form of *comedy* characterized by ridiculous exaggeration. The form and style of a burlesque may be either lower or higher than the dignity of the subject matter.

Business: a *character's* minor physical actions with his or her hands and face.

Catharsis: the emotional purification or relief experienced by the audience at the end of a *tragedy*. The word is from Aristotle's *Poetics*.

Centre Stage (or stage centre): a position approximately in the middle of the stage or acting area.

Character: one of the people—*dramatis personae*—in a play. The word also refers to the physical and psychological makeup of the character.

Characterization: the creation of *characters*; the process by which a playwright creates a personality for a character in a play.

Climax: the point of highest interest in a play. The turning point in the action. The climax may or may not be the *crisis* as well.

Clown: a comic figure present in plays through most of the history of theatre. The clown has often been called "fool."

Collective Creation: a script put together by a number of people, often the members of a theatre company, rather than a single playwright.

Comedy: as compared with *tragedy*, comedy is a lighter form of drama primarily designed to amuse and which ends happily for the *characters* involved.

Comedy of Manners: the term is commonly used to designate the *comedy* of the Restoration period. However, in a general sense, comedy of manners is comedy concerned with the manners and conventions of an artificial, highly sophisticated society.

Complication: an incident within a play which changes the direction of the play's action.

Concentration: complete attention to some aspect of a script or performance, such as the actions of a *character* or the accomplishment of an *intention*.

Conflict: the struggle which grows out of the interplay of opposing forces in a play. Conflict can take the form of one *character* against himself/herself, against other characters, against the world, nature, or supernatural forces.

Copyright: the exclusive legal right to perform, publish, or reproduce works of literature or art. (You may not perform a play without obtaining permission from the publisher.)

Counter: to shift the position of one *character* to compensate for the movement of another character in order to maintain an effective *stage picture*.

Cover: to conceal an action or object from the audience; or, to conceal the mistake of another performer through *improvised* speech and/or movement.

Crisis (or major crisis): the point at which the opposing forces that create the *conflict* interlock in the decisive action on which the *plot* will turn towards the *climax* and *denouement*.

Cross: movement of a *character* from one stage area to another. It is sometimes symbolized in scripts with an "X." (See *blocking*.)

Cue: a word, movement, or gesture, which is a signal for another *character* to respond in speech and/or action.

Curtain: a drapery used to conceal the stage area. The term is also used to denote the end of a scene, act, or play.

Cut: to delete some part of a script (dialogue, action, a role). It is also used as a command to stop a rehearsal.

Denouement: the final unravelling of the *plot* at the end of a play. This explanation or outcome resolves all the secrets and misunderstandings connected with *complications* of the plot.

Deus ex Machina: Latin for "a god from a machine." In classical Greek theatre "gods" were lowered to the stage from the "machine" or stage structure above, and solved problems beyond mortal powers. The term now refers to an improbable device or forced invention used by a playwright to solve a difficult situation.

Diction: the pronunciation and articulation of words.

Director: co-ordinator of all artists and technicians working on a theatre production.

Double: to play more than one role in a single play.

Downstage: the stage area closest to the audience.

Dramatis Personae: Latin for "masks of the play." The term refers to the *characters* in a play.

Dress the Stage: to furnish *props* and items to finish the setting. The term also refers to a *character* moving slightly to provide more space for others.

Dumb Show: a type of *mime* (a scene with actions but without words) used frequently in Elizabethan drama. It usually provided a spectacular element and was often accompanied by music.

Emphasis: putting a special force, stress, or importance on an action, word, line, or *character.*

Entrance: the act of entering the performance area that is in view of the audience. The term also refers to an opening in a set through which *characters* can enter.

Epilogue: in a play, a concluding speech which is addressed to the audience.

Exit: the act of leaving the performance area that is in view of the audience. The term also refers to an opening in a set through which *characters* can exit.

Exposition: introductory material which creates the tone, gives the setting, introduces the *characters*, and supplies other facts necessary for an understanding of the play.

Floor Plan (or ground plan): an outline drawing of a stage setting as it would look from above.

Focal Point: the place or stage area of greatest interest *on-stage* at any moment of a play.

Freeze: a period of time during which some or all characters *on-stage* remain motionless, fixed in a *tableau.*

Genre: a term used in literary critism to signify a literary form. Traditional genres include *tragedy* and *comedy*, and a modern understanding of genre includes such forms as the novel, short story, and essay. Plays written in the same genre are similar in structure, even though they may be totally different in *theme.*

Give: to move slightly to provide space for another actor; to respond or offer emotion, energy, or activity *on-stage* in order to direct more attention to another *character.*

Given Circumstance: a factor which must be known about a play in order to understand it.

Gothic: when applied to a play, the term refers to such things as a brooding atmosphere of gloom or terror, or to events which are uncanny, or macabre, or *melodramatically* violent.

Greenroom: in a theatre, a room in which performers, and their guests, can relax.

Ham: an actor who overacts or exaggerates his or her part.

Hero: the central *character* or *protagonist* in a play.

Hold: to stop or delay action because of laughter or applause or in order to emphasize a moment.

Hubris: from the Greek word for excessive pride. Hubris is the most common *tragic flaw* of the *hero* of a *tragedy.*

Impromptu: a speech or performance done without previous preparation.

Improvise: to invent dialogue and action spontaneously, based on an understanding of a role and a situation.

In: to move toward *centre stage.*

Intention: a term for a *character's* reason for an action or speech regardless of what reason the character gives in his or her dialogue. (See *motivating force* and *sub-text.*)

Interlude: entertainment, usually musical, presented between acts or plays while scenery is being changed. In sixteenth-century England, an interlude was a short farce.

In-the-round: a round stage on which actors are surrounded by an audience. *Exits* and *entrances* are made by way of the aisles. This type of stage is also called an arena stage or theatre-in-the-round.

Irony: in a play, a condition in which the truth is known by the audience but not by the *characters* involved; the words or acts of a character which carry a meaning unperceived by the character but understood by the audience.

Kinesics: the study of communication by means of gestures, facial expressions, etc., especially as they accompany speech.

Lead: a principal role.

Light Bars: the rows of lights which hang above a stage.

Masque: an elaborate form of court entertainment which flourished in England during the sixteenth and seventeenth centuries. It combined *poetic drama*, music, song, dance, splendid costuming, and stage spectacle.

Matinee: an afternoon performance.

Melodrama: a play based on a romantic *plot* and sensational development with little regard for convincing *motivation* and with an excessive appeal to the emotions of the audience.

Mime: an ancient dramatic entertainment in which acrobats, jugglers, singers, dancers, and actors perform without dialogue.

Monologue: a long speech delivered by one actor.

Mood: the dominant emotional atmosphere of a play. Mood is created by a combination of tempo, imagery, lighting, scenery, and costuming.

Motivating Force: the central drive of a *character* which pushes him or her toward a desired goal. (See *intention* and *sub-text.*)

Motivation: the reason a *character* does and says certain things. The motivation of a character is derived from an understanding of the psychological makeup of the character.

Mummings: a type of game or spectacle in medieval times. A procession of masked people (townsfolk) would go through the streets, enter house after house, silently dance, play games, and continue on to the next stop. A participant was called a mummer.

Musical Comedy (or musical theatre): a play in which songs and dances are integrated with action and dialogue.

Objective: the goal or desire towards which each *character*, through actions and/or dialogue, is working.

Off-stage: the part of a stage out of view of the audience.

On-stage: the area of a stage in view of the audience.

Overlap: to move or speak slightly ahead of *cue.*

Overplay: to act with exaggeration. (See *ham.*)

Pace: the speed with which a play or actor moves.

Parody: a play (or scene, or *character*, etc.) which *burlesques* or ridicules an original piece of work or idea, etc.

Pathos: a quality in a *character* which evokes pity, tenderness, or sorrow.

Pickup: to increase the *pace* of a scene, or to shorten the interval between *cues.*

Places!: a command for actors to get in position to begin a rehearsal or performance.

Play-within-a-play: a play presented within the play being performed.

Plot: the organization by which the story of a play unfolds.

Poetic Drama: a play whose language is metrical, or written in verse.

Practical: a functioning *prop* or piece of scenery which can actually be used by an actor and is not merely decorative.

Processional Movement: a co-ordinated and orderly method of walking used by a chorus or group of actors.

Project: to accentuate or intensify vocal delivery (volume or articulation), movement, or emotion.

Prologue: a speech directly addressed to the audience at the beginning of a play.

Prompt Cards: large boards or sheets of paper on which lines or key words that an actor has trouble remembering are printed.

Prompter: a person located *off-stage* who whispers lines to forgetful actors during a performance.

Property (or prop): an object or article used in a play. Hand props: props used by *characters*; set props: furniture and other standing props; trim or dress props: objects hanging on the walls of a set.

Proscenium Arch: the arch over the front of the stage from which the *curtain* hangs and which, together with the curtain, separates the stage from the audience. Such a stage is called a proscenium arch stage and is distinct from a theatre-*in-the-round*, for example.

Protagonist: the main *character* in a play. In early Greek drama, the protagonist was the name given to the first character to emerge from the chorus.

Rehearsal: a practice performance of a dramatic work or part of a work. Rehearsals usually follow this sequence: reading, blocking, working, polishing, technical, run-through, and dress.

Repartee: conversation made up of brilliant witticisms, usually spoken with rapid delivery.

Repertory (or repertoire): the body of dramatic works a company is trained to perform. A repertory company performs a number of plays daily, weekly, or monthly, rather than a single play for an extended run.

Resolution: the events which follow the *climax* in a *plot.*

Revival: a production of a play which has not been performed for a long time.

Revue: a theatrical entertainment with singing, dancing, skits, and a humorous treatment of happenings and fads of the year.

Rhythm: the combination of tempo, imagery, stress, beat, sound, accent, and movement which creates a recognizable pattern. A play has a rhythm; roles have a rhythm.

Ritual: a ceremonial act or performance.

Run-through: a rehearsal without interruption of a scene, act, or play.

Satire: a work ridiculing aspects of human behavior, usually socially corrective in nature and intended to provoke both laughter and thought.

Scenario: a detailed outline giving only the dramatic action of a story and not specific dialogue.

Share: to give equal attention to two or more actors. The term also refers to an informal presentation of dramatic material.

Sight Line: the line of vision from any seat in the audience to the performance area.

Soliloquy: a speech in which a *character* utters thoughts aloud while alone *on-stage.* It can be delivered directly to the audience or spoken as meditation.

Stage Directions: during a play, instructions for an actor to follow given either in the script by the playwright, or in *blocking.*

Stage Left: left of *stage centre*; determined by the actor's left when facing the audience.

Stage Picture: at any given moment, the arrangement of actors, setting, props, etc., to form a composition *on-stage.*

Stage Right: right of *stage centre*; determined by the actor's right when facing the audience.

Static: little or no movement; a slow *pace.*

Steal: one actor drawing the audience's attention to himself/herself when that focus should be on others. (See *focal point.*)

Stock Character: character types that recur repeatedly in a particular *genre*, and so are recognizable as part of the *conventions* of that genre.

Straight Role: a role without particular or unusual characteristics.

Style: the mode of expression of a particular play taking into consideration that play's *characters*, language, *theme*, and historical period.

Sub-text: the reasons behind what a *character* says and does. Sub-text is not part of a script; it must be discovered by the actor playing the part. (See *intention* and *motivating force.*)

Symbol: a person, place, or object which stands for or represents an idea or quality and which, when used or referred to, immediately summons an organized pattern of emotional and intellectual responses.

Tableau: during a scene a short interval in which the actors *freeze* in position and then resume action as before or hold their positions until the *curtain* falls.

Tag Line: the last line of a joke, or the line which comes before an *exit* or before the end of a scene or act.

Theme: a play's central idea or concept which reflects in general terms the meaning of the play.

Throw Away: a line or action which does not warrant special emphasis; to deliberately underplay a line of dialogue or action so that the audience's focus will be drawn elsewhere.

Timing: the art of delivering a line or doing an action at the moment of maximum effectiveness.

Top: to emphasize a line or an action in such a way that it is more emphatic than the preceding dialogue or action.

Tragedy: a drama which relates a series of events in the life of a person of significance, and which culminates in an unhappy catastrophe. Tragedy is a record of a man or a woman's strivings and aspirations, and is in contrast to *comedy* which is the amusing spectacle of a man or a woman's limitations and frailties.

Tragic Flaw: the flaw, error, or defect in the tragic *hero* which leads to his or her downfall.

Trilogy: a collection of three plays on the same or similar *theme.*

Type Casting: the practice of casting a performer whose age, physical characteristics, and personality match those of the *character* he or she is to play.

Underplay: to deliberately control or de-emphasize emotions when playing a role.

Understudy: an actor who learns a part in order to replace the regular performer of that part if necessary.

Up-stage: the stage area furthest away from the audience.

Vaudeville: originally a type of variety show developed in the eighteenth and nineteenth centuries. However, the word is usually used to refer to the American variety show developed in the early years of the twentieth century. Elaborate theatres were built for vaudeville actors and their performances.

Walk-on: a small role without lines.

Wit: a striking or clever and often amusing association of ideas and words.

Acknowledgments

For the use of the selections below, listed in the order in which they appear in *Interpretation*, grateful acknowledgment is made to the copyright holders as follows:

From *The Empty Space* by Peter Brook. Used by permission of Granada Publishing Limited.

Acknowledgment is made to Campbell Smith and Pulp Press Book Publishers for the use of the selection from *Juve*.

The Elephant Man by Bernard Pomerance. Reprinted by permission of Grove Press, Inc. Copyright © 1979 by Bernard Pomerance.

Come and Go by Samuel Beckett from *Cascando and Other Short Dramatic Pieces*. Reprinted by permission of Grove Press, Inc. Copyright © 1968 by Samuel Beckett.

What Glorious Times They Had—Nellie McClung © By permission Simon & Pierre Publishing Co. Ltd., Box 280, Adelaide Street Post Office, Toronto, Ontario M5C 2J4. Production rights are controlled exclusively by Simon & Pierre. No performances may be given without obtaining written permission in advance and payment of the requisite fee.

From *Barefoot in the Park*, by Neil Simon. Copright © 1964 by Ellen Enterprises, Inc. Reprinted by permission of Random House, Inc.

After Liverpool by James Saunders. Reprinted by permission of Margaret Ramsay Ltd. All rights whatsoever in this play are strictly reserved and application for performance, etc., should be made before rehearsal to Margaret Ramsay Ltd., 14A Goodwin's Court, St. Martin's Lane, London WC2, England. No performance may be given unless a licence has been obtained.

The Real Inspector Hound by Tom Stoppard. Reprinted by permission of Faber and Faber Ltd. from *The Real Inspector Hound* by Tom Stoppard. All rights whatsoever in this play are strictly reserved and professional applications for permission to perform it, etc., must be made in advance, before rehearsals begin, to Samuel French Ltd., of 3 Queen Square, London WC1N 3AU.

Jitters by David French. Reprinted by permission of Talon Books.

Whose Life Is It Anyway? by Brian Clark. Reprinted by permission of Dodd, Mead & Company.

Countdown by Alan Ayckbourn from *Mixed Doubles*. Reprinted by permission of Margaret Ramsay Ltd. All rights whatsoever in this play are strictly reserved and application for performance, etc., should be made before rehearsal to Margaret Ramsay Ltd., 14A Goodwin's Court, St. Martin's Lane, London WC2, England. No performance may be given unless a licence has been obtained.

The Farm Show by Paul Thompson. Reprinted with permission of Paul Thompson and Theatre Passe Muraille.

The Tragedy of Doctor Faustus by Christopher Marlowe. Reprinted by permission of Simon & Schuster. Copyright, ©, 1959 by Simon & Schuster, Inc.

Antigone by Jean Anouilh. Reprinted by permission of Methuen London, Publishers.

1837: The Farmer's Revolt by Rick Salutin. Reprinted by permission of James Lorimer & Company, Publishers.

A Midsummer Night's Dream by William Shakespeare, adapted by Peter Brook and published by The Dramatic Publishing Company. Reprinted by permission of The Dramatic Publishing Company.

From *The Shadow Box*, copyright © 1977 by Michael Cristofer. Used by permission of Drama Book Publishers, 821 Broadway, New York, N.Y., U.S.A. All rights reserved.

Professionals and Amateurs are hereby warned that "COUNT DRACULA" by Ted Tiller, being fully protected under the copyright laws of the United States of America, the British Empire, including Canada, and all other countries of the Copyright Union, is subject to a royalty. All rights including professional, amateur, motion pictures, recitation, public reading, radio and television broadcasting and the rights of translation into foreign languages are strictly reserved. Amateurs may produce this play upon payment of a royalty of Fifty Dollars for the first performance, and Twenty-Five Dollars for each additional one, payable one week before the play is to be given, to Samuel French (Canada) Limited, at 80 Richmond Street East, Toronto, Ontario. M5C 1P1.

Professional royalty quoted on application to Samuel French (Canada) Limited.

Particular emphasis is laid on the question of amateur or professional reading, permission for which must be secured in writing from Samuel French (Canada) Limited.

Copying from this book in whole or in part is strictly forbidden by law, and the right of performance is not transferable.

Whenever the play is produced the following notice must appear on all programs, printing and advertising for the play: "Produced by Special Arrangement with Samuel French (Canada) Limited".

Due authorship credit must be given on all programs, printing, and advertising for the play.

Us and Them © by David Campton. All rights reserved. Amateurs wishing to perform this play should make prior application as follows: USA and Canada: The Dramatic Publishing Company, 4150 N. Milwaukee Ave., Chicago, Ill. 60641 USA. Rest of the world: Samuel French Ltd., 26 Southampton Street, London WC2E 7JE, England. All enquiries concerning professional performing rights or any other use of copyright should be directed to: ACTAC (Theatrical & Cinematic) Ltd. 16 Cadogan Lane, London SW1, England.

"What is He?" from *The Complete Poems of D.H. Lawrence* by D.H. Lawrence. Reprinted by permission of Laurence Pollinger Ltd. and the Estate of Frieda Laurence.

"Whirlpool Garbage Disposer." Reprinted by permission of Whirlpool Corporation, Benton Harbour, MI 49022, U.S.A.

"Boy, Girl, Boy, Girl" by Jules Feiffer. Copyright 1982, Jules Feiffer. Reprinted with permission. All rights reserved.

"Two Friends" by David Ignatow. Copyright © 1963 by David Ignatow. Reprinted from *Figures of The Human* by permission of Wesleyan University Press. This poem first appeared in *The Nation*.

"Get Off This Estate" by Carl Sandburg. From *The People, Yes* by Carl Sandburg, copyright 1936 by Harcourt Brace Jovanovich, Inc.; copyright 1964 by Carl Sandburg. Reprinted by permission of the publisher.

"Battle Won Is Lost" by Philip George. Reprinted by permission of the author.

Reprinted by permision of Hill and Wang, a division of Farrar, Straus and Giroux, Inc. "Wait Till Then" from *That Shining Place* by Mark Van Doren. Copyright © 1969 by Mark Van Doren.

"A Frosty Night" from *Collected Poems* by Robert Graves. Reprinted by permission of the author and A.P. Watt Ltd.

"The Horn" from *The Blackbird in the Lilac* by James Reeves (1952). Reprinted by permission of Oxford University Press.

"Find Me A Hero" from *The Runaways* by Elizabeth Swados. Copyright © 1979 by Swados Enterprises, Inc. Published by Bantam Books, Inc. All rights reserved.

"Canedolia: An Off-Concrete Scotch Fantasia" by Edwin Morgan. Reproduced from *The Second Life* by Edwin Morgan, published by Edinburgh University Press.

A Rope Against the Sun by Al Pittman. Printed with the permission of BREAKWATER BOOKS LTD., St. John's, Newfoundland. Copyright Al Pittman 1974.

The Last Night of the World by Ray Bradbury. Copyright 1951 by Ray Bradbury. Copyright renewed 1979 by Ray Bradbury. Reprinted by permission of Harold Matson Company, Inc.

I Got a Tailor-Made Coat by Alvin Lewis Curry, Jr. Reprinted from *Stuff*, edited by Herbert Kohl and Victor Hernandez Cruz. Copyright © 1970 by Herbert Kohl and Victor Hernandez Cruz.

Professionals and amateurs are hereby warned that "STORY THEATRE" is subject to a royalty. It is fully protected under the copyright laws of the United States of America, the British Commonwealth, including Canada, and all other countries of the Copyright Union. All rights, including professional, amateur, motion pictures, recitation, lecturing, public reading, radio broadcasting, television, and the rights of translation into foreign languages are strictly reserved. In its present form, the play is dedicated to the reading public only.

"STORY THEATRE" may be given stage presentation by amateurs upon payment of a royalty of Fifty Dollars for the first performance, and Thirty-Five Dollars for each additional performance, payable one week before the date when the play is given to: Samuel French, Inc., at 25 West 45th Street, New York, New York 10036, or at 7623 Sunset Boulevard, Hollywood, California 90046, or to Samuel French (Canada) Limited, 80 Richmond Street East, Toronto, Ontario, Canada. M5C 1P1

"The Wolf and the Lamb" retold by Ann McGovern. Reprinted by permission of Scholastic Inc. from AESOP'S FABLES retold by Ann McGovern. Copyright © 1963 by Scholastic Inc.

"The Owl Who Was God" by James Thurber. Copyright © 1940 James Thurber. Copyright © 1968 Helen Thurber. From FABLES FOR OUR TIME, published by Harper & Row, New York.

The Seven Skinny Goats by Victor G. Ambrus (1969). © Victor G. Ambrus 1969. Reprinted by permission of Oxford University Press.

Excerpts from *The Pioneer Years* by Barry Broadfoot. Copyright © 1979 by Barry Broadfoot. Reprinted by permission of Doubleday & Company, Inc.

"School Thief" by Dennis Potter from *Nigel Barton Plays* by Dennis Porter. Reprinted by permission of the author.

"Good Old Days At School" by W.M. Kiley. Reprinted by courtesy of the London Free Press.

"The Loser" from *Where The Sidewalk Ends* by Shel Silverstein. Copyright © 1974 by Shel Silverstein. Reprinted by permission of Harper & Row, Publishers.

"The Fun They Had" copyright © 1957 by Isaac Asimov from the book *Earth Is Room Enough* by Isaac Asimov. Used by permission of Doubleday & Company, Inc. and NEA Service, Inc.

"What Did You Learn In School Today?" by Tom Paxton. © Copyright 1962 Cherry Lane Music Company. All rights for Canada controlled by Welbeck Music of Canada Corp. Toronto. International Copyright Secured. All Rights Reserved. Used by Permission.

"Off Base" by Barry Base. Published originally in the OSSTF *The Bulletin*, Vol. 50, No. 3, May 1970.

"Schoolhouse," by Dave Etter, from *Go Read the River*, University of Nebraska Press. Copyright © 1966 by Dave Etter. Reprinted by permission of the author.

"See Mother Run!" Story by Joan Mills. From *Reader's Digest*, September 1967, originally published by the Berkshire Eagle, Pittsfield, Mass. 01201 U.S.A.

"Vacation Trip" from *Stories That Could Be True: New And Collected Poems* by William Stafford. Originally appeared in *The New Yorker* and reprinted by permission of Harper & Row, Publishers, Inc.

Adaptation of Chapter 8, pages 40-48, from *Pardon Me, You're Stepping On My Eyeball!*: A Novel by Paul Zindel. Copyright © 1976 by Zindel Productions Incorporated. By permission of Harper & Row, Publishers, Inc.

"Who Works?" "The Workplace," "Workers," and "Not Having Work." From *Words on Work* by Stanley A. Nemiroff, Olivia M. Rovinescu, Cliffton B. Ruggles and David Booth. Reprinted by permission of Globe/Modern Curriculum Press.

"Should Teenager in Ghetto Quit School?" by Ann Landers, published in the Toronto *Star*. Reprinted by permission of Ann Landers and the Field Newspaper Syndicate.

"The Worker" by Richard W. Thomas, associate professor in History and Urban Affairs at Michigan State University. Reprinted by permission of the author.

"The Winnipeg Strike" by Gerry Kopelow from *Weekend Magazine* May 12, 1979.

"Job Characteristics" from *The Canadian Book of Lists* by Jeremy Brown. Reprinted by permission of Pagurian Press Limited.

"Cathy" by Cathy Guisewite. Copyright, 1982, Universal Press Syndicate. Reprinted with permission. All rights reserved.

"Jobs Rated According to Boredom" from: R.D. Caplan, et al. *Job Demands And Worker Health.* Ann Arbor, Michigan, Institute for Social Research, 1980.

The King's Rival by Adjai Robinson. Adapted by permission of G.P. Putnam's Sons from *Three African Tales* by Adjai Robinson.

The First People by Faye Davis and the Carousel Players. Reprinted by permission of Faye Davis & Company—Carousel Players, St. Catharines, Ontario.

Scenes, 2, 4, 7, 17, 20, 24, and 26 from *A Life In the Theatre* by David Mamet. Reprinted by permission of Grove Press, Inc. Copyright 1975, 1977 by David Mamet.

Coronation Event and Drama from *Technicians of the Sacred* by Jerome Rothenburg. Originally from a play from *Thespis* by Theodor H. Gaster. Reprinted by permission of Doubleday & Company Inc.

Savages by Christopher Hampton. Reprinted by permission of Faber and Faber Ltd. from *Savages* by Christopher Hampton.

Excerpt from Sophocles' *Oedipus The King*, translated from the Classical Greek by Kenneth Cavander. (Chandler) Copyright © 1961 by Harper & Row, Publishers, Inc. By permission of the publisher.

Seneca's Oedipus by Ted Hughes. Reprinted by permission of Faber and Faber Ltd. from *Seneca's Oedipus* adapted by Ted Hughes.

Murder in the Cathedral by T.S. Eliot. Reprinted by permission of Faber and Faber Ltd. from *Murder in the Cathedral* by T.S. Eliot.

The Creation of Man, Chester Cycle of Mystery Plays. Reprinted by permission of Heineman Educational Books Ltd.

The Serpent by Jean-Claude Van Itallie. Reprinted by permission of International Creative Management. Copyright © 1969 by Jean-Claude Van Itallie.

"Commedia Dell'Arte" by T.G. Kottke. First published in *Dramatics*. Reprinted by permission of the T.G. Kottke, professor of drama at SUNY-Oneonta.

"Lucy's Fake Illness; I Love Lucy" From *Lucy & Ricky & Fred & Ethel: The Story of "I Love Lucy"* by Bart Andrews. Copyright © 1976 by Bart Andrews. Reprinted by permission of the publisher, E.P. Dutton, Inc.

"A Day at the Races; The Marx Brothers" from the MGM release *A Day At The Races* © 1937 Metro-Goldwyn-Mayer Corporation. Copyright renewed 1964 by Metro-Goldwyn-Mayer Inc.

"Archie in the Hospital; All in the Family." Reprinted by permission of Tandem Productions, Inc. © Copyright 1972 Tandem productions, Ltd. All Rights Reserved.

Hamlet by William Shakespeare. Reprinted by permission of Cambridge University Press.

Rosencrantz and Guildenstern are Dead by Tom Stoppard. Reprinted by permission of Faber and Faber Ltd. from *Rosencrantz And Guildenstern Are Dead* by Tom Stoppard.

Marowitz's Hamlet by Charles Marowitz. Reprinted by permission of Marion Boyars Publishers Ltd.

Black Ey'd Susan by Douglas Jerrold from *Nineteenth Century Plays* edited by George Rowell (1972). Reprinted by permission of Oxford University Press.

programs, printing, and advertising for the play: "Produced by special arrangement with Samuel French, Inc."
Due authorship credit must be given on all programs, printing, and advertising for the play.

An Enemy of the People by Henrik Ibsen. Reprinted by permission of International Creative Management, Inc. Copyright © 1950, 1951 by Arthur Miller.

The Bald Soprano by Eugene Ionesco. Reprinted by permission of Grove Press, Inc. Translated from the French by Donald M. Allen. Copyright © 1956, 1958, 1965 by Grove Press, Inc.

The Good Person of Szechwan by Bertold Brecht. Translated by John Willett. Reprinted by permission of Methuen London, Publishers.

Six Characters in Search of an Author by Luigi Pirandello. By kind permission of Familiari Pirandello—Roma.

"The Old Gumbie Cat," "Mungojerrie and Rumpleteazer," "Gus: the Theatre Cat." Reprinted from OLD POSSUM'S BOOK OF PRACTICAL CATS by T.S. Eliot by permission of Faber and Faber Ltd.

Every reasonable effort has been made to acquire permission for copyright material used in this book, and to acknowledge all such indebtedness accurately. However, all errors and omissions called to our attention will be corrected in future printings. In particular, we would be grateful for any information regarding the copyright holders of the following: *I've Got Viktor Schalkenburg*; "A Litany for Rain," translated by W.E. Calvert; and "Some Excuses For Not Going to Work," from *Peter Gzowski's Book about This Country in the Morning*.

List of masks/makeup used: page 17 paper bag mask; page 29 neutral mesh mask; page 43 molded gypsum mask; page 45 Philippine Islands mask; page 61 Mexican festival mask; page 64 North American West Coast Indian mask; page 79 Iroquois corn husk mask; page 86 Hawaiian contemporary mask; page 87 Philippine Islands dancer's frog mask; page 94 old age makeup; page 105 contemporary stick-mask; page 106 traditional mime makeup; page 115 West African mask; page 125 North American West Coast Indian mask; page 141 Mexican sun mask; page 142 pageant wagon devil makeup; page 149 Commedia dell'Arte character makeup; page 168 Puerto Rican carnival fool's mask; page 170 lorgnette mask; page 180 Philippine tortoise-shell mask; page 191 cat makeup. (Masks from the collection of David W. Booth.) The cover is an interpretation in makeup of a tragic mask used in an Aristophanes play.